The Dharma's Gatekeepers

The Dharma's Gatekeepers

Sakya Paṇḍita on Buddhist Scholarship in Tibet

Jonathan C. Gold

State University of New York Press

Cover: Stone Manjushri—Namasangiti (Northern India, 1000–1099), item no. 65391 on himalayanart.org, Collection of Rubin Museum of Art

Published by
State University of New York Press, Albany

Printed in the United States of America

For information, contact State University of New York Press, Albany, NY
www.sunypress.edu

Production by Dana Foote
Marketing by Anne M. Valentine

Library of Congress Cataloging-in-Publication Data

Gold, Jonathan C., 1969–
The Dharma's gatekeepers : Sakya Pandita on Buddhist scholarship in Tibet / Jonathan C. Gold.
p. cm.
Includes bibliographical references and index.
ISBN 978-0-7914-7165-4 (hardcover : alk. paper)
ISBN 978-0-7914-7166-1 (pbk. : alk. paper)
1. Sa-skya Pandi-ta Kun-dga'-rgyal-mtshan, 1182–1251. Mkhas pa 'jug pa'i sgo. 2. Buddhism—Study and teaching—China—Tibet. I. Title.
BQ162.C52T55734 2007
294.3'923092—dc22

2006032683

10 9 8 7 6 5 4 3 2 1

CONTENTS

PREFACE

This book describes a Buddhist view of scholarship. It is a study of the *Gateway to Learning* (*Mkhas pa 'jug pa'i sgo*), a thirteenth-century Tibetan introduction to scholarship by the great luminary Sakya Paṇḍita. The *Gateway* is in many ways a unique product of its author's time, place, and worldview. Yet the brilliance with which Sakya Paṇḍita grasped the intellectual issues of that time and place, and the clarity and depth with which he expressed his worldview, make the *Gateway* a classic of world literature with lessons that resonate in our time.

The *Gateway*'s principal audience consisted of the most ambitious scholars among the Tibetan monastic establishment, and these were students who struggled, above all, with the complexities of understanding their scriptures in translations from Sanskrit. Sakya Paṇḍita consequently reflects with greater depth than any other premodern Buddhist on the nature of translation, and on the challenges that the dharma faces during its travels among diverse cultures and languages. The many translated Buddhist scriptures and treatises available to Tibetans during this time contained a bewildering variety of doctrines and practices. So Sakya Paṇḍita provides a unique hermeneutic theory that allows for a diversity of interpretive conventions, each legitimate and applicable in its own scriptural context, while yet defining true mastery as comprehension of all contexts. The intellectual repertoire that the *Gateway* describes is justified by its claim to continue the practices of the true original *saṅgha* established by the Buddha in India. So Sakya Paṇḍita explicitly elevates this scholarly community to the role of just arbiter not only of its elite membership but of the legitimate possibilities of linguistic meaning itself. These are distinctive views of learning and expertise that are rooted in traditional Indo-Tibetan Buddhist thought and entwined around the specific frameworks and needs of Sakya Paṇḍita's thirteenth-century readership. They are also sophisticated, Buddhist contributions to the wider philosophical study of language, translation, interpretation, and the functions of communities of learning.

At the same time, the more general ideals of literary and philosophical expertise that the *Gateway* advocates are by no means unique. Sakya Paṇḍita's vision of scholarship takes part in a Buddhist imagination of the perfection of knowledge that extends from the notion of the Buddha as ideal teacher to the many faces and forms of Mañjuśrī, the great bodhisattva of wisdom. As on the cover of this book, Mañjuśrī often carries not only the lotus of the perfection of wisdom scriptures, but also the sword that slices through false views. The scholar who wishes to emulate Mañjuśrī must be prepared to defend the dharma against its enemies and its misrepresentation—whether these appear in the form of illusory concepts, deluded pretenders to authority within the *saṅgha,* or detractors from outside the Buddhist traditions. Sakya Paṇḍita is by no means the first, let alone the only, Buddhist to hold aloft Mañjuśrī's sword of scholarship in the hopes of purging the monastic community of erroneous, innovative views.

In this role as master and guardian of a tradition in transition, however, Sakya Paṇḍita is not only an exemplary Buddhist, but also an exemplary window into religious motives for the development of learned societies across the world. His requirement that a true scholar must gain comprehensive mastery over every area of knowledge is reflected in the systematic intellectual pursuits of many great medieval scholars, from al-Ghazali to Zhu Xi. When he declares that the teachings are in decline and the situation is dire, requiring the guardianship of an elite community of master scholars armed with both traditional intellectual methodologies and endlessly subtle literary aesthetics, he, surprisingly, echoes the sentiments of scholars as distant as the translators of the King James Bible (see chapter 7, the conclusion to this volume).

This book thus describes a Buddhist view of scholarship, but it suggests that Sakya Paṇḍita's Buddhist motivations for learning may be only one enactment of human needs that are more widespread than any particular religious doctrine and yet specific to each individual's yearning for understanding and control. Because it provides such a unique and incisive set of arguments in favor of a particular form of literate learning in one place, in one time, from one perspective, the *Gateway to Learning* just may serve as a paradigm for intellectual development—a gateway through which we may begin to understand the nature and origins of scholarly learning itself.

Notes to the Reader

Most of the *Gateway* passages discussed in the body of the book are translated in appendix B. Readers can use the outline in appendix A to locate the appropriate sections within the translation.

Tibetan names that appear within the text are phoneticized into forms that can be pronounced without knowledge of Tibetan orthography. Tibetan orthographic equivalents are listed at the end of the book.

Acknowledgments

This book is based upon work conceived and developed as my PhD Dissertation at the University of Chicago, where I had the great fortune of studying with Paul J. Griffiths, Sheldon Pollock, and Matthew T. Kapstein. These three superlative scholars and teachers are the main source of my knowledge and interest in the topics of this book.

His Holiness Sakya Trizin and Khenpo Gyatso generously allowed me to study at Sakya College in Dehra Dun in 2000. While I was there, all the monks provided assistance to me in one way or another, without complaint over the extra alien burden that I was. My good friend Kunsang Wangchuk was particularly generous with his time and advice. Tenzin Chöpak, Losel Dundup, and Geshe Ngawang Gyatso were assigned the arduous task of guiding me through the *Mkhas 'jug* line by line. They were inspiring and energetic teachers, dedicated to their charge that I should not misrepresent Sakya Paṇḍita to the Western world. I hope I have not disappointed them. In a wonderful series of meetings at the Central Institute of Higher Tibetan Studies in Sarnath, Professor K. N. Mishra and Tashi Tsering helped to clear up many of my difficulties in understanding Sa-paṇ. During this time I also enjoyed the warm hospitality of the Negi family of Rajpur. In New York, Lama Pema Wangdak continues to share his encouragement and his insights into the Tibetan language. And my friend Jackie Sherman has generously provided me with a beautiful, quiet work space.

I am grateful to several people who have read this work at various stages in part or in full and offered their comments: Daniel Arnold, Mario D'Amato, Amy Lavine, my colleagues in the 2001–2002 Martin Marty Seminar and the 2002–2003 Chicago Forum on Scholarship in Theology and Religion, and two anonymous readers. Janet Gyatso deserves special thanks for her extremely helpful and detailed comments. David Jackson generously provided me a copy of his polished, unpublished translation of the second chapter of the *Mkhas 'jug*, which helped me resolve many difficult issues. I have also benefited greatly from conversations and contacts with Georges Dreyfus, Jay Garfield, John Dunne, Ngawang Jorden, Bruce Lincoln, and Elizabeth Morrison. The errors that remain are my own.

Finally, thanks above all to my wife, Heather Cristol, who is the best.

Chapter 2 contains a revised version of "Guardian of the Translated Dharma: Sakya Paṇḍita on the Role of the Tibetan Scholar," in Lynne Long, ed., *Translation and Religion: Holy Untranslatable?* (Clevendon, U.K.: Multilingual Matters), pp. 115–28. Chapter 3 contains a revised version of "Sa-skya Paṇḍita's Buddhist Argument for Linguistic Study," *Journal of Indian Philosophy* (2005) 33:151–84, used with kind permission of Springer Science and Business Media.

1

THE LION'S ROAR IN THE ASSEMBLY

Sa-paṇ's Scholarly Ideal

> It is agreed that there are these two truths: the conventional and the ultimate. Reality is beyond the scope of intellection. Intellection is said to be the conventional.
>
> —Śāntideva, *The Bodhicaryāvatāra*

Introduction

In the verse above, the ninth-century Indian Buddhist philosopher Śāntideva affirms a basic belief of the Mahāyāna: Ultimately, truth and reality are beyond intellection. The highest goal of Buddhist realization is ineffable—strictly, inconceivable. Some, building upon this notion, have claimed that Buddhism is (or ought to be) simply about practice. They declare that meditation, conceived as the very opposite of intellection, is the only appropriately Buddhist path of understanding. Yet the overwhelming majority of Buddhist practitioners have held an alternative vision, in which the intellect plays a decisive role in both Buddhist practice and history. The vast majority of the most influential and idealized practitioners in Buddhist history are not only great meditators, but great scholars as well. Indeed, Śāntideva's own verse begins one of the more intricate extended philosophical examinations of the nature of truth available in classical Sanskrit literature. He did not consider it a contradiction to be an intellectual, an accomplished scholar, pursuing what is beyond intellection; nor have most Buddhists who came before or after him.

The Buddha is often called "the teacher" (*bstan pa*), and his teachings, the dharma, became the model and guide for his followers after he was gone. Members of the Buddhist monastic community, the *saṅgha,* thus became teachers as well as students and practitioners of the dharma. The most prominent members of the community have been those of evident intellectual, not only meditative, accomplishment. For the Buddha, the two skills were intertwined; his ability to win debates and secure converts was taken as a sign of his spiritual greatness. Of course, when the intellect is seen to be an ultimately untrustworthy manipulator of half-truths, there remain problems as to how best to regulate its functions. To some questions, the Buddha famously responded with silence, reasoning that in certain circumstances any answer will be misleading. On most days, however, the Buddha spoke.

The Chinese Chan and Japanese Zen traditions claim that their lineages survive through nonlinguistic "mind-to-mind" transmissions of realization from masters to disciples. The so-called Southern School patriarchs are famous for having rejected the book learning that keeps one enmeshed in a net of false conceptualizations. Yet, as Bernard Faure has so ably shown, it would be a mistake to take this "rhetoric of immediacy" too literally—for it is only through rigorous training in the elite cultures of the monastery that Zen neophytes are transformed into masters capable to receive or bestow a lineal transmission.[1]

When we turn to Tibetan traditions, it is equally useful to note the rhetorical impact of different positions on scholarship and learning. Tibetan literature records many stories of great adepts besting arrogant and jealous scholars of logic and language. In a biography of Milarepa (1052–1135), for instance, one Geshe Tsakpūhwa challenges Milarepa by asking him to explicate a book of philosophy. In response, Milarepa says that he is not at all interested in the kind of learning and scholarly disputation that the Geshe represents, and supports this with a song describing how his own meditational skills are superior to any scholarship:[2]

> I prostrate myself before Marpa the Translator,
> May he bless me and keep me from dispute.
>
> The blessing of my lama penetrated my mind.
> I have never been overcome by distractions.
>
> . . .
> Having meditated on the instruction of the secret tradition,
> I forgot the books of dialectic.
>
> Having maintained pure awareness,
> I forgot the illusions of ignorance.
>
> . . .
> Having dwelt in the unaltered state of naturalness,
> I forgot the ways of hypocrisy.
>
> Having lived in humility in body and mind,
> I forgot the disdain and arrogance of the great.

These verses win over the crowd of observers with their implicit attributions of ignorance, arrogance, and hypocrisy to the disputational scholar, and the Geshe leaves humiliated and angry. He will return to poison Milarepa in revenge. In another similar disputational situation, Milarepa is even more dismissive of scholarly training in language and logic:

> Oh great teachers and scholars,
> Cling not to meaningless words and empty talk
> Deeming them to be the Truth!
> Even heretics can play with them.
> One can waste two-and-thirty lives and gain nought,
> If his mind but follows words.
> It would be much better, therefore,
> To conquer the devil of egotism.
> I have no time to waste in words, words, and still more words!
> Nor do I know logic or how to pose a proposition.
> Therefore, you are the one
> Who wins the argument today![3]

These stories draw their power from a long-standing Buddhist trope, with as much of a tradition in Tibet as elsewhere, in which authors declare their preference for realization through practice over mere book learning. Yet here, again, we should not jump to the conclusion that this text considers *all* learning foolishness, and values *only* meditation. Milarepa's own guru, Marpa (1012–1097), gained great fame and massive wealth through his reputation as a "translator" (*lo tsā ba*), an honorific designation reserved for the greatest scholars of the day. Indeed, if Marpa was not a great scholar, his "translations" would provide an inauthentic source for Milarepa's own teachings. This observation, rather than a general anti-intellectualism, puts us on the proper trail toward an explanation of the scholar's challenge. The scholar's arrogance and jealousy are the most evident targets worthy of Buddhist critique. But the scholar/murderer in Milarepa's life story represents a very serious threat not only to the proper practice of Buddhism, but to the legitimacy and survival of Milarepa's lineage. Indeed, in the story mentioned, a scholar plays the significant role of indirectly causing Milarepa's death—significant even though, like Socrates, Milarepa drinks the poison willingly, and the scholar himself ends up regretting his act and converting to become one of Milarepa's disciples.

In fact, the scholarly challenge here embodied in myth might well be that of the growing "neoconservative" intellectual movement—a movement that sought to "Indianize" Tibetan Buddhist traditions and to purge them of all forms of inauthentic, "self-made" Tibetan knowledge.[4] This movement was only in its youth when it challenged the authenticity of Milarepa's lineage, but it would grow to control the helm of Tibetan intellectual life in the centuries to follow. Its most vocal and influential advocate would be the great Sakya Paṇḍita Künga Gyeltshen (1182–1251, hereinafter Sa-paṇ). This book is a study of Sa-paṇ's masterpiece the *Gateway to Learning* (*Mkhas pa 'jug pa'i sgo*), in which Sa-paṇ provides his most comprehensive and compelling presentation of this new view of scholarship. The *Gateway* secured Sa-paṇ's reputation, in the eyes of Tibetans, as the model of a scholar—occasionally lampooned as excessively arrogant, but primarily revered as an ideal to which all students of the dharma should aspire.[5]

The *GATEWAY* IN THE HISTORY OF TIBETAN LEARNING

In order to understand the Neoconservative Movement and Sa-paṇ's position within it, we must go back to the very beginnings of Tibetan literacy—for Tibetan identities are shaped around the distinctive character of the language in which Tibetan Buddhism is written. The earliest Tibetan writings date from the imperial period (c. 650–850). Traditional histories of this period link the origins of writing and scholarship with the importation of Buddhism, in particular from India. King Songtsen Gampo (617–649/50), considered the first Buddhist king, is said to have sent the scholar Thönmi Saṃbhoṭa to India to devise a new alphabet for the Tibetan language on Indian models. The Tibetan alphabet is, indeed, derived from the Indic Brahmī script, though forms of this script were already in circulation in Central Asia. In the wake of the script, however, came Buddhist learning, imported from Tibet's neighbors beginning during this time, and officially adopted as the state religion by King Thri Songdetsen (742–c.797) a century later. It is not entirely clear why the Tibetan emperors decided to adopt and support Buddhism—it was certainly controversial in their time. Matthew Kapstein has pointed out that Buddhist systems of learning surely provided a powerful set of tools and models for how to organize and run a newly complex imperial administration.[6] Whatever the reason, though, the state-sponsored support of Buddhist institutions under the auspices of Thri Songdetsen and his successors, and in particular, their oversight and sponsorship of the translation of Buddhist scriptures from Sanskrit into Tibetan provided the foundation upon which all of Tibetan Buddhism is based.

This is true not merely because many hundreds of texts rendered into Tibetan at this time would, much later, be incorporated into the Tibetan canons for all time, but more importantly because the language and methods of the translators would provide the standard for all later translations, and indeed, the standard language of the dharma itself in Tibetan. Even when other, later translations became the central practice texts for other later Tibetan Buddhist traditions, the language would remain that of the early translators, and would accord with the rules of the "dharma language" (*chos skad*) formalized under King Thri Desongtsen (r. 804–815).[7]

This is not a claim as to linguistic determinism of the kind advocated by modern linguists such as Edward Sapir and Benjamin Lee Whorf.[8] Tibetan modes of thinking were never curtailed or limited by the structures of the "dharma language" for the very simple reason that the "dharma language" is not a natural language at all. It is a translator's language, designed for the exclusive purpose of rendering Indian, Sanskrit texts, mostly Buddhist ones, into Tibetan. But fluent speakers of Tibetan cannot read it without being trained to do so. Like the Sanskrit that it translates, it is always something like a second or third language, never a first. Tibetans grow up learning their local variety of Spoken Tibetan, and so have their thought mediated by that language, not by the dharma language (if language indeed mediates thought). What's more, the translation language is not even by any means identical with what is properly called "Classical Literary Tibetan"—the language of literate Tibetan composition.[9] Thus, although the imperial decrees (*bkas bcad*) governing the translations of Sanskrit texts into Tibetan have had an immeasurable influence on Tibetan literature, they have by no means limited what could be written any more than what could be thought.

My claim is of a different order. The official translation language was designed to allow for the capture and transmission of a Sanskrit source in a language perhaps not exactly like Spoken Tibetan, but relatively easily learned by speakers of Tibetan. In these purposes—especially in capturing the Sanskrit—the dharma language was quite successful. As David Ruegg has noted, this could hardly be better exemplified than by the fact that every once in a while, a modern scholar who has used the traditional dictionaries and rules to "back-translate" from the Tibetan translations into Sanskrit to create a model of the lost Sanskrit original, will find his work very closely verified by the discovery of some previously unknown Sanskrit exemplar—causing much delight for modern scholars who specialize in such things.[10] Yet the Tibetan success in generating a massive corpus of remarkably accurate renderings could not be bought without some sacrifice on the other end—namely, in the degree of learning necessary for speakers of Tibetan to comprehend the meaning of the "translated" texts. The official choice to prefer reflective authenticity over target language comprehensibility would prove a decisive factor in the development of later Tibetan intellectual traditions.

The issues surrounding this linguistic choice come into focus around the problem of textual "fabrications." Although designed for translation, and different in various ways from the language in which Tibetans ordinarily wrote, the dharma language could, like any code, be used to compose new texts. As Ruegg has noted, such independent compositions appeared quite early in Tibetan translation history—and so we find, along with orders that translators may not invent their own new translation terminology, parallel complaints and rulings against fabricated, "self-made" scriptures. There is no rule against writing religious texts. The issue here is using the *translation form* to compose texts. One can understand the complaint. What reason is there for standardizing translation methods other than to make scriptures available in their most authentic form possible? The whole point is to provide a system for ensuring that the translated scriptures authentically reflect their Sanskrit originals. To compose a text in this language, however, suggests the presence of a Sanskrit original where there is none.

Once again, Ruegg has made the issue crystal clear by distinguishing between texts that are historically "Indian" and those that are typologically "Indic."[11] Any text composed in the dharma language (*chos skad*), though it is not a translation of a genuinely "Indian" original, will nonetheless adopt characteristically "Indic" ideas, concepts, and forms of writing; and, if it is to be accepted as an authentic representation of the dharma, it must reiterate traditional views and lines of argument as well. Ruegg is right to note that the "Indic" came to dominate Tibetan modes of Buddhist text (as well as artistic) production. But, and here is the problem, once the Sanskrit originals are set aside, and Tibetans are studying translated texts, how are they to distinguish between texts purporting to be derived from an "Indian" source and texts that are, like most Tibetan productions, merely "Indic"? Every translator worth his salty tea ought to be capable of fabricating a very convincing forgery. This fact, and attendant anxieties, are what fueled the Neoconservative Movement during the Tibetan renaissance.

The fall of the Tibetan empire precipitated a century-long dark age in Central Tibet.[12] Ronald Davidson's most recent masterful work, *Tibetan Renaissance,* records how Tibetans drew upon the norms of late tantrism in India and Nepal to rejuvinate their culture after this dark period, establishing during only a few centuries the religious and political forms that would dominate Tibetan history to follow. One persistent theme that develops during this time is the notion that India was the sole authentic source of the true dharma.[13] This meant that many of the most important agents in this development would be, once again, "translators" (*lo tsā ba*). This second round of great translators made trips to India and Nepal to study Sanskrit language and the dharma with enlightened masters, and to bring new scriptures back to Tibet. Unlike the earlier period, the translations during this "later dissemination" (*phyi dar*) were not organized or overseen by any central authority. There were a tremendous variety of methods developed during this period by which scholars could generate "shortened" lineages for themselves—not only discovering new texts in India, but as Kapstein has put it, some scholars "may be said to have *found India within themselves*" either through visions or through discovering hidden treasures.[14] This alone would have provided cause for concern among those who would want a sharp line between authentic and inauthentic scriptures. But along with the means of forgery, translators had a substantial motive. As Davidson emphasizes, the greatest of these translators returned to Tibet with the ability to leverage their monopolistic mastery of secret tantric cycles into a form of spiritual authority that granted them great wealth and power.[15]

We are finally in a position to understand the significance of the Geshe's challenge to Milarepa: For Milarepa's master, Marpa, was of course one of the great translators of the day. But Marpa did not pass on his translator's knowledge, and Milarepa himself was neither a linguist nor a logician. The implication of the scholar's challenge, then, is that Milarepa has no independent means of verifying the authenticity of Marpa's "translations." In fact—perhaps more to the point—Milarepa's claim to have the Indian Siddha Nāropa as his guru's guru was a contested matter, a difficulty exacerbated by the fact that the teachings were exclusively oral.[16] Many teachings during this period consist in what Davidson terms "gray" texts—"neither definitely Indian nor identifiably Tibetan."[17] Indeed, many texts that would become central to the practices of major Tibetan lineages to follow seem to have resulted from collaboration among Tibetan translators and their Indian teachers. My suggestion is that when we read Milarepa's critique of the ignorance and arrogance of a scholar obsessed with technicalities, we should understand it as a counterattack, or at least, a foritification against a potential attack.

It is the practice of distinguishing authentic from inauthentic scriptures that characterizes what I am following Davidson in calling the Neoconservative Movement. Such practice perhaps began as simply a strategy employed by translators to shore up their own reputations and undercut their rivals. Some published lists of spurious texts, and some seemed simply to have spread a damning word. But these early attempts to verify authentic teachings and invalidate inauthentic ones lacked a system. Their only unifying method was the basic test of asking Indian *paṇḍitas* whether they knew of the texts in their Sanskrit originals.[18] The fact of the matter was that all lineages were vulnerable to an excess of scrutiny, and all translators were capable of occasionally identifying fallacies in the teachings of their rivals. It was only with the advent of a new form of scholar, trained like an Indian *paṇḍita* in linguistics and logic, that methods of scriptural analysis could be guided by systematic and rational procedures.[19] It was only with the advent of a new view of the scholar's knowledge as comprehensive that decisions of scriptural inclusion—which to allow in, which to keep out—became especially critical. It was only with this new skill set that a scholar could learn to perceive the difference between the merely "Indic" and the genuinely "Indian." This new view of scholarship, of course, is the one advocated and delineated by Sakya Paṇḍita in his *Gateway to Learning.*

The *Gateway* is Sa-paṇ's textbook on the basic skills of a good scholar, and my purpose in this book is to explain the philosophy of scholarship embedded within its first two chapters, which discuss, respectively, scholarly composition and exposition. This work will not focus on the *Gateway*'s third and final chapter, on debate, which has been expertly translated and studied by David Jackson.[20] Jackson's indispensable work also covers Sa-paṇ's education, career, and oevre in great detail. I will therefore focus only on those elements we need to know if we are to comprehend why and how Sa-paṇ comes to advocate a Tibetan variety of *paṇḍityam*. As we will see, Sa-paṇ believes that it is the responsibility of all legitimate scholars to defend the true Buddhist teachings (the dharma) against corruption and fabrication. He understands the dharma to be in constant competition with other doctrines and ideas, and under constant threat of misrepresentation. As might be assumed from the foregoing discussion, the latter is of particular concern to Sa-paṇ, since he believes the teachings to have been widely misunderstood and misrepresented by his Tibetan contemporaries, especially those from competing traditions.

In this context, Sa-paṇ believes that the great scholars must form a kind of elite Buddhist guard to protect the stronghold of the *dharma*—using, as their main intellectual tools, the great Indian traditions of grammar, literature, and philosophy. These are the traditions that Sa-paṇ is most concerned to promote among the Tibetans of his time. The *Gateway* therefore introduces the basics of these fields of learning, and, as I will show, it provides distinctive Buddhist arguments as to why scholars need to learn epistemology, philosophy of language, translation studies, hermeneutics, and literary theory. I will treat each of these topics in turn. It is remarkable enough to find a thirteenth-century Tibetan Buddhist addressing issues, such as translation and translatability, that are of central intellectual concern in today's academic community. What we will see is that Sa-paṇ's analyses of translation are grounded within a series of subtle, brilliant, and quintessentially Buddhist arguments about the nature of scholarship itself. For this reason, in each case, his arguments illuminate even current discussions in each field with a new perspective.

In the the remainder of this chapter, I discuss the origins of Sa-paṇ's new view of scholarship, and I lay out the general character of the scholar as Sa-paṇ presents it in the opening of the *Gateway*. In subsequent chapters, I will focus in turn upon Sa-paṇ's treatments of particular areas of scholarship: terminological expertise and translation theory (chapter 2), grammar and Buddhist philosophy of language (chapter 3), Buddhist hermeneutics (chapter 4), intellectual conventions (chapter 5), and poetics (chapter 6). In the concluding chapter (chapter 7), I pull together the themes of these chapters in the attempt to draw a complete picture of Sa-paṇ's comprehensive vision for Tibetan Buddhist scholarship. In the appendixes I supply (A) a summary and outline of the relevant sections of the *Gateway*, and (B) a translation of the first chapter of the *Gateway* up to, but not including, where Sa-paṇ begins to paraphrase the *Kāvyādarśa* of Daṇḍin.[21]

ŚĀKYAŚRĪBHADRA AND THE INDIANIZATION OF TIBET

In the *Gateway,* Sa-paṇ adopts a rhetoric of exasperation with the intellectual abilities of his contemporaries. As he writes, most Tibetans are badly educated at best, especially when it comes to issues of linguistic and textual analysis:

> Some here in the snowy mountain ranges [of Tibet] who claim to be learned are not well trained in the analysis of sound itself, in providing the grammatical affixes for nominal inflection of a formed word, in providing the grammatical affixes for inflections (*ti ngan ta*) in verbal formation, in applying the four, six, etc. *kārakas,* in distinguishing such things as the object (*dngos, vastu*) and the reversal (*bzlog pa, viparyāsa*) in an analogy, in the nature of verbal ornamentation, in distinguishing among such things as expressions of substance and quality, in the different methods for divisions and headings, in how to summarize based on the general and subheadings in a summary, in deciding among opposing [positions] in reckoning and ascertainment (*grangs nges pa*), in eliminating wrong views, in how to get a definitive ascertainment by way of the purpose, and in joining the order of words and meanings in a structure that is pleasant to say and easy to understand, and so [they] are, for the most part, mistaken. This *Gateway to Learning* is related for their benefit.[22]

The *Gateway* thus sets itself up as an attempt to rectify the dearth of proper scholarship in Tibet. This is the rhetorical stance of much of Sa-paṇ's work, in which he often dedicates space to correcting mistakes of Tibetan scholars and establishing what he sees to be the correct interpretation of the Indian masters.[23] Over against his rivals, Sa-paṇ paints himself as embodying the quintessence of Indian scholarship. This is articulated most dramatically in his poem *The Eight Affirmations of the Ego* (*Nga brgyad ma 'grel pa dang bcas*), wherein the ego affirmed is his own. He claims to be master of all of the esoteric and exoteric sciences, with no equal anywhere. In Kapstein's translation:[24]

> *I* am the grammarian. *I* am the dialectician.
> Among vanquishers of sophists, peerless am *I*.
> *I* am learned in metrics. *I* stand alone in poetics.
> In explaining synonymics, unrivaled am *I*.
> *I* know celestial calculations. In exo- and esoteric science
> *I* have a discerning intellect equaled by none.
> Who can this be? Sakya alone!
> Other scholars are my reflected forms.

In commenting upon the *Eight Ego* poem, Sa-paṇ challenges the doubtful reader to examine his many accomplished writings in order to test the great scholar's erudition.[25] One of those impressive works is, of course, the *Gateway*. A similar claim appears in the opening to the *Gateway*:

> By having heard, seen, and grown accustomed to many [teachings]
> And being able to give close instructions [upon them], the glorious
> Kun-dga'
> Rgyal-mtshan [371] is explaining something here;
> Scholars, make yourselves happy: Listen up![26]

Sa-paṇ's vision of the scholar, then, which he embodied but which he believed most other Tibetans of his time failed to meet, was that of the consummate Indian intellectual, the comprehensive virtuoso *paṇḍita*. In his autocommentary to this verse, Sa-paṇ justifies his claims to expertise by listing texts he has studied in each area of learning.[27] Even if the *Gateway* does not go in depth into all of these realms of scholarship, it is still the "Gateway" for them all, since it provides the basic tools for all scholarship.

Why was Sa-paṇ's intellectual vision different from his predecessors? As heir to the throne at Sakya, Sa-paṇ was given a first-class education, and he proved an outstanding student.[28] He began his studies at home with his uncle, the great tantric scholar Trakpa Gyeltsen (1147–1216), and then traveled to the upper Nyang Valley in central Tibet for study with several well-known masters, especially in epistemology and logic.[29] What finally changed the course of his education, and in turn, changed the course of Tibet's intellectual life, was that after returning home for his father's illness, Sa-paṇ met the great Kashmiri *paṇḍita* Śākyaśrībhadra.[30]

Buddhism had been in decline across northern India for some time before, but when Śākyaśrī first visited Magadha at the turn of the thirteenth century,[31] the sun had truly set on the great Buddhist monastic colleges of India. Indeed, before long Buddhism would essentially die out in the land of its birth. Odantapura and Vikramaśīla, once great centers of learning, had been destroyed.[32] Śākyaśrī and his followers had to continue on to Jagaddala for their studies. Even there it was only safe to stay for three years, after which they turned northward to Nepal and, when invited by the translator Thropu Lotsāwa, to Tibet. This is how India's tremendous loss turned out to be Tibet's good fortune. Still, though texts would continue to arrive throughout Tibet's history, the demise of Nālandā, Vikramaśīla, and the other major monastic centers of India desiccated the main sources for the flow of Buddhist Sanskrit literature into Tibet, "like a pond whose tributary streams have dried up."[33] The eleven years that Śākyaśrī and his retinue taught and studied in Tibet would represent one of the last major influxes of Buddhist texts and teachings from

India.[34] As a direct result of this "last word" on Indian scholarship, the students of Śākyaśrī would indelibly transform Tibet's intellectual life and history.[35]

For several years Sa-paṇ studied under Śākyaśrī, who was to become his preceptor (*upādhyāya*),[36] as well as with three other Indian *paṇḍitas* of Śākyaśrī's entourage: Sugataśrī, Saṃghaśrī, and Dānaśīla.[37] Sugataśrī, in particular, acted as Sa-paṇ's private tutor at Sakya for three years, teaching him Sanskrit grammar, poetics, *kāvya*, lexicography, and drama.[38] Sa-paṇ became a translator, was deeply interested and successful in Sanskrit language, and was among the first Tibetans to be granted the title *paṇḍita*—an expression of his having mastered the entirety of the traditional Sanskrit curriculum. It is this breadth of learning that distinguished Śākyaśrī's disciples from previous Tibetan scholars. Eventually, through promoting the logic and epistemology (*pramāṇa*) tradition of Śākyaśrī, Sa-paṇ became one of the most influential philosophers of Tibetan history. But more importantly for the purposes of our discussion here, Sa-paṇ and the other Tibetan followers of Śākyaśrī were able to act as *paṇḍitas* capable in the full scope of Indian learning—formalized, we will see below, as "the Five Sciences" (*pañca-vidyāsthāna*).

This book is an investigation of the ideals of Śākyaśrī's circle (the new wave in the Neoconservative Movement), as understood by its best known Tibetan advocate, Sa-paṇ. In order to get a sense of this movement from other sources, therefore, we should at least be aware of its two most prominent other members, among the best known scholar/translators of their time, whom Sa-paṇ would have identified as scholarly compatriots: Chak Lotsāwa and Thropu Lotsāwa.

As much as Sa-paṇ adopts a grandiose rhetoric of his own scholarly uniqueness, he is also recorded as having expressed his jealousy of Chak Lotsāwa for his scholarly abilities and experience:

> When the Dharmasvāmin [Chag Lo-tsā-ba] was staying in Nepāla, the Dharmasvāmin Sa-skya Paṇḍita requested him to send him the bDud-rtsi thigs-pa (Tg. bGyud, LXXV, I), a commentary on the *Nāmasaṅgītī*. The Dharmasvāmin sent him the Indian original of the text. Then the Sa-skya Paṇḍita again asked the Dharmasvāmin to send him the Tibetan translation prepared by the Dharmasvāmin. When it was sent, the Sa-skya Paṇḍita looked through it and became very pleased. Later when they met at Sa-skya and discussed (the text), the Dharmasvāmin Sa-skya-pa said, "Surely after the lo-tsā-ba Rin-chen bzaṅ-po there was no other scholar greater than you! When I also thought of becoming a scholar like you, my father and grand-father did not allow me to go to India. As a result of which their grace diminished. At the best they did not make me abandon religion and wealth, at the worst they did not send (me) to India." Later, in Mongolia the Sa-skya Paṇḍita is reported to have said, "Chag lo-tsā-ba is himself a scholar. If you wish to study, meet him!"[39]

This remarkable passage adds dimension to the appearance of egotism in Sa-paṇ's *Eight Affirmations of the Ego.* The story seems to record that Sa-paṇ was interested to test the translation abilities of his former student,[40] but one cannot help wondering whether Sa-paṇ had not simply asked for Chak's Tibetan translation because he himself had questions about its very difficult original Sanskrit. Whichever the reason, though, Sa-paṇ was convinced after receiving the document that Chak had succeeded, throughout his travels, in becoming a greater scholar than Sa-paṇ, stuck in Tibet, was ever able to become. At least, this is the point of this story, which comes at the end of Chak Lotsāwa's biography—a document that, among its many interesting qualities, teaches the lesson that great practical advantages can accrue to a great scholar through travels in India.

If the translators were the scholar's scholars of Tibet, Chak Lotsāwa was what might be called a "translator's translator," and he achieved this state by seeking out texts and teachers in India and Nepal. His biography records that "he mastered the entirety of, in general, the five sciences, and in particular, tantra, linguistics, and logic" as a result of his study with twelve great Indian *paṇḍitas.*[41] The story of his travels to India to see the great monasteries (*vihāras*), which he undertook in spite of the dangers of repeated military incursions from Turkey, are well worth reading, and I will tell only one highlight. The climax comes perhaps when Chak discovers the great *paṇḍita* Rāhulaśrībhadra at Nālandā, deserted by his students. The translator stayed with him to study, hid with him when the soldiers arrived, and eventually carried the aged *paṇḍita* on his back to safety. One can understand why Sa-paṇ's family prevented him from travelling in India as a youth. There were real dangers to this pursuit of *paṇḍityam,* but the result, evident in Sa-paṇ's praise of Chak's abilities, could well be worth the risk.

I mentioned that Sa-paṇ was one of Chak Lotsāwa's teachers. Another was the great Thropu Lotsāwa, famed not only as another great disciple of Śākyaśrī,[42] but also as a scholar who was able to bring three great *paṇḍitas* to Tibet from India.[43] This was no small achievement. Thropu Lotsāwa sent letters requesting Śākyaśrī to come to Tibet, and received a positive reply before he ever met the *paṇḍita.* When they first met, however, Śākyaśrī was apparently a bit surprised and disappointed by the youth of his host, and was rethinking his choice to follow him to Tibet. Informed of this, Thropu set up a display of his great intellect, questioning the nine lesser *paṇḍitas* before the learned assembly. This so pleased Śākyaśrī that he was ready to leave before Thropu could put together his own necessary arrangements.[44]

These scholars were avid searchers for original, authentic, Indian teachings and interpretations, and for them Sanskrit learning was the method of ensuring the veracity of the teachings. Unlike other, competing scholars, who would attempt to fortify their connection to India by a shortened lineage, by a vision, or by discovered treasures, these teachers sought to transplant the entire Indian tradition of learning itself. By studying for many years with the Kashmiri *paṇḍita* and his entourage, Sa-paṇ and his contemporaries gained a depth of Indian learning rarely seen among Tibetans. As for Sa-paṇ himself, he would retranslate Dharmakīrti's *Pramāṇavārttika* with Śākyaśrī and by promoting it transform the face of Tibetan philosophy; and, he would work to establish in Tibet what he saw to be the acme of Indian Buddhist scholarship even as it disappeared from its Indian homeland.

As to the question of Sa-paṇ's and Śākyaśrī's influence on future studies in Tibet, it would be difficult to overstate their success. This might partly be credited to the ideas themselves—in particular, to the way the five sciences serve the needs of rationalizing the neoconservative cause—but we must admit that the bulk of the cause rests in peculiar circumstances of history. For, in the last years of his life, Sa-paṇ was summoned by the Mongol Köden Khan, who was threatening to invade Tibet. Sa-paṇ brought his two young nephews, Pakpa and Chakna, both of whom therefore ended up spending their formative years living among the Mongol chiefs, as their captives. Some years after Sa-paṇ's death, Pakpa was chosen as the preceptor to Qubilai Khan, and consequently as religious and temporal leader of all of Tibet. Pakpa was thus the first in a series of figures in whom the combined leadership of the political and religious realms would be most permanently formalized in the tradition of the Dalai Lamas.

If Pakpa's relationship with Qubilai Khan followed from the fact of Sa-paṇ's having been summoned to Köden's court, it might seem appropriate to ask just why Sa-paṇ was summoned. Davidson is probably right to attribute the Mongol interests primarily to the Sakya lords' well-known monopolies on powerful tantric maṇḍalas, in particular their mastery of the *Lamdre* system of the *Hevajra Tantra.* Yet at least part of the Mongols' assumption that Sa-paṇ could prove a useful member of their court might well be attributable to the fact that he was widely reputed a great scholar—a reputation that he had secured for himself through composing the *Gateway,* among other works. The specifics of Sa-paṇ's literary interests, which we will have occasion to discuss in later chapters, are particularly suggestive in this regard. But this cause hardly predicts the incredible result: More than a century of Sakya overlordship of a unified Tibet, during which Pakpa and his Sakya successors promoted Sakya scholarship and oversaw vast translation enterprises dedicated to the development of Sa-paṇ's vision of *paṇḍityam* among Tibetans. This is the period during which nearly all of the Tibetan canon's works of Sanskrit poetry (*kāvya*), literary theory (*alaṅkāra*), and metrics were first translated. It is the period during which Sakya monastery became established as the preeminent site for training in logic and epistemology (*pramāṇa*), the tool that Sa-paṇ considered the most crucial for distinguishing correct from incorrect doctrines. Indeed, great scholars of every tradition would come to study at Sakya monastery, including such influential luminaries as the editor of the Tibetan canon, Butön Rinchendrup and the founder of the Gelukpa, Je Tsongkhapa. These scholars—indeed, all of Tibetan scholarship to follow—would come under the influence of the vision of learning articulated by Sa-paṇ and promoted by his Sakya successors. I do not mean to overstate this ifluence. Sa-paṇ's unified curriculum was never practiced as he articulates it in the *Gateway*, and never had exactly the effect he had hoped. Yet Sa-paṇ is rightly credited with having consolidated the study of the "five sciences" across Tibet, and with having made the linguistic sciences—poetry (*kāvya*) in particular—the crown jewel in a great scholar's intellectual repetoire.[45] The manner in which this took place, however, must be seen as something of an accident of history.

THE FIVE SCIENCES AND THE GOAL OF SCHOLARLY PERFECTION

Sa-paṇ does not think that a scholar's education is, or should be, limited to topics that contribute directly to the practitioner's advancement on the Buddhist path. Instead, he provides us a better model when he describes the purpose of debate, which is intended to preserve the true dharma against the false, to defend the correct interpretation against the incorrect:

> A noble person should debate as proponent or respondent for the sake of dispelling error and for making understood the unmistaken facts of the matter, with the aim of maintaining his own doctrine.[46]

My analysis in the chapters that follow will illuminate why Sa-paṇ believes that the full panoply of scholarly abilities fit together and how they allow the scholar to protect the "unmistaken facts of the matter"—that is, the true dharma. We will see that the linguistic skills that Sa-paṇ studied with Sugataśrī are no more and no less a necessary part of the scholar's abilities than the *pramāṇa* studies for which he was most famous, and they all work together, reinforcing and supporting one another.

A traditional statement of this view appears in the *Mahāyānasūtrālaṅkāra* (*The Ornament to the [Buddha's] Discourses on the Great Vehicle*, MSA), which Sa-paṇ quotes in the opening to the *Gateway*:

> Without becoming a scholar in the five sciences
> Not even the supreme sage can become omniscient.
> For the sake of refuting and supporting others,
> And for the sake of knowing everything himself, he makes an effort in these [five sciences].[47]

The first half of the verse tells us that even an advanced bodhisattva must study the five sciences, or he can never achieve omniscience. Contrary to my opening claim, this does seem to place the *paṇḍita*'s education within the context of the Buddhist path. But we must investigate further. What are these five sciences (*vidyāsthāna*), which here represent the comprehensive knowledge of a true scholar, and which across Tibet in the centuries to follow would become the touchstone for judging a scholar's educational achievement?[48] Sa-paṇ glosses with a traditional list:

> Grammar is [the science of] language; reasoning is [the science of] logic; the outer science is crafts; the inner science is the transmitted [Buddha's] teachings (*dharma*); and medicine is the science of remedies—[so are the five sciences] explained.[49]

The five are linguistic science (*śabdavidyā*), logical science (*hetuvidyā*), medical science (*cikitsāvidyā*), science of fine arts and crafts (*śilpakarmasthānavidyā*), and the spiritual sciences (*adhyātmavidyā*) of the dharma. The second half of the MSA verse, as further explanation, divides up these five sciences into the three purposes served by the Buddha's studies: Two goals for others—to refute others and support others—and one goal for the Buddha himself—to come to know everything. As the commentary tells us, and as I represent in Table 1.1, linguistics and logic are studied to refute others; medicine and crafts are studied to assist, or support others; and the dharma itself is studied for one's own sake, in order to attain omniscience.[50]

Now, it is clear how a doctor with medical training can help other people, and the fascinating question of why Buddhism values the arts as a way of helping others is, unfortunately, a question for another study. But the main topics of the *Gateway* are the first two sciences: linguistic and logical studies. The *Gateway*'s first and second chapters are introductions to the linguistic sciences, and its third chapter introduces logical debate.[51] What makes "refuting others" such

Table 1.1. MSA 11.60 on the five sciences (*pañcavidyā*): first interpretation

Five Sciences	Purpose	For the Sake of
linguistic science, logical science →	refuting →	others
medical science, science of fine arts and crafts →	supporting →	others
dharma, "inner science" →	knowing everything (omniscience) →	oneself

a meritorious act that it befits an aspiring Buddha? Why is this said to benefit "others"? Well, the most evident possibility is that the bodhisattva has to serve the *saṅgha,* the Buddhist community, in this case by refuting wrong views—either as a teacher or in public debate against heretics and non-Buddhists. The point, as I take it, is that the true dharma, the Buddha's teachings, needs to be protected against the corrosion of false views. So, the purpose of logic and linguistics are not to explore and create new ideas, but to protect and defend the correct Buddhist view against misunderstandings and against the attacks of non-Buddhists. It is an essentially conservative view of scholarship.

Now, to complicate things, notice that there's an apparent contradiction between the first and second halves of the MSA verse. How can it be claimed in the second part that the 'inner science' of *dharmic practice* is what brings omniscience, when it was already said that the bodhisattva cannot attain omniscience without *all five* sciences? In fact, both appear in the commentary, as well. It says first that "All [are to be investigated] together for the sake of achieving omniscience,"[52] and then goes on, when setting them out separately, to say that specifically "[one studies] spiritual science for the sake of knowledge for oneself."[53] Why do you need all five if you've already got omniscience? The solution to the puzzle is in Table 1.2, where I've shifted the "others" and "oneself" up into the header row.

On this reading, the verse seems to be saying that the two *goals* of the bodhisattva's study that are directed toward *other* beings—refuting wrong views and helping others—come earlier, and are necessary stages on the path toward omniscience. So when the verse says that the bodhisattva needs to study in order to gain omniscience, this is not meant to say that the bodhisattva has to gather together all of the various knowledges until he has acquired omniscience. Instead, the point is that the compassionate acts of a bodhisattva, the acts that help one to progress, spiritually, on the Buddhist path, require scholarly study.

To summarize the two points I take from this verse, and I believe Sa-paṇ would agree: First, logical and linguistic study are understood to work together,

Table 1.2. MSA 11.60 on the five sciences (*pañcavidyā*): second interpretation

Five Sciences	For Others	For Oneself
linguistic science logical science	→ refuting	→ omniscience
medical science science of fine arts and crafts	→ supporting	→ omniscience
dharma, "inner science"		→ omniscience

conservatively, to preserve the authentic teachings; and second, this defensive practice of protecting the Buddhist dharma is an essential act on the path of the bodhisattva, the path to Buddhahood. This second point places the intellectual practices noted in the first point within the framework of the path, and thus imbues them with practical Buddhist value. This does place scholarship within a soteriological framework, since it is valuable to whatever degree it may contribute to defending the truth of the dharma. But this is entirely different from saying that the intellectual practices themselves are in any way distinctive Buddhist practices or paths. I believe that this is the general view that Sa-paṇ is advocating in the *Gateway,* and I will attempt to show in increasing particularity just how the various aspects of linguistics and philosophy he presents fit into this structure.[54]

Before we move on to specific skills, though, we can gain a better general understanding from the opening of the *Gateway.* Early on, Sa-paṇ defines the scholar in two ways:

> If you should ask, Who is called a "scholar"? Someone who knows all knowable things unmistakenly; alternatively, whatever specific teachings you know, in that and that alone you get called "scholar."[55]

The second definition, that a scholar is always a scholar *of* something, is in agreement with a modern secular academic understanding of the term. But we do not ordinarily accept the existence of the first, the all-knowing scholar. Who is this omniscient scholar? It may be said that the entire opening of the *Gateway* is about this question. First, we need look no further than the *Gateway*'s opening verse of reverence. Sa-paṇ begins the *Gateway* by praising the guru and Manjuśrī for possessing two lists of qualities shared in the essence of all Buddhas, the Four Specific Knowledges and the Four Fearlessnesses. As Sa-paṇ explains, these are the qualities of knowledge that allow the Buddhas to teach the dharma:

> This partial [listing] of qualities [of the guru and Manjuśrī] begins the treatise with [their] own attainment of confidence in the four specific knowledges, and [their use] for others [of] the four fearlessnesses to roar like a lion in the midst of the assembly.
>
> These [qualities] are, furthermore, the four specific knowledges—meanings, classifications, confidence, and definitive wording—by means of which [the guru] has attained mastery over everything that can be known; and, both for his own (*rang*) sake and the sake of others, the four fearlessnesses—realization, abandonment, [teaching] the path to Buddhahood, and teaching its obstacles—which [he] has achieved by being invincible to others [such as] the *tīrthikas* together with [their] gods (*lha dang bcas pa'i mu stegs*). Through this method, in composing texts himself, explaining them to others, and clarifying wrong views, he fears nothing;

> and since this is the complete basis for the perfection of the lion's roar, [I] explained this at the beginning.[56]

The lion's roar in the midst of the assembly—an assembly that might include followers or opponents—is the perfect characterization of the Buddha's unwavering and invincible power to teach and protect the dharma. Sa-paṇ makes explicit that it is "through this method"—that is, the method of the four fearlessnesses and the four specific knowledges—that the perfect Buddhas fearlessly engage in the *Gateway*'s three topics of composition, exposition, and debate. The Buddhas are, thus, the paradigmatic scholars. Clearly, these are the powers to be sought and emulated by all protectors of the dharma who seek to engage in these scholarly activities.

The modern commentator Tashi Chöpel gives a description of the four specific knowledges that explains the topics condensed in this brief passage with the central issues of the *Gateway*:

> The four specific knowledges are:
>
> 1. The specific knowledge of true meanings, in which, having understood just as it is the essential nature and taxonomic grouping (and so forth) of everything in samsara and nirvana, one gains mastery over these teachable meanings, without even a shred of the faults of misunderstanding, wrong-thinking, or doubt;
> 2. The specific knowledge of classifications, in which one understands just as they are [both] the perfect words that are used to express these knowable meanings, and a full listing of the names of every thing, and so forth;
> 3. The specific knowledge of confidence, in which, having developed confidence in exposition, debate, and composition on all knowable things—skills that are summarized in the ten sciences—one has an inconceivable ability to uphold what is right and defeat mistaken views;
> 4. The specific knowledge of language, in which, in accord with the national language [Chinese] and the minority languages[57] one is able to teach [one's] meaning with the right words, without faults such as using unclear words, being less than thorough, or confusing causes and results.
>
> These four, the lion's roar (declaration) in the assembly, are the uncommon inner cause of attaining the confidence that fears nothing of composing [texts] oneself, giving teachings to others, or clarifying mistaken understandings.[58]

This comment shows the specific knowledges to be in a kind of cumulative order. First, one comes to know all things individually as they truly are, then one understands how to express these classifications through language. Then, the third specific knowledge declares the virtue of confidence. A kind of extreme certainty comes as a result of having acquired perfect knowledge of all the sciences, and allows one to engage in teaching and defending what is right. Finally comes the fourth specific knowledge, which is not merely the linguistic knowledge necessary to express ideas (which was the second specific knowledge), but the very special linguistic knowledge necessary to express each idea in a way appropriate to its context and its hearer.

Likening the guru to Manjuśrī, along with all the Buddhas, refers specifically to Sa-paṇ's own root guru, his uncle Trakpa Gyeltsen. It is an ordinary part of tantric Buddhist practice to envision one's guru as equivalent to the Buddhas of the three times, and we do not want to place too heavy an emphasis on this occasion. Still, claiming that his own guru was equivalent to Manjuśrī *in teaching ability* suggests that Sa-paṇ was well positioned for a perfect reception of the teaching. This sets up the discussion that follows.

Next, Sa-paṇ explains his reason for composing the *Gateway,* which, as I have already noted, was to fill a gap in Tibetan learning. Sa-paṇ provides his list of categories on which he has seen Tibetans to be, "for the most part mistaken." Then, to declare his own ability to teach and clarify the issues on these topics, Sa-paṇ gives a resume of his own abilities. The following are the topics on which he claims to be expert, having "seen, heard, and grown accustomed to" major texts (which he lists) on each one: (1) Grammar, (2) Logic, (3) Poetry, (4) Metrics, (5) Poetics (*alaṅkāra*), (6) Synonymics, (7) Drama, (8) Medicine, (9) Crafts, (10) astronomical calculations of various kinds (including the vital energy analyses of the *Kālacakra*), and (11) all of the Buddhist "Inner Sciences," including Sutra, Vinaya, Abhidharma, and the four Tantra classes.[59]

After this list, Sa-paṇ turns to the central topic of the nature of a scholar, citing the two types of scholar mentioned above. Which, we might wonder, is Sa-paṇ claiming to be? Well, it is immediately after these definitions of scholarship that Sa-paṇ cites the famous verse from the MSA discussed above, which says that omniscience (*sarvajñatvaṃ*) is unattainable by one who has not studied the "five sciences." Sa-paṇ says that these five sciences are "the subjects to be learned by that scholar"—meaning, perhaps, the one "who knows all knowable things unmistakenly."[60] Thus, the *Gateway,* as a key to the five sciences, is a crucial first step in attaining omniscience; it is a "Gateway" to omniscience, which is itself an essential characteristic of the bodhisattva path. And, Sa-paṇ, the guide into this material, is clearly a master of all of the sciences.

Does this mean that Sa-paṇ is claiming to be an all-knowing Buddha? Of course, the MSA verse does not say that the all-knowing scholar is, necessarily, an advanced bodhisattva; omniscience is not described as a sufficient but only a necessary condition for the bodhisattva's advancement.[61] Yet by equating the "five sciences" with the objects of knowledge of "that scholar," Sa-paṇ does seem to suggest that mastering the five sciences is a *sufficient* condition for attainment of a kind of scholarly omniscience. Then, if the five sciences are what the omniscient scholar knows, Sa-paṇ does seems to be claiming, indirectly, to be all-knowing. We have, then, with the *Mahāyānasūtrālaṅkāra* reference and the references to the lion's roar, two homomorphisms between the scholarly ideal —Buddha as scholar—and the living scholar, and sandwiched between them a suggestion that Sa-paṇ, among few other Tibetans, evinces that ideal.

A clearer answer to the question of Sa-paṇ's own claim to knowing everything comes from the life story of Sa-paṇ's disciple Martön, the author of the *Zhib mo rdo rje,* as recorded by Lowo Khenchen. When he showed Sa-paṇ his *Lamdre* commentary, the *Gsung sgros ma,* Sa-paṇ is reported to have said:

> You have gained an understanding of the words in my explanation, without leaving out a single word. You will become a great expert who achieves mastery of everything knowable.[62]

If Martön is to achieve mastery of everything that can be known as a result of his studies with Sa-paṇ, it is no stretch to imagine that Sa-paṇ considers himself to have achieved such mastery as well. Indeed, Sa-paṇ also seems to hold the view that the disciple can only be as good as the master.[63]

But if Sa-paṇ believes this to be his own achievement and also a likely future for his student, surely we must use the English word "omniscience" with caution. We should remember that omniscience in Buddhism is not the same as the omniscience attributed to the God of the Hebrew Scriptures, eternal knower of everything. Buddhist omniscience (*sarvajñatā*), for instance, is not a state of awareness that includes all things simultaneously. The Indian Buddhist philosopher Vasubandhu writes in the *Abhidharmakośa* that "we do not declare the Buddha to be omniscient owing to manifest knowledge of everything," but rather "owing to potentiality."[64] Whatever the Buddha takes as an intentional object, he knows perfectly, as fire consumes whatever fuel comes into contact with it. Another explanation says that the Buddha knows all dharmas (*sarvadharmajñatā*), but in the sense of knowing every *class category*—every *kind* of dharma, with its proper application. So he knows perfectly what he needs to know to respond appropriately to every situation, but this does not require of him the knowledge of every particular.[65] The Buddha knows everything he needs to know, when he needs to know it: I will call this *relative omniscience.*

Sa-paṇ gives every indication that the "five sciences" consist in a vast but still finite scope of knowledge that *is* attainable by humans. Sa-paṇ may truly believe that it is possible, through ordinary scholarly training in the five sciences, to learn *everything that you'll ever need to know.* This may not be identical to the complete knowledge of a Buddha. In fact, in the *Treasury,* Sa-paṇ explicitly says that knowledge of ultimate truth is beyond what can be conceived (*bsam gyi mi khyab pa*).[66] But before achieving perfect Buddhahood, scholarship may provide the next best thing: a kind of omniscience that is available in this world, the relative omniscience of a scholar. Perhaps the ability to negotiate all known fields with a knowledge that is "active and useful" justifies the scholar's claim to comprehensive mastery. Butön, after all, was also to be known as "the all-knowing one" for his scholarly—as well as religious—accomplishments.[67]

How does this notion of relative omniscience conform to an ideal of learning actually sought in the circles Sa-paṇ wanted more Tibetans to emulate? I have already quoted Chak Lotāwa's biography where it is said that he, too, "mastered the entirety of . . . the five sciences."[68] Yijing reports of the Indian Buddhist "Method of learning in the West" that included "all the vinaya works and investigat[ing] the *sūtras* and *śāstras*"; extensive study in grammar and language (*śabdavidyā*) preceded that of logic (*hetuvidyā*) and metaphysics (*abhidharmakośa*). As a result of this breadth in learning, the learned monks were able "to oppose the heretics as they would drive beasts . . . and explain away disputations as boiling water melts frost."[69]

But, as Yijing writes, not everyone is expected to fulfill this education agenda: "Of such persons in every generation only one or two appear."[70] Xuanzang concurs in his description of Nālandā, writing that the slim odds of even passing the test to enter the debate court only limit the number of people subject to inevitable failure:

> If men of other quarters desire to enter and take part in the discussions, the keeper of the gate proposes some hard questions; many are unable to answer, and retire. One must have studied deeply both old and new (*books*) before getting admission. Those students, therefore, who come here as strangers, have to show their ability by hard discussion; those who fail compared with those who succeed are as seven or eight to ten. The other two or three of moderate talent, when they come to discuss in turn in the assembly, are sure to be humbled, and to forfeit their renown.[71]

The community of learning at Nālandā thus had an exceptionally high standard for inclusion. The result was that those who could pass muster could be counted among the elite of Buddhist learning:

> But with respect to those of conspicuous talent of solid learning, great ability, illustrious virtue, distinguished men, these connect (*their high names*) with the succession (*of celebrities belonging to the college*) such as Dharmapāla (Hu-fa) and Chandrapāla (Hu-yueh), who excited by their bequeathed teaching the thoughtless and worldly; Guṇamati (Tih-hwui) and Sthiramati (Kin-hwui), the streams of whose superior teaching spread abroad even now; Prabhamitra (Kwang-yeu), with his clear discourses; Ji-

> namitra (Shing-yeu), with his exalted eloquence; the pattern and fame (*sayings and doings*) of Jñānachandra (Chi-yueh) reflect his brilliant activity; Śigrabuddha (?) (Ming-min), and Śilabhadra (Kiaï-hien), and other eminent men whose names are lost. These illustrious personages, known to all, excelled in their attainments (*virtue*) all their distinguished predecessors, and passed the bounds of the ancients in their learning. Each of these composed some tens of treatises and commentaries which were widely diffused, and which for their perspicuity are passed down to the present time.[72]

In a similar passage, Tāranātha names the six famed "gatekeepers," or *dvāra-paṇḍitas,* at Vikramaśīla: Ratnākaraśānti, Vāgīśvarakīrti, Naropa, Prajñākaramati, Ratnavajra, and Jñānaśrīmitra.[73] I have these passages in mind when I call Sa-paṇ a "gatekeeper." Sa-paṇ is describing the standard of learning held by those whose job it is to keep ragged, itinerant ideas from entering the intellectual stronghold. As Jackson quipped, the *Gateway* is a difficult gateway to pass through, and only a few virtuoso scholars in Tibetan history have tried.[74] This may be overstated (the *Gateway* was, after all, taught in general lectures to all monks at the Sakya College in Dehra Dun when I visited there in 2000), but surely it is correct that Sa-paṇ considered mastery of the five sciences a very special ideal of scholarship. It seems reasonable to say that part of the purpose of the *Gateway* was to show the way for elite scholars seeking to emulate those previous famed "gatekeepers." In a story said to be Sa-paṇ's own words, the *Zhib mo rdo rje* records the words of the great translator Drokmi's *paṇḍita* teacher who recommended that he meet with Śāntipa, saying that he was "famed as a second Omiscient one in the age of strife," and that he was "one of the six experts at the gates of the temple of Vikramaśīla."[75] The term applied to these six "experts" is, of course, *mkhas pa,* which I am translating as "scholar" and "learning." Thus, though the word used in Tibetan for a gatekeeper of Vikramaśīla is *sgo-srung,* Skt. *dvāra-pāla,* which is not the term Sa-paṇ uses for the gateway in the *Gateway*'s title, there is an implicit link between the ideal scholars who were the gatekeepers at Vikramaśīla, considered "omniscient ones" on earth, and the ideal scholar of the *Gateway to Learning.*

Sa-paṇ writes, in a concluding verse to the *Gateway*:

> (III 73) So that the Sage's Doctrine may widely flourish and so that it may remain for a long time in this world, I have opened the three entrance doors for the wise who uphold the traditions of scholarship. May the wise enter within![76]

In this verse the "three entrance doors" are, clearly, those of composition, exposition, and debate. One might think, then, that it is the *pupil* who is invited to enter in, learn these methods, and begin to attain to a state of wisdom. Surely the pupil who seeks the highest of goals is intended as well, but Sa-paṇ especially extends his invitation to the wise—the already wise—who want to attain still higher states of learning:

> This treatise, the *Entrance Gate for the Wise,* which establishes the procedures of composition, teaching and debate, is a gateway by which intelligent persons enter into the great city of liberation; it is a passageway to be crossed over by noble persons.[77]

And, since the state of the dharma is in decline, Sa-paṇ believes that such noble persons are hard to come by, and that diligent study among the ignorant is hard to do:

> (III 77) Nowadays this doctrine of the Śākya Lion diminishes day by day, like a pond whose tributary streams have dried up. Those who have bright minds [and] who desire liberation must exert themselves for an excellent understanding of this procedure.[78]

Sa-paṇ sees himself as a protector of the doctrine, not merely as a link in the chain of the lineage, but a trainer for "those who uphold the traditions of scholarship." This suggests the elite corps of scholars that Sa-paṇ envisions as the last bastion, protectors of the fortified city of proper scholarship.[79] It begins to make a bit more sense to speak of these persons—the virtuoso, scholar-intellectuals—as "omniscient" at least in a relative sense, in the hope that they really can protect the doctrine against all comers. Sa-paṇ is simply claiming, with a detailed resume of his own abilities, to be one of the greatest Tibetan representatives of this well-established tradition of elite Indian scholars.

A final citation from the *Gateway* places us, once again, on the line between an appeal to scholars in the world and a projection of an imagined realm of perfect knowledge. After an arduous and detailed discussion of potential errors in interpretation that might arise for untrained scholars, Sa-paṇ cites, once more, the importance of general training in the linguistic sciences, but then moves immediately into another topic, from which all knowledge may be approached "in general":

> If you desire to understand well the meaning of such words, you need to be suitably trained in the five sciences. Specifically, you should be well acquainted with grammar, metrics, poetics, and lexicography, etc. In general, you need to know the dharaṇī doorways into mastery over everything that can be known.[80]

The "mastery over everything that can be known" is the same object as the four specific knowledges, and thus is the ultimate object of all intellectual occupation. But here the method of practice, far from the context of teachers and students and texts that are the common topics of the rest of the *Gateway*, involves the meditation upon *dharaṇī*, magical incantations, in order to perfect one's knowledge. Sa-paṇ is not saying that one method works and the other doesn't; rather, using both methods is best. Even if it is possible for ordinary beings to achieve this knowledge, we should not forget that one of the five sciences is Buddhist practice, which includes such extraordinary methods.

The belief in *relative omniscience* would appear to reflect two cross-culturally characteristic elements of "scholastic" traditions, as José Cabezón has summarized the concept: Scholastics hold a strong belief in "completeness and compactness," that "nothing essential to the project of salvation has been neglected," together with the idea of the "epistemological accessibility of the world," that every fact is knowable.[81] As I understand Cabezón's argument, the two concepts of completeness and compactness are linked because they sit under a common aegis of authority: nothing has been overlooked by the tradition in its formalization and canonization, and so nothing new need be added and nothing old can be removed. This, together with the fact of the world's transparency to analysis, allows us to make still greater sense of Sa-paṇ's notion of the omniscient scholar: it suggests that *to understand properly is to understand the whole, and such understanding is attainable.*

Thus Sa-paṇ and his colleagues who sought to formalize the ideals of the neoconservative movement through "Indianizing" or "Indologizing" Tibetan modes of learning did not need so much to *invent* a scholastic tradition, as they needed to discover and comprehend it as a properly comprehensive scholastic unity, and then translate and reconfigure it for their Tibetan contemporaries. It is this project that we might call their building the fortifying walls, and training the gatekeepers, of the proper Buddhist intellectual tradition. A crucial element of this, and perhaps all, scholastic traditions, then, is the belief that the tradition, once mastered, qualifies one to be such a necessarily invincible gatekeeper. It provides one a religiously sound position sufficient to silence the opponent—sufficient to grant one the "lion's roar" of victory—in any and every assembly in which one may appear. Surely Sa-paṇ would like his readers to believe that he was such an invincible lion. But he was not the only one. And those who read on might learn how, with work, they could achieve this perfect intellectual mastery for themselves.

2

BEWARE OF THE DHARMA IN TRANSLATION

A Warning to Interpreters

INTRODUCTION: TRANSLATION IN TIBET AND IN THE *GATEWAY*

Since the time of the Tibetan renaissance, Tibetan Buddhism has looked back to India, the home of the Buddha, as the original, authoritative source of scripture and learning. This is a powerful reason that special veneration has always been reserved for the great translators, the scholars who brought the dharma from India to Tibet, and made available in Tibetan language what had once been inaccessible in Sanskrit. Indeed, translation was often considered the quintessential scholarly ability, and translators the greatest intellectuals. Surely this was the opinion of Sa-pan's family tradition: "Ma gcig [Zang mo] said [to Sa Chen], 'Your father's teacher was a translator. You must also learn Dharma from a teacher who is a translator.'"[1] Early on, Sa-paṇ himself, along with other great scholars of the day, was called by the honorific title, "Master Translator."[2] As I will discuss below, his later honorific title "Sakya Paṇḍita" is also directly connected to his expertise as a translator from Sanskrit.[3]

It is not difficult to understand the importance Tibetans placed upon translators.[4] Sa-paṇ and his fellow translators represented an intellectual bridge between the dharma of the past and the dharma of the present, and in Sa-paṇ's day between India and Tibet. Yet amid all the veneration of translators, there are precious few discussions of just what translators do, and why it is so important that their work is good. In fact the *Gateway* may have been the first systematic and detailed discussion of translation to apear in Tibet since the publication of the official translation rules decreed by Thri Desongtsen.[5] But whereas that ruling provided an essentially pragmatic regulation of translators' conduct, Sa-paṇ's analysis provides a theory of translation along with a pragmatic interpreter's guide. For this reason, Sa-paṇ's distinctively Tibetan view of India and his distinctively Buddhist understanding of the role of the scholar come through in his analysis of translation, making this one of the most thoughtful practical and theoretical discussions of translation in any language before the modern period.

In particular, Sa-paṇ is interested in the specific problems facing the Tibetan Buddhist scholar working in the thirteenth century, wherein nearly all of the properly authoritative texts are translations—but translations that are full of dangers. As I have discussed in chapter 1, Sa-paṇ believes the scholar principally to be a guardian of the Buddha's teachings, a breakwater against the dharma's inevitable decay. In this context, the decay is cataloged in the form of extensive lists of potential misinterpretations of the dharma that are due to its shift into Tibetan language. The Tibetan scholar who seeks to fulfill his role as protector of the dharma must be aware of the distinctive hazards present in interpreting the dharma in Tibetan translation.

Throughout this chapter, I distinguish between two scholarly roles: the translator, who produces a translation, and the expositor, who reads and teaches the translated text. The *Gateway*'s second chapter, "Entry into Exposition" (*bshad pa la 'jug pa*), contains most of Sa-paṇ's discussion of translation. There he emphasizes the scholar's role not as a writer or debater, but as a teacher of scripture. It is, therefore, primarily in the context of the scholar's role as teacher that Sa-paṇ is discussing issues of translation. More specifically, these discussions come from Sa-paṇ's vast and diverse treatment of lexical exegesis, literally "explaining the meaning of the statement" (*ngag gi don bshad pa*).[6] Most of these translation issues are thus, for Sa-paṇ, issues of scriptural interpretation—proper interpretation of translated texts. For this reason, I will often speak simply of "interpreters" where Sa-paṇ would say "expositors" or "teachers."

Sa-paṇ's emphasis on the needs of the thirteenth century interpreter distinguishes the *Gateway* from all previous (perhaps *all*) known Tibetan discussions of translation. Although there was no central authority in charge of translation during the "second diffusion" of Buddhism in Sa-paṇ's time, the process of translation had been systematized early in the ninth century under the auspices of the Tibetan emperors, and the official works on Buddhist translation produced then were still essential tools of the translators' trade.[7] As themselves translators (*lo tsā ba*), Sa-paṇ and his colleagues would certainly have studied and taken to heart the standard works on Buddhist translation, especially the *Mahāvyutpatti* with its commentary, the *Two-Volume Lexicon*.[8] These were lexicographical works, consisting primarily in categorized lists of specific translation terms in source and target languages, but they also contained general rules for translators. Sa-paṇ draws upon his knowledge of these texts in his presentation of translation issues in the *Gateway*, but he is approaching the issue from the opposite perspective. He asks, given that all of these texts have been translated in a given manner, how is a Tibetan interpreter to make sense of these translated works? At one point in the *Gateway*, in order to explain how to interpret different levels of honorific terms, Sa-paṇ cites "the new language determination (*skad gsar bcad*)" rule of Thri Desongtsen on the use of honorifics from the *Two-Volume Lexicon,* which says "'In relation to the honorific level of Tibetan expressions, translate so as to [achieve] ease of understanding.'"[9] The point is that, whereas the Sanskrit language has far fewer status markers, Tibetan language honorifics can be usefully employed to enhance the meaning of a passage —for instance, in a conversation, to indicate whether a servant or a master is speaking. This is an important rule for the translators to know, of course, but why would an interpreter, teaching the text, need to know it? Sa-paṇ places this rule under the heading of aspects of a text that "the scholar does not need to explain."[10] That is, the honorific character of a Tibetan term does not necessarily reflect the honorific character of the Sanskrit original, and so is not an appropriate topic of analysis. To rely too heavily upon such markers might even lead to an interpretive mistake.

Such complications in interpretation are many, and to negotiate them an interpreter must have wide experience not only with texts in translation, but also with aspects of Sanskrit language and Indian literary norms. Two points that will come up repeatedly should be made clear from the outset: First, these interpretive difficulties are not to be blamed on the translators. On the contrary, as we will see, Sa-paṇ appears to be in agreement with the translators about their translation strategies, regardless of the resultant potential for misunderstanding.[11] In fact, the only time that Sa-paṇ criticizes the translators as a whole is when, based on ignorance, they sacrifice the Sanskrit meaning in order to make Tibetan comprehension easier. Sa-paṇ believes that the translators have done their job in preserving the original meaning of the dharma in its movement from Sanskrit to Tibetan. It is now the properly trained expositor's job to perceive and pass on an authentic teaching.

Second, Sa-paṇ makes no claim that Tibetan teachers must know the texts in their original Sanskrit versions. Although some interpretive problems will be difficult to solve without such knowledge, Sa-paṇ never suggests that the translations are unreadable in Tibetan. Instead, we must assume that Sa-paṇ believes that the translations are intended to be read by interpreters with special training that compensates for such difficulties.

I will analyze two sections from the *Gateway,* one where Sa-paṇ is troubled, and one where he seems optimistic about the dharma in translation. His worries, however, take up far more space. He is extremely concerned that the differences between Sanskrit originals and their Tibetan translations are misleading to inexperienced Tibetan interpreters. As usual, Sa-paṇ dedicates most of his space to correcting mistakes of other Tibetan scholars and establishing what he sees to be the standard interpretation of the Indian masters.[12] Interpretive mistakes are thus for Sa-paṇ a source of life-long irritation. But they are also a corrosion of the dharma and the arch enemy of the scholar. When the ignorant give teachings, he says,

> This dharma is a [mere] reflection of the dharma, or a so-called "dharma-like fabrication." Teachings of such a kind, on top of being of no benefit, bring about the destruction of the dharma.[13]

So the stakes are high.[14] As we review the variety of potential interpretive mistakes, we are also enumerating the skills required of any scholar who wishes to protect and not destroy the dharma.

For the sake of this discussion, I have divided Sa-paṇ's numerous concerns about difficulties in interpretation into four broad categories.[15] The interpreter must be familiar with (1) difficult words; (2) the techniques of translation used by Tibetan translators; (3) the common mistakes in translation from Sanskrit to Tibetan; and (4) elements with an unintelligible or invalid context.

OBSCURE VOCABULARY

In the first category, (1) for those unfamiliar with difficult Tibetan translation terms, Sa-paṇ suggests studying a good word list. As he says, "A good knowledge of synonyms such as [those in] the *Amarakośa* and the *Viśvaprakāśa,* etc. settles doubts about all word meanings."[16] He also suggests that, as an introduction, the beginning scholar might study Sa-paṇ's own lexicographic work, the *Word Treasury* (*tshig gi gter*).[17] This kind of study helps prevent four types of errors.[18]

First off, the uneducated interpreter is often unfamiliar with "the differences between new and old conventions [employed] by translators of the early and later traditions."[19] Thus:

> For example, when *bye ma ka ra* [is used] for *hwags; glo gor zho sha* for the *go yu* herb; *rin chen tog* for *rin chen dbal; nam yang* for *gzhar yang*—such are old Tibetan signs that are difficult to understand today.[20]

These are instances of old and new translation terms for Sanskrit words. The uneducated reader, encountering *hwags* and *bye ma ka ra,* both words for sugar, might be familiar with one but not the other and imagine that they translate different Sanskrit terms. Similarly, *rin chen tog* and *rin chen dbal* are two translations for the same Sanskrit term *ratnaketu,* meaning "jewel pinnacle." As Sa-paṇ explains in detail in his *Clear Differentiation of the Three Codes,* the problem is that while in the newer translations *dbal* has been replaced by *tog,* some interpreters look at the old translations and read *dpal* ("radiance") for *dbal,* and take it to mean not "jewel pinnacle" but "jewel radiance."[21] These are problems best solved by memorizing a list of translation terms.

Next, Sa-paṇ points out that:

> By virtue of being translated into local idioms (*rang rang gi yul gyi skad*), [for instance, translating] "arrow" (*mda'*) as *nyag phran*; "bow" (*gzhu*) as *gnam ru* . . . and so on—since they are translated [into words] not well known one place to another, they are difficult to understand.[22]

Here again the issue is clear: A knowledge of the variety of potential translation terms could prevent confusion when faced with obscure words. To avoid these errors, the interpreter needs to know the rare Tibetan words used to translate from Sanskrit.

Third, Sa-paṇ mentions that sometimes proper names are translated into Tibetan, and sometimes they are left untranslated. For instance, sometimes "*Magadhā* is translated into 'bearing all people' (*byings 'dzin*); *Vārāṇasī* into 'destroyer of attendants and family' (*'khor mo 'jig*),"[23] and so forth. The interpreter who is unfamiliar with translation terms has no way to know that an expression like "bearing all people" is the name of a place, not an abstract quality.

Fourth, and finally, sometimes Sanskrit terms are translated into Tibetan with a semantically faithful transformation of the term,[24] with a kind of description of the meaning instead of a literal rendering of the Sanskrit terms. Looking at the expression "the one that changes everything" there is no way that an uneducated reader could know that it means "prayer," or looking at "the one that turns evil away," know that it means "merit."[25] And, even if an interpreter knows that "the one that turns evil away" means "merit," he does not necessarily know that the notion of turning evil away does not appear in the Sanskrit word it translates.[26]

Thus to read the dharma the scholar must have a sure grasp of the often obscure vocabulary used to translate Sanskrit terminology into Tibetan. Sa-paṇ is not complaining about the translation practice that burdens the reader with the requirement of an unusually large and obscure vocabulary. It is to be expected that such unusual and obscure terms will appear, since "When beauty appears (*mdzes pa byung na*) in the Sanskrit language, Sanskrit [words] are used that are not, for the most part, well known in the world."[27] "Well known in the world" is traditionally contrasted with "well known in treatises"—the latter being knowledge that many scholars, but only scholars, possess.[28] Sa-paṇ recognizes that in order to translate the elevated style of Sanskrit texts, translators have imposed a new, elevated vocabulary on the Tibetan language. The Tibetan translation terms are designed to reflect the unique beauty and character of the Sanskrit. This suggests Sa-paṇ's understanding that the new vocabulary is, therefore, intended to be part of a new distinguished, perhaps aristocratic, Tibetan literate culture.

THE TECHNIQUES OF TRANSLATORS

Errors in interpretation of the second category (2) result from Tibetan interpreters being unfamiliar not with unusual vocabulary and expressions but with the techniques of translation used by the Tibetan translators. These are all mistakes of excessive glossing—ignorant scholars give expositions on expressions that in fact do not exist in the original Sanskrit. They fall under five basic types. The first two occasions for error are similar: they are terms that present, in Tibetan, a word that is merely a clarification and not a direct substitution for a Sanskrit term. When an Indian flower or jewel is named, even though the terms "flower" and "jewel" do not appear in the Sanskrit, they are often translated as, for instance, "Vaidūrya jewel" or "Saugandhika flower."[29] Also, Sa-paṇ writes, with terms such as

> "divine flower" and "divine incense," etc., some [translators] have added the expression "property" (*rdzas*), translating [them thus] as "flower offering" (lit. "divine property flower") and "incense offering" (lit. "divine property incense").[30]

These are terms that are unclear when translated word for word, and so the translators have strategically inserted an extra word to clarify the meaning.

The third translation strategy noted is similar to these, but involves compound words that represent uncompounded, simple terms in Sanskrit. In terms such as *ye shes* (*jñāna,* wisdom) and *phyag rgya* (*mudrā,* seal), the first syllables *ye* and *phyag* represent no proper part of the Sanskrit; the translators have inserted these in order to facilitate understanding in Tibetan.[31] Sa-paṇ chastises interpreters who gloss *ye shes* as "primordial wisdom" in spite of there being no word corresponding to "primordial" in the Sanskrit source. Thus, whenever a pseudo-scholar gives a commentary on a Tibetan syllable that fails directly to reflect a Sanskrit original, Sa-paṇ levels the charge of innovation—"fabricated dharma."

Sometimes, in order to reflect the Sanskrit wording, the translators have included words that appear redundant in Tibetan. As an example, Sa-paṇ cites the *Eight Thousand Line Perfection of Wisdom Sutra* as having the Sanskrit term *pakṣi,* "winged one," together with the term *śakuna,* "bird." Both terms are translated into Tibetan, so that the translated term reads, essentially, "winged one bird" (*'dab chags bya*). A Tibetan interpreter who comments on these words may be tempted to read the verse as "the winged one and the bird," reasoning that there is no justification for the redundancy unless two creatures are meant. But Sa-paṇ explains that in Sanskrit the terms *pakṣi* and *śakuna* are each ambiguous on their own, and only together mean, exclusively, "bird."[32] It would seem that the translator has sacrificed ease of comprehension in Tibetan to a very close adherence to the Sanskrit. But Sa-paṇ takes this translation strategy for granted, and places the burden on the interpreter. As I see it, the only way for the interpreter to avoid being fooled by this type of translation change will be either to know something of the Sanskrit terms reflected in the Tibetan, or to be warned by a teacher of the significance of this specific translation. Perhaps this is why Sa-paṇ points out that, realistically,

> If you desire to understand well the meaning of such words, you need to be suitably trained in the five sciences. Specifically, you should be well acquainted with grammar, metrics, poetics, and lexicography, etc.[33]

Errors of exposition will continue to arise until the interpreter masters all the sciences, and especially the full complement of linguistic sciences.

As the last aspect of this category, the scholar expositor must be aware that translators of Sanskrit into Tibetan have adopted the use of honorific and nonhonorific language in accordance with proper Tibetan usage. As mentioned above, Sa-paṇ notes that very few Sanskrit terms have honorific and nonhonorific forms, and he cites the "new language determination" of Thri Desongtsen that "In relation to the honorific level of Tibetan expressions, [one must] translate so as to [achieve] ease of understanding."[34] A Tibetan interpreter who does not know this rule might place too strong an emphasis on the use of a particular honorific or nonhonorific form.

Translation Mistakes

In the third category (3), errors arise from an unfamiliarity with common mistakes in translation from Sanskrit to Tibetan. These are of three types, but all are mistakes that occur in decoding the Sanskrit, as opposed to recoding the meaning into Tibetan. In fact, it is fair to say that Sa-paṇ criticizes translators only when they have performed errors of decoding (Sa-paṇ does not consider it an error of translation when the translators place the word "bird" twice in succession in Tibetan). This section is particularly interesting for what it suggests about Sa-paṇ's approach to his readers: the passages are remarkably opaque to a reader who is ignorant of Sanskrit. For instance, for the first type of error, where Sanskrit words are mistaken for their synonyms, he writes:

> Words with [errors of] Sanskrit reckoning [include] a translation of "rhino" as "sword" or "sword" as "rhino";[35] a translation based on a reversal of the expressions "footprint" (*rjes*) and "foot" (*rkang pa*); a translation that respectively mixes up "child," "sand," and "hair,"[36] and so on.[37]

If we don't know that the Sanskrit word *khaḍga* can mean either "sword" or "rhino," and that *bāla* can mean "child," "sand," or "hair," we cannot follow these examples; what we do understand is that in Sa-paṇ's estimation we are underqualified for explicating difficult passages in the dharma.

Second, sometimes translators mistake a word for a similar word, writing, for instance, *brgya byin byang chub* instead of *'byung po'i dbang po*—that is, misconstruing the Sanskrit name Indrabhūti as if it were *indrabodhi*.[38] And third, sometimes they divide words improperly, for instance taking the *na* of the instrumental case ending and misreading it as a separate word, the negative particle (perhaps reading *mahāyānena vidyate* as *mahāyāne na vidyate*).[39] Such translators' errors are frustrating, but Sa-paṇ points them out primarily to place interpreters on their guard, saying that, for the ignorant, "wrong translations are difficult to *understand*."[40] How could an interpreter without access to the original and without knowing Sanskrit correct these kinds of translation errors? Probably Sa-paṇ believes it possible to become familiar with the common errors in translation—perhaps Sa-paṇ hoped other scholars would add to the *Gateway*'s compilation of translation mistakes. Still, even to understand the errors the interpreter must know at least the basics of Sanskrit, and be familiar with the linguistic forms in which a variety of potential errors might appear. This interpretation fits with the relatively limited presentation of Sanskrit grammar in the *Gateway*, and it would appear thus to understand the scholarly community as separated into two classes: ordinary scholars who will memorize lists of errors and learn the basics of Sanskrit grammar, and experts who can *discover* the errors and so must know a good deal more than the basics of Sanskrit.

UNINTELLIGIBLE CONTEXT

The fourth (4) and final category of hazards for interpreters is, in fact, a category of my own making. Sa-paṇ describes these three categories separately, but I join them together to show their commonality as problems which arise from an unfamiliarity with contexts that the translators have left unexplained. I point them out here because they are, indeed, issues of translation and problems that arise for interpreters as a result of translation. I will refer to them again in a later chapter (chapter 5), when I take up the issue of scholarly practice in more detail. The three categories are: methods of commentary, common tropes, and literary characters or places.

First, Sa-paṇ explains many methods of commentary that are "well known in treatises" but not "well known in the world."[41] For instance, it is a common practice to gloss a word through appeal to its morphological root. Sa-paṇ says that if the word *kāya* is given a straight gloss, it means "body"; but if it is glossed as a derivative from the root *kai,* to shout, then it is perfectly legitimate to explain "the body" as "a shout."[42] Yet a passage from a scriptural commentary that claims that the body is a shout is, on its face, incomprehensible to anyone unfamiliar with the Sanskrit terminology that lies beneath the word-for-word Tibetan translation. Many other examples of glossing are listed that require some knowledge of the original linguistic context. I'll give two more examples. As Sa-paṇ writes, one commentator glosses the term "body" as "god." For body, the Sanskrit had *deha,* which he replaced with *deva.*[43] And when the expression "Thousand *bindu*-ed, hundred-syllabled" from the *Manjuśrīnāmasaṅgīti* is glossed in the *Kālacakra,* the hundred is changed to six by replacing the *śa* and *ta* of *śatākṣara* with the retroflex *ṣa* and *ṭa.*[44]

The interpreter who reads these glosses in Tibetan translation must first be familiar with the protocols of such commentary—to know the general principles of glossing that might make it legitimate to call the "body" a "shout." This knowledge consists in a set of culturally specific expectations for what satisfies a particular type of text.[45] But more importantly, it is difficult to imagine that an interpreter who knows no Sanskrit could come to understand the *particular* gloss, unless an explanation of the Sanskrit comes down in a separate commentary—oral or written. Without an additional explanatory tradition accompanying these translations, these elements are left completely unexplained—and, I would submit, they are in fact made more obscure—when the Sanskrit words have been changed into Tibetan.

The second and third varieties of what I am calling "unexplained context" consist, respectively, in common tropes and proper names that assume knowledge of Indian literature. Sa-paṇ explains a number of standard phrases that, translated literally, are confounding and misleading, unless the scholar is familiar with their meaning:

> Calling [someone] "pleasing to the gods," since what are pleasing to the gods are sacrifices of goats and buffalo, etc., is understood as an ironic expression of "You've got a mind like a beast." The expression "Like spirit[s] with [a] necklace," just as the spirit offerings bind a single thread—a string of flowers, etc.—on the necks of many different statues of beings, is an illustration [evoking the idea of] many different things pervaded by a single generality. The expression "The way of the crow and the plantain," [referring to] where a crow [has] landed on the very branch of the plantain that was [already] broken and the world declares that "the crow has broken the plantain," is an example of an accidental accomplishment.

> The expression "A crow's question" is a rash question, [for example,] during the exposition of scripture, without thinking ahead, considering it suddenly imperative and asking, "What's that?"[46]

Let this kind of expression stand as the paradigmatic instance of a translation that requires a scholarly community of interpreters to maintain its proper interpretation. There is simply no way for a reader to know the "meaning of the words" here without being given a direct interpretation from his teacher—or, from a work like the *Gateway* itself. Sa-paṇ's treatment of these tropes is quite extensive, suggesting that, in addition to proving beyond a doubt that scholars must be familiar with such Indian literary tropes, Sa-paṇ is hoping largely to fill that knowledge gap here and now. At one telling point Sa-paṇ instructs the reader in the particular intention behind a standard phrase, and, at the same time, provides an example of exactly why this kind of instruction is necessary:

> The expression "the adulteress wins with audacity" [refers to] when the husband saw an adulterous woman acting wrongly. When her lord confronted her, she said "Will you trust your eyes, inanimate bubbles? I am true as [your own] heart." For instance, [people] saying, "Why do you rely upon scripture and reasoning? I trust myself or the speech of my master."[47]

One can imagine the latter statement coming from a critic of Sa-paṇ's pedantic insistence upon scholarly precision. It is a mockery of exactly the kind of criticism that Milarepa levels at Geshe Tsakpūhwa in the poem discussed above in chapter 1. Sa-paṇ's answer comes in the very analysis that sets up the criticism itself, which the uneducated would fail to understand. Only a careful knowledge of the scriptures defends one against a fabricated, false version of the dharma. And, only a careful study of these kinds of conventional tropes of Indian literature provides one a true understanding of the scriptures.

Finally, as to proper names, Sa-paṇ mentions these as mistakes in translation—names that are mistranslated. But I count them as unexplained context because whether or not the names are correctly translated, they mean nothing without a knowledge of the context. Sa-paṇ says that Dāmodara (*Dha mo da ra*), a name for Kṛṣṇa, gets translated as *khyab 'jug*, the ordinary translation term for Viṣṇu. Dāmodara, which means "rope belly," is an epithet for Kṛṣṇa because when he was a child Yaśodā tied a rope around his belly.[48] The Tibetan translators did not know the story, and so mistranslated the name. Sa-paṇ suggests *tha gu lto* ("rope belly") as a better translation.[49] The Tibetan name for the goddess Sarasvatī is *dbyangs can ma*, which means basically "She of the Melody." But as Sa-paṇ points out, Sarasvatī only becomes "She of the Melody" if the expression is altered to make "Svaravatī."[50] A more correct translation, he writes, is *mtsho las byung ba*, "The Ocean-Born One," which preserves not only the Sanskrit name, but also the story behind the name. Sarasvatī was born from the ancient churning of the cosmic ocean. But, Sa-paṇ writes, "not having seen the story, and for the sake of making it easier for Tibetans to understand, it is translated 'She of the Melody.'"[51] Ease of Tibetan comprehension is insufficient to justify fabricating a name that fails to resemble the Sanskrit name, especially—and this is the sticking point—when the change is made out of ignorance of the Indian convention.

Here Sa-paṇ is finally criticizing translators as a group, including even the best of translators (who can avoid the howlers?). He writes:

> As for the [standard] words for different names of living beings and places in the non-Buddhists' ancient lore and the various *avadānas* in the sutras, one sees that even expert translators (*lo tsā ba mkhas*) have translated them incorrectly because of not knowing the ancient tales.[52]

The fact that this is the only place where Sa-paṇ points out a general problem in the translations (a problem for "even expert translators") makes it the exception that proves the rule: the translations are made for a community of expert interpreters. It is the only case where even the educated translators have introduced a Tibetan interpolation in favor of a Sanskrit original. In every other instance, complex and potentially misleading translation—in the form of obscure vocabulary and phrasing, redundancy, concepts left unexplained, even predictable mistranslation—is tolerable because it is easily countered by scholars who have mastered the structures of Indian texts and the standard practices of the translators.[53] But here the translators' ignorance has led to a systematic fabrication of the dharma. By changing the term, the translations represent a shift in meaning that is unrecoverable from the translated record. This makes it clear that Sa-paṇ takes the translators' main job to be to preserve in Tibetan as much of the Sanskrit as possible, notwithstanding the interpretive difficulties this causes. Once the translators have done their part, then it is the responsibility of the community of interpretation to maintain familiarity with the necessary conventions, in order to compensate for all the problems in shifting from one cultural/linguistic setting to another.

For this reason, I maintain the coherence of a category of translation problems that arise due to the translators' having left the context unexplained. In the chapters that follow, I will continually argue that Sa-paṇ views the scholar's central role to be to maintain this proper interpretive context in the face of increasing difficulties.

Untranslatability Denied

From what we have seen so far, then, it is clear that Sa-paṇ views the Tibetan translations of Buddhism to be a minefield of interpretive difficulties. Western discussions of translation with this kind of emphasis on mistakes and loss in translation have often fallen into skepticism about the very value and utility—even the possibility—of translation.[54] But it is clear that Sa-paṇ stands by the viability of translation. The biography of early masters of the *Lamdre* recently translated by Cyrus Stearns, called the *Zhib mo rdo rje,* is considered to be a record of Sa-paṇ's own words, and contains the following well-known anecdote:

> When the teacher [Sa skya Paṇḍita] spread out his Tibetan texts and listened, the lesser paṇḍitas ridiculed him, and laughed, and master [Śākyaśrī] said, "What use is it to spread out Tibetan texts?"
>
> Master [Śākyaśrī] read to a stopping point, and after that said, "You read!"
>
> When the teacher [Sa skya Paṇḍita] read out the Tibetan text in the Sanskrit language, [as though he were] reading an Indian [manuscript], it is said that [Śākyaśrī] was extremely pleased and exclaimed, "What are you laughing at? The one from Sa skya understands."[55]

Of course the purpose of the story of Sa-paṇ's impressive spontaneous back-translation into Sanskrit from a Tibetan translation is to display the mastery of the reader.[56] Stearns mentions an annotation in the manuscript that says "that Śākyaśrī gave him the name 'Sa skya Paṇḍita' on this occasion."[57] The ideal to which Sa-paṇ's name points is that of a Tibetan who is able to read Tibetan texts without any loss in translation, as though they were still in Sanskrit. But the trick can't work unless the translations, in the right hands, are functional. The Tibetan must contain, somehow, the meaning of the original Sanskrit.

In the final passage under discussion in this chapter, from the *Gateway*'s first chapter, Sa-paṇ recognizes that shifts in phonetic qualities, grammatical relations, and etymological implications are the inevitable result of the translation process. But rather than taking this to show a decay in the dharma, Sa-paṇ uses the occasion to argue that linguistic meaning operates not through the words themselves, but through the speaker's intention. As long as that intention is preserved, the linguistic changes are insignificant.

The argument I am describing is framed by Sa-paṇ's brief study of the two main categories of Sanskrit words: nouns and verbs. Sa-paṇ lists and defines the categories of case, number, and gender for nouns, and person, number, and tense for verbs, but he stops short before detailing the specifics of Sanskrit morphology, saying:

> These are completely necessary for Sanskrit terms, but inflection does not exist in Tibetan language, and moreover, because there is understanding [in Tibetan] owing to the force of established convention (lit. "well known to the ancients").[58]

Since Tibetan words do not undergo inflection—at least not in the same way as Sanskrit words—the translations cannot replicate Sanskrit morphology and syntax in Tibetan. Thus, instead of learning Sanskrit grammar, interpreters must familiarize themselves with scholarly conventions.

Then Sa-paṇ entertains an objection: "If the morphological constructions are not made in this way [i.e., according to Sanskrit rules], how is one to understand the meaning of a Sanskrit expression from a translation into Tibetan?"[59] This question asks, essentially, how can one language's meaning be understood in another's syntax? In answer to this question, Sa-paṇ first gives several examples of loss in translation between Sanskrit and Tibetan that he sees as both inevitable and unproblematic, and then he argues that, in fact, strong theories of untranslatability are non-Buddhist.[60]

The examples are of three kinds. Sa-paṇ's first, simple point is that the length and strength of a word's sound—phonetic qualities that are important in metrics—are different in Sanskrit and Tibetan terms.[61] Second, he notes that sometimes a grammatical particle, even when it represents the same Sanskrit case ending, might be written in several different ways in Tibetan—for instance the genitive case particle might be written as *yi*, *kyi* or *'i*, depending on the suffix letter of the word it follows.[62] Finally, he points out, sometimes in order to prevent mistakes, or to conform with the patterns of Tibetan understanding, the cases or the arrangement of Sanskrit words have been changed. For instance, while in Sanskrit the "reason" (*hetu*) of a logical syllogism is placed in the fifth case, in Tibetan it is always translated into the fourth case.[63]

As much as these changes resemble the kinds of hazards of which interpreters are warned in the section already discussed, in this section they are said to be free of fault:

> Even in cases like this, these very [expressions]
> Are consistent even though they are constructed differently.
> There is no such thing as an essential relation.
> Therefore they are made only as a speech intention (*brjod 'dod*).
>
> Since there is no substance to the connection between a sound and a meaning, its [linguistic] application (*'jug*) relies on the power of a speech intention. For this reason, no matter how it is applied there is no contradiction.[64]

We can state the basic argument of this passage fairly simply. There is no eternal, substantive connection between a word and its meaning. Words have to be given meanings by speakers, who invest the sounds with particular intentions. So any sound can be applied to any meaning. When Sa-paṇ says that there is no contradiction, he means that there is no *natural* contradiction between any particular sounds and meanings—which means that anything that can be expressed in one set of sounds can also be expressed in another.

This argument, as I've just stated it, is consistent with a number of modern philosophies of language, perhaps with common sense as well, and there is nothing in it that would necessarily appear distinctively Buddhist. Yet the significant terms that Sa-paṇ uses to state his argument—"essential relation" (*ngo bo nyid kyis 'brel*), "linguistic application" (*'jug pa*) and "speech intention" (*brjod 'dod*)—have their roots in basic Buddhist metaphysics, philosophy of language, and soteriology. Properly understood, this passage is, in fact, a distinctively Buddhist philosophy of translation. The technical terms just listed will occupy our analysis in the next two chapters (chapters 3 and 4), so I will conclude this chapter only by suggesting how Sa-paṇ's defense of translatability relates to the translation issues already discussed. All that is initially relevant, then, is the clear point that Sa-paṇ is distinguishing between a purported "essential relation" between words and meaning, and the accepted Buddhist view that language is constructed based upon the speaker's intention or supposition.[65] Linguistic use is a pragmatic activity, and linguistic meaning is constructed in dependence upon convention alone. It is this relative nature of language that Sa-paṇ calls upon to justify the stability of meaning as it moves through the transforming processes of translation. Translation changes only the context-bound, linguistic conventions. Since it is the intention, and not the word, that determines meaning, certain kinds of loss in translation are acceptable—as long as the translations preserve the speech intention (*brjod 'dod*) of the original.

But how can this intention be preserved, especially given that Sa-paṇ believes so many things to have been altered in the translation process? We have already seen the beginnings of Sa-paṇ's answer: Through an intellectual community that preserves the intentions in conventions called "well known in the world" or "well known in treatises."[66] Translation difficulties, it would seem, are overcome in the same way as all Buddhist knowledges are preserved; namely, through a valid lineage. The translations were made to preserve the dharma, but only in partnership with a continuous Buddhist community—the *saṅgha*—to teach it and guide its reception. The translations can be properly read, therefore, only by a direct inheritor of the authoritative tradition of interpretation. The ideal scholar ought to have inherited the true interpretation of the translated texts at the feet of his teacher, his guru.

Both sections, then, suggest a similar conclusion. If Tibetan interpreters train in the full complement of intellectual skills, like Indian *paṇḍitas,* the dharma will be protected against the corrosive tendencies of the change in linguistic and cultural context. The conventional nature of language means that translation is possible in principle, but only successful when the readers of the translation are trained to discover the same "speech intention" in the translation as was apparent in the original.

Sa-paṇ's analyses thus enclose the Buddhist scriptures within a particular set of social practices—primarily educational—that describe the range of both valid interpretations and authoritative interpreters. To put it this way shows that this is surely a political act, yet Sa-paṇ's transparent method of articulating his intellectual authority is simply to analyze translation choices. To a significant degree, then, the implicit interpretive context was, in fact, encoded in the Tibetan scriptures by the translators themselves. This point, then, returns us to the issue with which I began chapter 1: In a very specific sense, it would appear that Tibetan attitudes about religious authority and authority in general may be traceable back to translation choices made by the early translators of the dharma. Matthew Kapstein has recently noted that literacy in Tibet most likely persisted during the so-called dark age between the collapse of the old Tibetan empire and the period of renewed translation activity a century later, but only the form of literate usage characteristic of the Buddhist translations:

> Thus, it seems plausible that following the collapse of the dynasty, as the archaic language used by the civil and military administration became obsolete and a literate culture was preserved largely among Tibet's Buddhists, Buddhist usage gradually emerged as the standard, even in writing about subjects such as history that had previously been written in the language employed by the state bureaucracy. Some such development would have contributed to the iconizing of Buddhism and its originally Indian context as the paradigms of learned (that is, literate) and prestigious culture.[67]

After our above discussion, we can add that, when we note thus the centrality of Buddhist institutions in the preservation of literacy in a particular form, we should also turn our attentions to the character of the Tibetan Buddhist translations themselves, which by their difficulty require and so by implication project an elite community of interpretation as the paradigmatic guardian of the true Indian dharma—and, perhaps, literacy and learning itself.

3

THE DHARMA IS ONLY WORDS

A Philosophical Authorization of the Linguist

Introduction

In this chapter, we turn our attention to Sa-paṇ's attempts to convince his contemporaries to gain expertise in the linguistic sciences, beginning with Sanskrit grammar. In order to establish the importance of grammatical study, Sa-paṇ strategically intertwines grammatical concepts with standard ideas in Buddhist philosophy of language. In particular, he appeals to an extensive tradition in Buddhist thought that understands the Buddha's teachings not as a necessary and static set of doctrines, but as *upāya,* "skill in means." The great teacher used language as a method of moving disciples forward on the Buddhist path, and we have, in the dharma, the written form of that linguistic means. As I argue in this and the next chapter, what is notable in Sa-paṇ's argument is not his acceptance of this doctrine, but that he uses it as the basis for his articulation of the scholar's role in Tibet. It would not be immediately evident to Buddhists generally that a *skill in means* view of the doctrine would necessarily provide an argument for scholarly expertise, much less for Sa-paṇ's specific scholarly program. On the contrary, this doctrine has more often been used to support, if not a relativistic perspective, at least the legitimacy of a multiplicity of viewpoints.[1] Sa-paṇ, however, uses the relativity of the dharma as evidence that the doctrine requires expert scholarly interpretation, and that linguistic study in particular is crucial to the preservation of the teachings in their truest form.

The argument I describe is extracted from a short section from the *Gateway* on the basic categories of grammar.[2] In the course of this passage, with which Sa-paṇ introduces his linguistic analyses, Sa-paṇ employs as technical terms the expressions "term generality" (*sgra spyi*), "portion of the dharma" (*chos kyi phung po*), and "speech intention" (*brjod 'dod*) at what I take to be crucial and telling junctures. These terms, used as Sa-paṇ uses them, amount to a kind of "covert" argument—that is, one that we can discern once we know the terminological implications, but that Sa-paṇ never makes explicit. In what follows, then, I will first very briefly present what I consider Sa-paṇ's rather strict "skill in means" view. Then, in order to understand these terms in their Sakyapa philosophical reading, it will be necessary to take significant detours, comparing the *Gateway* passage with passages from Sa-paṇ's *Treasury of Reasoning* (TR) and his uncle Sönam Tsemo's *Gateway to the Dharma* (GD). Ultimately we will see that Sa-paṇ is using the particulars of Sakyapa epistemology, together with a well-established notion of the dharma, to provide a kind of Buddhist justification for grammatical study. Sa-paṇ believes that grammatical analysis of the dharma is neither perfunctory nor merely supportive of more consequential analysis; it is, instead, a direct method for revealing the intentions of the Buddha, crystallized and preserved as they are in the forms of language.

SKILL IN MEANS IN THE *GATEWAY*

Much of Mahāyāna Buddhist doctrine is, in one way or another, associated with the notion that the dharma is a result of the Buddha's skill in means (*upāya-kauśala; thabs mkhas*).[3] One approach to this complex view begins with the recognition that a Buddha's every act is undertaken in order to help sentient beings move forward on the path to enlightenment. The speech of the Buddha, recorded as the written dharma, is no exception. It is the method by which the Buddha removes obstacles to enlightenment in his listeners. The real *skill* comes in the Buddha's having recognized, in his omniscience, that sentient beings exist at numerous levels of understanding, and so it is not fitting to provide just one teaching for all; rather, a variety of lessons must be given that apply to the different levels of sentient beings. Any one teaching, then, is intended to remove one type of obstacle to enlightenment, one that happens to be preventing the enlightenment of the disciples to whom the Buddha is speaking.[4]

In the *Gateway*, the doctrine of the Buddha's skill in means comes up most often in the context of separating out the dharma's evident plurality of doctrines. Several of Sa-paṇ's writings are dedicated to isolating the doctrines of distinct Buddhist schools and clarifying the different contexts in which the Buddha's true "intention" (*dgongs pa*) can be understood.[5] Each tradition, Sa-paṇ writes, is valid, but only in its own context. Each canonical Buddhist text is directed at a particular audience with its particular needs. For this reason, while every teaching has its proper audience, to mix the teachings leads to mistakes:

> For example, in activities such as farming in different places and seasons, [each activity] will be successfully realized through its own system of practice, whereas if one mixes them up one will not succeed. The Buddha's teaching of different classes of scripture according to the particular mental dispositions [of different creatures] was also done with that in mind.[6]

Sa-paṇ often devoted space in his works to correcting what he took to be the erroneous views of his contemporaries. Here, he is preoccupied with arguing against opponents who imagine or worry that differences between the doctrines of the Mahāyāna and the Hīnayāna,[7] or between Pāramitāyāna and Vajrayāna, display inconsistency in Buddhism itself. On the contrary, Sa-paṇ points out, each was a perfect teaching for the disciples to whom it was taught. Each teaching served to remove a particular afflictive negative state (*kleśa; nyon mongs*).[8] For this reason, it is perfectly reasonable for a Buddhist to adopt and defend any of these positions, as long as she does not switch from one position to another within a single round of debate.

Sa-paṇ's view of the Buddhist doctrine is, therefore, an orthodox Mahāyāna view: the Buddha's teachings were composed "according to the particular mental dispositions [of different creatures]," not according to the truth values of their propositional content. Just after the passage cited above, an objector raises an inevitable question in this context: If one allows that so many Buddhist teachings are acceptable within their context, how does one establish one teaching as the absolutely right, ultimately correct teaching? In reply, Sa-paṇ is supremely clear: One cannot. For even the so-called ultimate truth of Mādhyamika doctrine is liable to error when it is subjected to critical examination, simply by virtue of its being a conceptualization: "For whatever is established as the object of mind becomes, upon examination, liable to faults. Nothing is [then] suitable but silence."[9] All mental objects are liable to the faults characteristic of beings who have yet to attain freedom from the afflictions, and any doctrine is essentially a mental object. All doctrines, therefore, are only provisional. Everything that rests in language, including the dharma, is corrupt by virtue of being a conceptual construction. In what follows, we will see how Sa-paṇ uses this view of language and the dharma as a justification for developing linguistic expertise.

THE "TERM GENERALITY" AT THE FOUNDATION OF GRAMMAR

Sa-paṇ's linguistic analyses from chapter 1 of the *Gateway* fall into two broad sections. The first, smaller section, which is my concern here, is Sa-paṇ's brief discussion of the "three assemblages which are the causes of language."[10] These three assemblages are, in turn, the assemblages of letters (*yi ge,* more accurately "phonemes"), words (*ming,* lit. "names"), and phrases (*tshig,* lit. "words, wording"). According to this view of language, briefly stated, language requires that letters be gathered into basic lexical word units, and then that those forms—essentially uninflected stems—be inflected and gathered into meaningful phrases and statements.[11] These three groupings are called the linguistic *causes* because each grouping is the cause for the next, and because they bring about linguistic understanding. These are basic linguistic concepts for the Indo-Tibetan world.[12]

Perhaps the locus classicus for this view of the causes of language is chapter 2 of Vasubandhu's *Abhidharmakośa,* where they are described as three of the "compositional factors dissociated from the mind" (*cittaviprayukta saṃskāras*).[13] This categorization is a kind of catch-all for leftover dharmas that fail to fit into other categories. Saying that they are "dissociated from the mind" distinguishes letters and words from, on the one hand, properly mental compositional factors such as the emotions; calling them "compositional factors" distinguishes them from, on the other hand, properly material phenomena such as the elements.[14] Vasubandhu's general practice in the *Abhidharmakośa* is to present the orthodox Vaibhāṣika view, and then to refute that view from the perspective of the Sautrāntika school. On this issue, the Vaibhāṣika argue that these linguistic causes (i.e., words) have a reality distinct from their sounds, but bring about understanding only when vocalized; the Sautrāntika respond that it is superfluous to posit the existence of words in excess of mere sound, and that sound is only a material form.[15] Biardeau has noted that this debate in the *Abhidharmakośa* reflects practically every important issue in non-Buddhist Indian philosophy of language.[16] For my purposes here, it is sufficient to note that, in both accounts, (1) the causes of language are considered extramental causes of understanding, and (2) the causal story is left unexamined.

Sa-paṇ's *Gateway* presents a new perspective on the causes of language. For comparison, let us look at another of Sa-paṇ's texts, the *Entry into Words* (*sgra 'jug,* EW), which is also a first textbook on language, but is not dedicated to the *Gateway*'s larger project of defining and justifying a comprehensive vision of scholarship. In the EW Sa-paṇ introduces his readers to a fair amount of detail about the three building blocks of language. The EW is, in turn, based upon a text that Sa-paṇ cites in his *Gateway* section as a good source for further study, the *Sword Doorway into Language* (*Smra sgo mtshon cha,* SDL) by the Indian scholar Smṛtijñānakīrti.[17] Compare, then, the definitions of the causes of language from Sa-paṇ's EW with those from his *Gateway,* and then with two passages from the SDL on which both of Sa-paṇ's analyses are clearly based.[18]

Sa-paṇ's *Entry into Words* has:

> ["Letter"] is defined as "whatever sounds are combined into a syllable."[19]
> ["Word" (*ming*) is defined as] "what is able to designate the real substance of a meaning."[20]
> ["Phrase" (*tshig*)] is defined as "what is able to indicate a specific meaning."[21]

Sa-paṇ's *Gateway to Learning* has:

> "Letter" is defined as "the appearance of a term generality that does not indicate a meaning."[22]

"Word" (*ming*) is defined as "the appearance of a term generality that indicates the substance of a meaning."[23]

"Phrase" (*tshig*) is defined as "the appearance of a term generality that indicates a specific meaning."[24]

The *Sword Doorway into Language* by Smṛtijñānakīrti has:

In brief, what is capable of indicating merely the very substance of a thing, being an assemblage of letters which separately do not indicate [the substance of a thing], is called a "word" (*ming*).[25]

The nature of a "phrase" (*tshig*) is to indicate a specific meaning with an assemblage of those [words].[26]

I have taken these passages out of their respective contexts in order to show the parallel movement from letters, which are building blocks that fail to express a meaning, to words, which denote the substance (*ngo bo*) of a meaning, to, finally, phrases, which indicate meanings in specific cases.[27]

The obvious difference in the definitions, then, is the expression "the appearance of a term generality" (*sgra spyi snang ba*), which accompanies all three definitions in the *Gateway*, but is entirely absent from the EW and the SDL. The mystery is not in the expression's absence from the more strictly linguistic texts: "term generality" is a technical term of Sakyapa epistemology, and it does not appear in other discussions of these terms or in other Buddhist grammatical texts.[28] But if this term is unexpected in the context of linguistic study, why does Sa-paṇ place it at the root of language study in the *Gateway?* In order to answer this, I will first examine the meaning of the term "term generality" for Sa-paṇ, and then show that a parallel use of this term, similarly out of context, appears in a text by Sa-paṇ's uncle Sönam Tsemo.

THE "TERM GENERALITY" IN SAKYAPA EPISTEMOLOGY

One issue that distinguishes the Sakyapa interpretation[29] of the Buddhist epistemologists from that of other Tibetan schools is its characteristic use of the terminological pair "term generality" (*sgra spyi*) and "object generality" (*don spyi*).[30] In this section I will analyze, philosophically, the meaning and purpose of both of these terms, citing the passage from Sa-paṇ's monumental epistemological work, the *Treasury of Reasoning* (*tshad ma rigs gter,* TR), in which Sa-paṇ documents his view of these terms.[31] For the sake of clarity, I will speak of this view as Sa-paṇ's own, rather than attempt to trace its connections to other sources.[32]

Suppose I say a word that you have never heard before, say, *roandus*. I might even say it in context, such as, "Have you ever seen a *roandus?*" What Sa-paṇ wants us to notice, first of all, is that when you hear the new word, you recognize it as a word and immediately form a verbal concept based on that sound. If you ask me, in turn, "What is a *roandus?*" you have used this verbal concept. When I said the word *roandus,* I created a unique sound that vibrated at a frequency specific to my own voice, with many other particulars in tone, pacing, volume, and so on. This unique sound, which occurs only once, is a bare particular (*svalakṣaṇa, rang mtshan*). But your immediate response showed that you understood *roandus* not as a particular sound, but as a term, so that you were able to reproduce the *same* word using *your* verbal signature. The conceptual bridge necessary for this act is what Sa-paṇ calls a "term generality"—the general concept of a particular term or sound. He would say that when you spoke, you *conceived* (*zhen pa*) your vocal vibrations to be identical to the term generality that you constructed, or, what is the same, he might say that you conceptually *superimposed* (*sgro btags*) the term generality on your own vocalization.[33] But, as Sa-paṇ writes, in truth there is an important distinction to be made between the word itself—that is, the sound itself—which you think you are using to signify a meaning, and the concept you have of the sound, which you are in fact using to signify a meaning:[34] "[The term's] real signifier, which is the term generality, [is different from] the conceived signifier, which is the sound as a bare particular."[35]

To clarify briefly, imagine the difference in your conceptualization process if instead I had said "Have you ever seen a . . . *cough* . . ."—that is, coughing instead of finishing my sentence. You would never think to ask the meaning of the cough. Instead, you hear the cough not as a term, but as a sound. Your conceptual mechanisms created no term generality for the cough.[36] The point to remember is that you cannot connect meaning to a particular sound, only to a term generality. Once you have a term generality, you are ready to ask for its meaning.

To give a bit of background, it is useful to know that the ontology that accompanies Sakyapa Buddhist epistemology allows only two kinds of things: particulars and generalities (*sāmānyalakṣaṇa, spyi mtshan*). The particulars are real, simple perceptions, whereas the generalities are false mental fabrications. Everything that is not a bare particular, then, is a false mental fabrication. The typical mistake of all nonenlightened sentient beings is to confuse their mental fabrications with their simple perceptions, imagining that, for instance, their idea of a "good job" is identical with the countless external stimuli that are presented to them as discrete perceptual moments. Because beings engage in conceptual construction, assembling momentary perceptual stimuli into conceptual categories, they can be deluded into imagining that they *have* one of these good jobs, and eventually they suffer when it turns out, inevitably, not to be the case. "Good jobs" only exist in the mind. The same is true of term generalities, such as the one that you constructed upon first hearing my use of the word *roandus*.

Continuing on, suppose a *roandus* is a kind of animal and I happen to have a picture of one, which I show you in response to your question. Looking at the picture, even if you have never seen a *roandus* before, you immediately recognize that it is an animal, that it has certain kinds of feet and eyes, and so on. You begin to form a concept that you will forever associate with the term *roandus*. This concept is what Sa-paṇ calls the "object generality." Notice that, just as you formed the term generality based on a single sound pattern, you have now formed the object generality based on a particular image. Although I show you a single photo, it is clear that the term *roandus* refers not to that photo, but to any animal of the sort pictured there. As with the term generality, there is an important distinction to be made between the thing itself—in this case, your visual perception—which you imagine to be signified by the word *roandus*, and the general concept you have of the animal, which is what the term *in fact* signifies: "The term's real signified, which is the word meaning [i.e., the object generality], [is different from] the conceived signified, which is an object as a particular."[37]

Sa-paṇ believes that both the term generality and the object generality, since they are conceptual constructions, are false. Nonetheless, we cannot have meaningful communication or conceptualization without them. Such is the unsatisfactory nature of human understanding within samsaric existence: all linguistic reference is dependent upon false conceptualization. False conceptualization is not only inevitable, it is necessary in order for humans to operate normally, and, for instance, to succeed in actually understanding one another and encountering the objects of which they speak. If you say, for instance, "Please bring me the dumplings," you are engaging in a tremendous number of false conceptualizations, including, especially, your belief that you are referring to the dumplings on the table across the room: in fact, you are referring to your own falsely constructed conception of dumplings as an object generality, and merely superimposing this concept on your visual perception so that a particular appearance appears to you as an instance of the generality *dumplings*. Nonetheless, since I, too, have generated a false conceptualization that I associate with the term "dumplings," and since I, too, will superimpose my conceptualization onto the sensory phenomena that I am receiving from the dumplings across the room, it is likely that *you will get your dumplings*. This view of language ultimately consigns all reality to the ineffable; yet at a conventional level, it allows the ordinary use of language to proceed in a manner more or less in accord with our intuitions.[38]

Therefore, while there are real distinctions between term or object generalities and the particular phenomena upon which we superimpose these concepts, they are distinctions that have relevance only from a descriptive perspective. We cannot speak without *forgetting* (so to speak) these distinctions and simply proceeding with the business of error-wrought communication. For this reason, Sa-paṇ makes a strict distinction between our knowledge *that* language depends upon false constructions and our ability to *use* language properly in the face of, indeed through, these errors:

> When explaining, one discerns reality by understanding the divisions. . . . When using [language], without making a distinction between the generalities and the bare particulars, one mistakes them as one; when the application of signs [produces] a conventional designation, one is able to achieve the thing itself.[39]

We can now look at the full passage from Sa-paṇ's *Treasury of Reasoning.* The passage begins with the word "Second . . ." because it is the second section of Sa-paṇ's chapter on "How to understand the signified and the signifier."[40] In the first section of the chapter, Sa-paṇ refutes alternative positions on this terminology, and in the third and last section, he refutes potential objections to his own position. In between, here in the second section, Sa-paṇ briefly presents his own position (*rang 'dod*). Please note that each indented verse is explained in the commentary that follows it:

> Second, my own position [will be presented] in three parts: Definitions, divisions, and determination of their meanings.[41]
> First,
>
> > From the sign, the understood and the understanding.
>
> The definition of *signified* is *what is to be understood from a sign; signifier* is *the sign that brings about understanding of an object.*
> Second, the divisions:
>
> > A person's [linguistic] explanation and use—by dividing them by two and by two, [each make] four kinds.
>
> The signified and signifier, when explaining or using [language], two [times divided in] two are four.
>
> > When explaining, by separating out the kinds, be discerning (*mkhas*). When using, by mistaking them as one, achieve.
>
> When explaining, one discerns reality by understanding the divisions thus: "The term's real signified, which is the word meaning [i.e., the object generality], [is different from] the conceived signified, which is an object as a bare particular; and [the term's] real signifier, which is the term generality, [is different from] the conceived signifier, which is the sound as a bare particular." When using [language], without making a distinction between the generalities and the bare particulars, one mistakes them

as one; when the application of signs [produces] a conventional designation, one is able to achieve the thing itself.[42]

The word *mkhas,* which I have translated here as "be discerning," is the same word, used as a verb, that appears all over the *Gateway to Learning,* including in its title (*mkhas pa 'jug pa'i sgo*), and which, as a noun, I ordinarily translate as "scholar," "scholarship," or "learning." Sa-paṇ uses the term in the above passage to say that these terminological distinctions are the proper topic of expert *analysis,* but that the *use* of language proceeds properly without such an understanding. We may safely take this to mean that linguistic expertise (*mkhas*) is unnecessary for ordinary speech acts to succeed. Yet to use this term is by no means to denigrate such learning. On the contrary, the term *mkhas* is also the word for *skill* in the Tibetan translation of the term "skill in means" (*thabs mkhas*). The special skill mentioned here is the ability to discern what is really *meant,* what signification actually occurs in a speech act. Of course, Buddhist experts in linguistic analysis focus their energies on the dharma, which is the *result* of the Buddha's skill in means, the Buddha's particular linguistic intentions directed toward particular disciples. Thus the "skill" of the linguistic scholar reflects quite directly the skill in means of the Buddha. Through grammatical analysis, as we will see, the linguist discerns and brings to light the particular linguistic intentions of the Buddha.

What remains to be drawn out from this passage is the structure of the two twos that make four—that is, the two pairs of divisions that apply to both the explanation and the use of language. We have already made these distinctions in our discussion: they are *signified* versus *signifier* on the one hand, and *particular* versus *generality* on the other. The chart below shows the four elements that, Sa-paṇ writes, the discerning scholar is able to separate out in order to explain the workings of language:

Table 3.1. Terminological analysis of *Treasury of Reasoning* 167.1–19, on signifier (*rjod byed*) and signified (*brjod bya*)

	Signifier (*rjod byed*)	**Signified (*brjod bya*)**
Generality (*spyi mtshan*)	term generality (*sgra spyi*)	object generality (*don spyi*)
Particular (*rang mtshan*)	sound (*sgra*)/conceived signifier (*zhen pa'i rjod byed*)	object/thing (*don*)/conceived signified (*zhen pa'i brjod bya*)

My discussion above began with what appears here in the *signifier* column, distinguishing between the sound of the word *roandus,* the particular phenomenon, and the term generality you generated upon hearing that sound for the first time. Now, the term "conceived signifier" appears in the box along with "sound," since this is the term Sa-paṇ uses to denote how the sound itself is mistaken for the signifier. I then discussed what appears here in the *signified* column, where the *roandus* itself was shown in a photograph—a visual bare particular "thing" upon which you based your conception of the animal, your "object generality." Now, the term "conceived signified" appears in the box along with "thing," since this is the term Sa-paṇ uses to denote how the thing itself is mistaken for the signified. The paired terms share their boxes because Sa-paṇ takes them to be identical. As I see it, the need for these two different terms points to the central difficulty in this system: If you have only *conceived* that you were referring to the *thing*, why do you end up getting your dumplings? I will return to this difficulty in several contexts below. For the time being it must suffice to point out that Sa-paṇ, at least, considers it a significant issue that he must face. It is only after several arguments and scriptural citations that he will conclude this section of the *Treasury of Reasoning*: "Thus, even though the word's real signified does not exist, the conceived signified is the actual object of engagement."[43] We are deluded, and yet language works.

SA-PAṆ AND SAUSSURE ON THE CONCEPTUALITY AND CONVENTIONALITY OF LANGUAGE

The discerning reader will perhaps have noticed that my treatment of Sa-paṇ has benefited from Saussure's linguistic terminology: *signifier, signified,* and *sign.* In this I am following Georges Dreyfus,[44] who saw the utility of these terms for translating, in the Sakyapa context, the terms *brjod bya* (*vācya*) and *rjod byed* (*vācaka*), literally "to be said" or "sayable" and "saying," respectively.[45] This translation is justified by a basic similarity between Saussure's and Sa-paṇ's reasons for using these terms.[46] And, the juxtaposition of elements from Sa-paṇ's and Saussure's linguistic lexicons will bring to the fore the motives behind some of Sa-paṇ's usages.

Sa-paṇ and Saussure share the conviction that there is an important distinction between linguistic acts in the mind and the things in the world that we generally take them to be. As Saussure writes: "The linguistic sign unites, not a thing and a name, but a concept and a sound-image."[47] Saussure assigns to this *concept* the term "signified [*signifié*]," and to the *sound-image* he assigns the term "signifier [*signifiant*]." It is worth citing his introduction of the sound-image in full:

> The psychological character of our sound-images becomes apparent when we observe our own speech. Without moving our lips or tongue, we can talk to ourselves or recite mentally a selection of verse. Because we regard

> the words of our language as sound-images, we must avoid speaking of the "phonemes" that make up the words. This term, which suggests vocal activity, is applicable to the spoken word only, to the realization of the inner image in discourse. We can avoid that misunderstanding by speaking of the *sounds* and *syllables* of a word provided we remember that the names refer to the sound-image.[48]

Saussure wants us to shift our understanding of *sounds* and *syllables* so that when the terms come up we always understand them to refer not to the sound vibrations, but to our conceptual representations of sounds. It seems to me Sa-paṇ is doing the very same thing. In the *Gateway*, when he defines the causes of language as term generalities, he is, at the very least, urging the reader to understand all linguistic terms in their conceptual, and not their extramental, forms:

> "Letter" is defined as "the appearance of a term generality that does not indicate a meaning."[49]
>
> "Word" (*ming*) is defined as "the appearance of a term generality that indicates the substance of a meaning."[50]
>
> "Phrase" (*tshig*) is defined as "the appearance of a term generality that indicates a specific meaning."[51]

Thus, we can see that Sa-paṇ's placement of "the appearance of a term generality" at the root of his grammatical analysis encloses an argument in the philosophy of language. To define the three linguistic causes as a very precise form of conceptual construction provides a significant improvement on Vasubandhu—but without explicitly disagreeing with the Indian master. Remember, Vasubandhu had characterized phonemes and words as extramental causes of understanding, without indicating how that understanding comes about. By defining them as term generalities, Sa-paṇ brings them entirely into the mental sphere, and somewhat clarifies their character as *causes* of linguistic understanding, since term generalities are causally connected to object generalities.

This comparison with Saussure has thus uncovered one layer of what I am calling Sa-paṇ's "covert argument." Simply by placing one term in a new context, Sa-paṇ takes a stand on the nature of language. I began this discussion by asking why the term "term generality" should fail to appear in Sa-paṇ's general linguistic treatises—and the question is particularly pressing now that it appears that Sa-paṇ is arguing a point of "general linguistics"—but we can now begin to provide an answer.

First, notice that the linguistics argument only becomes evident when accompanied by a lengthy discussion of some of the more technical arcana of Sa-paṇ's epistemology. These definitions consequently serve different purposes for different audiences. In the complexity of the terms, evident to all, the definitions display Sa-paṇ's broad technical mastery. To those who are familiar with the general context of the terminology but have no detailed understanding of the notion of the "term generality," they show that grammatical concerns are not separate from epistemological. Passages such as these are crucial in Sa-paṇ's efforts to make the various sciences cohere into a single ideal of learning. Finally, to the learned scholar, the argument embedded in these definitions shows exactly *how* linguistics fits into the complete scope of a scholar's knowledge. The learned scholar who is familiar with the TR, for instance, knows that these terminological distinctions are the proper subject of expert descriptive analysis, not ordinary linguistic use. But to fully understand this third purpose, I will have to uncover yet another layer of meaning enfolded in Sa-paṇ's terminological use. As we will see, Sa-paṇ's designation of all language as rooted in a term generality is an argument for his understanding of both the Buddha's use of language in articulating the dharma, and the scholar's role in perpetuating it.

The basis for this covert argument rests in yet another parallel between Sa-paṇ and Saussure: Saussure's famous first principle of "The Arbitrary Nature of the Sign."[52] Sa-paṇ and Saussure agree that nothing essential unites a word and its meaning. Saussure would presume such agreement, for he remarks that, "No one disputes the principle of the arbitrary nature of the sign."[53] But Sa-paṇ knows that in the Indian philosophical tradition this is anything but true. Certainly the Mīmāṃsā and the Vyākaraṇa (grammatical) philosophers in India believed in an "essential relation" (*ngo bo nyid kyi 'brel; svabhāvika-sambandha*) between words and their meanings.[54] In his discussion of the hazards of translation, Sa-paṇ cites the *absence* of such an essential relation as support of the legitimacy of translation from Sanskrit into Tibetan language.[55] Since the relation between words and their meanings is arbitrary, there is no rule preventing one meaning from being expressed in two different languages, in spite of unavoidable phonetic and other changes.

Like Saussure, Sa-paṇ recognizes that the arbitrariness of the sign suggests not the *independence* of signifier and signified, but their *dependence upon convention.* The comprehension of meaning and the attainment of whatever goals are associated with the use of language arise in the mind not due to some essential character of the words, but due to a familiarity with conventional use of terminology: "When the application of signs [produces] a conventional designation, one is able to achieve the thing itself."[56] It is only through convention, then, that terms have their meaning. This is one piece of Sa-paṇ's answer to the conundrum of how it is that you will end up getting your dumplings: I understand your meaning because the conceptual mistakes that *I* make are the same mistakes that *you* make; we share the same erroneous patterns of conceptualization and linguistic convention.[57]

Sa-paṇ and Saussure share the belief, therefore, that the determination of meaning relies upon linguistic use: words themselves are arbitrary, but become fixed by convention. In what follows, we will see how this understanding of conventionality in thought and language dovetails with central themes in Buddhist doctrinal speculation. The Buddha's teachings recorded in the written dharma are understood to be merely conventional because they are directed toward the needs of specific disciples. Such conventionality must be distinguished from the ultimately true realization of a fully enlightened Buddha. Yet the recognition of convention at the root of language is also the first step in understanding the *proper* approach to the written dharma. Since it is merely conventional, we can only understand the dharma once we have learned the conventions through which it operates.

SA-PAṆ AND SÖNAM TSEMO ON THE DHARMA AS LANGUAGE

At the beginning of the second chapter of the *Gateway*, Sa-paṇ gives a brief exposition on "the methods of teaching and learning" the Buddhist dharma. He describes the basic qualities of a good teacher, of a good student, and of the Buddhist dharma itself. After this introduction to the dharma's nature, Sa-paṇ recommends a work for the interested reader's in-depth study, and here gives the most extensive description of another work that appears in the *Gateway*:

> If [you] desire to know [about this] at length, [you] should refer to the *Gateway to the Dharma* (*chos la 'jug pa'i sgo*) written by the great-souled Sönam Tsemo (Bsod-nams rtse-mo), in which definitions of master and disciple, methods of explaining and listening to the dharma, and incantations that destroy the demonic hordes, etc. are well addressed.[58]

This Sönam Tsemo whose work is so highly recommended is Sa-paṇ's uncle, a previous throne holder of the Sakyapa. In this section, I will analyze two brief portions from the *Gateway to the Dharma* (*Chos 'jug*, GD) which use the expressions *term generality* and *object generality* in a manner comparable to Sa-paṇ's use of *term generality* in the *Gateway*.

The GD as a whole is a discussion of the nature of the dharma, and much of the opening section of the work is dedicated to characterizing the meaning and purpose of the Buddha's teachings. Before dividing up the subject, Sönam Tsemo addresses the general nature of a religious system:

> What is the 'religious system'? It is an individualized means (*rang rang gi thabs*) and the scriptural system of doctrines that arises from [that] means. It is called religious because it *relegates* the mind, or because of disciplining the mind.[59]

Although Sönam Tsemo is referring to the Buddha's religious system, this passage could almost just as easily refer to any religious "means" (*thabs*) in the Indian landscape, not only to the Buddha's *skill in* means. But a Buddhist believes that only the Buddha's doctrine is sufficient to provide genuine discipline for the mind. The Buddha's doctrine always has its proper origin in the Buddha's means, and always succeeds in taming the mind. These two sides are always at play in the dharma's definition: it links the authentic source to the authentic result.[60]

In a passage a bit further down, Sönam Tsemo cites a basic division of the dharma from Vasubandhu, which thematizes these two authenticities:

> As the *Treasury* (*mdzod*; [*Abhidharma*]-*kośa*) says:
>
> The supreme teacher's dharma is of two kinds:
> With the nature of (a) realization and of (b) scripture.[61]
> They are grasping and speaking, [respectively].
> Only [these two] are established.[62]

The two kinds of dharma are (a) the kind that is, itself, the experience of enlightenment—that is, true realization—and (b) the kind that articulates the path to that realization. One is the Buddha's "grasping" reality with his awareness, the other is the Buddha's "speaking" the scriptural dharma. The statement that the realization itself is one form of the dharma, and the scripture that arises based upon it is the other, makes of the Buddha's teachings a mere reflection. Sönam Tsemo's commentary makes it clear that the first is infinitely more significant than the second. The realization is perfect and emphatically *final*, whereas the scriptural articulation consists in a contingent, temporary, and ultimately false conceptual construction.

> On these, (a) the realized dharma is what arises among noble persons:
>
> > The final cessation, free from incidental defilements of the realm, and
> > The final path, generated through the awareness of the non-existence of the conceptual appearance of that [cessation].
>
> (b) Scriptural dharma is a means (*thabs*) for achieving that [realization]: One's own conceptual construction (*rang gi rnam par rtog pa*) has appearances (*rnam par snang ba*) associated with term generalities and object generalities. What act as conditions for those [appearances] are sounds as particulars (*sgra rang gi mtshan nyid*) and books, etc., which one imputes and defines.[63]

The picture of the two kinds of dharma could not be more starkly different. In the realized dharma, the two kinds of liberation are reached, at the end of either the Hīnayāna or the Mahāyāna path.[64] The scriptural dharma, on the other hand, in spite of being a means for achieving this ultimate liberation—in spite of being the Buddha's skillfully executed method for bringing about the liberation of beings—is saddled with the imperfections of language. This should not be a surprise, since the whole purpose of speaking of the Buddha's teachings as a *means* is to distinguish the expressions in the dharma from the ultimate truth, which is beyond language. But it is still important to note that here the scriptures are described in Buddhist terminology loaded toward the negative. Sönam Tsemo's passage emphasizes that scripture is only a means to an end.

Looking more closely at this passage, we see that Sönam Tsemo, like Sa-paṇ, has integrated the terminology of the *appearance of term generalities and object generalities* into a more general linguistic causal story. Sounds as bare particulars and books (visual phenomena equivalent to sounds in their cognitive effects), are the basis upon which one *imputes* and *defines* the conceptual appearances of term generalities and object generalities. This description of the linguistic process is consistent with the theory outlined in Sa-paṇ's *Treasury of Reasoning,* though somewhat more compact. Yet Sönam Tsemo is not in the process of explaining the nature of language, but rather giving a *definition of the Buddhist scriptures.* The dharma is, simply, conventionally constructed language; through the use of the expressions *term generality* and *object generality,* Sönam Tsemo distinguishes the temporary, contingent, linguistic dharma from the ultimately true and unchanging reality that can only be known through realization.

The same point is being made by Sa-paṇ's use of *the appearance of a term generality* in the *Gateway.* Two differences would seem to separate Sa-paṇ's characterization of language in the *Gateway* and Sönam Tsemo's characterization of the dharma in the GD. First, Sa-paṇ's definitions of the causes of language in the *Gateway* appeared to be referring to all language, not merely to the dharma. But such is not the case. Second, Sönam Tsemo's causal story placed the term generalities and object generalities together in the appearance of the conceptual construction that is the *means* for producing realization. In the *Gateway,* Sa-paṇ mentions only the appearance of the term generality. This difference follows from the difference between Sönam Tsemo's goal to elucidate the mechanics of the dharma and Sa-paṇ's goal to elucidate the role of the scholar.

How do we know that Sa-paṇ's passage from the *Gateway,* like Sönam Tsemo's from the GD, is using the basic structures of language as a means to explain the nature of the dharma? I have mentioned that the causes of language—the groupings of letters, lexical stems, and inflected structures—are described in turn, each building upon what has come before. But the building does not stop after the basic causes of language are formed. Continuing on, Sa-paṇ says that by combining inflected structures one builds a *statement* (*ngag*). Sa-paṇ then groups these, proceeding through larger and larger linguistic assemblages:

> By combining statements, [if] one indicates one's intended meaning from a particular perspective, it is a specialized thesis (*prakaraṇa*); indicating a few aspects, [it becomes] a chapter (*le'u*); giving it a full reckoning, it is a treatment (or treatise, *brjod byed*); then a complete dissertation, or a compendium of stages—such linguistic formations are achieved, all the way up to a verbal portion of the dharma.[65]

The largest grouping, then, which is the goal of all of these smaller linguistic conceptualizations, is a *portion of the dharma* (*dharmaskandha*). This term, on which Cabezón has written, is defined by Vasubandhu in the *Abhidharmakośa*.[66] A *portion* of the dharma is a unit of measurement, like a pound or an ounce. It is said that the Buddha taught 84,000 portions of the dharma. How can we tell what is a portion of the dharma? It is said that one portion of the dharma is sufficient as an antidote to one of the 84,000 afflictions that beset sentient beings. Just as Sönam Tsemo defined the scriptural dharma as what causes full realization, a *portion* of the scriptural dharma is defined as what causes a portion of realization, that is, the removal of one obstacle to enlightenment. A portion of the dharma is, therefore, the smallest possible unit of scripture that succeeds in being dharma—anything less would have no effect in producing realization.

This notion of a "portion of the dharma" being a measurement of text seems to conflate two meanings of the term "dharma": dharma as soteriological vehicle and dharma as a set of scriptures. Sa-paṇ's jump from discussion of words and sections of texts to a *portion of the dharma* seems odd for its apparent shift in units of measurement. One minute we were just discussing units of language, and now we are discussing the dharma. The confusion disappears once we understand that, all along, we were discussing the words and statements that were building blocks in the formation of the dharma. Once they are combined in such a way as to be capable of producing a realization, they can be measured as a unit of the dharma. As Cabezón has pointed out, the scripture is linguistic matter, but comes to be measured soteriologically. For what is the scriptural dharma, after all, but the linguistic means for the attainment of realization? Sa-paṇ's shift in units to a measurement of the dharma shows that all along, Sa-paṇ's *appearance of the term generality* was designed to invoke the linguistic means of the dharma.

Why, then, does Sa-paṇ write only of the term generalities without mentioning object generalities? When Sönam Tsemo writes that the dharma consists in term generalities and object generalities, he is emphasizing that the dharma is conceptually constructed, a "generality" rather than a "particular" (the vertical axis in our chart of Sa-paṇ's four linguistic elements). This emphasis highlights the dharma's conventionality, relativity and impermanence. When Sa-paṇ limits the scriptures to term generalities alone, he is declaring the scriptures to be *signifier* rather than *signified* (the horizontal axis in our chart above), words rather than meaning. This limitation reminds the reader that there is no "essential connection" between words and meanings. The causal connection between language and understanding (between the term generality and the object generality) is arbitrary and relies upon linguistic convention. In the dharma, that understanding is a means for enlightened realization. Thus, as I see it, Sa-paṇ's use of the term generality in the definitions of the causes of language has, enfolded within it, a full statement of the importance of linguistic study: If we are to move from a merely surface understanding of the words of the dharma to a full comprehension that might bring about realization, we must understand the linguistic conventions present in the language of the dharma. Only with knowledge of such conventions will we be able to move from the dharma's words to its proper meaning, and from that merely verbal meaning to the realizations that make the scriptures worthy of the name "dharma."

LINGUISTICS AS THE STUDY OF CONVENTION: THE "SPEECH INTENTION"

The section of the *Gateway* on the linguistic causes contains frequent reference to a speaker's "speech intention" (*brjod 'dod, vivakṣā*),[67] a term which describes the role of the speaker, rather than the role of the interpreter. A brief look at this term will tell us something more about the causal force behind the causes of language, and will allow us to see something of how Sa-paṇ understands the conventions of linguistic formation.

Unlike the notion of a "term generality," the speech intention appears in grammatical as well as epistemological discussions of language, and seems always to be employed in a precritical sense, rather than as a technical term.[68] The speech intention conveys, essentially, the speaker's intention to convey one meaning rather than another. For instance, the *Cāndravyākaraṇa*—one of the grammatical systems in which Sa-paṇ claims to be an expert[69]—cites a speaker's speech intention as the reason for the selection of particular word forms: "The desired inflection results always from the speech intention."[70] And, from among the epistemologists, Dharmakīrti cites the conditioned nature of the speech intention as proof that words are arbitrarily assigned to meanings: "Since they are relative to the speech intention, what words may not be [given a particular meaning]?"[71]

These grammatical and epistemological points are both present in Sa-paṇ's repeated appeals to the speech intention in the section of the *Gateway* that describes the causes of language.[72] Sa-paṇ imagines an interlocutor who objects to his definition of letters. Where Sa-paṇ has defined letters to be incapable of expressing meaning, the interlocutor points out that there are in fact cases where individual letters do express meaning:

> Suppose [the following objection is raised]: [There is a problem] when [letters are defined] like this. When definitively stated, the letters, "a" and "ka" and so on are said to be [equivalent to] Mañjuśrī and Brahmā, and so forth, [in tantric symbolism]. And in Tibet as well, it is seen that individual letters can be words, so this [definition] is uncertain.
>
> [Response: In fact] there is no mistake. Comprehension comes as a result of case endings or the speech intention (*brjod 'dod*), but no comprehension comes from the individual letters taken separately (*yi ge ldog pa*). For, [such an argument] would issue in an extreme consequence.[73]

The objector protests that some letters are considered, in tantric symbolism, to be equivalent to certain deities. Are they not expressive of meaning? What about single-letter words in Tibetan, such as the word *nga,* which means "I."[74] Sa-paṇ's response is to indicate that it would be an extreme consequence (that is, an *atiprasaṅga,* too broad a definition) if all uses of the letter *nga* issued necessarily in the meaning *I.* It is the speaker's intention that determines when a letter is being used as a whole word rather than as a part of a word.[75] Without case endings or the speech intention that chooses them, Sa-paṇ writes, "they will not become a word merely by being an assemblage of letters."[76] This point is repeated again and again in this section, as words and then phrases are joined into larger and larger groupings. Sa-paṇ takes great care to emphasize that language is infused with the speaker's intentions at every level. It is the presence of a speaker's intention that distinguishes words from meaningless sounds, phrases from mere lists of words, and texts from mere strings of statements.

Since, as we have determined, Sa-paṇ is at every level considering his linguistic analyses to be dharmic analyses, we know that the speaker whose intentions are at stake is the Buddha. With this, we can at last definitively describe Sa-paṇ's Buddhist justification of linguistic study: First, it is now clear that grammatical analysis of the dharma is, in fact, analysis of the Buddha's intention. The same speech intention that makes mere letters into words also makes mere words into the true dharma, the cause of realization. I take this to be yet another "covert argument" encapsulated in Sa-paṇ's linguistic definitions. Sa-paṇ is suggesting that the Buddha's intention is just as much present in the linguistic formation of the dharma as it is present in the dharma's meaning. The grammarian who analyzes the word formations of a sutra is therefore uncovering the Buddha's speech intention. Second, this point impels us to ask what conventions have guided the Buddha's speech intentions. This is an issue we will take up in detail in the next chapter, but even to pose the question is to recognize that, since the Buddha lived in India, the dharma of our world was spoken according to the conventions of Sanskrit language and Indian culture. Thus Sa-paṇ will say that the true Buddhist scholar must be learned in the grammar, literature, and philosophy of India. For, the term generalities that make up the dharma were formed out of the Buddha's specific intentions, intentions guided by the conventions of Indian culture and language. Sa-paṇ seeks to keep that context alive by educating Tibetans in just those conventions.

This is why, I believe, Sa-paṇ opens his linguistic analyses with the short passage that has been the object of study of this chapter. It presents, in a nutshell, covertly, a philosophical statement of the Buddhist value of linguistics in general, and more specifically of Sanskrit literary studies for Tibetans: (1) The dharma, made of term generalities, is above all conceptual, and thus imperfect and subject to the errors characteristic of all conceptualization; (2) the conceptual nature of language is guided by *convention*, so that our successful understanding and realization of the dharma depends upon our properly understanding the conventions at play in the language of the dharma; (3) the intentions in the language of the dharma were the intentions of the Buddha, making linguistic analysis of the dharma Buddhist analysis; and (4) the conventions present in the language of the dharma, employed by the Buddha in formulating the dharma, were the conventions of Indian language and culture. Thus, only the scholar with expertise in linguistic science can preserve the possibility of true realization hidden within the conventional designations of the dharma.

4
THE EXPERT KNOWS THE CONTEXT
Sa-paṇ's Appeals to Buddhist Hermeneutics

> Different contexts of communication and different communicative settings will clearly make for different sorts of communicative ground rules. Suppositions that are taken for granted among practitioners of a certain sort or specialists in a certain field may fail to be operative elsewhere. We can assume that in dealing with people hairstylists and haberdashers will give priority to different sorts of issues. Even the same facts may be seen in a very different light. In dealing with an old man, the physician will care for the person's diet; the lawyer will ask whether he has a will. In communication there are but few universal priorities. A cry of "Fire!" by the actor on the stage carries messages different from that by the usher in the aisle.
>
> —Rescher, *Communicative Pragmatism* . . .

Introduction: Sa-paṇ's Contribution to Buddhist Hermeneutics

In recent decades, scholars have found it useful to discuss a constellation of issues in Buddhist intellectual practice under the rubric of "Buddhist hermeneutics," noting with this term that a number of problems Buddhist intellectuals have faced in interpreting the dharma, and a number of solutions they have devised, resemble similar problems and solutions found by the scholastics of medieval Christendom attempting to interpret the Bible.[1] For Buddhist interpreters, the relevant issues nearly always shape themselves around the famous doctrine of the Buddha's *skill in means* discussed in chapter 3. Given that the Buddha provided so many different teachings directed toward the needs of different kinds of students, how are the faithful to understand—interpret, describe, explain, use—the dharma, when it provides so great a variety of contradictory views, all of which are, in any case (to many interpreters), merely "conventional"? Buddhist hermeneuts attempt to systematize, and so make order out of, the variety of doctrines, and provide methods for determining which scriptures and which views belong in which categories of analysis. The most famous, and perhaps foundational, bifurcation in Buddhist hermeneutics is the distinction between provisional and definitive meaning (*neyartha* and *nītārtha*). Often, a hermeneutic theorist will articulate a set of graded levels in the dharma, with some scriptures providing the most perfect, complete, and definitive teachings, and others providing lesser, provisional doctrines.

As is true of hermeneutics in the West, issues in Buddhist hermeneutics touch upon a broad range of problems, including the nature of scripture, doctrine, and truth, as well as of course the relation between text and interpreter.[2] But centrally, Buddhist hermeneutics is concerned with the "reconciliation of inconsistencies" in the scriptures[3] and with the methods for ascribing the proper Buddha-intention to the scriptural signifiers.[4] Modern scholarship has catalogued numerous methods according to which Buddhists of different schools have sought to set the scriptures in order and to articulate the interpreter's proper methods of analysis. Among these many interpretive rules and scriptural categorizations, however, very little *general theory of interpretation* has come to light. And, when a general theory is reported, it is nearly always an expression of modern scholarly interpolation. Theory of interpretation is not a common theme of Buddhist texts.[5]

Sa-paṇ is, once again, something of an exception. Although his contribution to hermeneutic theory is no sprawling dissertation, he does provide the careful reader with a discernable, compact argument. The argument draws its impetus from the causal, conceptual theory of language discussed in the last chapter. There, we saw Sa-paṇ explaining that since all terms and all concepts are ultimately unreal constructs, language should not be thought of as establishing accurate correlations between concepts and reality, or between mind and world. On the contrary, what defines *success* in interpretation and understanding, and leads to the correct apprehension of "the object itself," is in fact a proper ordering of *erroneous concepts*—the correct movement, that is, from a term generality to an object generality. Each of these is a mistaken conceptual construct—or, more properly, each is a concept that is ordinarily mistaken for an external reality. But it is possible to move from one (signifier) to the other (signified) "correctly"—in fact, most of the time we do.

The crucial question that this raises is obvious: How could this possibly work? How can we secure the proper movement from "term" to "object" under a conceptualist, causal theory of language, where all concepts are erroneous constructs? What criteria could possibly determine the "correct" movement from one erroneous concept to another? The answer that Sa-paṇ gives, which we began to unpack in the last chapter, involves an appeal to linguistic conventions. Language is thoroughly conventional. For this reason, while language has no purchase on ultimate reality, it *is conventionally* useful. Sa-paṇ's theory of meaning and interpretation is fundamentally a theory of conventions.

Sa-paṇ in fact uses two different words for two different but related senses of "convention": *tha snyad,* which I translate as "conventional," and *grags pa,* which I translate as "well known." The first term is the opposite of *don dam,* "ultimate." To say that something is "conventional" (*tha snyad*) is to say that it is *not ultimately real.* The second term is, really, more or less equivalent to the common English word "conventional." As when someone says that the word "marriage" *conventionally* refers to a union between a man and a woman, to say a term is "well known" (*grags pa*) is simply to say that people have some general agreement about what it means (but this does not imply ultimate reality or definitive truth).[6] For most contexts, "conventional" is a more natural and readable English translation of *grags pa* than "well known." Yet among contemporary scholars of Buddhist studies, "conventional" is a well-established translation of *tha snyad* (itself the standard Tibetan translation of the Sanskrit *vyavahāra*). Since this book is intended to be of interest to such scholars, I consider it an important duty to adhere to that "well-known" scholarly convention. For this reason, and for the reason that Sa-paṇ regularly takes advantage of the implications of "fame" and "renown" in the term, *grags pa* will here be translated as "well known."

Very briefly, then, Sa-paṇ's theory of meaning is one that says that language, while merely conventional (*tha snyad*), succeeds in communicating meaning because of the persistence of communities that preserve well known (*grags pa*) interpretations. Thus the conventionality of language is the basis of its proper function. Sa-paṇ writes that "To be well known somewhere is to be well known."[7] To put this less obliquely, linguistic conventions are valid in their appropriate contexts. There is no ultimate arbiter of the validity of a linguistic interpretation, but each linguistic context provides its own conventions. This is semantic relativity, which makes the community of interpretation paramount in judging and adjudicating the meanings of expressions.

Such a view is in some ways philosophically unsatisfying, because it may be accused of avoiding the important question by shifting it to another level. If the stability of linguistic meaning rests not in the words themselves, but instead is maintained by the conventions of the interpretive community, then the question of linguistic meaning simply becomes: How can the interpretive community guarantee the accuracy of a given interpretive act, and how is the stability of the interpretive community itself guaranteed? Sa-paṇ indeed addresses himself to these questions, and they will become our focus in chapter 5. First, however, there is significant work to be done simply in grounding semantics within communities of interpreters.

Like his covert argument analyzed in chapter 3, here too Sa-paṇ synthesizes a variety of related but previously distinct issues in Indian thought. Sa-paṇ's innovation shares its starting point with all Buddhist hermeneutics. That is, it is based upon the doctrine of *skill in means* and the concomitant need to interpret the dharma differently in different contexts. Other hermeneutic theorists have also taken advantage, as Sa-paṇ does, of the primacy of lineage for authorizing a community of interpreters of Buddhist texts. But a number of things are distinctive about Sa-paṇ's presentation. Most importantly, Sa-paṇ strategically extends the tantric hermeneutics articulated in his uncle Sönam Tsemo's *General Analysis of the Tantra Classes* (*Rgyud sde spyi'i rnam gzhag,* hereafter GATC). In the GATC, Sönam Tsemo had integrated some grammatical terminology into one aspect of his hermeneutics. Sa-paṇ takes this practice to a logical extreme, interweaving his entire presentation of linguistic and interpretive practices with hermeneutic categories. The result is to suggest that hermeneutics is the basic scholarly skill, the foundation and impetus for all the others. Such a merging of disciplines under hermeneutics allows Sa-paṇ to expand and invigorate the concept of "well-known" designation—what would otherwise be merely a term for nonliteral or uncommon language—into a principle that demonstrates the contextual nature of all meaningful expression. By defining all language as context dependent, Sa-paṇ legitimizes the meaningfulness of the peculiar, "secret" language of the tantric scriptures, while simultaneously justifying the authority of scholars who embody an old, original lineage—in other words, who are living representatives of an authoritative community of interpretation.

In what follows, then, we will see that, for Sa-paṇ: (1) words and their objects are connected by "reasons" (*rgyu mtshan*); (2) those "reasons" are in turn established and protected by expert scholars; and (3) scholars are defined as those who have a familiarity with well-known (*grags pa*) linguistic conventions. We have already seen that the scholar is a preserver of the dharma, in its authentic language (chapter 2) and correct understanding of linguistic formation (chapter 3). Here, we advance the scholar to the level of semantics: The scholar is an essential mediator between words and their objects. Sa-paṇ's final notion of the "well known" combines Sanskrit linguistics, Buddhist epistemology, and tantric hermeneutics into a concise theoretical statement that makes scholars the guardians of linguistic meaning.[8]

TANTRIC HERMENEUTICS IN THE BACKGROUND OF THE GATEWAY

The *Gateway* has long been recognized as an important key to understanding Buddhist practices of interpretation. Leonard van der Kuijp wrote in 1983 that not only have "the presuppositions of biblical studies and classical philology . . . been applied to the study of oriental thought in general . . . without serious reflection on their suitability or adequacy to understand the latter," but "significantly, neither have the texts of the Buddhist tradition that are really pertinent to its hermeneutic possibilities, been studied in detail."[9] Van der Kuijp cited three texts that deserved such study, two written by two of the most important Buddhist philosophers of India, and one by Sa-paṇ. They are the section from Asanga's *Abhidharmasamuccaya* on *vyākhyāviniścaya*, Vasubandhu's *Vyākhyāyukti* with its commentary by Gunamati, and the second chapter of the *Gateway*, which, van der Kuijp writes, "must be considered as an update of Vasubandhu's work."[10] As van der Kuijp noted, the second chapter of the *Gateway* is entitled "[On] Explication," an overtly hermeneutical title. And, no doubt, van der Kuijp had noticed that this chapter makes use of the versified table of contents from the *Vyākhyāyukti*, and thus covers the same issues in a way "designed to render the latter relevant to the Tibetan scene."[11] The passages and the issues that van der Kuijp had in mind occupy a large segment of the *Gateway*'s second chapter, and do, in fact, build upon the Indian antecedents in interesting ways. We will take up some of these issues of *practical hermeneutics* in chapter 5.[12]

For a characterization of the hermeneutic *theory* of the *Gateway*, we must look not to the *Vyākhyāyukti*, but the tantric hermeneutics of the *Pradīpodyottana* of Candrakīrti[13] and, centrally, the work of Sa-paṇ's uncle, Sönam Tsemo. Sa-paṇ is not generally considered to have made much of a unique contribution to Tibetan, let alone Buddhist, "methods of explanation of the tantras," but Sönam Tsemo is indeed of special note in this regard,[14] and Sönam Tsemo's writings had a significant influence on the notion of the dharma described in the *Gateway*.[15] What we must do, therefore, is search the *Gateway* for resonances derived from the hermeneutical categories of Sönam Tsemo's GATC. As it turns out, the *Gateway* is littered with these hermeneutic categories and terms, and is to a large degree even organized by them. This is particularly true of the two sets of six hermeneutic terms called the "Six Alternatives" (*mtha' drug*) and the "Six Instructions" (*gdams ngag drug*).

The Six Alternatives, thematic for Sönam Tsemo, appear at the end of the second chapter of the *Gateway*. The Six Alternatives consist in three pairs of opposing terms that help to define the interpretive matrix of a given scriptural passage: (1) "with special intent" (*dgongs pa*) and (2) "without special intent" (*dgongs pa ma yin pa*); (3) "provisional meaning" (*drang don*) and (4) "definitive meaning" (*nges don*); and (5) "literal language" (*sgra ji bzhin pa*) and (6) "figurative language" (*sgra ji bzhin ma yin pa*). These terms have been treated in some detail by several modern scholars, so what is important here is only to explain their relevance and interest for Sa-paṇ.[16] Their primary significance is evident in Sa-paṇ's ongoing arguments with his rival, the Drigung Jigten Gonpo. Jigten Gonpo's doctrine of "single intention" (*dgongs gcig*) rejects the Six Alternatives in favor of the view that all of the Buddha's teachings are of perfect, definitive meaning.[17] Under the *Gateway*'s description here of *provisional meaning* and *definitive meaning*, Sa-paṇ says of those who hold Jigten Gonpo's views:

> Some say that the Buddha's words are only of definitive meaning, so provisional meaning is not possible. If there is provisional meaning, [they say,] the Buddha [458] will have spoken falsehoods. These [people] simply do not understand the intent of the sūtras and tantras. If definitive meaning is all there is, analytical distinctions such as the three bodies and the three baskets and the three precepts, etc., will for the most part be in contradiction. [Then] where will the definitive meaning of the ultimately true analytical distinctions be? They work by relying on designated use, conventional truth, provisional meaning.[18]

The meaning of this passage is clear: Sa-paṇ's intellectual adversaries read all doctrines and all passages with a single, direct intention; but such a perspective fails to take into consideration the variety of doctrinal systematizations present in the scriptures.[19] Instead, Sa-paṇ and the majority of Buddhists accept not only that the Buddha spoke, on varying occasions, with both provisional and definitive meaning, but also *with special intent* and *without special intent,* and with both *literal language* and a *figurative language:*

> Explanation of the special intent includes the four special intentions such as "identity" (*mnyam pa nyid*), etc. and knowing the four indirect special intentions, such as the indirect special intention with regard to the object of application (*gzhug pa la ldem por dgongs pa*). Where there are apparent contradictions in the Buddhas' and Bodhisattvas' word meanings, an understanding of the special intention will [find] no contradiction. For fear of extending the text too far, I will not write about these. One should look in the *Mahāyānasūtrālaṃkāra,* etc. Explanation without special intention is [where] the word meaning itself gives the Buddha's intention directly, without any need to seek out other special intentions such as those [just mentioned].[20]

> Literal language consists in statements such as those on the accumulation of virtue, merit and wisdom, such as "Wealth comes from giving, happiness from discipline," which apply to their meaning in accordance with the words. Figurative language consists in expressions such as "You should kill [your] father and mother," which apply to a meaning other than those words. They are as they come about in some sūtras and tantras and poetic treatises. For fear that an extensive [treatment of] these methods will be too long, I will not write [about them].[21]

Sa-paṇ does not explain these other four alternatives in detail, referring the reader instead to other sources for further research. But it is clear in his argument against Jigten Gonpo above and in the last passage that these are methods of exposition that apply whether one is approaching sūtra or tantra literature, and so are essential skills for all scholars:

> If one does not understand the Six Alternatives, whatever one explains in the sūtras and tantras will be erroneous. As Candrakīrti said, "Whatever is called a 'definitive conceptualization' without [reference to] the Six Alternatives is like looking at the tip of the [pointing] finger when desiring to see the moon."[22]

The remainder of this chapter will show how these hermeneutic issues are not only emphasized in these passages from the end of the second chapter, but in fact provide the backdrop for linguistic discussions in parts of the *Gateway* that *do not* explicitly follow from Vasubandhu's "hermeneutic" categories. Before entering into a lengthy investigation of the issues, however, the essential point of their presence in Sa-paṇ's discussion of linguistics may be established easily and quickly. In the following passage from early in the *Gateway*'s linguistic section, Sa-paṇ makes no reference to hermeneutical categories, yet he clearly foreshadows his own above critique of those who believe in a *definitive meaning* only, and uses the very same example he later uses to show the dharma's employment of figurative use:

> Expressions in the sūtras and tantras such as "father and mother should be killed," "where the ocean changes," and "*kotakṣa*" are signs made up by the Buddha. Even though some people appear to understand a trifling explanation [of these], [such expressions] do not have a definitive explanation (*nges pa*) from only one side. Consequently, since those who look [only] from their own perspective have a hard time fathoming them, they should be understood just as they were spoken.[23]

The argument and structure of this passage, which is sandwiched within a discussion of literary terms, is derived from the *Pradīpodyottana* by Candrakīrti, the same text cited by Sa-paṇ as evidence of the importance of a scholar learning the Six Alternatives.[24] Sa-paṇ is using hermeneutics to illuminate but also to ground his discussion of literary composition. The examples of Buddha's figurative language prove that it is important for Buddhists to learn these literary categories. At the same time, the elaboration of literary figures under common use proves that Jigten Gonpo's ultraliteralist interpretation is absurd. Once we see this implicit connection between literary and hermeneutical categorizations, it becomes clear that a large number of the verses in Sa-paṇ's linguistic analyses in the *Gateway* correlate with one or another of the categories of the Six Alternatives: A distinction between expressions that need special explanation and those that are read literally parallels the hermeneutic distinction between expressions with and without a hidden intention; a distinction between "autonomous expression" (*'dod rgyal sgra*) and "supervenient expression" (*rjes sgrub sgra*) and the varieties of the latter can be read as forms of literal and figurative use; and, most importantly, a series of differences described between special classes of terminological usage in the sutras and tantras can be seen as, essentially, a generalized form of the distinction between provisional and definitive meaning.[25] Further examples are to be found in the *Gateway*'s use of the Six Instructions (*gdams ngag drug*), another set of hermeneutic categories discussed by Sönam Tsemo, which I will treat below. But the basic point is already shown: the hermeneutic categories sit unnamed behind the linguistic ones.

Taking a wider view from this perspective, it quickly becomes clear that the first two chapters of the *Gateway* can legitimately be called a dissertation on Buddhist hermeneutics—but not simply because of the second chapter title or its categories from the *Vyākhyāyukti*. The first chapter discusses the scholar's role in the preservation of the dharma, the utility of standard text openings, the proper employment of linguistic terminology, and the complexities of linguistic philosophy—all of which, while classified under the rubric of "composition," might well be described as forays into theoretical hermeneutics. The second chapter's discussions of the teacher's relation to the student, methods of scriptural analysis, and difficulties of interpretation due to the dharma's translation—explicitly on "exposition"—can all be seen as issues in practical hermeneutics. This reading helps to make sense of the fact that the most explicit discussion of traditional hermeneutics in the *Gateway* (its discussion of the Six Alternatives) provides, if not a culmination, at least a cap to the second chapter. What's more, this final section includes two statements that, together, claim hermeneutics as the basis for scriptural interpretation, and thus as the defining characteristic of the true scholar:

> He who understands by way of the Six Alternatives
> Is extremely discerning (*shin tu mkhas*) in the exposition of treatises.[26]

> If one does not understand the Six Alternatives, whatever one explains in the sūtras and tantras will be erroneous.[27]

I am suggesting that these chapters apply lessons from Buddhist hermeneutics to every stage and every mode of interpretation, and that hermeneutics is thus the basic scholarly skill in a work that dedicates itself to the basics of all scholarly skills. As it stands, I admit, this is a rather diffuse claim, simply casting a wide net and calling it "hermeneutics." By clarifying the terms of Sa-paṇ's general theory of interpretation, however, we will see that Sa-paṇ is intentionally integrating hermeneutics and literary studies into a unifying vision of scholarship.

The main passage that I will use to make this argument appears early on in the first chapter of the *Gateway* on "Composition." It follows immediately after the section discussed in chapter 3 that describes the so-called causes of language—namely, letters, words, and phrases—which were described in neat and logical progression.[28] On the surface, it would seem that the *Gateway*'s linguistic analyses then fall into disarray, shuttling quickly from one topic to the next.[29] In a brief period of thirty-five verses (or so) Sa-paṇ treats topics as wide ranging as: the distinction between ordinary words and technical terms; the Buddha's use of unusual expressions in the sutras and tantras; the epistemological doctrine of "elimination of other" (*gzhan sel; anyāpoha*); and the structure of Sanskrit case endings. By the end of the discussion, the reader is overwhelmed by the variety of technical terms and theories from the linguistic and epistemological sciences. While I do not claim to have found an ordering principle to these numerous brief treatments, they share a very definite theme: each articulates a new complexity in the relation between signifiers and their signifieds. And, in each case, the scholar—or, more precisely, the scholarly community—is understood to be the mediator of this complex relation. Such a presentation displays the difficulties of interpretation. Remember, Sa-paṇ believes that only scholars with a broad comprehension of the dharma's original cultural and linguistic context—specifically, the scholarly traditions of India—can protect the teachings in their movement from Indian to Tibetan soil. When his chaotic presentation of the difficulties of interpretation is paired with a comprehensive, unifying theory of interpretive methods across hermeneutics and literary studies, the result is a potent, if covert, argument that the dharma in Tibet needs just this kind of elite, interpretive community.

HOW WORDS GET THEIR MEANING

Sa-paṇ's extensive discussion of linguistics follows immediately upon, and under the same general heading as, his discussion of assemblages of letters, words, and phrases—what he calls the "linguistic causes" (*sgra rgyu*). The reader will recall that, exemplifying his Sakyapa approach to Buddhist philosophy of language, Sa-paṇ defined these linguistic elements as "term generalities" (*sgra spyi*)—that is, as conceptual generalizations for classes of similar sounds. Although each particular sound is unique, we nonetheless conceive of two different people's vocalizations (I say, "Cat." You say, "Cat.") as being "the same" word. Once we have a term generality, we can connect that generalization with a meaning (what "Cat" means). A meaning is also a form of conceptual construction. It is a classificatory generalization of distinct elements (no two cats are really the same) into an "object generality" (*don spyi*). This much was covered in chapter 3. Moving on, then, Sa-paṇ writes repeatedly of the "reasons" for a word's meaning (or a sign's signification), using the term *rgyu mtshan*. Both this term and the term *rgyu*, which Sa-paṇ used to refer to the linguistic "causes," can mean "cause," "principle," or "reason"; in all circumstances the purpose is to elucidate the principle according to which a term generality is associated with an object generality. Thus the basic question of this section is, How do linguistic expressions bring about meaning or comprehension of meaning? Each topic in this section of the *Gateway* provides another obstacle on the difficult path from signifier to signified, and each obstacle requires a scholar's guidance.

While the commentaries make no such division, I read the section in two large subsections. The first subsection[30] deals with categories of words that might appear meaningless or mislead one to the wrong signification, including: a wide variety of types of figurative or "supervenient" expressions; well-known versus relatively rare conventions for word use; and special onomatopoetic and onomatopoetic-like sounds. The second subsection[31] includes primarily epistemological issues, such as: the distinction between naming and classificatory expressions; the formation of linguistic conceptualization; the nature of expressions that assert and negate to varying degrees; and the persistence of the Buddha's intention through inevitable shifts in the dharma's form due to the translations of Sanskrit texts into Tibetan. These latter issues display complexities in understanding *just how signification works,* and how an improper or incomplete *concept* of language might prevent the proper grasp of the Buddha's true intention, which is the ultimate signified in all Buddhist scriptures.[32] I will discuss these issues selectively, focusing on the first, more properly linguistic, category of issues.[33]

The section begins with a simple verse on the crucial distinction between primary and secondary word meanings, which informs the whole first subsection:

> What the old [linguistic inventors] (*rgan po*) of these words
> and phrases
> Initially associated [with them] is [called] "sign";
> What is later analyzed [in them] is [called] "term."

> Joining words and phrases with things, the old [linguistic inventors] made [such] associations by force of mere speech intention (*brjod 'dod*)—such are [called] signs. Later, secondary analysis of these is [called] "term."[34]

Sa-paṇ uses the term "speech intention" (*brjod 'dod*) to describe the motivation for a speech act. The distinction defined is between words whose usage relies only upon the speech intentions of the linguistic inventors of old—the people who invented the basic words of the language (Sa-paṇ gives "wood" and "ox" as examples), and those that rely upon some additional analysis. The distinction is clarified immediately below:

> The first of these is an autonomous expression (*'dod rgyal sgra*);
> Based on that, later on, [what is made to]
> Signify another meaning is a supervenient expression (*rjes sgrub sgra*).

> The first, where whatever sign is [chosen] casually without looking to [any] reason (*rgyu mtshan*), is an autonomous expression—such as "wood" or "ox." [The second type of expression] is a subsequent expression, [which is] made based upon that [autonomous expression] for reasons such as similarity, association, and so on—as where [the meaning of] steadfastness[35] is superimposed on [the word] "wood," or stupidity on "ox."[36]

These terminological distinctions are straightforward, and derive from a well-established tradition in Indian literary analysis and, as noted above, occasionally thematized in Buddhist philosophical and hermeneutic writings.[37] What is of note is not Sa-paṇ's mention of these relatively well-established particulars, but his peculiar use of them in a kind of covert argument. Having divided all words into two categories, Sa-paṇ declares each to be the domain of a specific kind of expert. First, in regard to autonomous expressions, which are the result of a mere speech intention, he writes:

> In latter days [new signs] are not used, because even if the sign applies to the meaning, it is not understood.

> If scholars of grammar should see that if they do not use a new sign, the meaning will not be established, there is no contradiction in using a new [sign]. Nevertheless, they do not use a new sign for [some] small purpose, because of it being the cause of incomprehension, misconception, and doubt. For instance, the signs [invented by] doctors and magicians.[38]

Here we find, placed foremost, the distinction between the expert and the unqualified. We find before us the specter of improper word use and subsequent misinterpretation. The fact that words have been invented by the "old ones" in the past should not be taken to license the casual invention of words "in latter days (*slan chad*)." That privilege is granted only to experts who have legitimate reasons for inventing words, such as to doctors who must make up new terms for their medicinal products. Scholars trained in grammar can also claim the right to invent new words, but only if they are aware of all the possibilities of speech and have determined that no other method will establish their intended meaning. This would seem to imply that to be counted a scholar of grammar one must have a complete, comprehensive knowledge of the semantic as well as syntactic possibilities of a language. To put a fine point on it, the scholar must have a comprehensive awareness of how other scholars will interpret his usage.

Sa-paṇ is worried that even if words do have proper meanings that *apply* correctly (in a technical sense), the connections between words and their meanings will not be widely known and properly understood. Users of language are responsible to the community of interpreters, even—perhaps *especially*—when acting in accordance with a mere "speech intention."

If an "autonomous expression" is one that is chosen (or was chosen) according to the speech intention alone, the terms and supervenient expressions are defined as having "reasons such as similarity, association, and so on" according to which the word use is justified. The important distinction is that some words are selected with no reason in mind, whereas others are given meanings for very specific reasons. Of course, the superimposition of meaning on existing words ought to be no more haphazard than the invention of new words. The expert must be able to discern the reason:

> Signs that the scholars [can] understand
> Are supervenient (*rjes sgrub nyid*),
> Because they [can] see [their] reasons.[39]

Thus the division between primary and secondary meaning of words is articulated in such a way as to show that all word use relies upon the differing special roles of experts. Signs first become signifiers when qualified experts invent them in order to fill a gap in the language's lexicon. When choosing the particular sign and assigning it a primary meaning, the linguistic inventors rely only on their casual, unreasoned desire (though not without respect for the community of interpretation). All other word uses are chosen for some reason. The focus on "reasons" embedded within word usage highlights the scholar's interpretive role. If the writer or speaker is responsible to know the potential interpretations available to the linguistic community, the reader is responsible to know the principles by which actual word meanings operate. From the fact that words are supervenient if they have a reason that scholars can understand, we can deduce that it is the scholar who is able to give the reason for each legitimate expression. This deduction is underscored by the extensive and elaborate lists of such reasons that appear in Sa-paṇ's autocommentary:

> [Supervenient expressions made for the reason of] being mutually related are: Naming the cause after the result, as in [calling a] water spring "leg sickness";[40] naming the result after the cause, as in "known thing" (*shes pa*) or "object-possessor" (*yul can*);[41] naming the group after a member, such as "sound of a drum" or "sprout of a seed";[42] naming a part after the whole, such as calling one side of a stretch of cloth that has been burnt a "burnt stretch of cloth" or, when seeing one side of a house, [saying we're] seeing the house. [Supervenient expressions] made by reason of similar-

> ity are, for instance, the medicine [called] "crow's leg"[43] or calling a stupid person an ox. [Supervenient expressions made by reason of] a reversal of similarity are, for instance, calling a stupid person "pleasing to the gods," and the reversal of a relation [gives us something] like "auspicious" for Tuesday,[44] or "good" for the viṣṭi-karaṇa[45]—[381] all these ways of giving names should be understood after a thorough investigation.[46]

The categorical intricacy and conceptual complexity of many of these "reasons" would appear to suggest that reason-identification is a learned skill requiring special training.

SA-PAṆ'S PREVIOUS POSITION: LINGUISTIC ANALYSIS IN THE *TREASURY*

Nothing will give us a better vantage point on just how innovative is Sa-paṇ's treatment of these reasons in the *Gateway* than to contrast it with the position that Sa-paṇ himself adopted in his epistemological masterpiece, the *Treasury of Reasoning*. As we have already seen, Sa-paṇ wrote in the *Treasury* that the terminological distinctions between terms and term generalities, or objects and object generalities, are the proper subject of *expert analysis* (*mkhas*), but that the *use* or *application* (*'jug*) of language proceeds ordinarily without such an understanding:

> When explaining, one discerns reality by understanding the divisions. . . . When using [language], without making a distinction between the generalities and the bare particulars, one mistakes them as one; when the application of signs [produces] a conventional designation, one is able to achieve the thing itself.[47]

This point in the *Treasury* seems to suggest that analysis of language is less than crucial for practical linguistic use, and other sections in the *Treasury* seem to agree.

One relevant passage appears within the *Treasury*'s discussion of the relation between words and their definitions. As part of a larger section on "divisions" within the category of *a word's meaning* (*sgra'i don* or *ming don*), Sa-paṇ writes of a word's meaning that:

> Words have two kinds [of meaning]: explanation and application. An expression that has an explanation reason (*bshad pa'i rgyu mtshan*) is one where [word meaning] is achieved through explaining individual letters, such as "omniscient" (*thams cad mkhyen pa*). And one that has an application reason (*'jug pa'i rgyu mtshan*) is a word such as "tree" (*shing*).[48]

"Explanation" and "application" here are two kinds of reasons or principles (*rgyu mtshan*) for a word's meaning. The word *thams cad mkhyen pa*, "omniscient" or "all-knowing," can be analyzed and understood by breaking the term into its parts: "all" (*thams cad*) and "knowing" (*mkhyen pa*). No such analysis is possible on a word such as "tree," which has only an "application reason"—that is, it merely *applies* to a thing directly, without any intervening analysis.[49]

This latter point shows our first difference between the terminological use in the *Treasury* and the subsection of the *Gateway* under discussion. In the *Gateway*, Sa-paṇ writes specifically that there is *no* reason for a word such as "tree" to apply to a tree, except that it was designated to be so: It was "[chosen] casually *without* looking to [any] reason." When Sa-paṇ says in the *Gateway* that supervenient meanings are legitimate because "scholars can see their reasons," he means scholars can see what the *Treasury* calls "explanation reasons" and not "application reasons." Words with only application reasons require no such scholarly intervention. Thus, whereas in the *Treasury* Sa-paṇ takes the term *rgyu mtshan* in this context to refer to whatever causal principle sustains a term's meaning, in the *Gateway* Sa-paṇ has dropped the notion of an application reason, instead reserving the term "reason" for terminological uses that have reasons scholars can "explain." What in the *Treasury* gets called "application reason," then, becomes shortened simply to a term's "application"—as in the case where a newly invented term might *apply* correctly but still not be understood. In the *Gateway*, as we will see, a term's application is its proper referent, independent of whether the referent is correctly understood. I will argue that it is his focus (in the *Gateway*) on the scholar's role that makes Sa-paṇ want to distinguish words' *applications* from their *reasons*.

Continuing in the *Treasury*, Sa-paṇ provides an analysis of the "four logical possibilities" (*mu bzhi, catuṣkoṭi*) for the use of these two terms "explanation" and "application":

> Expressions with explanation and application in contradiction are [words like] "sesame-eater bird," or "shepherdess bird," etc. Expressions with no contradiction [between explanation and application reasons] are [words like] "omniscient" and "consciousness." Contradicting or not contradicting brings together three logical possibilities (*mu*). The example is "lake born." The application is that it applies to a lotus. If you explain it, it is "lake born" because it is born from a lake. This [example] has three logical possibilities. For, while the lotus that is born in a lake has both explanation and application, the lotus born on dry land has only application, and insects born in a lake have only explanation. [Objection]: Is there not the fourth logical possibility of not having explanation or application, with respect to a stump of wood on dry land? [Reply]: That may be, but

since the word "lake born" has no such use, it is not counted as a fourth logical possibility.[50]

These examples help to clarify what distinguishes a word's explanation reason from its application reason. We must assume that the expression "shepherdess bird" refers to a bird, but not to one that herds sheep. The reason that this term is an example of "contradiction," then, is that a linguistic explanation of the parts of the term would contradict the *application* of the term as a whole. In modern parlance, the term's meaning violates expectations of semantic *compositionality*. The opposite is the case for the term "omniscient" which, when analyzed into its parts, can only be explained as something like "one who knows everything"—which will guide us to the correct meaning of the term. The third "logical possibility"—which is a term that has both a contradiction and a noncontradiction—is embodied in the example of the expression "lake born," which is itself given three logical possibilities (in fact, only two would be required to have both "a contradiction and a noncontradiction"—as it is, we have a noncontradiction and two contradictions). The reader is expected to know that the term "lake born" is a term for a lotus flower. The noncontradiction in the term "lake born" is its use in reference to a lotus born in a lake; the explanation of the parts of the word, "a thing born from a lake," fits. The contradictory examples, then, are of two kinds. A lotus that is *not* born in a lake is still referred to as "lake born," even though it does not fit an explanation of the words. This usage is identical to the "shepherdess bird." Finally, insects that are born in a lake do, in fact, match the words "born in a lake," but the term "lake born" can never be used to refer to them, because, as a term for a lotus, it *does not apply/refer* to insects. That's not what the term "lake born" means.

The fourth element of a standard *catuṣkoṭi,* with *neither* explanation *nor* application, is raised by an imagined objector and acknowledged to be a logical possibility, but denied relevance to this case on the grounds that such a usage has nothing to do with the example "lake born." It is, of course, logically possible to discover for any given term a reference that fails utterly to be a relevant meaning of that term, but this logical possibility hardly makes the examples worth discussing. The point is to discover what explanations and applications the word *has,* not those it *fails* to have. For this reason, while it is true that wood on dry land has no legitimate explanation or application in the term "lake born," Sa-paṇ judges this fact irrelevant to the example.[51] For presumably the same reason, Sa-paṇ also does not provide a fourth *example;* any word with *neither* contradiction nor noncontradiction between explanation and application would have to be a word with no meanings at all.

In the *Treasury,* then, the application reason (*'jug pa'i rgyu mtshan*) of a term is the principle of the term's reference—that is, to what the term "applies."

The explanation reason (*bshad pa'i rgyu mtshan*) is a linguistic description of the meaning that is derived from the parts of the term.[52] Any term ought to have a description under each category, but the two descriptions will not necessarily meet. The principle of a term's application is that description which *allows a proper reference to take place,* as opposed to what we might call a *merely linguistic description* of a term's parts, which may or may not allow one to succeed thus.

To put it this way helps us to see that the distinction just described comes hand in glove with a potential challenge to the utility of linguistic analysis. When the *Gateway* writes of expert analysis, it emphasizes the importance of scholarly learning on the implicit argument that linguistic application is fraught with error, and *proper application relies upon proper explanation.*[53] This we have seen in the context of the interpretation of scripture and in the explanation of the speech intentions implicit within the grammatical forms of the dharma. Yet here we see Sa-paṇ himself, in the *Treasury,* saying that a term's *explanation* may fail to meet its *application,* which would seem to undermine the trustworthiness of the linguistic explanation—and, perhaps, the scholars who give such explanations. When we turn back to the *Gateway,* however, we will see how this apparent contradiction is resolved. Of course, not all grammatical explanations are sufficient, because not all meanings are sufficiently explained through such analysis. For this reason, the *Gateway* does not say that the scholar's interpretive needs are met by a circumscribed set of skills. Instead, ideal scholars are familiar not only with a term's proper linguistic breakdown, but also with its range of conventional interpretations across a full complement of linguistic contexts.

SA-PAṆ'S PREDECESSORS ON "WELL KNOWN IN THE WORLD" AND "WELL KNOWN IN TREATISES"

The terminological differences between the *Gateway* and the *Treasury* are best exemplified in the *Gateway*'s characterization of a term that is related to the "reasons" for terminological use, namely a term's classification as "well known" (*grags pa*). This is a term that plays a central role in the *Gateway*'s theory of interpretation. Words that are used indirectly, obliquely, or in a technical sense can be understood only by a scholar who is familiar with the special well-known meaning ordinarily attributed to that word. The distinction between ordinary meanings and special terminological use has a long and complicated history in Buddhist theory of textual interpretation.[54] In fact, the link between the terms "reason" (*rgyu mtshan*) and "well known" (*grags pa*) is quite clear and straightforward in both Smṛtijñānakīrti's *Sword Doorway into Language* (SDL)[55] and Sönam Tsemo's GATC. Sa-paṇ complicates the issues, and draws upon this tradition and terminology in his own new and sophisticated way, in order to articulate and justify his belief that scholars are the guardians of linguistic conventions. A somewhat intricate discussion here is necessary in order to reveal just how Sa-paṇ is presenting his new position through a deft manipulation of these terms. I will begin, therefore, with the most traditional of his predecessors, and work up (by the end of this chapter) to Sa-paṇ's own view.

To call something "well known" suggests a natural question: Well known to whom? Smṛtijñānakīrti discussed the term "well known" (*grags pa*), in his SDL, making there a traditional distinction between "well known in the world" (*'jig rten la grags pa*) and "well known in treatises" (*bstan bcos la grags pa*):[56]

> "Well known in the world" are, for instance, conventional designations such as "pillar" and "pot." "Well known in treatises" are, for instance, mentioning the *kārakas* (*byed pa'i tshig*) such as "*karman*" (*las*).[57]

The *kārakas* are syntactic-semantic class categories used in all of the major Sanskrit grammatical systems.[58] But most people are not grammarians, and have no reason to be familiar with the *kārakas* and the special grammarians' use of the term *karman* (*las*). The term *karman* as a *kāraka* is thus a particularly apt example of a technical term "well known in treatises," since the word also has so many other meanings that are "well known in the world." A reader who is unfamiliar with grammar might, for instance, be tempted to misread a scholar's technical analysis of a term's grammatical function as somehow referring to the "karmic" effect of actions in this life on the next. But the fact that most people do not know the *kārakas* does not disqualify the usage from being called "well known," because anyone who is familiar with Indian textual study can be expected to know it. As I mentioned at the opening of the chapter, the term *grags pa* could more colloquially be translated as "convention"; the two categories of well-known terms are simply categories of persons among whom this particular kind of usage is conventionally understood. For Smṛtijñānakīrti, then, the two classes of well-known knowledge also describe two classes of people: the ordinary and the learned. When we call a term "well known": (1) the term is indexed to its interpretive context, and (2) that context is associated with a class of interpreters with predefined abilities.[59]

Such a reading is supported by Sönam Tsemo's GATC, which provides a classification of well-known usages that resembles the SDL's, but also sheds light on Sa-paṇ's terminological treatments in both the *Gateway* and the *Treasury*. In fact, the passage is supremely clear and brings together nearly all of the significant terms in question in this chapter. It comes as part of the GATC's treatment of the six-fold hermeneutic scheme called the Six Instructions (*gdams ngag drug*, not to be confused with the Six Alternatives, *mtha' drug*, also discussed in the GATC).[60] The Six Instructions fall into two groups of three, and apply to any given passage two at a time, with one from each set. The first set describes three different scriptural categories, referring to three different levels of the tantric path. The second set, which I will elaborate upon here, describes explanations with three different interpretive approaches: (a) interpreting literally or directly so as to reveal linguistic signification, called "explanation by way of a meaning's linguistic elements" (*yan lag gi don gyis bshad pa*); (b) interpreting obliquely to reveal patterns or coded meanings in linguistic signs, called "explanation by way of a meaning's letters" (*yi ge'i don gyis bshad pa*); and (c) interpreting "Terms of the Tathāgata," a name for extremely oblique signs that only *āryas* can understand, called "explanation by way of concise meaning" (*bsdus don gyis bshad pa*) or "explanation by way of a meaning's esoteric instruction" (*man ngag gi don gyis bshad pa*). As is typical of Buddhist hermeneutic categorizations, these are all considered methods of "explanation" (*bshad pa*)—that is, how one describes or classifies a passage of scripture.

The first of these three is of particular relevance to our discussion, since within it Sönam Tsemo includes both of Smṛtijñānakīrti's types of well-known usages as well as both of Sa-paṇ's types of "reasons" from the *Treasury*.[61] This category includes within it all analysis of the direct, literal meaning of a passage, as opposed to analysis that seeks out an oblique or hidden intention:

> Explanation by way of a meaning's linguistic elements means entering into the meaning of a text made manifest (1) by having an expression (*sgra*) well known in the world, (2) by having an expression well known in treatises, and (3) by having a linguistic analysis (*nges pa'i tshig*) of the application reason (*'jug pa'i rgyu mtshan*) of the expression. On these: (1) An example of well known in the world is what is established with the fire crystal as its cause, dwelling in the sky, hot, [with] light rays—that [thing] has the well-known [designation] "sun." (2) And, for instance, in treatises that very [same thing] is well known as "the twelver," "100 light rays," "the lotus' friend," "illuminator," "bringer of the day," etc. (3) The [linguistic analysis of the] application reason of the expression is [that] the sun's many qualities such as having twelve houses, opening the lotus, dispelling darkness, subduing the night, etc., make these [names] each suitable to designate [the sun]. Thus, in methods such as these one gives an explanation by way of a meaning's linguistic elements.[62]

This passage recalls several points from the above discussion. First, the general hermeneutic category, "explanation by way of a meaning's linguistic elements," is quite close to Sa-paṇ's definition of a word with an "explanation reason" from the *Treasury*, as one where "[word meaning] is achieved through explaining individual letters."[63] The whole GATC passage, then, would appear to be an analysis of explanation reasons—with "well known in the world" and "well known in treatises" as two possible modes or subsets. To provide a breakdown of the words of a passage is to provide its explanation reason.

Then, the passage provides a series of helpful examples to show the relation between the well-known terminology and the reasons that the scholar calls upon to explain the use of the term. The GATC's third category, "a linguistic analysis of the application reason" provides an explanation for all but one of the terms "well known in treatises":

Table 4.1. Sönam Tsemo on "well known in treatises" (*bstan bcos la grags pa*) and "linguistic analysis of the application reason" (*'jug pa 'i rgyu mtshan nges pa 'i tshig*)

Well Known in Treatises	Analysis of the Reason
the twelver	having twelve houses
100 light rays	—no explanation—
the lotus's friend	opening the lotus
illuminator	dispelling darkness
bringer of the day	subduing the night

Each of these analyses is said to "make these [names] each suitable to designate [the sun]"—that is, to justify the use of the term in reference to the sun. In this hermeneutic category, wherein meanings are essentially direct, an interpreter's job is, thus, to explain what makes a particular term "suitable to designate." By explaining the linguistic elements that form the expression, the interpreter succeeds in explaining "the application reason (*'jug pa'i rgyu mtshan*) of the expression"—that is, in *explaining why the expression applies to a given reference.* This requires an appeal either to one or the other kinds of well-known linguistic convention, or to a reasoned explanation. Thus there is a direct relation between the principle of the term's *application* and the principle of the term's *explanation.* For words that everyone knows, they are the same. For terms that only scholars know, the effect of a linguistic explanation is to account for the term's application.

In the *Gateway*'s second chapter, on "exposition" or "explanation" (*bshad pa*), Sa-paṇ seems to have made quite direct use of the SDL and the GATC:

> Initially, the words are classified and explained according to [types of] expression. These are threefold: (1) [Expressions] well known in the world, (2) well known in treatises, and (3) expressions well known in special contexts. (1) The first, commonly well known to all the world, are [expressions like] "pot," "pillar," etc. (2) The second, well known to linguists (*sgra pa dag*), are established through [scholarly classifications] such as "case" (*rnam par dbye ba*) and "*kāraka*" (*dbye pa'i tshig*)—that is, terms under-

> stood by scholars. (3) The third are [expressions] not well known in the world or in treatises. The linguistic analysis (*nges pa'i tshig*) of the reason for the application of such expressions is difficult to explain. They have a very great purpose for *āryas*. There may be a small number of such expressions in the Sūtra Basket, and there are many in the Tantra Basket. They are well known as "terms of the Tathāgata." If one is explaining the Tantra Basket this is necessary, but since here is not [such a] context, for the time being I will set it aside.[64]

This passage reiterates the SDL's division between "well known in the world" and "well known in treatises," even to the point of using the same examples "pillar," "pot," and "*kāraka*." Interestingly, Sa-paṇ defines the second category as "well known to linguists," implying the set of persons whose conventions are necessary for the interpretation of "treatises." Then, Sa-paṇ adds a third class of words ("[expressions] not well known in the world or in treatises") that parallels Sönam Tsemo's third hermeneutic category (from the Six Instructions), "explanation by way of concise meaning" (*bsdus don gyis bshad pa*). Sönam Tsemo's and Sa-paṇ's explanations of this category both call such expressions "terms of the Tathāgata." By saying that for these terms, "the linguistic analysis (*nges pa'i tshig*) of the reason for the application of such expressions is difficult to explain" Sa-paṇ suggests, as Sönam Tsemo's examples do (see above Table 4.1), that the category of "a linguistic analysis (*nges pa'i tshig*) of the application reason (*'jug pa'i rgyu mtshan*) of the expression" is a description of the method of explaining terms that are well known in treatises. The above passage from the *Gateway* makes no reference to Sönam Tsemo's category for oblique terms, "explanation by way of a meaning's letters" (*yi ge'i don gyis bshad pa*). But in fact Sa-paṇ includes these types of explanations along with other forms of "linguistic analysis of the application reason of the expression" as the third in his threefold division of methods of scriptural exegesis "well known in treatises":

> On expressions well known in treatises, [there are three kinds]: (1) Expressions explained directly, (2) explained by derivation, and (3) explained by complementary transformation.[65]

These divisions provide the governing structure of the majority of chapter 2 of the *Gateway* on exposition. All three are included under the general heading of methods of interpretation of expressions well known in treatises. Thus, it may safely be said that Sa-paṇ expands the notion of well known in treatises beyond the hermeneutic categorization in the GATC, where the third form of well-known usage above, explanation through "complementary transformation," was separated out in the hermeneutic category for oblique interpretations. But aside from (1) expanding the notion of "well known in treatises" to include non-literal interpretive schemes, (2) giving the interpretive role to "linguists" (*sgra pa dag*) and (3) making the notion of "well known" a governing term for all of the categories of linguistic analysis, there are few evident differences between the GATC and this passage from the *Gateway*.

Yet we already know, from the *Treasury* passage discussed above, that Sa-paṇ cannot accept the simple view propounded by the GATC when it assumes a direct identity between a term that is "'suitable to designate" and one that "applies" to its referent. Nothing in the GATC passage suggests that Sönam Tsemo is interested in the problems of shepherdess birds and lake-born insects—that is, the problems of distinguishing the results of linguistic analysis from actual meanings. Sönam Tsemo recognizes the basic point that some terms need explanation and get explanation reasons, and other terms are transparent and so any reason or explanation must simply be a naming (or description) of the meaning, a mere "application reason." But this is only a simplified version of the *Treasury*'s distinction between explanation reasons and application reasons, which allowed for linguistic descriptions of the signifier that nonetheless *fail to justify* the signifier (the GATC would be forced to say that "lake born" is "unsuitable to designate"—though it *does* designate—a lotus born on land). If, as the GATC seems to categorize it, terms that have a special explanation reason all fall under the category "well known in treatises" instead of "well known in the world"—that is, all terms with special explanations are technical terms, and vice versa—then this is exactly the same bifurcation of terms that the *Gateway*'s linguistic subsection classified as a division between "autonomous expressions" (*'dod rgyal sgra*) and "subsequent expressions" (*rjes 'jug sgra*). So, we should not be surprised when we find that Sa-paṇ makes somewhat different use of the term "well known" (*grags pa*) in his linguistic subsection of the *Gateway*. The theme of well-known scholarly conventions is of obvious and central importance to the entirety of the *Gateway*, and Sa-paṇ provides the ground for his general *theory* of the well known quite early in his first chapter.

WELL-KNOWN TERMINOLOGY AND LINGUISTIC CONVENTION

In the context of these forays into the *Treasury*, the SDL, the GATC, and Sa-paṇ's own classificatory scheme from chapter 2 of the *Gateway*, Sa-paṇ's analysis of the term "well known" (*grags pa*) in his linguistic sub-section of the *Gateway* appears clear and yet surprising. Here he starts by contrasting *grags pa* with the term *'jug pa*, which I translate (in this context) as "direct application." This passage has so many resemblances to the *Treasury* passage discussed earlier that it is difficult to avoid concluding that Sa-paṇ has lifted the passage from his own previous text[66] and transformed it for a new purpose. As in the *Treasury*, here Sa-paṇ gives examples of the four logical possibilities (*mu bzhi; catuṣkoṭi*) surrounding usage of a pair of terms, one of which is *'jug pa*. Again, Sa-paṇ uses the example of the expression "lake born" as a term that means "lotus" but can be variously interpreted, correctly or incorrectly, with regard to four references: a lotus born in a lake, a lotus not born in a lake, water-born creatures, and wood on dry land. Here, however, the examples are used to distinguish not between explanation reasons and application reasons, but between ordinary and special terminological use. I highlight the terms *grags pa* and *'jug pa* here by translating them fairly literally as "well-known use" and "direct application," but they might just as appropriately be translated as "conventional meaning" and "literal meaning":

> Having no contradiction between well-known use (*grags pa*) and direct application (*'jug pa*) is, for instance, calling a lotus that was born from a lake "lake born." Having a contradiction between direct application and well-known use is, for instance, using the expression "lake born" for [a lotus] that is not a lotus born in a lake. Direct application but not well-known use is like saying ["lake born"] of such things as lake-born plants and water animals that, though born in a lake, are not well known as "lake born." Having neither well-known use nor direct application is like saying ["lake born"] of rocks and wood on dry land.[67]

Several points distinguish this passage from the *Treasury* passage discussed above. First, the one term "lake born" is used as the example of all four logical possibilities (*mu bzhi, catuṣkoṭi*), rather than merely being an example of *both contradiction and noncontradiction.* This is done by separating out the four possible *references* of the term "lake born" and making a separate example of each signifier/signified pair. This shift allows the example of "rocks and wood on dry land" to play a meaningful part in the discussion (whereas in the *Treasury* it was deemed irrelevant). Also, the second half of the passage abandons the use of the *contradiction/noncontradiction* structure in favor of a *presence/absence* structure. This suggests that it is appropriate to read the first logical possibility, the *noncontradiction,* as a *presence of both* well-known use and direct application, and the second logical possibility, the *contradiction,* as a *presence* of well-known use and an *absence* of direct application—both of which also fit with the examples provided.

Thus important differences are evident, but similarities predominate. Yet a close analysis reveals that the term *'jug pa,* which is in both passages, has switched sides; and the new term "well-known use" (*grags pa*), instead of substituting here for the missing term "explanation" (*bshad pa*) from the *Treasury,* is in fact a substitute for the *Treasury*'s *'jug pa.*

Table 4.2. Comparison of uses of *bshad pa, 'jug pa,* and *grags pa* in *Treasury* and *Gateway*

	Treasury		**Gateway**	
	"explanation reason" ***bshad pa***	**"application reason"** ***'jug pa***	**"well-known use"** ***grags pa***	**"direct application"** ***'jug pa***
lotus born in a lake	✓	✓	✓	✓
lotus not born in a lake	×	✓	✓	×
insects born in a lake	✓	×	×	✓
wood on dry land	N/A	N/A	×	×

The term *bshad pa* in the *Treasury,* meaning "explanation reason," referred to a reading that analyzed the term according to its linguistic make-up ("through explaining individual letters," as Sa-paṇ wrote there). An "explanation" for "shepherdess bird" failed to meet up with the actual meaning of the term. The GATC had used the term "linguistic analysis (*nges pa'i tshig*) of the application reason (*'jug pa'i rgyu mtshan*)" to refer to such an explanation, but *on the assumption that such an explanation would always fit with the real meaning.* The *Gateway* passage thus seems to combine these perspectives in the term *'jug pa,* meaning "direct application." This term highlights the notion of a form of explanation that *applies* the literal or surface meaning of the term, while suspending the question of whether or not the term *really* "applies" in the *Treasury* sense of *'jug pa.*

The *Treasury*'s *'jug pa,* in turn, indicated the term's reference, which the GATC called the "application reason," but again naively, assuming it to be equivalent to any and all linguistic analysis. Now, in the *Gateway,* this notion of a term's real meaning is given to the term *grags pa,* meaning "well-known use." The implication of this terminological shift is that words *apply* because they are *well known*—in the sense that they are ruled by linguistic convention. The proper use of terminology is subject to convention, and the term "well known" implies (as it always does) the existence of a speech community that shares a particular understanding of the term. Terms do not simply apply *automatically,* as the *Treasury* meaning of *'jug pa* might suggest. Nor, as the GATC suggests, is basic linguistic analysis sufficient to provide knowledge of a term's proper object. A community of interpretation—a scholarly community—maintains the proper relation between signifier and signified. Sa-paṇ here protects scholarly analysis from the charge of irrelevance and misconception that might fall upon it if all of its "reasons" were only *explanation reasons* as opposed to *application reasons*. Instead, Sa-paṇ's reversal of terms grants to scholarly convention the ability to govern the *correct use*, not just the grammar, of language; thus not only the *description*, but also the *application* of the dharma depends upon the scholarly community.

Finally, this *Gateway* passage provides an excellent teaching example to show how even ordinary language relies upon scholarly convention. An ignorant writer who uses the term "lake born" to refer to frogs and fish would inadvertently mislead a properly educated reader. And, an interpreter who does not know the well-known meaning of "lake born" is in danger of mistaking a denotation for a figure, or vice versa. Later in Sa-paṇ's subsection on linguistics, he points out that, unlike Sanskrit, Tibetan language carries very little information in its word forms, and in any case Tibetan translators had to create forms comprehensible in Tibetan language.

> Scholars of such linguistic applications
> In the olden days were concerned only with well-known use.

> For these expressions in Tibetan, the old ones had well known use as their main concern, but [word] formation was not the main concern.[68]

Consequently, it is essential for Tibetans to familiarize themselves with the linguistic conventions employed by the translators—that is, the conventions of the very heroes of scholarship, the best educated and best respected scholars within the community of interpretation.

SA-PAṆ'S GENERAL THEORY OF THE "WELL KNOWN" AND TANTRIC HERMENEUTICS

Although chapter 2 of the *Gateway* reiterates the distinction between "well known in the world" and "well known in treatises" and their association with methods of scriptural exegesis articulated in the SDL and the GATC, the linguistics subsection from chapter 1 does not mention it. Instead, Sa-paṇ extrapolates to a general principle of the contextual nature of all well-known terminology:

> As for differences among signs: What in some [texts]
> Is well known, in others is not well known
> [And] thus not understood. What in some [texts]
> Is well known is clearly well known.

> Some signs, while well known in scriptures, are not well known in reasoning; and some are well known in reasoning but not well known in scriptures. And even though the [terminology of the] three baskets of the sutras and the four tantras are not mutually well known, each in the other, there is no fault, since to be well known somewhere is to be well known.[69]

Sa-paṇ's position here is that the well-known character of a term's use depends upon its context. The general principle that "to be well known somewhere is to be well known" means that a famous Italian actress is still called famous, even if she is not famous outside Italy. On the surface this would seem to fit with the spirit of the distinction between "well known in the world" and "well known in treatises," since that distinction rests upon separating out the distinct, well-known conventions operating in two different interpretive contexts. Yet this passage stands *against* the idea that there is some unified category of well-known usage that applies across all treatises. In fact, there are significant consequences of adopting Sa-paṇ's general principle instead of the binary pair, as Sa-paṇ's Buddhist scriptural examples make clear.

The fact that Sa-paṇ adduces Buddhist examples in explaining a point of ostensibly secular linguistic terminology is in itself significant, since it suggests that Sa-paṇ is trying to "Buddhicize" language science by using terms that apply to language in general to argue about the peculiar needs of the Buddhist dharma.[70] In this case, however, the use of Buddhist examples is especially significant because, I believe, Buddhist hermeneutic doctrines account for Sa-paṇ's shift to a general principle of well-known terms.

Why should the use of Buddhist scriptures as examples force Sa-paṇ to adopt the general principle instead of the division between "well known in the world" and "well known in treatises"? Buddhist hermeneutics distinguishes between different levels of interpretation of the doctrine, with each treatise occupying a rung in the ladder of well-known interpretations. Smṛtijñānakīrti's *kāraka* example and Sönam Tsemo's numerous terms for the sun consist in knowledge available and necessary to all scholars. But, whereas the *kārakas* may be well known to all *paṇḍitas*, Buddhist terminology is peculiar to Buddhist interpretive methods. Buddhist hermeneutics understands that different methods of textual interpretation apply to different kinds of texts, due to the variety of speech intentions (*brjod 'dod*) exercised by Buddhas and Bodhisattvas in a variety of contexts. When scripture exists in different forms and with different possible interpretations for different audiences, and when a single term may legitimately be interpreted with several intended meanings, what does it mean to say that a term is employed in accordance with a well-known linguistic context?

This issue is particularly salient in the context of not just Buddhist, but tantric hermeneutics. Tantric hermeneutics are concerned not only to distinguish among a variety of doctrines across the various paths of practice, but must explain the special character of meaning *within* tantric texts, which often contain terms in "secret" codes that cloak the true meaning from the uninitiated. What's more, one of the basic principles of the "secret mantra" path is that the utility of the practices depends entirely on the practitioner's having "received" the meaning of the scripture through the ritual process of initiation. This means that not only is it important to understand the secret code in which the language of the tantras is cast ("*bodhicitta*" means "semen," etc.)—but *one must also be initiated* into any given tantric practice or cycle that one hopes to "understand."

It would seem that such a tantric view necessitates the conclusion that there is never any single context that allows for every term to be considered "well known." Thus, where Smṛtijñānakīrti's "well known in treatises" applied to the full range of scholarly textual study, Sa-paṇ's use of the term must allow for divisions among treatises into the major categories of Buddhist treatises: first "scripture" (*lung*) and "reasoning" (*rigs*), and then sutras and tantras. Sa-paṇ might, then, have continued dividing, listing numerous categories of well-known terms, but to do so coherently he would have had to make many quite difficult arguments for his divisions. And, with each division, there would be an increasing risk of it seeming absurd to call the category of treatises "well known." Much easier and much clearer is the general principle, which accounts for the special training necessary for each type of Buddhist text, even while explaining Sa-paṇ's general view that each science has its own experts: ". . . for someone who knows teachings in some specific field, in that and that alone he gets the name 'scholar.'"[71] Each kind of text, including each category and subcategory of Buddhist text, has its specialists who, alone, are capable of comprehending its special terminology. Each specialist knows the well-known terms, the linguistic conventions, of that form of literature, and is therefore privy to the speech intentions that they represent. The proper interpretive context for each form of text, then, is passed down through the scholarly community: the scholarly conventions *are* the proper context.

If the reader doubts that tantric hermeneutics is a motive for this general theory, recall that I began this chapter by showing that tantric hermeneutic categories lie behind and structure this subsection of the *Gateway*. The relevant hermeneutic distinction from the Six Alternatives, which this verse and commentary (on "differences among signs") reflect by describing the differences between special classes of terminological usage in the sutras and tantras, is none other than the distinction between provisional and definitive meaning (*neyartha* and *nītārtha*).

The argument of Sa-paṇ's I have brought out here, which bases the scholar's legitimacy upon the importance of special knowledge of context, is only the linguistics-inspired hermeneutical branch of an argument that appears in many forms across Sa-paṇ's writings. Sa-paṇ's famous polemical work, the *Clear Differentiation of the Three Codes*, is explicitly dedicated to this notion of the importance of context. The "differentiation" that that work's title commands is the discrimination among the three Buddhist paths. The *Differentiation* catalogues and corrects dozens (hundreds?) of errors that Sa-paṇ discerns in Tibetan misinterpretation of the dharma, most of which are the result of taking texts and practices out of context. A single example will make this point clear, though many could be cited. As Sa-paṇ explains, some say that practitioners who take a one-day Individual Liberation vow of abstention (from sex, food, etc.) must also perform meditations upon deities and mantra recitations as part of their practice.[72] But Sa-paṇ points out that since the vow of abstention is an Individual Liberation vow, it is fulfilled simply by doing the abstention. The mantra recitations and meditations upon deities are Mantra Vehicle instructions, which enhance the resulting merit but are not required as part of the Individual Liberation vow.[73] Here, and across his works, Sa-paṇ shows how the scholar must be able to distinguish between the various scriptural positions and various practices in order to understand each view in its context.

In the *Gateway*, Sa-paṇ is declaring the same to hold for specific terminology: each type of scripture or reasoning provides its own rules that provide for terminology's being legitimately called "well known." This is a linguistic principle that corresponds to the general principles of Buddhist hermeneutics. A community of interpretation, through whom special terminological usages must be evaluated, holds each interpretive context in place.

Which Scholars Form the Community of Interpreters?

If each intellectual context provides its own interpretation of a term or concept, there is a sense in which each intellectual context has its own "scholars"—what we call "specialists." Although these scholars have their proper range of purview, they are not the kind of scholar that the *Gateway* is seeking to train. On the contrary, Sa-paṇ believes that the fact of difference among different contexts has, as a necessary corollary, that it is rarely sufficient to be an expert in only one category of knowledge. No scholar who knows only the rules of the Individual Liberation vows could have cleared up the confusion that came from mixing the Mantra Vehicle with the Individual Liberation vehicle. Since each category of Buddhist texts employs its own specialized well-known interpretive conventions, the scholar needs to have a comprehensive understanding of *all* contexts, or be in danger of misinterpreting one kind of term as another, that is, of mistakenly interpreting a term in one context through the conventions of another.

But even if it is possible for one scholar to know all of the well-known contexts, there are some contexts that are not really 'well known' anywhere: they are special terms called "speech of the Tathāgata." These are special expressions used in tantric contexts that are only explained to initiates in esoteric instructions (*man ngag*)—in chapter 2 of the *Gateway* Sa-paṇ begs off explaining them on the excuse that "If one is explaining the Tantra Basket this is necessary, but since here is not the occasion, I will leave off [the explanation] for now." For Sönam Tsemo these expressions consisted in a third, separate category distinct from both of his well-known methods. In the following verse from the *Gateway*, however, Sa-paṇ explains why these esoteric expressions qualify as well known even when they are not at all well known:

> A fully enlightened Buddha in front of his disciples
> [Says things] that do not exist in mundane treatises.
> Such signs are beyond the ken (*spyod yul min*) of ordinary people.
> The omniscient one's intention is incomprehensible.

> Expressions in the sutras and tantras such as "father and mother should be killed," "where the ocean changes," and "*kotakṣa*" are signs made up by the Buddha. Even though some people appear to understand a trifling explanation [of these], [such expressions] do not have a definitive explanation (*nges pa*) from only one side. Consequently, since those who look [only] from their own perspective have a hard time fathoming them, they should be understood just as they were spoken.[74]

Sa-paṇ's claim that these confounding expressions of the Buddha "do not have a definitive explanation from only one side" suggests that I am not far off in saying that Sa-paṇ requires a scholar to have a broad, multicontextual understanding of scripture. I have already noted that this passage provides an oblique, but definite, rejection of Jigten Gompa's "single intention" theory. But can the scholar truly understand the Buddha's words "just as they were spoken"? Here we see Sa-paṇ applying the philosophical basis of the technical term "well known"—that is, that the requirement of the interpreter is to understand, via the context, the speech intentions of the speaker—to a realm beyond the comprehension of ordinary sentient beings. If I understand the point of this statement, Sa-paṇ is reserving the right of interpretation of at least *some* of the Buddha's signs for those who are beyond the ordinary, if not themselves omniscient. The effect of Sa-paṇ's having placed this verse immediately after the verse explaining the general principle of well-known words, then, is to reiterate his notion that "well known in the world" and "well known in treatises" are then complemented by the category of terms "that are not in accepted usage either among ordinary men in the world or in technical treatises"; some terms are known only to the omniscient. This usage would also appear to parallel Sa-paṇ's two kinds of scholar, the omniscient one who knows all knowable things, and the scholar who has mastery of a particular field of knowledge:

> If someone should ask, who gets called "scholar"?—He is someone who knows without error everything that can be known. Alternatively, for someone who knows teachings in some specific field, in that and that alone he gets the name "scholar."[75]

It seems to me that the most likely and sensible interpretation of these passages is that Sa-paṇ is suggesting something fairly obvious, which is that the ideal hermeneut and teacher is omniscient. It is unclear whether we are also to believe that certain scholars exist *in the world* for whom even the most perplexing words of the omniscient Buddha are well known, but if they do exist, they must surely have learned the many interpretive contexts only available to master scholars such as Sa-paṇ and his colleagues.

There is a certain irony in the desire to call the intentionally baffling terminological use of the tantras "well known." Why should there be a concern—Sa-paṇ says defensively that "there is no fault"—about scriptures being well known or not? Perhaps the basic answer comes from recognizing that, as much of the preceding analysis suggests, a term that is not well known is in danger of being misinterpreted. Just like new terms and terms generated according to specific recognizable rules, well-known terms are allowable only within the strictures established by scholars for their proper use. Thus, it would appear that Sa-paṇ is answering a potential charge of contradiction between principles of literary analysis and principles from Buddhist hermeneutics. If it is required that literature be clear and use well-known terminology, the question arises as to the legitimacy of the Buddha's "skillful" method of proffering so wide a variety of teachings with a wide range of terminological uses that appealed to different audiences with different needs.

Several traditional principles of Indian poetics (of which Sa-paṇ may well have been aware)[76] require terms to be as widely comprehensible as possible. The "defects of words" (*padārtha-dośa*) described in Vāmana's *Kāvyālaṃkārasūtravṛtti* include, for example, the "unknown word" (*apratītam*), which is "used only in learned (technical) treatises [and not in common uses]."[77] Another defect is a word that is "difficult of comprehension" (*gūḍhārtha*), one that is "used in such a meaning as is not generally known (*aprasiddha*)."[78] It is considered inappropriate to use obscure and technical language in poetic treatises. One can see why it would be tempting to use these terms to elucidate Buddhist hermeneutical issues, since the poetic principle that lies behind the terms *pratītam* and *prasiddha,* and so their Tibetan translation *grags pa,* is that each form of literature has its appropriate audience. But the use of the term in poetics makes a distinction that Sa-paṇ will not accept: That between the learned and the literary. Vāmana's example of the poetic fault called "unknown word" is the use of the Buddhist technical term *rūpaskandha* in a poem. Sa-paṇ, however, says explicitly that the use of technical terms simply indicates the appropriate audience, and "there is no fault" in the scriptures. What can be meant here except the potential faults that are leveled at *literary works?* Sa-paṇ wants to be able to apply the lens of poetics to Buddhist texts. Thus, he must address and counter the potential charge that the Buddhist scriptures use terminology that fails the test of being well known, whether among ordinary persons or among scholars. Sa-paṇ might have circumvented this potential criticism by limiting the use of "well known" as a category of analysis to only nonesoteric texts, as Sönam Tsemo did; but, since he accepts the tradition that claims the Six Alternatives as principles for understanding sutras and tantras, he must allow for one continuous interpretive scheme to cover all interpretations. Thus he accepts the concept that all terminological use must be well known, but explains the well-known character of the dharma by appeal to the community of interpretation within which it is, indeed, known well:

> The dharma being heard must also be spoken by the Buddha, transmitted by scholars, meditated upon by adepts, explained by paṇḍitas, translated by translators, and well reputed (*legs par grags pa*) among all the scholarly keepers of the scriptures (*sde snod*) of India and Tibet—such a dharma ought to be heard and explained.[79]

This principle allows Sa-paṇ to write of the scholar's need to learn special terms which are not well known in the world without sacrificing the appropriateness of the dharma to its every context. It allows him to explain, for instance, that although the Tibetan translations from Sanskrit use difficult and obscure terms, there is no fault: "When beauty appears (*mdzes pa byung na*) in the Sanskrit language, Sanskrit [words] are used that are not, for the most part, well known in the world."[80] Terms have been used which are appropriate to convey the elevated style of the Sanskrit.

It is for this reason, finally, that not only must the dharma itself be well known, but the scholar who teaches it must be a part of the well-known community of interpretation that is responsible for the protection of the dharma. If you learn the dharma from someone not themselves well known, Sa-paṇ says, your own teachings will be held in doubt:

> In general, the master (*bla ma*) is a scholar, he acts justly, and he is known to be one who is famous for scholarship. If he is not a scholar, he cannot remove doubts. If he is undisciplined, he will be ineffective in constraining his students' behavior. If he is not famous as a scholar, they will be ridiculed, "Where does your [learning] come from, when [your] teacher has none?[81]

Thus, the well-known dharma is the true dharma and the well-known scholar is the true master: This conservative principle seeks to preserve the purity and authenticity of the dharma by claiming exclusive interpretive rights of a hegemonic community of interpretation.

CONCLUSION

The terms under special focus in this chapter— *rgyu mtshan, bshad pa, 'jug pa* and, centrally, *grags pa*—are by no means refined or precise technical terms in the literature here discussed. Nonetheless, their characteristic uses carry a range of suggestions that have allowed us to uncover a philosophical position underlying Sa-paṇ's linguistic analyses. Sa-paṇ's terminological use in the *Gateway* suggests that the extremely complex and forking paths that stretch between words and their intended objects require that scholar interpreters be legitimate heirs of a community of interpretation. There is no sure method of navigating these pathways, except with an experienced guide. It would seem that the scholar as interpreter inherits and passes on a tradition of interpretation in much the same way that the Buddhist teacher receives and passes on the dharma. Sa-paṇ's theorization of context and linguistic convention creates a homomorphism, if not an equation, between the interpretive community of linguistic scholars (*sgra pa dag*) and the Buddhist *saṅgha.* In a sense, this method recapitulates the master-disciple relationship, but on a culturewide scale. Only the perfectly aware teacher's understanding both of the truth and of the interpretive needs of the disciple can protect the dharma as it moves from one generation to the next. Only the continuation of the community of interpretation can protect the dharma as it moves from one context to the next.

This theory, and the catalogue of scholarly skills that it justifies, is the *Gateway*'s contribution to Buddhist hermeneutics. To comprehend the scriptures at a level that authorizes you to explain them, you must be a member of the community of interpretation that sees the words in their context, the context which *is* the knowledge provided through the community of interpretation, and which consists, minimally, in the set of skills delimited in the *Gateway.*

5
THE MESSAGE IN THE MEDIUM
Intellectual Norms and Protocols

Introduction

In the last three chapters I have emphasized Sa-paṇ's view that the Buddhist scholar must be an excellent interpreter. Sa-paṇ believes that scholars are mediators between texts that serve as repositories of the Buddha's intentions and the proper understanding and application of those intentions. I have underlined Sa-paṇ's view that a scholarly interpreter must be a part of, and draw from, a traditional community of interpretation, and that that community must do its best to preserve the conventions and contexts through which and in which the dharma has been taught. With this emphasis on the scholar as interpreter, we have naturally focused upon the scholar's intellectual activity in *decoding* the Buddhist textual corpus. In this chapter and the next, our focus shifts toward Sa-paṇ's presentation of processes involved in *recoding* the dharma for public consumption—whether as a teacher or a writer.

Sa-paṇ himself makes no such distinction between *decoding* and *recoding.* In fact, the subjects of the *Gateway*'s three chapters—composition, exposition, and debate—all fall squarely within the category of *recoding.* This is one reason I call Sa-paṇ's arguments about translation, linguistic conventions, and interpretation, "covert." They are implicit in the arrangements of materials and in certain (often repeating) passages and terms. But although these arguments provide the foundation and some of the structure of the *Gateway,* the bulk of the work details scholarly activities not of private study and rumination, but of public presentation before students, assemblies of learned peers, and opponents of Buddhism.[1]

In truth, to distinguish thus between decoding and recoding is, at least in Sa-paṇ's Buddhist worldview, a heuristic fiction. Sa-paṇ's pragmatic, conventionalist understanding of language (described in chapter 3) prevents any reification of the decoded meaning itself—which is, in any event, only at best relatively correct. If the dharma is always only *skill in means,* the scholar's understanding is only valid either because it leads toward, on the one hand, his deeper appreciation of the ultimate nature of reality (itself beyond language), or, more immediately, because it allows him to engage in fruitful interchange within an authentic Buddhist intellectual community. If, indeed, to be a scholar *simply is* to be engaged in such an intellectual community (my suggestion in chapter 4), there seems reason to say that in this case, at least, *there is no decoding without recoding.* This makes for an inseparable unity of the dharma's form and content.

In this chapter, therefore, we will see that Sa-paṇ considered a number of ostensibly formal intellectual conventions—in particular, introductory verses and exegetical methodologies—to be crucial to the dharma itself, properly understood and practiced. Sa-paṇ takes great pains not merely to describe these protocols, but to justify them as well. Sa-paṇ believes that, like good methods of *decoding,* these methods of *recoding* provide protections against the decline of the dharma. They are practices that constitute, or reconstitute, the dharma's legitimate interpretive context, and therefore in a very real sense make the dharma *work.* A proper encoding of the dharma provides the vehicle for its proper reception, and, at the same time, perpetuates the intellectual community that allows it to continue. Sa-paṇ comes very close to articulating, in a mode that is self-conscious and yet not at all ironic, the elsewhere implicit purpose of hermeneutics; namely, to maintain the comprehensive and authoritative character of the community of interpretation.

My goal in this chapter, then, is to show that two philosophical positions underpin Sa-paṇ's concerns in describing traditional compositional and expository protocols. First, we are to understand that the dharma in the form of a text is explicitly a tool for teachers and students—in fact, a text is best understood as a composer's method for establishing, framing, and stabilizing future teaching and learning opportunities. Second, we are to understand that standard formal and structural elements of texts, and standard protocols for interpretive performance, are intended to verify the authenticity and effectiveness of the text's composition and interpretation.

As many scholars who have studied these materials have noted, the *Gateway* here reflects and resembles Vasubandhu's extensive and detailed treatise on scriptural hermeneutics, the *Vyākhyāyukti.* In fact, these methods have a long and varied history in Sanskrit literature, and the exact relationship between the *Vyākhyāyukti* (itself an extremely difficult text), its reception in India and Tibet, and the *Gateway,* is too intricate a topic for this chapter. Here I am only seeking to characterize Sa-paṇ's general conceptualization of scholarship, which he was of course presenting for Tibetans of his time. Nonetheless, there is little reason to doubt that Sa-paṇ's understandings of introductory verses and methods of exposition express views shared, if only implicitly, by many of his Indian Buddhist predecessors.[2]

THE THREE KINDS OF MEANING IN A GOOD VERSE OF REVERENCE

At the start of his first chapter, "Entry into Composition," Sa-paṇ provides a brief but penetrating analysis of five standard forms of introductory verses: Verses of Reverence, Oaths of Composition, Expressions of Humility, Summary Outlines, and Statements of Purpose. Sa-paṇ uses his explanation of these verses to build and develop a consistent understanding of the relationship between the two scholarly roles of composition and exposition. For each type of introductory verse, Sa-paṇ provides (in his autocommentary) a standard threefold explanation of the purpose (*dgos pa*), the summary (*bsdus pa*), and the meaning of the words (*tshig gi don*). On each verse, I will discuss Sa-paṇ's use of this threefold analytical typology.[3] Since this section on text openings is the first topic in the *Gateway's* first chapter, it comes immediately after the *Gateway's* own verses of introduction. These opening verses provide examples I will use to illuminate Sa-paṇ's analysis.

To begin, we can see how Sa-paṇ describes the first type of introductory verse, a verse of reverence (*mchod brjod, maṅgalaśloka*), through a particularly clear use of the threefold analytical typology:

> An excellent author of a treatise [373] should give a verse of reverence to the teacher [i.e., the Buddha]. In order that the teachings may flourish, pure words are here seen to be proper and good.

> Verses of reverence have three [aspects]: the purpose, the summary, and the meaning of the words. There are two kinds of purpose: that which arises in the composer's own continuum, and that which is realized in the continua of others—[including both the people] who have explained and [those who have] listened to [the treatise]. The meaning in summary form is to whom, by whom, and in what manner the praise is offered, and so on. As for the meaning of the words: Once [the composer] has examined the statement meaning (*ngag don*) in the manner of a lion's glance, [he can then proceed to] explain the subject matter (*gzhung don*) with the gait of a tortoise.[4] Each subject matter must be understood at length in the context of its own composition and exposition.[5]

Here the root verse makes two interesting points. First, Sa-paṇ says that verses of reverence are something the best authors offer to "the teacher"—an epithet of the Buddha, but one that potentially invokes both the author's *own* teacher (or guru) as well as the role the author adopts *as* teacher when composing a teaching. Second, he says that verses of reverence should use language that is clear or purified, because they play a role in the success of "the teacher's" teachings. What role? It is possible that clear language will help ordinary people understand and pass along the teaching, but this is not the main point. We have a clear example of the benefits envisioned only four pages earlier, when Sa-paṇ analyzed the *Gateway*'s own verse of reverence, which praises the guru and Mañjuśrī for having the "four specific knowledges" and the "four fearlessnesses," as follows:

> Suppose someone should ask, what is the point of this verse of reverence at the beginning of the treatise? Well, the guru together with Manjughoṣa is the essence of all the Buddhas of the three times. So if you say even a part of his[6] qualities, the final result will be Buddhahood, and the temporary result will be the pacification of obstacles. The initial statement is said with this in mind.[7]

The verse of reverence is thus designed to provide a positive karmic effect for all who come in contact with it. The verse of reverence is a prayer, and it requires the greatest of attention to purity of language because the right words will make it most effective.[8] The commentary makes this point clear by bringing to mind not just the benefits to the author's own karmic "continuum," but also to the expositor and the student who will later engage the text. And here we see Sa-paṇ placing text composition in its proper place as a link, a binding among lineages of teachers and students, gurus and disciples. For Sa-paṇ, textual exposition consists in a kind of closed system with three interlocking elements: the teacher, the student, and the dharma. "The one who gives the exposition is the teacher. The object of the explanation is the student. It is the dharma that is to be explained."[9] These three elements are distinct, but each depends upon the others for their proper functioning. Ideally, the teacher is a pure and perfect scholar, and the student is always respectful and bright.[10] But Sa-paṇ recognizes that things are not always so, and he writes that teachers ought to have strategies for inspiring indolent students (such as putting the fear of samsara in them)[11] and energizing tired ones (such as telling exciting stories).[12] He says that teachers should teach differently to meet the various abilities of different students. That is, the teacher is to be aware of the particular needs of the student. And, although it is thematic of the *Gateway* that many teachers are less than ideal scholars, this in no way undermines the obligation that students venerate both teacher and teaching. The ideal educational situation is one of mutual respect and admiration, where all are united in service of the common goal of promoting a proper comprehension of the dharma.[13] In a verse of reverence, then, we see that the composer of the treatise is to consider the (karmic) needs of both teacher and student. In paying homage to the teacher, the composer reminds himself that the raison d'être of a treatise is to provide the topic (specifically, the dharma) on which a teacher instructs a student.

Thus Sa-paṇ's first statement about composition coheres directly with our discussions from previous chapters: A writer, like an interpreter, should keep in mind the community for which he is writing. It is, after all, the transmission of the dharma that makes his teaching a teaching. When he indicates, in addition, that pure and appropriate language is a key to the success of the verse of reverence, Sa-paṇ is once again suggesting the central importance of the linguistic sciences in protecting the dharma.

Next, describing the verse of reverence's "meaning in summary form," Sa-paṇ makes reference to another topic he will treat in the chapter on exposition: "The meaning in summary form is to whom, by whom, and in what manner the praise is offered, and so on."[14] Here Sa-paṇ is mentioning, in brief, his own watered-down version of *kāraka* analysis, which he says is necessary for Tibetans to learn—what he calls the strategy of "linking the meaning with the words" (*tshig don sbrel*) according to "object (*karman*), agent (*kartṛ*) and action (*kriyā*)."[15] I will discuss this method below, but for now we should register that Sa-paṇ's second point on composition, like his first, reminds the composer of the text's interpreters—here, their specific method of exposition.

Finally, to explain the "meaning of the words" of a verse of reverence, Sa-paṇ uses the analogy of the broad and comprehensive lion's gaze as opposed to the close, slow turtle's gait. One might think that the point is that, once the lion's gaze of the verse of reverence is taken in, one can proceed to the details of the treatise. In fact, this analogy will appear again in the chapter on exposition, again associating the comprehension of a general "statement meaning" (*ngag don*) with the lion's gaze—but contrasting it to the turtle's gait of particularized linguistic analysis *of the same passage*.[16] The point of the analogy is not to contrast the verse of reverence with the rest of the treatise, but to distinguish two (and later, three) levels of interpretation available within a single verse. A well-composed verse should bear new fruit under each new form of analysis. This is yet another reason the author ought to be aware of the analytical methodology of his readers.

The introduction to how to compose the verse of reverence is thus also an introduction to how to interpret it—in fact, it is an introduction to interpretation itself. When Sa-paṇ explains the verse of reverence's purpose, he does not tell us any *particular* benefits accruing to the continua of the author, expositor, and student. That should be determined on a case-by-case basis, depending on the verse in question—that is, depending on the benefits suggested in the verse by the author. When he gives the "meaning in summary form" of a verse of reverence, he does not tell us, in summary form, what a verse of reverence is. Instead, he gives us the *form alone* in which we should place the particular meanings of any given verse of reverence. When he gives us the "meaning of the words" of a verse of reverence, he is once again telling us of the different modes in which the words of such a verse should be interpreted. In the chapter on exposition, he will give particular examples of each of these three hermeneutic methods. For now, this is methodological meta-talk, and it issues only in a general statement about the value of employing these strategies—a statement which explicitly links the two roles of author and interpreter, composition and exposition: "Each subject matter must be understood at length in the context of its own composition and exposition."[17]

As I have already suggested, scholars who are actually planning to compose their own treatises will surely succeed best if they know the needs and interpretive methods of the teachers and students who use Buddhist treatises. And, scholars who might never compose their own verses of reverence can still use this typology to determine the quality of a verse's composition, simply by measuring the degree to which it yields to analysis of purpose, summary, and meaning of the words. The best of scholars, however, understand the process from both sides, since the same structures of interpretation can then constitute a single, continuous frame for both composition and exposition.

INTRODUCTORY VERSES AND THE SOCIAL FUNCTION OF RHETORIC

The second type of introductory verse is the "Oath of Composition" (*bshad par dam bca' ba*), which is a verse in which the author states what he intends to write. Sa-paṇ entertains an objection that this kind of statement is redundant, and then counters it by saying that such a verse has its own, distinct effect:

> As for the oath of composition and so forth, suppose someone should think that if you are going to give an exposition, it is unnecessary [to say what you are going to say again anyway], and if you are not going to give an exposition, [a promise to do so] is meaningless:
>
> Oaths, exhortations, and so forth
> Show one's determination (*spro ba*) to give the exposition.
> Since it will bring about the achievement of supreme realization,
> There is no inconsistency (*'gal ba med*) in the promise.[18]

Far from being merely a redundant statement of what is to come, an oath has the *effect* (as with verses of reverence, the *purpose* of these verses is primarily a causal effect) of making the treatise achieve the best possible result: "It will bring about the achievement of supreme realization." How can a mere introductory verse have so great a positive effect on the treatise as a whole? If we need to ask this, we have already forgotten that the verse of reverence also improved the ultimate result of the whole treatise by calling upon the "essence of all the Buddhas of the three times." In this case, however, the result is brought about in an entirely different way. The oath serves as a lever in the mind of the author for the exercise of social pressure. Although the expression "social pressure" is anachronistic, this seems the most direct interpretation of this passage. Sa-paṇ explains three ways that social pressure exerts itself on the author through the promise, beginning with an interpretation of a promise's linguistic range:

> First, the promise "[I] will give an explanation," indicates one's enthusiasm to give an exposition on this subject matter, and the cause of the enthusiasm is that one is starting in on a good topic. For instance, a king promises to give away the throne, or to turn the wheel of the dharma, but even though he does engage in lesser activities, such as playing dice and checkers, he does promise to do so in the middle of the assembly.[19]

If what you intend to do is wrong, you do not promise to do it. It is simply not done. It would not be a promise (the term "promise" doesn't even really make sense in reference to playing checkers, except as a joke). Thus, the act of promising limits what is promised to the morally right. This is as explicit a statement as we should hope to find that the form governs the content. And the phrase "in the middle of the assembly" is key. One can mumble anything to oneself. But the assembly keeps one's linguistic use within acceptable bounds.

Here we can begin to see Sa-paṇ's resolution to the crucial question of the nature of linguistic meaning, postponed from the last chapter. There, I suggested that it was perhaps philosophically unsatisfying to see the burden of linguistic meaning shifted from the conceptual to the social realm, because this evaded the question without meeting the essential point. Even if the movement from term generality to concept generality is "merely" conventional, the assertion that conventions are social agreements will not satisfy the question of how this movement succeeds until it is answered how the interpretive community can validate a given employment of those conventions, and how the stability of the interpretive community—and its conventions—is itself guaranteed. Sa-paṇ's first answer to the first point, then, is to indicate a simple fact about the nature of language: It is impossible to promise something immoral. The interpretive community, here represented by the assembly, regulates the "illocutionary act" of the promise, and restricts it to the morally right.[20] This is one way that the community regulates the proper employment of linguistic conventions.

Public promises are, of course, special cases. Not every speech act is a public action directly regulated by a judgmental collective. Yet Sa-paṇ next points out that the act of promising before an assembly can in fact extend its governing force beyond the act of the promise itself. The "action" of the promise is only the tip of the iceberg. A valid public promise claims a kind of public authorization, and therefore one can only promise what one is recognized (cf. "well known") to be capable of accomplishing:

> Additionally, because of the promise one is recognized by others as himself a scholar in that topic. If he is not a scholar how can he make the promise in the middle of the assembly?[21]

Thus not only does the assembly require that you promise only good deeds, it requires that you be capable of living up to your oath. What provides the promise with its driving force is therefore not merely the structure of the linguistic form, but the pressure to maintain one's reputation within learned society. The assembly knows what constitutes a proper composition, and is capable of judging a person's abilities and character, upon which reputation is built. If the assembly has good judgment, scholars in its midst cannot possibly be frauds. A scholar's presence as a fruitful member of the community is definitive of his legitimacy. As Sa-paṇ's next point indicates, this dynamic creates a community where each individual is ineluctably tied into the social structure:

> Furthermore, the oath will be the cause of achieving the [goal]. For, as it is said, "Noblemen will give up their life, but not their promise."[22]

The power of the assembly to keep the composer in line gives us a wonderfully clear picture of Sa-paṇ's ultimate goal in writing the *Gateway*. The goal is to produce scholars who will be of great mutual benefit to one another, and together to the dharma, through their scrupulous requirement that each be their best and nothing less. It is a society of noblemen bound to each other in perpetual defense of the dharma. Participation in such a society makes one enthusiastic to accomplish goals that are accepted as good goals, and to proclaim publicly one's intention to achieve such goals. Once one has made the promise, one's reputation hangs upon the proper completion of the goal. This is how the social order regulates each scholar's conceptions of the dharma. It is also how the social order guarantees the preservation of its goals.[23]

Now, there is no verse in the opening of the *Gateway* in which any explicit promise is made. But there is a verse that provides the same effect, of setting upon the author a lever for social pressure toward excellence. It seems likely, therefore, that when he writes his next lines of commentary, Sa-paṇ has the third verse of his own treatise in mind (which I place immediately below):

> Likewise, exhortatory expressions such as "Come here to listen to the supreme dharma," or "Make yourself happy: Listen up!" and so on should be understood in the same way as these [promises].[24]

By having heard, seen, and grown accustomed to many
[teachings]
And being able to give close instructions [upon them], the
glorious Kun-dga'
Rgyal-mtshan [371] is explaining something here;
Scholars, make yourselves happy: Listen up![25]

In this verse Sa-paṇ lays claim to his own membership in an elite group of scholars who are capable of teaching the learned, but he is also invoking the full authority of those scholars as a community that should judge the worth of his work. Sa-paṇ seems quite aware, therefore, of the rhetorical force of his own verse, in which he is claiming to be subject to, and approved by, the noble community of the learned.

The third type of verse of introduction is the "expression of humility" (*kheng bskyung ba bshad pa*) which, as Sa-paṇ writes, appears "in some treatises."[26] The *Gateway* is not one of those treatises. In fact, this is the only one of the five opening verse types under discussion that could not arguably be said to appear in the *Gateway*. It is the precise opposite of the self-aggrandizing rhetoric that Sa-paṇ adopts in his opening (as in the verse just discussed). Nonetheless, it is a standard trope, and Sa-paṇ considers it a valuable indication of the nobility of both author and treatise:

Even though I may not have the ability, in accord with my effort
I yet begin the treatise—such expressions exist,
With respect to treatise and author,
In order to demonstrate the nobility (*dam pa*) of both.[27]

Such an opening statement shows the nobility of the treatise because it suggests that the project is worth attempting even if the scholar might fail to accomplish it, "Like the merchant who goes to get a jewel from [across] the ocean."[28] Likewise, it shows the greatness of the scholar, who sets extremely high standards for himself:

> If one examines the humility like this, in which even such as a scholar of words and meanings (*tshig don*) [says] "I don't know," there is the [inevitable] recognition that the composer is a noble person.[29]

When we read an expression of humility we are not, of course, expected to put the book down and seek out a work with a more capable author. Sa-paṇ knows this. Thus, while this type of verse does not appear in the *Gateway*, Sa-paṇ perceptively explains expressions of humility as a part of the same rhetorical world in which he, on the other side of the same coin, lists his own accomplishments in something akin to claiming relative omniscience (see chapter 1). Both are rhetorical stances that simultaneously on the one hand place the author subject to the judgment of the scholarly expertise of the reader, and on the other hand indicate that the author accepts (and deserves) a high level of scholarly responsibility[30]—twin guarantors of linguistic reliability.

SYNOPSIS AS A DISPLAY OF MASTERY

Sa-paṇ understands the final two types of introductory verses as written primarily to facilitate the activity of teaching and studying the treatise, so here we will see Sa-paṇ underline the connection between composition and teaching even more strongly than in the above discussion of verses of reverence. The central scholarly characteristic that unites composer and expositor in these verses is the ability to synopsize, summarize, and introduce a topic without hesitation and without misleading the student. We should take Sa-paṇ seriously when he says that this ability is a requisite to saying a scholar has a proper *understanding* of the topic, since it appears to be a genuine and legitimate application of his pragmatic theory of meaning. To put this in terms of the community's regulation of linguistic meaning, we could say that the scholar's ability to synopsize (and summarize and introduce) constitutes a public test of his knowledge, which allows the community to determine his degree of comprehension.

The fourth type of introductory verse provides an outline of the treatise, and Sa-paṇ says that it should have three virtues that fit with the three purposes of an outline:

> There are three benefits to placing an outline of the body [of the treatise] up front: easy explanation by the expositor; easy comprehension by the listener; and generating certainty about the treatise.[31]

A good outline thus provides a kind of textual basis for success in each of the three interrelated aspects of exposition:

> The giver of the exposition, the object of the explanation [i.e., the student]
> [And] the thing to be explained, [428] are the three.[32]

Unlike all of the previous types of introductory verses, the outline is not said to benefit the composer of the treatise. Rather, the outline provides a reliable structure to keep the processes of exposition in order:

> First, [376] knowledge of the outline of the body [allows the expositor to] pinpoint what needs to be said, keep the order undisturbed, and form the meaning easily using what was said above—so, three benefits.

> Second, easy comprehension by the listener has three benefits: when hearing, easily pinpointing what's to be said; when contemplating, ease of comprehension without disturbing the order; and when meditating, due to the practice being in summary form, the quick arising of meditative wisdom.
>
> Third, generating certainty about the treatise is where, since the body and branches are properly fit together, the conviction arises that "This treatise is perfect," because it is free from the faults of being disordered, broken, or unnecessarily long.[33]

Outlines allow both teacher and student to "pinpoint what's to be said" in the moment of exposition. This is the moment when, as Sa-paṇ says in the chapter on exposition, the teacher "should make a pure explanation with every feature of verbal expression clear"[34] and the student should be keeping his mind from wandering. The outline helps keep both on track. For the student, the outline also helps keep order during the processes of contemplation—asking questions and solving doubts about the meaning—and during meditation on the treatise. The outline might assist the meditation process in much the same way as it assists the expositor: by guiding one's attention smoothly from one topic to the next. This is why the outline must be "easy to comprehend"—or, an equally legitimate translation, "easy to memorize" (*gzung bde ba*).

Finally, Sa-paṇ writes that an outline represents the orderliness of a treatise in an immediate and compelling way, and that orderliness in a treatise inspires faith and confidence. This is a convincing argument for the rhetorical effect of an outline, and it would seem to place us yet again very close to the *Gateway*'s motivational core. The maintenance of order and the systematic, full treatment of every topic satisfy the characteristic scholastic obsession with completeness. They serve as a counterweight to the rhetoric of doctrinal decline and self-doubt, and the fear of failing to maintain pristine, authentic teachings.

This point is reiterated in the chapter on exposition, where Sa-paṇ discusses the orderly outline as a benefit provided by a good expositor (as opposed to a good composer). Here, the (oral) outline counteracts a surprising number of the potential faults of an expositor, many of which are faults of disorder and misplaced emphasis (I list them all):

> Not giving an exposition, not giving a proper exposition, giving an exposition with a doubt, scratching your head in difficult places,[35] not elaborating where it is necessary, elaborating where it is not necessary, not fitting together a disorder of earlier and later [sections], making unnecessary disorder with an explanation, thus moving to the end what should be explained at the beginning, taking to the beginning what should be explained at the end, [443] explaining without putting in context, not

> explaining [what should be] put in [a particular context], speaking [overly] loud and soft, unclearly, mumbling, too quickly, too slowly, not properly glossing (*brda mi sprod pa*) the words and meaning, etc.—abandoning [these] faults of the expositor, scholars give a proper explanation.[36]

With our attention thus on Sa-paṇ's section on exposition, we see that his interest in the outline that opens a text was only one side (the composition side) of a scholar's general ability to synopsize and systematize a treatise or an idea. The expositor himself must also have this ability. Sa-paṇ provides more details in a subsection of the chapter on exposition on "Summarizing the Meaning."[37] This is the same phrase as the second in the listing of "purpose, summary, and meaning of the words" already discussed. To summarize an entire treatise requires significantly more care and detail than simply summarizing one verse, but the method is essentially the same. Sa-paṇ lists eight characteristics of a good summary as follows (numbers inserted):

> (1) The meaning summarized, (2) the words clear, (3) the utterance easy to say,
> (4) The discourse brief, (5) uniform in expression, (6) and easy to remember,
> (7) By the summarized meaning alone the treatise is understood.
> (8) Whoever understands it this way is a scholar.[38]

Each of these points is important enough to merit separate treatment in Sa-paṇ's autocommentary. (1) and (7) have to do with the skill of capturing the essence of the meaning of the treatise in a single summary. As Sa-paṇ writes, commenting on the first point:

> (1) The entire meaning of what is said is summed up in one point (lit. "one side"). The internal subdivisions should not be lost inside the general meaning. The designation of the general meaning should not be lost among the internal subdivisions. Don't mistake the boundaries of the different things to be said. What is to be said of the meaning, [432] without mixing one point with another, is in sum one great interrelated explanation.[39]

Care is to be taken to represent the treatise exactly, without misplacing subheadings or splitting continuous discussions. The goal is that the expositor (and later, his student) should be able to use the summary to move through the treatise with fluency and ease, grasping and explaining each new passage quickly:

> (7) Through the summarized meaning itself one understands the treatise: The words [make one] able by delving into the summarized meaning it-

> self to quickly understand what should be said, "The intention of the treatise is like this."[40]

Point (2), on the importance of clear words, is straightforwardly for the benefit of the student. All of the other points (3–6) benefit the expositor himself. (3) and (4) consider the expositor's physical vocal apparatus. Smooth, elegant phrases that allow one to take a breath here and there are far preferable to long-winded tongue twisters. The fifth (5) and sixth (6) points speak to the flow of the exposition. "Uniformity of expression" means that the summary should use the same terms as the summarized text, so that the expositor will be able to move smoothly into the topic when it arrives. Otherwise, the expositor will have to explain how the treatise fits the frame he has set up in the summary, which then breaks the flow of the treatise. As Sa-paṇ puts it, in such a case "The summarized meaning does not fit with the words [of the text], so by losing the context before and after it is unattractive in verbal arrangement."[41] Finally, the summary should be "easy to remember" so that the expositor will always have it readily available to apply each new section:

> (6) Easy to remember: pleasant words are agreeable to the ear and impress themselves upon the mind. Taking expressions from the earlier summarized meaning enables [you] to present a later expression without need of effort.[42]

All of these points, then, have been practical advice for expositors on how to go about summarizing a treatise. The last point, (8), combines the others and says that the ability to create a successful summary makes a scholar a scholar. There are many points in the *Gateway* where Sa-paṇ says that a scholar must know some topic or other, but it is rare that he says that a particular skill is *definitive* of being a scholar. An example we've already discussed is the opening verse where Sa-paṇ defines one type of scholar as a master of a particular topic: "Someone who is knowledgeable in a specific field is a scholar in that."[43] Recall that this verse followed Sa-paṇ's long list of scholarly fields and texts that he claimed to have mastered. Now we are being told that to be "knowledgeable in a specific field" is, essentially, to be capable of giving successful summaries of texts in that field: "Thus, easy for oneself to say, easy for others to understand, and pleasing to the ears of both—if you know this, you're a scholar."[44] To be a scholar is to be capable of holding forth comfortably in a clear discourse that is comprehensible to one's audience. Once again, we see here a collapsing of the form with the content, the meaning with the message, which makes sense in a pragmatic worldview where to be a scholar is to be productively engaged with the educational community. Sa-paṇ gives a lengthy comment on this point, which provides criteria according to which the nonscholar or the pseudo-scholar can be discerned and rejected:

> Whoever understands it this way is a scholar. The opposite of this is a nonscholar: Not summarizing the meaning that should be spoken. Not clarifying the expression of the summarized meaning. Where there's a teaching, it is not easy to say. One is compelled to speak a long speech in a single breath. The summarized meaning does not fit with the words [of the text], so by losing the context before and after it is unattractive in verbal arrangement. It is difficult to grasp—that is, since the point is not delivered (*'phrod*), it has difficulty settling in the mind, and is difficult to put into speech. [433] [This leads to] not having the intention of the treatise understood by saying the summarized meaning. Since the point of the summarized meaning and the treatise are not delivered, there is no ability to understand the treatise by relying on the summarized meaning. Many summarized meanings like this are seen all over. Some such basic divisions even misconstrue the meaning. Even if they do not misconstrue the meaning, they are difficult for the teacher to speak, and difficult for the student to remember. For this reason, I have set it out impartially (*btang snyoms su*).[45]

This kind of confused, long-winded, misleading summary gives evidence of "nonscholarship"—someone not knowing what they're talking about—which is the very opposite of the comprehensive mastery of a treatise necessary for proper summarization:

> Take as a mental object the entirety of the text, without exception. Having distinguished in [your] mind what conforms and does not conform with what category within the exposition, list off individually the large general headings. Distinguish, without any mistakes, the internal divisions. Individually summarize, where necessary, the divisions of their branches (i.e., the subdivisions). Some, which are not necessary, are summarized and explained inside their branches.[46]

To summarize, then, is to display mastery. If one wishes to be a scholar, one must subject oneself to the critical judgment of the scholarly assembly. Public display of mastery is thus the basic criterion for expertise. This explains further why the Six Alternatives, whose application entails a comprehensive display of mastery of interpretive positions, are in Sa-paṇ's judgment the test of a scholar's mettle with regard to exposition:

> He who understands by way of the Six Alternatives
> Is extremely discerning (*shin tu mkhas*) in the exposition of treatises.[47]

Like an expository summary, a good outline, to return to our verses of introduction, displays the very same degree of mastery, on behalf of the treatise it summarizes. The *Gateway* does contain a verse of introduction that very much resembles an outline:

> Some people, in [the fields of] language (*śabda*), and nominal inflection (*vibhakti*),
> Verbal formation (*dhātu-siddhi*), the ending's inflective impetus (*kāraka-pada*), examples (*upamā*), verbal ornamentation (*śabdālaṅkāra*),
> Divisions and summaries, reckoning, ascertainment, and arrangement,
> Are predominantly perplexed; seeing [this, I've written] this [treatise].[48]

The topics listed above are all covered, to varying degrees, in the *Gateway*. Yet the verse hardly reflects the main topics and headings in the *Gateway*, and it would be difficult to argue that an expositor would benefit greatly from having this verse in mind. On the other hand, we would be hard pressed to find a better verse to display comprehensive mastery of the topic (of scholarship).

ENSURING EXCELLENCE BY DECLARING A LEGITIMATE PURPOSE

The last of the five verses of introduction, the "statement of purpose and relations" (*dgos 'brel gyi ngag*)[49] ties this theme of public display of mastery back to the question of how the social order guarantees the preservation of its goals. The expression "purpose and relations" is shorthand for a standard fourfold list of hermeneutic categories, which Sa-paṇ expands under his discussion of this type of introduction's "summarized meaning": "The intended meaning (*brjod bya*, lit. 'what is to be said'), the purpose, the ultimate purpose (lit. 'the purpose of the purpose'), and the relation."[50] Sa-paṇ does *not* explain these four terms in the *Gateway*, though he does list them a second time in the chapter on exposition, where he says that since they are universally "well known" (*thams cad la grags pa*), he will not treat them at length.[51] All he does there is repeat that they are the "purpose" of exposition. But if we look at his earlier discussion of the introductory statement of purpose, the parallel between expositor and composer is clear once again. While "the purpose and relations" from the expositor's perspective may be the way to state the purpose of an *exposition*, the purpose and relations from the composer's perspective is the way to state the purpose of a *treatise*:

In order to indicate the nobility of [his] treatise,
The teacher [i.e., the Buddha] indicates the purpose up front.
If one with supreme knowledge is seen [doing] this,
Why not begin [one's own] analysis as well?[52]

This small argument calls upon two reasons that we have already seen for composing a particular kind of introductory verse: the Buddha's previous example as evidence of "best practice," and the desire to indicate the excellence or nobility (*dam pa*) of the treatise. In his autocommentary, Sa-paṇ provides three other possible purposes for stating the purpose up front, including (citing the *Vyākhyāyukti*) that "having heard the greatness of the sūtra . . . it will generate faith in the listener,"[53] that it will "generate a beautiful text," and that it will "refute a wrong understanding of [some] meaning."[54] All of these, Sa-paṇ says, are perhaps "not inappropriate as temporary goals." But his own opinion, upon which he settles, is that "the [final] purpose is the creation of an initial beginning (*'jug pa*)."[55]

What are we to make of this rather mundane comment, that the point of a statement that appears across Buddhist literature, not least in words of the Buddha himself, is merely "to enter" or "to begin" the text? The term "beginning" (*'jug pa*) is the "entry" from each of the *Gateway*'s chapter titles ("Entry into Composition," "Entry into Exposition," and "Entry into Debate") and, of course, is prominent in the title word "Gateway" (*'jug pa'i sgo*) itself. The term is quite common, and has many related meanings ("begin," "engage in," "introduce," "insert," etc.), so we should be careful not to force any particular interpretation. We can stretch the interpretation to mean that an entry into the treatise is something fairly significant, perhaps not only a beginning, but an opening that sets one forth in a particular direction, with a particular motive. Indeed, the "entry" that is the *Gateway* itself is more than merely an introductory textbook, as I have been at pains to argue. But it is, still, also a beginner's work. And Sa-paṇ does not seem to be saying anything much more significant here than that a statement of the purpose of the treatise is a good way to begin. But why?

In light of our earlier discussions, we can perhaps improve our reading of Sa-paṇ's question, "If one with supreme knowledge is seen [doing] this, why not enter into [one's own] analysis as well?" I have been taking this simply to mean that since the Buddha puts opening verses expressing his purpose in the front of his texts, so should everyone who respects the Buddha. (What better way are you likely to find—or, what reason have you got *not* to follow this method?) Yet perhaps the "this" (*de*) refers not to the Buddha's practice of placing a statement of purpose up front, but to *"that" goal or purpose, which the Buddha pursued.* In this case the lines should be read as asking, "Given that this was a goal pursued by one with supreme knowledge, why wouldn't you at least begin an investigation into it?"[56]

Under this interpretation, the statement of purpose justifies the treatise by indicating up front how the treatise fits with traditional, accepted goals—goals that the Buddha has adopted in the past. This is why it indicates the "nobility" or "excellence" (*dam pa*) of the treatise, and thereby ties the treatise to the same social network as the oath of composition. The oath limited the speaker's promised acts to the morally right, and placed the speaker under obligation to complete it. All that was left then to ensure the perpetuation of the social order's own dharmic goals was an explicit guarantee that the proposed or promised exposition would, in fact, satisfy an authentic, socially sanctioned goal. This is what the statement of purpose provides. It subjects the treatise to public scrutiny not only on the correctness of its tenets, but on the legitimacy of its goals.

Since in the chapter on exposition Sa-paṇ treats this same issue together with the other "summarized meanings," we can (again) look there to find a last clue as to its importance and justification. Sa-paṇ tells the expositor to begin with a verse that summarizes the main point of the treatise, but he is not very concerned about the *particular* verse: "If it needs [a summary], even where none is manifest, take [one] from another text of scripture and reasoning."[57] The evident assumption is that the basic purposes of the treatises a good scholar teaches are interconnected and cohere each with the next. One should not find oneself teaching a treatise that is so far outside the range of standard teachings that one cannot explain its purpose under some other more general category of justification covered in other Buddhist treatises. If one has trouble finding a standard verse that explains the reason for studying a particular text, that in itself is perhaps evidence that the text is of questionable value.

Sa-paṇ has not composed a verse stating the main point of his treatise up front, but he does act as expositor in his autocommentary, where he cites the famous *Mahāyānasūtrālaṅkāra* verse that justifies the broad approach to scholarship he advocates:

> Without becoming a scholar in the five sciences
> Not even the supreme sage can become omniscient.
> For the sake of refuting and supporting others,
> And for the sake of knowing everything himself, he makes an effort in these [five sciences].[58]

This verse shows the proper motives for becoming a scholar according to Buddha-dharma (see my chapter 1), and thereby draws the faithful into the treatise—thus, it provides an "entry" into the *Gateway* by indicating up front what the ultimate result of the treatise might be. It therefore serves exactly the purpose of a "statement of purpose": It justifies the treatise by indicating how it will satisfy traditional, accepted goals.

How to Make Meaning Evident

Although Sa-paṇ's comments on these verses of introduction make use of the threefold hermeneutic of "purpose," "summary" and "meaning of the words," nearly all of my discussion thus far has treated only the first two of these three categories. This was simply to follow the emphasis of Sa-paṇ's autocommentary, which generally mentions the third category only in passing, saying, for instance, "The meaning of the words [375] should be understood each according to their own text."[59] The reason for this scant treatment is that in these statements Sa-paṇ is not actually applying the hermeneutic categories, but only instructing the reader on their use. Thus instead of telling us the "meaning of the words" of his own verses, Sa-paṇ is telling us that we must elucidate the meaning of words that we will come across in the future.

What then does it mean to understand the meaning of the words? Again, Sa-paṇ's discussion of exposition provides the detail. In fact, the bulk of Sa-paṇ's chapter on exposition is dedicated to this detail, including strategies of glossing as well as all of the analyses of translation issues discussed in (my) chapter 2. To delve into these many varieties of scriptural analysis would take us too far off track, but just one example can provide us significant insight into Sa-paṇ's understanding of scripture. In particular, we can deepen and substantiate many of the points of this chapter by a glance through Sa-paṇ's exemplary exposition on the opening verse from Nāgārjuna's *Mūlamadhyamakakārikā* (MMK).[60]

Before turning to the actual analysis of the MMK, Sa-paṇ introduces the topic by stating that the form of analysis under discussion has a complex Sanskrit grammatical pedigree, and he cannot address the necessary details in an introductory work such as the *Gateway*:

> When some treatise [434] is explained, apply the six *kārakas*, etc. Properly conjoin the words with the meaning, and do not say anything unnecessary. Without missing anything necessary, give a complete explanation. This is the linguists' (*sgra pa*) way. Since even a good explanation to those who do not know Tibetan grammar[61] is difficult to grasp, I will not explain it here. If you want to know, you should look in the grammatical treatise that I've written.[62]

We might expect, then, that Sa-paṇ would move on to another topic. But he believes that even in an introduction it is important to get the basics of this topic, so he continues, "Here I should say a little bit about methods of explanation most useful in Tibet."[63] What follows is a watered down version of the Sanskrit *kārakas*, using three instead of the standard six:[64]

> For object (*karman*), agent (*kartṛ*) and action (*kriyā*),
> Having linked the meaning with the words, you get the meaning of
> the statement.

The object is cooked rice, etc.
The agent is Devadatta (*lhas byin*), etc.
The action is cooking.[65]

After this simple example, Sa-paṇ proceeds to analyze the following verse of reverence from the MMK (which he does not provide since he assumes his readers know it by heart already):

> By whom dependent arising, [which means being]
> Without cessation, without creation,
> Without nihilism, without eternalism,
> Without coming, without going,
> Without distinction, without identity,
> The peaceful pacification of all elaborations—was taught,
> To the perfect Buddha, among speakers
> The best: To him I bow down.[66]

The exegesis comes in two parts: the basis of characterization (*khyad par gyi gzhi*) and the qualities of characterization (*khyad par gyi chos*). It would appear that the basis is the fundamental, basic meaning of the verse as a whole, understood in the frame of the three *kārakas:*

> The first words are "by whom" and the sixth [line] has "was taught," and the eighth has "to him I bow down"—and when these are put together, you get "I bow down to the one who taught," which is the basis of characterization (*khyad par gyi gzhi*).[67]

Here Sa-paṇ is using an abbreviated *kāraka* analysis together with his distinction between "basis" and "qualities" of characterization to provide a comprehensive and precise system for analyzing the verse. According to more standard *kāraka* analysis, the entirety of a given sentence could be analyzed at once, applying one of the several *kārakas* to each element. In Sa-paṇ's system, one proceeds by stages through the analysis, applying at most three *kārakas* at once (It turns out one only needs three *kārakas!*). Once the basics have been established, the "qualities of characterization" must be enumerated by inquiring into the elements revealed in the basic analysis:

> Then, the qualities of characterization (*khyad par gyi chos*) are explained: Having inquired into the meaning, "What is taught, by whom is it taught, and how is it taught?" one answers: "For what is taught, dependent arising is taught. For who taught it, [435] the perfect Buddha taught it. For the question how was it taught, it was taught as peaceful."[68]

Through the continued interrogation by means of the three *kārakas*, taking each new issue and topic as worthy of investigation, the expositor moves through the verse until every word is thoroughly explained. Thus the "What" (dependent arising), "Who" (the Buddha), and "How" (peaceful) are interrogated in turn:

> If you are to explain these meanings well, to the question, Just what is dependently arising?—[you answer with the verse lines:]
>
> Without cessation, without creation,
> Without nihilism, without eternalism,
> Without coming, without going,
> Without distinction, without identity.
>
> [The fact that] things arise dependently in this way, free from the Eight Extremes,[69] is applied as a quality of characterization (*khyad par gyi chos*) of dependent arising.
>
> To the question, just who is that Buddha who taught [dependent arising]?—[the expression] "best of speakers" is applied. "Speakers" are such great gods as Shiva and Indra, or great old sages like Kapila (*ser skya*) and Kaṇāda (*gzegs gzan*). But whatever speakers are relevant, the ordinary are not considered.
>
> To the question, how is this dependent arising taught?—[the expression] "The peaceful pacification of all elaborations—was taught" is offered. Depending on that, that too arises. All elaborations are pacified with peace. But [gods] such as Shiva, who are called peaceful, are not peaceful. Rather, [real peace] is pacification of all elaborations, such as existence and non-existence—this should be explained.[70]

These three expository paragraphs thereby shape the verse into a series of answers to questions that are of the basic form of the three *kārakas*. Could one explain the basic meaning of the verse without this kind of technical analysis? Of course. But the use of technical terminology allows one to be extremely clear and concise in indicating the meaning and use of each term under analysis, and the desiderata of *kāraka* analysis provide a systematic frame for addressing the entirety of the verse. It provides the expositor with an analytical fluency that allows him to translate whatever verse comes up into a series of answers to questions of the required form.

It is evident that a scholar who gives such a systematic presentation needs to have an accurate comprehension of every term and concept in the scripture or treatise under discussion. Like a good summary, this method is simple and transparent to teachers and students alike. By following such an exposition, even a beginning student would be able to see where the instructor had gaps in understanding (though not where the instructor had misunderstandings), and so would be able to stand in judgment as part of the critical assembly. The form is also sufficiently easy to learn that a beginning student could be expected to give an exposition on any text that he or she had come to understand. It is in this context, therefore, that after exemplifying the method, Sa-paṇ explains, at great length, the potential difficulties and pitfalls that can come when trying to apply this method. This is where Sa-paṇ begins to analyze difficulties for interpreters—mostly, difficulties due to translation—that were the subject of my second chapter.

As I argued there, Sa-paṇ indicates these difficulties through a close analysis of Buddhist treatises themselves. Just as Sa-paṇ's advice to composers of treatises consists largely in explanations of exegetical method, his advice to interpreters consists largely in explanations of the methods of the composers and translators of treatises. In this view, to be a scholar is to be aware of the needs and expectations of the scholarly community at all points and levels. Now that we understand how the methods of composition and exposition call upon the judgmental assembly to perpetuate the dharma's well-established meanings and goals (via the scholar's reputation), we can see why Sa-paṇ's linguistic analyses of the dharma make it the *saṅgha*'s responsibility to maintain standards of linguistic scholarship. The dharma itself depends upon the judgmental assembly preventing expositions by all but those who pass through the gateway of scholarship.

CONCLUSION

It is not surprising to find Sa-paṇ so fond of introductions, outlines, summaries, and exegetical systems. What Sa-paṇ calls "the faults of being disordered, broken, or unnecessarily long" can arguably be said to characterize the style of much of Tibetan composition up to Sa-paṇ's time. Against this Sa-paṇ advocates the very orderly, systematic style of writing and interpretation that was to become so standard in Tibetan scholastic writing that twentieth-century Tibetan scholars find Sa-paṇ's thirteenth-century works largely quite readable. What is widely understood today as a Tibetan penchant for outlines and tables of contents surely precedes Sa-paṇ and his uncles,[71] but the systematicity and clarity that characterize Sakyapa writing must be credited with a wide influence, via Sa-paṇ, upon Tibetan literature.[72]

One way of putting what I have argued in this chapter is that Sa-paṇ was aware that systematicity, regularity, and order in composition and exposition have significant rhetorical effects, which dovetail with the doctrinal considerations discussed in the last two chapters. Above all, regularity of form gives the impression of conservation of content, and so conveys authenticity and legitimacy. The vow to explain a topic in full suggests that one is subjecting oneself to the judgment of a traditional scholarly community, and therein it suggests that (unless the reader hears otherwise) the scholars accept that the vow has been kept. The constant linkages between compositional and exegetical requirements suggest a continuity in expectations as to how readers are to approach texts. Thus, first Sa-paṇ suggests that a *composer* of treatises must consider the "meaning of the words" according to *kāraka* analysis and then he applies that kind of analysis to the opening verse of the MMK as an exemplification of good *exegesis*. This effectively unites the two sides of the text (author and reader) into a single process, implying that the community's current methods of analysis are exactly what the author of the MMK would have expected to be done with his text. If we engage in exegesis according to the traditional modes, our interpretation, thereby, becomes a mirror reflection of (at least part of) the author's compositional intention.

Readers familiar with recent studies in critical theory will wonder whether Sa-paṇ was an early "reader response" theorist. Literary critics such as Stanley Fish and others are like Sa-paṇ in that they want to describe the functionality of language and the proper interpretation of texts under a view that the language itself has no ultimate referent. In their case, of course, the language clearly has no ultimate referent because the literature of their analysis is fictional, which the dharma is not. Yet the desire to stabilize meaning in communities, rather than in the apparent linguistic object itself, makes for notable congruence. When I have written of Sa-paṇ's belief that communities govern modes of interpretation, I have repeatedly (and perhaps too uncritically) used the term "interpretive communities," which is borrowed from Stanley Fish.[73] Like Sa-paṇ, Fish believes that interpretive methods and the community's regulation of those methods act as the arbiter of meaningfulness, and that to interpret properly one must be a well-trained "informed reader."

Similarly resonant are the German reception theorists Wolfgang Iser and Hans Robert Jauss. When Sa-paṇ describes a treatise as though it were an instruction manual for a precise exposition, for instance drawing implicit interpretational acts out of the MMK, he comes close to positing Iser's famous doctrine of the "implied reader."[74] Sa-paṇ's view that proper training places a scholar in the position to respond to whatever interpretive scenario arises resonates with Jauss's view that well-trained readers approach texts from within predictable "horizons of expectations."[75] Also like Jauss, Sa-paṇ believes that historical and cultural context matter greatly; he will claim that scholars who wish to understand the literary conventions of foreign texts must immerse themselves in those texts and thereby gain familiarity with their standards of interpretation.

These intriguing parallels result from a similarity of purpose among differing theorists of different times: They all seek to secure the referential capacity of words that are admitted to have no ultimate referent.[76] Yet such similarities should not distract us from the crucial difference between postmodern literary theories and Sa-paṇ's premodern dharmic view, which is in their distinct notions of reality. Sa-paṇ would never go so far, as Fish does, to say that methods of interpretation not only mediate, but *constitute* the "text," and that therefore the selection of interpretive methods is ultimately "arbitrary." For, that would imply that the *saṅgha*'s interpretation is no more suitable to the dharma than any other. While Sa-paṇ rejects the belief that "ultimate reality" is accessible through language or concepts of any kind, he accepts the *reality* of "conventional reality." The conventionality of conventions does not make them false or unreal. Sa-paṇ's relativistic, pragmatic, conventionalist view is paired with an unswerving faith that the Buddha achieved a perfect realization and passed it on in the best way possible through the dharma and the *saṅgha*. The Buddha-dharma is therefore legitimate not because it is perfectly preserved, but because it is the causal result of a Buddha's actions, maintained through the best efforts of a Buddha's disciples.

One can imagine that Fish might criticize Sa-paṇ for not having gone far enough in his recognition of the community's power in the governance of meaning. Yet in response, Sa-paṇ could say that he has in fact gone much farther than Fish. Fish might well have cast the interpretation of literature into an abyss of uncertainty, but he nonetheless retains a solid belief in tables and chairs. The reality that literary criticism calls into question is the merely conceptual "reality" of fiction. Sa-paṇ has taken the conceptual construction of *ordinary* reality to heart. For him an interpretation which *really is* better than others is one that is more likely to help teachers and students move toward the pragmatic end of Buddhahood.

A more apt criticism would be to point out that Sa-paṇ relies upon a hidden assumption that the community of interpretation somehow resists the changes inherent in all things. When he advocates a particular exegesis of the MMK he implies that the community of interpretation is, for all (dharmic) intents and purposes, relatively continuous and unchanging—and, that this is largely *because* of the persistence of the kinds of interpretive practices he advocates. A modern critic might point out that the exegetical practices available to the disciples of Nāgārjuna are lost, and surely were quite different from the methods employed by thirteenth-century Tibetans. What's more, the original form of the MMK verse does not in any way recommend Sa-paṇ's approach. That is, there is no reason for a modern interpreter to expect that Nāgārjuna thought to himself that he would create a verse which indicated, basically, "I bow down to the one who taught," then upon that frame placed, "The perfect Buddha taught dependent arising," and then expanded upon that with characterizations of dependent arising, the Buddha, and teaching.

Still, true as this criticism may be, it is hardly a convincing defeater of the utility of the interpretive method, much less Sa-paṇ's conservative stance. Sa-paṇ's Mahāyāna view of the emptiness of all conceptual constructs is rooted in perhaps the most basic Buddhist doctrine, that of impermanence. Sa-paṇ will not be caught holding the view that there is something eternal and unchanging about the dharma that can be captured in or wrested from language, even under the strictest of grammatical regimes. Instead, comfortable in the reality of impermanence, Sa-paṇ might ask, in reply to the historicist criticism, In a changing world such as this, *what better method does anyone have?* Surely what has been inherited by Tibetans is of great value and is worthy of being preserved in its best current form, even if it is not a pristine, unadulterated original. Accepting "skill in means" may prevent a naive fundamentalism, but it does not make one a postmodernist. On the contrary, it is here an argument for conservative traditionalism.

Sa-paṇ is aware that a linguistic act takes place when a speaker intends to shape the understanding of his or her audience, and the audience's reception of that linguistic act depends entirely upon whatever social conventions happen to be at play. Thus, it is upon the conventions that Sa-paṇ focuses our attention. Sa-paṇ proposes methods of composition and exegesis that tie a scholar into the intellectual community with bonds of public reputation, personal responsibility, and countless mechanisms for checking and cross-checking each scholar's abilities. Even this is no guarantee that understandings will not change; in fact, if they did not change, they would be in violation of the principle of impermanence (*anitya*). Yet perhaps Sa-paṇ's envisioned intellectual community, with a mandate to preserve their understanding of the teachings, is the closest thing to persistence of meaning we are liable to find, this side of nirvana.

6

APPEALING TO THE TRANSLOCAL

Sanskrit Poetics for a Tibetan Buddhist Elite

> One of the great challenges of a history of literary cultures in South Asia, as elsewhere, is to exhume the conditions that make possible and desirable the creation of new literatures and to understand more subtly what other choices, social, political, religious, are being made when a given language is chosen for literature.
>
> —Pollock, "Literary History . . ."

INTRODUCTION

If it was in the imperial period that Tibetan elites made the choice to adopt Buddhism as the national religion, it was in Sa-paṇ's time that they chose to adopt Sanskrit poetry (*kāvya*) as the model of refined literary expression. It is almost fair to say that Sa-paṇ made that choice, though of course it would take his nephew Pakpa's royal support of the project to make it stick. Sa-paṇ provides an extensive treatment of Sanskrit poetics that is very much the heart of the *Gateway*. It follows immediately upon his discussion of grammar and fills out the remainder of chapter 1. Covering over 35 pages of a work that is only 132 pages in its entirety, it takes up 60 percent of its largest chapter.[1] This discussion of poetics is in many ways the *Gateway*'s most original and unprecedented contribution to Sa-paṇ's intellectual milieu, and indeed also its most influential section, for it seems to have initiated an enduring cultural form. This was Tibet's first extended discussion of Sanskrit poetics, and it was followed, less than half a century later, by a massive flowering of Tibetan interest in poetics. This new interest in Sanskrit poetics, guided by the Sakyapa rulers of Tibet under their Mongol patrons, shaped itself around Daṇḍin's *Kāvyādārśa* (*Poetry's Mirror*)—the very work that the *Gateway* first introduced to the Tibetan world in extensive paraphrase, translation, and summary.[2]

There is a danger, in examining Sa-paṇ's treatment of poetics, to lose the forest for the trees. Indeed, were it not for this section, the *Gateway* might well be used as an introductory textbook across Tibetan scholastic traditions—surveying, as it does, so many important Indic terms and concepts. With Daṇḍin's poetic examples, however, the details are overwhelming and highly specialized. In order to keep my own work within a reasonable limit I will not dwell upon the details or upon the history of Sanskrit *kāvya* at great length, but rather (as is my purpose in this book) simply seek out Sa-paṇ's apparent motivation in describing literary theory as he does. In fact, since even to explain these elements of the *Gateway* sufficiently would have overburdened this text, I have chosen not to provide a retranslation of Sa-paṇ's translation of Daṇḍin. My translation in appendix B therefore ends just before Sa-paṇ begins to summarize Daṇḍin's poetics.

To be more precise, my translation includes the first two of the four subsections into which I divide Sa-paṇ's poetics section. The first subsection[3] is where Sa-paṇ deals with the nine main poetic emotions that characterize a literary scene or work, what in Sanskrit dramatic and literary theory are called the *bhāvas* (Tib. *nyams*) and, when heightened and sustained, are called *rasas* (Tib. *ro*, literally "tastes" or "flavors"). These appear at the beginning of subsection 1 in a form reminiscent of a verse from the *Hevajra Tantra*.[4] This seems a significant choice, for it indicates Sa-paṇ's intention to assimilate Indian literary practices with Tibetan expectations—in particular, Tibetan Buddhist expectations. This interest seems to have brought Sa-paṇ to a new and distinctive Buddhist literary theory, and is consequently one of the more remarkable sections of the *Gateway*. Sadly, although Daṇḍin, with his many literary figures, was translated and became influential shortly after Sa-paṇ's death, Tibetans never seem to have translated any Sanskrit theorists who developed the theory of the *rasas*. Sa-paṇ's creative approach to literary criticism "evidently fell dead from his pen," as Leonard van der Kuijp has put it.[5]

If Sa-paṇ's first interest was simply to engage Tibetan hearts and minds with the possibilities of such literary theorizing, the second subsection[6] indicates Sa-paṇ's second main interest in laying out the details of poetics: It is essentially about proper and improper language for use in the royal assembly, or amid an assembly of learned scholars. Poetics becomes the highest benchmark for expertise within the very same community of interpretation described in chapters 4 and 5. In fact, the *rasas* were also shown to support very much the same set of goals. It is, indeed, a standard characteristic of the poetic emotions, across Indian traditions, to be defined through what Ingalls calls "conventions of portrayal"—more precisely, appropriate and inappropriate combinations.[7] The "argument" in this second section, then, is intended to connect up the first subsection's *rasa* theoretics, and the sense of propriety that it evinces, with the details of poetics exemplified in the third and fourth, on Daṇḍin.

The third[8] and fourth[9] subsections, then, are those that paraphrase and summarize Daṇḍin's *Kāvyādarśa*. I separate them because they represent somewhat different approaches in Sa-paṇ's writing style: The third subsection, which is Sa-paṇ's treatment of issues from the first chapter of the *Kāvyādarśa,* also includes a few issues not covered by the *Kāvyādarśa* and shifts Daṇḍin's order here and there to accommodate something of Sa-paṇ's own argumentative flow. Also, like most of the *Gateway,* the autocommentary in this subsection regularly cites Sa-paṇ's own root text and generally provides only a few paragraphs of commentary before returning to it. The fourth subsection, on the other hand, is almost entirely a verse-by-verse summary of *Kāvyādarśa* II.8–200, with almost no editing, insertion, or commentary. In addition, it is predominantly autocommentary. At one point the autocommentary goes through twelve pages of Tibetan without citing a single word from the root text. Here Sa-paṇ is using the autocommentary as an opportunity to expand his poetics section from the basic introduction it is in the root text into the most extensive and detailed treatment of any issue of the *Gateway.*

Above all, Sa-paṇ's goal in this section of the *Gateway* is to present traditional poetic concepts in a mode that will satisfy the likely tastes of his Tibetan Buddhist readership, and at the same time, to show them that literary expertise can be used to display the very height of refinement. If Sa-paṇ could have simply made this argument without translating and summarizing extensively from the *Kāvyādarśa,* perhaps he would have. But at the point of the exposition where on other topics the *Gateway* instructs its readers to seek further explanations elsewhere, Sa-paṇ instead feels obliged to lay out a great amount of detail. For no other Tibetan texts yet existed for Sa-paṇ's readers to pursue for further study of *alaṅkāraśāstra.* Sa-paṇ chose to save space by referring to other texts wherever he could, but judged that since no existing Tibetan texts provided the required exposition of poetics, his own detailed, original exposition was necessary.

SA-PAṆ'S BUDDHICIZATION OF THE *RASAS*

In the *Gateway,* Sa-paṇ mentions two texts on literary theory that he claims to have read and mastered. He identifies the author Daṇḍin and the text the *Sarasvatīkaṇṭhābharaṇa (dbyangs can gyi mgul rgyan)*, meaning Daṇḍin's *Kāvyādarśa* and the *Sarasvatīkaṇṭhābharaṇa* by the great polymath king Bhoja. The *Gateway* shows clear and extensive evidence of Sa-paṇ's mastery of Daṇḍin. But Daṇḍin provides no theorization of *rasa* as a special mode of poetic expression distinct from, or over and above, the other literary ornaments (*alaṅkāras*), and in any event, Sa-paṇ does not cite Daṇḍin's treatment of *rasa.*[10] Thus one would expect to find Sa-paṇ's separate treatment of *rasa* echoing Bhoja's. Indeed, much in this section seems to draw upon Bhoja's *Sarasvatīkaṇṭhābharaṇa.* For instance, as I have mentioned, Sa-paṇ catalogues the proprieties and improprieties involved in combining the different poetic emotions, a theme that Bhoja also treated in great detail.[11] And Sa-paṇ makes three explicit references to the *Sarasvatīkaṇṭhābharaṇa,* quoting it twice.[12] Perhaps most interestingly, Sa-paṇ's initial introduction to the section on poetics seems to reflect Bhoja's distinctive thematization of *śṛṅgāra* ("Passion" or "Seductiveness") as the central emotion of all poetry:

> With directly and indirectly [stated] analogies, etc., good language and ornamentation becomes superimposed [with exaggerated meaning] (*sgro btags*), and in applying the nine emotions (*bhāvas, nyams*) the poetry of Passion (*rol sgegs dang bcas pa'i snyan ngag, śṛṅgāra-kāvya*) is written.[13]

This is indeed suggestive of some influence of Bhoja's views on Sa-paṇ. Yet this brief summary is *the only passage* where Sa-paṇ uses the term *rol sgegs,* as a translation of *śṛṅgāra,* in a passage clearly referring to a characteristic of all well-composed poetry (Bhoja's special sense), rather than in the more common translation *sgegs pa,* where it indicates only one of the several poetic emotions. No one would expect that Sa-paṇ, in this first, basic presentation of poetic themes for Tibetans, should give the kind of thorough treatment of *śṛṅgāra* that is found in Bhoja's encyclopedic treatises. Yet the above passage is only just barely enough for us to surmise that Sa-paṇ was probably aware of the two different uses of the term *śṛṅgāra.* By no means does it show him to have been an advocate of Bhoja's distinctive view of poetry, nor can we say that he formed his view of *rasa* predominantly under Bhoja's influence.[14] Like many theorists of his time and preceding him, Sa-paṇ does not maintain a consistent distinction between *rasa* and *bhāva,* and he seems far more interested to characterize the distinctive literary types than he is to theorize poetics itself.

It seems to me, therefore, that the much older tradition of theorization on drama represented by Bharata's *Nāṭyaśāstra* is at least as perceptible as the *Sarasvatīkaṇṭhābharaṇa* in the background of Sa-paṇ's discussion of the *rasas.* The traditional dramatic distinction between *dharma rasas* and *loka rasas,* in particular, is prominent in Sa-paṇ's analysis—though greatly transformed. In truth, I am not content that I have discovered any single source for Sa-paṇ's presentation. Rather, the *Gateway*'s presentation of *rasa* theory seems to have been guided not specifically by Bhoja's or Bharata's or any other known Sanskrit scholar's approach, but instead by Sa-paṇ's own intellectual goals, which led him to pick and choose appropriate points from a variety of sources.[15]

Before continuing, it is perhaps worth explaining the nature of the *rasas.* I think this will become more clear as we go on, but the idea is that the poetic emotion of *horror,* for instance, is constituted through various effects of the setting and the appearance and behavior of the characters—dark forests, fires, dangerous animals, hideous monsters, and the like, combined with confused and frightened people, and so on—so that when these things are present in the appropriate form the emotional intensity of the scene or the work reaches a kind of peak, that then is called a *rasa*, a "flavor"—the "flavor" of horror. The same kind of thing will be true for the other poetic emotions, such as, for instance, *passion*, where the intensity of the romantic flavor is heightened by the presence of spring flowers, buzzing bees, cool breezes, characters in the peak of beauty, meeting secretly, expressing themselves playfully and indirectly, and so on. All of this is delineated and systematized by Sanskrit literary theorists.

It would appear that when Sa-paṇ explains the *bhāvas* he has to do some work in order to present this theory in a way that will be of obvious use and interest to his Buddhist contemporaries. Since this is a theoretical model that is largely new, he is careful to make it as palatable as possible by connecting it to familiar Buddhist themes and goals, and by skipping over the racier parts. More importantly, though, he wants this theory to appear relevant and grand. In order to accomplish this, he describes poetics in a way that links the community of elite, knowing poetics scholars with the community of the great bodhisattvas, and distinguishes both classes of great beings on one side from the ordinary, the unlearned, and the non-Buddhist on the other. This connects us back to the themes covered in previous chapters because it puts *kāvya* at the very peak of the learned curriculum that makes one an active member of a community of interpretation that distinguishes the valid, the appropriate, and the refined from their opposites. The result is a distinctively Mahāyāna version of *rasa* theory, and a distinctively Tibetan motivation to study Indian literature.

The *Gateway* is designed for a broad readership, and is certainly not a work on esoteric topics. For this reason, Sa-paṇ is careful not to reveal anything that might be considered a Vajrayāna secret, even when he is mentioning topics that pertain to tantra.[16] In chapter 4, I argued that Sa-paṇ's hermeneutic theory is based in the tantric hermeneutic tradition of Candrakīrti's *Pradīpodyottana*, but although Sa-paṇ makes mention of incomprehensible terms from the tantras, he gives very few citations. It seems significant, then, that Sa-paṇ opens his discussion of *rasa* theory with a list of the nine poetic emotions derived directly from the *Hevajra Tantra:*

> Passion (*śṛṅgāra, sgeg*), heroism (*vīra, dpa' ba*), repulsiveness (*bibhatsa, mi sdug pa*),
> comedy (*hāsya, dgod*), violence (*raudra, drag shul*), horror (*bhayānaka, 'jigs su rung*),
> compassion (*karuṇa, snying rje*), awesomeness (*adbhuta, ngam*), and tranquility (*śānta, zhi ba*) are the nine.[17]

In Tibetan, these words invoke a verse universally memorized and recited by Sakyapa monks as part of the standard *Lamdre* liturgy.[18] One could not hope to find lines on poetic theory more "well known" to Tibetans. What this means is that Sa-paṇ's words bring to mind the one verse on the obscure topic of Sanskrit poetics that much of his thirteenth-century Tibetan audience would find familiar. This is true even though, as I've said, Sa-paṇ's was the first significant treatment of Sanskrit poetics in Tibet (and the *only* extensive treatment of *rasa*).

Sa-paṇ's decision to reference the *Hevajra Tantra* is therefore a way of highlighting a Buddhist source for the significance of the study of poetics, and grounding the unfamiliar in the familiar. What might otherwise seem entirely new and perhaps even irrelevant to accepted Buddhist intellectual pursuits is through this method shown to have roots in a text absolutely central to the practice of every Buddhist in Sa-paṇ's tradition. This would seem to be a good enough reason for Sa-paṇ's having made an exception to his rule against tantric citation.

When Sa-paṇ turns to define the poetic emotions, we find the clearest instance of his attempt to "Buddhicize" poetic theory—by which I mean he is attempting to incorporate poetics into the interpretation of the dharma. Here, for six out of the nine he articulates two distinct categories of their use: as a *dharma rasa* or as a *loka rasa,* that is, as a moral/ethical or worldly instance of the poetic emotions:

> Heroism (*vīra*) is a kind of fearlessness. If we further divide it, the one who is fearless in practicing giving (*dāna*) and moral behavior (*śīla*), etc. [i.e., the six *pāramitās*], is the hero of dharma. The worldly hero is fearless with respect to enemies in battle, wild beasts and demons, etc.[19]
>
> Violence (*raudra*) is subduing the enemy with roughness. "He pulls out negative afflicted emotions from the root," and so forth. (1) Cutting out the roots of such afflicted obscurations and obscurations of wisdom, with their latent tendencies (*vāsanā*), and (2) the Buddha's subduing the Maras, and (3) Vajrapāṇi subduing Rudra, etc., are [all instances of] violence conducive to the dharma. As a way to suppress the opponent, to subdue the enemy with rage—a great commotion of body, speech and mind—is worldly violence.[20]
>
> Horror (*bhayānaka*) is driving away the opponent and making [him or her] frightened. It may be a quality of mind, but is generally best [exemplified] through gestures of body and speech. To relate examples in the six perfections (*pāramitās*): The cutting away of son and daughter by Vessantara; of [his] eye by the king of the Śibis; of [one's] flesh through the power of love (compassion); of [his] head by king Moonlight; and of the upper and lower parts of the body by Suvarṇavarṇa, for example. Likewise for the other perfections, such as moral behavior, etc. For others (ordinary people), [these acts that are] difficult to perform surpass even the

> imagination. All [these things] that bring about "terror" (*skyi bung*) are dharmic horror. Other than that is worldly [horror], such as the appearance of demons and ogres, and the terrifying behavior of wild animals, etc., [vertigo in] canyons [and] mountain slopes, and dark forests, oceans, great fires, frightening winds, etc.[21]
>
> Feeling loving kindness in the heart for one who has fallen into evil, into the three lower existences, a lack of refuge, disease, misery, hunger, poverty, being tormented by others, old age, trouble, and death, etc., is the arising of compassion (*karuṇa*) for an inferior person. Having heard of the splendid acts of the bodhisattva, the heart is overwhelmed, one's hair stands up. Tears flow. Being amazed, loving kindness arises; this is the compassion that arises for the superior person.[22]
>
> Caste, physical appearance, power, wealth, sovereignty, etc., are worldly awesomeness (*adbhuta*). When, by being singly superior to others in intelligence, virtue, confidence, renunciation, and attainments, etc., one suppresses the opponent with splendor, it is dharmic awesomeness.[23]
>
> Tranquility (*śānta*) is the abandonment of the qualities of pride, haughtiness and conceit. If we divide it, there is abandonment of worldly pride and dharmic pride; [each] dispels the mentality [associated with one of the types] of awesomeness explained above.[24]

While these type distinctions are present in traditional *alaṅkāraśāstra,* no known Sanskrit text makes so much of the distinction between worldly (*loka*) and dharmic versions of the poetic emotions as these passages. Here we are not merely presented with a typology, but with a consistent characterization, not to say theorization, of this distinction. If we assume therefore, for the time being, that Sa-paṇ (or Śākyaśrī with his entourage) deserves credit for articulating this distinction so extensively, with such an explicitly Buddhist ethical palate, several observations are in order.

First, it should be clear that here "dharma" means *Buddha-dharma.* The dharmic versions of the poetic emotions are exemplified with distinctively Buddhist instances of those emotions. The Sanskrit poetic tradition represented in, for instance, the theorist Dhanika's analysis knows three types of heroes: Heroes of giving (*dānavīra*), heroes of compassion (*dayāvīra*), and heroes in battle (*yuddhavīra*).[25] When Sa-paṇ combines the hero of compassion with the hero of giving, this would appear to be a clear instance of Sa-paṇ's Buddhicization of these categories: In a Buddhist worldview, giving (*dāna*) is one of the crucial heroic acts of dharma, a quintessential compassionate act. The "hero of dharma" is a bodhisattva practicing the six perfections. The heroism involved in slaying wild beasts and demons might well fall under a broader conception of dharma as "justice," but here it is explicitly described as nondharma, that is, not in the service of Buddhist dharma.[26]

Second, we should note that after combining the *dānavīra* with the *dayāvīra,* Sa-paṇ turns the *yuddhavīra* ("hero in battle") into a *lokavīra* ("worldly hero"). All heroes are thus either Buddhist heroes or worldly, ordinary heroes. This is the same term "world" (*'jig rten*) that is familiar from the expression "well known in the world"—meaning well known according to ordinary, nonscholarly conventions (see chapter 4). Thus the term meaning "ordinary" which was applied above to language (to distinguish it from expert, technical language) is now being used in a moral sense: ordinary in the sense of not extraordinary, not special, not the act of a great being such as a buddha or a bodhisattva. Sa-paṇ would of course have been aware that the "ordinary" heroes of Sanskrit poetry are by no means ordinary people. The standard example of a hero called upon in Sanskrit poetics is Rāma, the hero of the *Rāmāyana.* But for Sa-paṇ, Rāma would be just such a "worldly" hero: "The worldly hero is fearless with respect to enemies in battle, wild beasts and demons, etc."

Third, these terms provide an occasion for Sa-paṇ to show us what makes a Buddhist (dharma) story different from a non-Buddhist (*loka*) one. Sa-paṇ's Buddhist examples tend to emphasize the heroic practices of a bodhisattva, though he also includes references to stories from the *Nikāyas* and *Jātakas* acceptable to all Buddhists, and one reference the tantric Buddha Vajrapāṇi. At the very least, each of these stories might be called upon to show that the poetic emotions exist and are applicable in the analysis of Buddhist stories. Sa-paṇ's distinction between dharmic and worldly poetic emotions might simply be a matter of classifying the literary in a way that appealed to an audience for whom *dharma was Buddhadharma.* But another possibility is that Sa-paṇ uses his distinctions and examples in order to make a literary-theoretical point, to help us to understand some distinctively Buddhist emotional registers.

This latter approach seems most successfully applied where Sa-paṇ adduces examples of the *rasas* of horror and compassion. A non-Buddhist "horror" story tells of basically frightening events (dark forests, demons, etc.). But Buddhist "horror" has an entirely different character: One is horrified, but also somehow uplifted, at the tale of a great being who cuts off his own flesh as a gift, an act so "difficult to perform" as to "surpass even the imagination."[27] This is truly horror with a Buddhist (or, perhaps, religious) flavor. Similarly, compassion in the ordinary sense is the emotion that we normally associate with the term, taking as its object a person who has undergone difficulties. But the superior form of compassion comes about only in response to hearing of the achievements of the Bodhisattva, at which "the heart is overwhelmed, one's hair stands up. Tears flow. Being amazed, loving kindness arises."[28] This is not the ordinary experience of compassion; on the contrary, it is the experience of *true* compassion that only arises in superior beings who encounter the teachings and have a deep recognition of their power.[29] In these examples Sa-paṇ has done what I take to be some rather sophisticated religious literary criticism. We can recognize these stories as exemplifying distinctively religious poetic emotions, and Sa-paṇ (understandably for a Buddhist) reserves them for the Buddhist dharma alone.

If we apply this recognition to the other poetic emotions described as having a dharmic version, it is not difficult to find still more cases where Sa-paṇ exercises a subtle literary perception. Fearlessness in practicing the six perfections is fearlessness in a distinctively religious mode—in its own way superior to bravery on the battlefield. The violence of wrathful bodhisattvas "cutting out the roots of . . . afflicted obscurations and obscurations of wisdom, with their latent tendencies (*vāsanā*)"[30] is surely an example of "roughness," but its violence is related only figuratively to the violence of the battlefield. Sa-paṇ's distinction between the qualities that make the ordinary person appear intimidating (caste, physical appearance, power, wealth, sovereignty etc.) and those that make the Buddhist adept appear intimidating (intelligence, virtue, confidence, renunciation, and attainments, etc.) provide us with a well-articulated distinction between religious and worldly values.[31] Thus, we could say, the moment when Mara's armies flee before the Buddha is a moment where worldly awesomeness loses to dharmic awesomeness. What is "awesome" or intimidating in the Buddha's presence is quite different from what made Mara appear awesome. Tranquility, finally, is defined as an abandonment of one of the two kinds of pride associated with awesomeness: whether pride in one's worldly attainments or pride in one's dharmic attainments. The abandonment even of pride in dharmic attainments is, of course, a necessary part of the Buddhist path, but one that occurs far later on the path than the abandonment of (worldly) pride that allowed one to renounce the world and become a monk in the first place.

Thus, Sa-paṇ's division between worldly and dharmic poetic emotions: (1) shows that the poetic literary emotions exist within and apply to the analysis of Buddhist texts; (2) bifurcates the poetic world into non-Buddhist and Buddhist, ordinary and extraordinary; and (3) provides a subtle reading of the distinctive character of Buddhist religious literature, which read properly glorifies the Buddha's achievements above those of all other heroes.

There are only three remaining poetic emotions that Sa-paṇ chose not to divide into dharmic and ordinary varieties: passion (or the erotic), repulsiveness, and comedy. It might be suggested that these could all be more than appropriately exemplified by stories from the tantras. One could even evince the story of the great siddha Virūpa, founder of the *Lamdre,* who is said to have stopped the sun so that he could keep drinking beer. Other stories of the great siddhas include plenty of passion and repulsiveness, as well as more comedy. Why, if Sa-paṇ draws upon the *Hevajra Tantra* to describe the *rasas*, does he not use these examples to describe the analytical possibilities of Sanskrit poetics? It seems to me that such questions give evidence of the exception proving the rule. These are left out because the intention is to elevate the Buddhist path above other paths, and to elevate its interpreters above ordinary interpreters. Such popular stories are fun, but their very popularity undermines their effectiveness as a support for the elite.

APPLYING THE *RASAS*

After this initial introduction to the poetic emotions, Sa-paṇ's *rasa* subsection runs through the poetic emotions three more times: Once to say for each emotion which of the others to avoid in the context of its use; once to say for each emotion which *can be used* in conjunction with it; and once to treat extra issues that are not simply about what can and cannot be combined. Like subsection 2 to follow (and like so much of the *Gateway*), this part of subsection 1 is concerned with propriety—that is, proper and improper uses of the *rasas*. An analysis of proper and improper combinations shows, once again, how Sa-paṇ is integrating Buddhist themes into his presentation of the poetic emotions.

Since Sa-paṇ lists contradictory and noncontradictory emotions for each of the poetic emotions, there is no reason that he should necessarily have missed

Table 6.1. Properly combining the poetic emotions

	Using These Emotions								
In These Contexts	**Passion**	**Heroism**	**Repulsiveness**	**Comedy**	**Violence**	**Horror**	**Compassion**	**Awesomeness**	**Tranquility**
Passion			x		x		o	xo	o
Heroism				x	o	o	x	o	x
Repulsiveness	x				o	o	x		x
Comedy	o	o	o		x	x	x	o	x
Violence		o	o				x	o	x
Horror		o	o				x	o	x
Compassion	x	x		x	x	x		x	o
Awesomeness	o			o	o	o	x		x
Tranquility	x	x		x	x	x	o	x	

x—does not fit
o—does fit

the opportunity to explain some contradiction or consonance between each given pair. But he does not treat all of the emotions equally. In Tables 6.1–3, I lay out Sa-paṇ's statements of how each poetic emotion should be used in the context of other poetic emotions. Table 6.1 shows an 'x' for each combination that Sa-paṇ declares as unacceptable, and shows an 'o' for each he says is acceptable. For those that Sa-paṇ does not mention, I leave the box blank. These combinations are interesting in themselves, but for the sake of brevity I summarize the results in Table 6.2. As we can see there, Sa-paṇ tells us of only four emotional contexts (out of the eight other *rasas*) in which it is appropriate or inappropriate to use repulsiveness and comedy, and only five each for passion and heroism. For the other contexts, we are left to our own devices to determine whether these emotions are appropriate. As it turns out, only compassion and tranquility are explained exhaustively. This indicates that Sa-paṇ had a special interest in these two poetic emotions. If we attend to Sa-paṇ's consideration of compassion and tranquility in the following verses, the reason becomes clear:

> In both violence and horror, avoid,
> Similarly, compassion and tranquility.

> Violence and horror, being vicious, are qualities of doing harm to others. Since compassion and tranquility, being tender, benefit [others], they are mutually opposed.

> In both compassion and tranquility, avoid
> the six: passion, heroism, comedy,
> violence, horror, and awesomeness.

Table 6.2. Summations of Table 6.1

	Fits with Others	Doesn't Fit	Total Mentioned*
Passion	2	3	5
Heroism	3	2	5
Repulsiveness	3	1	4
Comedy	1	3	4
Violence	3	4	7
Horror	3	3	6
Compassion	2	6	8
Awesomeness	5	3	8(7)*
Tranquility	2	6	8

* Awesomeness is said both to fit and not to fit with passion. Thus its propriety is mentioned eight times, but with reference to only seven different other poetic emotions.

> Since, while compassion and tranquility, being beneficial, are kinds of discipline, passion—quivering and distracting—is a quality of extreme disquiet. And since, on the one hand, compassion and tranquility, with the mind serene, are disciplines, and on the other hand, heroism, comedy, violence and horror are hindrances to those [disciplines].
>
> If some of them, like heroism and horror, etc., do not oppose the perfections (*pāramitās*) such as giving, etc. in contexts associated with the dharma, then the application in context is explained as was explained in the context of heroism above.
>
> In the ornament of awesomeness, completely
> avoid both compassion and tranquility.
>
> Because, while awesomeness is a kind of pride, compassion and tranquility are kinds of discipline.[32]

Sa-paṇ emphasizes three qualities of both compassion and tranquility: (1) both are tender and serene, thus associated with an atmosphere that could be disrupted by the disquiet of violence, passion, and so on; (2) both are beneficial for others, thus opposed by any kind of harm to others; and (3) both are kinds of discipline, thus opposed by any kind of distraction. I need hardly emphasize that these (at least 2 and 3) are fundamental characteristics of the path of the bodhisattva. Indeed, the commentary on the middle verse cited here is quite explicit about it: Those emotions which are potentially distracting *might* be allowed in contexts of compassion and tranquility, as long as they "do not oppose the perfections such as giving, etc., in contexts associated with the dharma." But if we still need to be reminded of the internal relation between the dharma and discipline, recall that Sa-paṇ's uncle Sönam Tsemo had analyzed the term "dharma" (*chos*) itself as derived from the dharma's ability to discipline the mind, using the same term for "discipline" (*'dul ba*) as Sa-paṇ uses above: "It is called religious (*chos*) because it *relegates* (*'chos pa*) the mind, or because of disciplining (*'dul ba*) the mind."[33]

It would appear that Sa-paṇ's treatment of compassion and tranquility is rather different from any previous known authors on *rasa*. We cannot properly understand his choices without a clearer sense of his indebtedness to other works to which he might have had access, but unfortunately this is research that remains a desideratum for the future. For the time being, let us simply notice that the poetic emotion *karuṇa* that I am translating as "compassion"—to reflect Sa-paṇ's translation and discussion—is often translated "pity." While it is surely considered morally appropriate for Rāma, for instance, to feel pity, this is something entirely different from Buddhist compassion.[34] "Compassion" (*snying rje*) is, needless to say, an extensively thematized Buddhist technical term, and

Sa-paṇ treats it here as though it needs no separate new redefinition in the poetic context. Thus, by simply treating the word *as is,* Sa-paṇ has completely reconfigured this one emotion to reflect the needs of an audience interested in Buddhist composition, not insignificantly including *two* distinctively Buddhist (religious) emotions in his nine where other theorists had left the religious sentiment to tranquility alone.

After delineating the contradictions and noncontradictions among the poetic emotions, Sa-paṇ runs through the list one more time, giving six verses on topics special to particular emotions or groups of emotions. In this section, as well, Sa-paṇ gives special attention to the emotions of compassion and tranquility, treating each under two separate topics (see Table 6.3). As it turns out, the only emotions aside from compassion and tranquility that are treated more than once in this section are those that are said to be *in contradiction with* compassion and tranquility (passion twice, heroism and violence once each)—which makes these emotions the exceptions that prove the rule of Sa-paṇ's special interest in compassion and tranquility. But nothing shows this interest more vividly than the following, which also shows Sa-paṇ exercising a subtle literary sensibility:

> With regard to compassion and tranquility:
> Both are destroyed if they are mixed with verbal ornaments
> Such as passion and heroism.
> Therefore, abandon fabricated ornamentation!

> Compassion and tranquility are both by nature soothing. Thus, expressions which come from the main ornament with a nature in conformity with that [natural serenity] are able to generate love and discipline (*dul*).

Table 6.3. Additional special topics

	Topic No. Treated	Special Topics
Passion	1, 5, 6r	1—use attractive ornamentation
Heroism	2, 5	2—use rough ornamentation
Repulsiveness	3	3—kinds of repulsiveness
Comedy	1, 4	4—kinds of comedy (fools and scholars)
Violence	2, 6c	5—these are special: no fabrication!
Horror	2	6—mutually contradictory examples
Compassion	5, 6c	(r = root text; c = commentary)
Awesomeness	1	
Tranquility	5, 6r	

> Therefore, the noble ornament is unfabricated, like what is said by parents to a suffering child. Here, fabricated verbal ornaments should not be mixed in, because if they are mixed in, the spontaneously arisen compassion and discipline become as if fabricated. Examples of compassion should be understood by looking at the *All-liberator* (*thams cad sgrol*), and examples of tranquility [should be understood by looking at] the *Iron House Jātaka*.[35]

We have already seen that Sa-paṇ considered storytelling a useful pedagogical tool.[36] Frightening stories of the dangers of samsara can help to motivate a lazy student, and exciting stories can grab the attention of one who is tired. In the above verse and commentary, however, we come close to a distinctive religious literary theory. Here Sa-paṇ writes that "expressions . . . are able to generate love and discipline." It is possible that Sa-paṇ means that the reader experiences this "love and discipline." In that case, this verse would be saying that a particular style of writing—that which is not fabricated—can directly advance the reader on the bodhisattva path. This seems unlikely to me, though I find the interpretation tempting enough to mention.[37] More likely, Sa-paṇ is advocating a particular "unfabricated" method of composition to *represent* the generation of love and discipline, and arguing that a "fabricated" ornamentation fails to convey the reality of the bodhisattva's path. Either way, though, the words of a proper Buddhist tale should be natural, gentle, and consoling: "The noble ornament is unfabricated, like what is said by parents to a suffering child." This elegant statement takes a common trope for explaining the ideal, spontaneous character of Buddhist compassion and uses it to explain the ideal of *expression* that Sa-paṇ seeks in the composition of Buddhist poetry.

Poetics in Defense of the Dharma

Sa-paṇ's love of unfabricated ornamentation is a literary aesthetic to match his rejection of all dharma-like fabrications (*bcos*), which are the opposite of the true "gift of the dharma" from master to disciple:

> As the Buddha says: "Masters who don't know the dharma give explanations of false constructions and whatever they think up themselves. This negates the intention of the sūtras and tantras, and is not a gift of dharma. The one who gives those expositions—he is a friend of non-virtue." Also, it is said, "This dharma is a [mere] reflection of the dharma, or a dharma-like fabrication." Teachings of such a kind, on top of being of no benefit, bring about the destruction of the dharma. It is a gift of non-dharma, not a gift of dharma.[38]

This passage refers not to literary fabrication but to false constructions in scriptural interpretation. Nonetheless, I believe it is reasonable to assume that Sa-paṇ believes that too much ornamentation of the wrong kind is potentially damaging to the dharma in ways similar to interpretive fabrication. This seems especially the case since Sa-paṇ moves immediately from his discussion of the dangers of disrupting the proper application of the Buddhist poetic emotions (through mistaken combinations) to a more general discussion of how poetic knowledge is important if one is to prevent the dharma's misrepresentation and embarrassment in front of non-Buddhist critics. This second, small subsection thus provides a justificatory transition between the Buddhicized literary theory that precedes it and the detailed analyses of poetic ornamentation that follow it. The details of poetic analysis—drawn almost exclusively from Daṇḍin's *Kāvyādarśa*—are not, for the most part, explained in terms that justify their own importance to a Tibetan Buddhist audience. If, however, we accept the argument from this subsection—that proper Buddhist scholars need to know and use standard, well-known poetic conventions—then the details appear justified simply as literary conventions of which Buddhist poets should be aware. It tells us, in short, why Sa-paṇ is so concerned with literary theory.

This subsection is rather short, straightforward, and of a piece. Sa-paṇ makes only three basic points: (1) One must be careful to use literary figures that are appropriate to their subject, especially in reference to the dharma; (2) a good way to do this is to learn and use the standard tropes of Sanskrit poetry; and (3) another way is, conversely, to be sure to avoid inappropriate or nonstandard uses. All three points suggest that Tibetan authors ought to be able to satisfy the elite literary tastes of an ever-critical assembly of outsiders.

Sa-paṇ's first point is that a writer must use literary figures that (of course) express the correct meaning, but that also are appropriate to their object. The following is a nice example of how one might make a basically good point with unfortunate implications:

> Geese (*chu skyar*), cats, and thieves
> By advancing silently and stealthily,
> Attain the object of their highest desire.
> The sage [i.e., the Buddha] always behaves like this.[39]

While stealth may be a useful skill, the poet who compares the Buddha to a thief not only sets himself up for ridicule, he also lays the dharma open to attack. In reference to examples such as this, Sa-paṇ says that the danger is that "If there is [such a mistake] in the context of poetry, the non-Buddhists will question [you] and tease, 'Does your Buddha act like this?'"[40] This point is driven home at the end of the subsection:

> If one hears [such mistakes] from many people of faith,
> What need is there for the burning expressions of opponents?[41]

The *Gateway*'s third chapter is about public debate, but here the point is that the opponents of Buddhism don't even need to show up if foolish Buddhists themselves make Buddhism appear foolish. Thus a parallel is drawn between the fields of debate and poetry: Both are occasions in which Buddhism and Buddhists are judged for their reasoning, values, and learning. The debate court would, of course, be more familiar to Tibetan Buddhists of Sa-paṇ's time than the "competitive" aspect of poetic composition. Here Sa-paṇ is suggesting, by implication, that poetic expertise helps the scholar impress the same kind of critical audience that attends a debate.

To start, Sa-paṇ gives only two very basic methods for avoiding this kind of shame: Use standard tropes and avoid inappropriate language. As to standard tropes, Sa-paṇ provides the following safe examples:

> Use the example of a lion, etc. for fearlessness; a fox, etc., for cowardice; Manjuśrī, etc., for scholarship; Narāyana, etc., for power; the bull for foolishness; the snake for aggression; the sun for clarity; and, likewise, such things as the lotus for being unstained by error.[42]

Then, with regard to inappropriate language:

> [Words] which are inappropriate for use in the assembly, even if they make fools happy, are expressions that are likely to bring ridicule from the scholars upon [oneself], and do not apply.[43]

Sa-paṇ gives examples from both Sanskrit and Tibetan language:

> If you should ask just how these sounds are unsuitable for use in the assembly: "the body of the excellent one" is, in the Sanskrit language, *varāṅga;* "stand by" is *upasthā,* which means the male and female organs; the word for "excite" is *codana,* which in common usage means to be adulterous; "light movement" is said *haraṇa* in Sanskrit; so, you could enter into a shameful situation.[44]

> In Tibet, occasionally it is possible even to go to ridicule. "Kinds of colors of flowers," "wanting to make distinctions," "incense cup," "smelling the incense," and such expressions—even though they are faultless—since in some circumstances they become words unsuitable for use in the assembly, you should examine the context and apply them appropriately.[45]

Sa-paṇ does not entirely explain the Sanskrit expressions, but he says nothing at all of the Tibetan expressions, whose erotic implications he very likely expects his readers to know. The point is that you need to "examine the context" when you're speaking—namely, the context of the always-judgmental public assembly.

All of this is good advice. Yet if we are to compose poetry that will impress a learned assembly, we need to know more than a few standard tropes and a few words to avoid. This is only a taste, and Sa-paṇ uses it to show the importance of being aware of the assumptions of the poetic assembly. Thus, to end this section, Sa-paṇ states that poets must raise their standard of composition even beyond that of many Buddhist scriptures and treatises, because they must keep in mind the elite poetic sensibilities of the assembly:

> In some treatises of scripture and reasoning the examples are not beautiful, and the sounds, arising in a manner unsuitable for use in the assembly, do indicate the meaning, and are therefore faultless. In poetry, since the main thing is the sound, it must fit [the meaning] without fault in any way.[46]

These are the last words of commentary before Sa-paṇ turns to his treatment of Daṇḍin's *Kāvyādarśa.* They justify the lengthy treatment that follows with the claim that the language of poetic composition "must fit without fault in any way." The scholar who seeks to impress such company must be aware of the complete range of poetic virtues and faults.

Before turning to the next section, however, I would like to dwell just for a moment on Sa-paṇ's interesting distinction between "treatises of scripture and reasoning" on the one hand (where the *meaning* is the thing) and "poetry" on the other (where the *sound* or *wording* is the thing). I want to draw attention to two points. First, this may seem a rather different position than the one that I claimed (in chapter 4) Sa-paṇ was advocating as to the importance of "well-known" terminology in the Buddhist scriptures. Sa-paṇ was careful to point out that there is "no fault" when the scriptures use obscure terminology, and I suggested that the potential "fault" against which Sa-paṇ was defending the scriptures was a poetic fault. Here, however, Sa-paṇ is saying that the goal of the scriptures is different from that of poetry, and the two are not subject to the same criteria of propriety. How can we reconcile these two interpretations? I think the point is simply that Sa-paṇ recognizes that not all Buddhist texts are poetry, but some can be. It is important both for Tibetan Buddhists to be able to *compose* elegant poetry according to the criteria of the poetic specialists, and to be able to distinguish between aspects of the dharma that are appropriate for an elite poetic audience and aspects that are not. Perhaps not all of the dharma is appropriate for a poetic audience, but much is and can be, and a deep knowledge of poetic composition can only enrich one's ability to promote the teachings among the most refined company. Again, the defining character of a scholar is the ability to know the appropriate act for the appropriate context.

Second, I wish to underline an apparent difference between how Sa-paṇ characterizes the relation between the literary (*kāvya*) and the Buddhist scriptures and reasoning (*śāstra* and *vitarka, lung* and *rigs*) and the equivalent distinction in traditional Sanskrit literary theory. As Sheldon Pollock writes, citing Bhoja's *Śṛṅgāraprakāśa:*

> Bhoja, for example, invokes this older conception when he says, "People traditionally define (āmananti) literature (kāvyam) as the 'unity' (sāhityam) of word and meaning, cf. 'Word and meaning unified (sahitau) constitute poetry' [Bhāmaha]".[47]

This is the norm Sa-paṇ evokes when he says that "In poetry, since the main thing is the sound (or wording, *sgra*), it must fit [the meaning] without fault in any way." Later in the *Śṛṅgāraprakāśa,* however, Bhoja once again "reproduces a very wide-spread cultural conviction"[48] when he writes:

> A Sanskrit sentence [is itself of three types:] "relating to revelation" (śrauta), "relating to the seers" (ārṣa), "worldly" (laukika). Sanskrit sentences relating to revelation have two subdivisions, mantra and brāhmaṇa. Those relating to the seers are of two types, "memory" (smṛti) and "accounts of the past" (purāṇa). Worldly sentences have two subdivisions, "literature" (kāvya) and "scientific discourse" (śāstra). (ŚP pp. 165–66)

> The essence of transcendent texts is their actual wording . . . the essence of texts relating to the seers is their meaning . . . and the essence of human texts [i.e., literature] is both the wording and the meaning. (ŚP pp. 376–77).[49]

Surely Sa-paṇ was aware of this typology. Yet his presentation subtly alters the categories and blurs the traditional line between "worldly" and religious texts. We should hardly be surprised that Sa-paṇ does not mention texts "relating to revelation" (*śrauta*) in this context—an expression that refers to the "sound" of the Veda. In Sa-paṇ's Buddhist worldview, no significant linguistic category exists whose essence is "their actual wording" alone. He has already argued that even syllables from mantras produce a meaning via the speaker's intention, and that "they will not become a word merely by being an assemblage of letters."[50] More significant is how Sa-paṇ, having thematized *rasas* as inclusive of both worldly (*laukika*) and dharmic modes, here reiterates the point of Bhoja's statement that what is important "for seers" (in this case, for Buddhist scripture and reasoning) is "the meaning"—but without suggesting that this characteristic prevents its potential, partial inclusion within the category of *kāvya.* Once again, *kāvya* is not necessarily "worldly." Space is left for Buddhist use of poetics.

Introducing Poetics to Tibetans

I have mentioned that an immense portion of Sa-paṇ's opening chapter, "Entry into Composition," is simply translation—or, more accurately, paraphrase—of a large number of verses from Daṇḍin's *Kāvyādarśa,* with very few original comments and interpolations.[51] Since this is largely the case, a close study of this section—unless it is a careful study of Sa-paṇ's translation itself—will amount more to a study of Daṇḍin than Sa-paṇ, a piecemeal study at that, since Sa-paṇ's translation is only partial. Although I have provided some of my thoughts on the translation elsewhere, I do not have any general comments on Sa-paṇ's version of Daṇḍin's words that speak significantly to the issues of this book. What is relevant, however, is the question of just *why Sa-paṇ included so much of the* Kāvyādarśa *in the* Gateway.

To begin, we should note that Sa-paṇ begins this section like other sections with a basic "entry" into the topic (subsection 3), but that the gateway soon opens up to allow a casual stroll through some of the topic's interior rooms (subsection 4). As no previous discussions of the *Gateway* seem to have noted, Sa-paṇ's translation of *Kāvyādarśa* I (subsection 3) is entirely different in selection and ordering from his translation of *Kāvyādarśa* II (subsection 4).[52] The verses from *Kāvyādarśa* I seem to follow smoothly from the previous discussions, and Sa-paṇ's autocommentary sticks relatively close to his verses. But the verses from *Kāvyādarśa* II are translated in Daṇḍin's order, almost exclusively in the autocommentary with no intervening root text verses. The result is that the discussion of poetics is dramatically different in the root text and the autocommentary. If all we had was the root text, we would probably assume that Sa-paṇ was only interested in introducing a few basic terms from the *Kāvyādarśa,* most from its first chapter. With the autocommentary, however, the *Gateway* provides a full translation of the *Kāvyādarśa*'s treatment of each of the main poetic ornaments from its second chapter.

To make this clearer, I summarize the difference graphically below. Using numbers to represent the verses (and the letters a through d to represent quarter-verses where necessary) from *Kāvyādarśa* I and "*" to represent each passage that Sa-paṇ writes which does *not* directly reflect a passage from the *Kāvyādarśa,* we can represent subsection 3 (GL 405.2–410.15) as follows. I place in bold every verse number that is represented in Sa-paṇ's root text, leaving his autocommentary in ordinary type:

> {**11.a–b,** *, *, *, **11.c–d,** 12, **10,** *, *, *, *, **20, 21, 22, 40,** 41, **42,** *, **55, 68, 69, 93,** 98, 100, **101, 102**}

Using the same form with verse numbers referring to *Kāvyādarśa* II, subsection 4 (GL 410.15–427.16) looks as follows:

> {**8,** 9, 10, 11, 12, 13, **14,** *, 15, 16, 17, 18, 19, 20, 21, 22, 23, 24, 25, 26, 27, 28, 29, 30, 31, 32, 33, 34, 35, 36, 37, 38, 39, 40, 41, 42, *, 43, 44, 45, 46, 47, 48, 49, 50, 51, 52, 55, 56, **57, 58, 59, 60, 61, 62, 63, 64, 65,** *, **66,** 67, 68, 69, 70, 71, 72, 73, 74, 75, 76, 77, 78, 79, 80, 81, 82, 83, 84, 85, 86, 87, 88, 89, 90, 91, 92, 93, 94, 95, 96, 97, 98, 99, 100, 101, 102, 103, 104, 107, 108, 109, 110, 111, 112, 113, 114, 115, 117, 118, 119, 120, 121, 123, 125, 126, 127, 129, 131, 132, 133, 134, *, 135, 136, 137, 138, 139, 140, 141, 142, 143, 144, 145, 146, 147, 148, 149, 150, 151, 152, 153, 154, 157, 158, 161, 162, 163, 164, 159, 160, 165, 166, 167, 168, 169, *, 172, 173, 175, 176, 177, 178, 179, 180, 181, 182, 183, 184, 185, 186, 187, 188, 189, 190, 191, 192, 193, 194, 195, 196, 197, 198, 199, 200, *, *, *, *}

The differences are clear. Subsection 4 sticks extremely close to the order of the *Kāvyādarśa,* whereas subsection 3 selectively picks and chooses, even jumping around in Daṇḍin's order at the beginning. Aside from one long section in the middle,[53] subsection 4 has only three of Daṇḍin's verses represented in the root text—this as opposed to thirteen in subsection 3, which is obviously also much shorter.

We can see the relationship between the root text and the commentary in subsection 4 more clearly by examining what happens after Sa-paṇ introduces Daṇḍin's explanation of "analogies" (*upamā*) in II.14. This is one of the rare bold numbers in the above representation of section 4, so it means that Sa-paṇ includes this verse in his root text:

> Analysis of analogies like that (*de lta'i dpe*)
> Previous scholars have explained in this way.[54]

After this brief introduction, Sa-paṇ provides a verse of his own invention (also in the root text) that lists a number of these analogies:

> Quality (*dharma*), object (*vastu*), reversal (*viparyāsa*),
> Mutuality analogies (*anyonya*) and definite analogies (*niyama*),
> Indefinite (*aniyama*) and combination analogies (*samuccaya*)—
> Analogies such as these are adduced and explained.[55]

This sets up the discussion to follow, in which Sa-paṇ summarizes examples of each of these *upamās* from *Kāvyādarśa* II.15–21. Up to this point, he is sticking to his root text, and simply using Daṇḍin as a source for his commentary. But then he continues on. Daṇḍin gives dozens of types of analogies, and Sa-paṇ includes them all, extending all the way up to verse II.56 (but skipping II.53–54). Of course, Sa-paṇ is free to comment as he pleases, but was all of this implicit in his "analogies such as these are adduced and explained"?

The commentary takes off again, even more dramatically, after his verse summarizing II.66:

> The kind of analogy that is inexplicit
> Itself, is accepted as *rūpaka*.[56]

After these two lines, Sa-paṇ first summarizes Daṇḍin's verses on *rūpaka* all the way up to II.97, and then writes:

> These are only the initial [forms of *upamā* and *rūpaka*]. You should consider for yourself at length, and understand, As the *Ornament* says:
>
> > Since there is no limit to conceptions,
> > *Rūpaka*-s and analogies are
> > Only explained in part. The scholars
> > [Must] judge whatever others are said.[57]

This passage sums up what has come before, and allows the possibility that Sa-paṇ might be moving on to another topic. If he had, then the commentary would be an extensive treatment of the root verse, but still within its purview. Instead, he continues to follow Daṇḍin, but this time in a new direction, since Daṇḍin moves from *rūpaka* to *dīpaka, akṣepa, arthāntara-nyāsa, śleṣa,* and more. After paraphrasing nearly two hundred verses from Daṇḍin's second chapter, Sa-paṇ finally moves on, but not without suggesting that he has only scratched the surface:

> Although poetry such as this is extremely prized in India, since it has not had an influence on the methods of Tibetan poetry, I break off this discussion here and cut it short.[58]

What, then, is Sa-paṇ's intention here? He has, of course, only scratched the surface of Indian literary theory, as he says. But he has expanded so far beyond the frame of his root text that he is no longer merely providing a "gateway." It is possible to think, therefore, that Sa-paṇ intended all along to use the root text only as a frame in which to place his treatment of Daṇḍin. Does the closing passage above suggest that he may have considered translating *all* of Daṇḍin here? Why would he have felt this necessary as part of an introductory text? The following passages should give us a clue. They are only a selection of the numerous points where Sa-paṇ cuts his discussion short and turns to another topic:

> If you desire to understand this, you should look in the *Poetic Floral Bouquet* (*sdeb sbyor me tog gi chun po*) which I have composed.[59]
>
> If [you] desire to know [about this] at length, [you] should refer to the *Gateway to the Dharma* (*chos la 'jug pa'i sgo*) written by the great-souled Sönam Tsemo (Bsod-nams rtse-mo), in which definitions of master and disciple, methods of explaining and listening to the dharma, and incantations that destroy the demonic hordes, etc. are well addressed.[60]
>
> Since one cannot understand the meaning when it is explained with a summary, you should look in the other grammatical treatise that I have written and the [*Sword*] *Doorway into Language* (*smra sgo* [*mtshon cha*] of Smṛtijñānakīrti), etc.[61]
>
> Such linguistic explanations are limitless, and though quite proper for scholars, they are difficult for fools to understand. So I won't write about it at length here. If you want to look into this a bit, you should look at commentaries on the sūtras and tantras.[62]
>
> A good knowledge of synonyms such as [those in] the *Amarakośa* and the *Viśvaprakāśa*, etc. settles doubts about all word meanings. Some of this can be known as I have explained it in [my] *Word Treasury* (*tshig gi gter*).[63]

We must remember that in the *Gateway* Sa-paṇ is not only analyzing and presenting scholarly methodology, he is exemplifying it as well. Part of that good scholarly practice would appear to be that a scholar should not beg off his treatment of a worthy topic without sending the reader somewhere else for further study. This is what makes the *Gateway* such an excellent "gateway" into all of the methods of learning Sa-paṇ promotes. He provides a tour around the great entrance hall of scholarship, showing for each topic the doorway into deeper understanding. But for Tibetans of Sa-paṇ's time, there was nowhere to turn for a deeper knowledge of poetics. Sa-paṇ thus had to provide extensive detail himself, and regretted having to stop.[64]

Conclusion: Who Benefits from Aesthetic Cultivation?

Matthew Kapstein has argued convincingly that the Indian literary sensibility is a kind of linguistic "hyperrefinement" built upon the "refinement" that is Sanskrit language (*saṃskṛta*), and that Buddhists accepted this general Indian "assumption of a fundamental relationship between education emphasizing the refinement of language and the formation of the morally refined individual." Citing a passage well loved by Buddhists, Kapstein quotes Daṇḍin's ninth verse as saying that "the 'brilliantly varied pathways of speech,' were intended for the formation of cultivated persons."[65] This is a most appropriate frame in which to place Sa-paṇ's analyses of poetics, and much else that appears in the *Gateway* as well. In particular, Sa-paṇ's analysis of the *rasas* displays a subtle perception that combines literary with moral refinement. Also, this notion provides another explanation for Sa-paṇ's extensive treatment of poetics in a work with merely introductory passages on most other topics. For Tibetans, the argument still needs to be made *that literary knowledge is a hyperrefinement.* A few examples of similes and metaphors would hardly suffice to indicate the expressive power of the Indian literary world. It would certainly fail to indicate that such speech exemplifies the highest level of refinement, the kind of speech one would expect from an omniscient bodhisattva, a protector of the dharma. Yet when Sa-paṇ fills the *Gateway* with the *Kāvyādarśa*'s amazing variety of figures, the fact of literary refinement becomes easily grasped. It floods the reader with subtlety, power, and depth, and therein exemplifies precisely the refinement of taste that Sa-paṇ hoped Tibetans would adopt.

At the same time, if my reading is correct, then Sa-paṇ has presented Sanskrit poetics (*alaṅkāraśāstra*) to Tibetans in a mode that is not only different from all previous Sanskrit literary theories, but one that interestingly parallels the well-known Tibetan union of the political with the religious. As discussed in the first chapter, Sa-paṇ and his nephew Pakpa were instrumental not only in establishing the ideal of scholarship under the "five sciences" and the development of *kāvya* as the height of scholarly expertise, but also in establishing the broad pattern of rule that combined the political and the religious across a unified Tibet.[66] If, therefore, as Pollock writes, the literary in premodern South Asia must be understood as a central aspect of "the game of elite cultural politics,"[67] it stands to reason that Sa-paṇ (both a religious and a political leader) should be at pains to include the religious mode of composition within the literary. Sa-paṇ has not Buddhicized *all* of *kāvya,* but he has blurred the line between religious and secular literature—which may mean that he is importing the methods of *kāvya* into politico-religious structures. The Tibetan merging of the religious and the political—at Sakya, then across a united Tibet under Mongol patronage, and eventually under Dalai Lamas—perhaps required a poetics that encompassed religious literature together with *kāvya,* for the "politics" of *kāvya* to be of use. It seems likely that the well-known elite literary conventions under discussion ("well known" according to the logic of chapter 4) provide another arena of scholarly expertise that is envisioned on a translocal *political* playing field, wherein the dharma is understood to be in perpetual contest with other faiths, overseen by the great leaders of the day. One is tempted to draw a connection between the ideal of scholarship suggested here in the *Gateway* and the tremendous success "on the ground" that Sa-paṇ and his nephews would enjoy some thirty-five years later in winning the Mongol rulers over to Buddhism and to patronage of the Sakyapa establishment.[68]

7
CONCLUSION
Thoughts on a Future Comparative Intellectual History

> From this perspective the popular anthropological image of discrete cultures—each of which is stably fixed as a mosaic stone in a disconnected dot-pattern of humanity—becomes gross misrepresentation. For example, Kannada literary culture, which I study as a paradigmatic instance, shows itself to be no "thing" but rather a series of processes comprising individuation from proto-Dravidian up to the fifth or sixth century, Sanskritization through the thirteenth, de-Sanskritization for some centuries thereafter, Anglicization, Europeanization, globalization in swift succession thereafter, with supplementary and typically highly self-conscious sub-processes (textualization competing with orality, the "popular" with the court, Jaina with Brahmanical with Śaiva and Vīraśaiva with, latterly, socialist, Dalit, feminist), each of which is fed by a cultural current whose source is always elsewhere and ultimately nowhere.
>
> —Pollock, "Literary History . . ."

> To understand a sentence means to understand a language. To understand a language means to be master of a technique.
>
> —Wittgenstein, *Philosophical Investigations*

We have surveyed the main issues of the first two chapters of the *Gateway*, revealing with each treatment a new aspect of the scholar's identity and a new reason that the dharma in Tibet needs linguistic and philosophical masters like the great Sakya Paṇḍita. As much as this appears, and is, self-aggrandizing, it is also a sincere attempt to inspire the teachers and students who will encounter this teaching to emulate this master, for their own sake and for the sake of protecting the Buddhist teachings:

(III 76) I, the Śākya bhikṣu Kun-dga'-rgyal-mtshan-dpal-bzang-po who have great reverence toward the Doctrine here at the termination of the Doctrine and who wish to defend and uphold the Doctrine, have composed this for the benefit of the Doctrine.

(III 77) Nowadays this doctrine of the Śākya Lion diminishes day by day, like a pond whose tributary streams have dried up. Those who have bright minds [and] who desire liberation must exert themselves for an excellent understanding of this procedure.[1]

Sa-paṇ's picture of himself as the ideal, "hyperrefined" scholar is intended not to intimidate, but to inspire faith and confidence in the reader. Even though his scholarly achievements are masterful, perhaps even perfect, he does not set himself beyond the reach of the aspiring student. The only reason he says others are incapable of achieving great knowledge are that they are not willing to exert themselves. The great rhetorical success of the *Gateway,* then, is that it combines self-aggrandizing rhetoric with a complete, systematic, program of study. It simultaneously argues for the necessity of an elite community of noble, expert scholars, and systematically inventories those scholars' behaviors and abilities. This precise enumeration of skills, readable by a beginner, combined with "suggested readings" to allow readers to expand their knowledge, intimates that the path to comprehensive mastery is available to students at any level. The lion's roar that comes from mastering the five sciences—the confidence that one feels upon having memorized and understood a treatise that covers all issues in a given field, multiplied by the number of fields there are—is available, through study, to the diligent and intelligent student. As I suggested in chapter 1, this belief that practical methods of study can lead one to perfect and complete knowledge—as evidenced by the great accomplishments of a historical individual—may be a general characteristic of scholastic traditions, a fundamental assumption underlying the "completeness and compactness" that, as José Cabezón has pointed out, scholastics ascribe to the tradition itself.

Thus we find Sa-paṇ believing that the difficulties facing the doctrine can best be compensated by the elite scholar's comprehensive knowledge, and his participation in a community of like experts. The ideal scholar is not merely a composer or an exegete; he understands textual conventions from both sides. He is not educated in only one of the dharma vehicles; his complete mastery of all of the dharma's modes allows him to interpret each technical term within its proper context, and to separate doctrines that have become intermingled. He understands terminology as it applies in various fields of knowledge, such as hermeneutic terms that appear in grammatical analysis and vice versa. His complete knowledge means that he is aware of the language use of all relevant communities—whether this means that he is able to teach to the needs of his students, or that he is aware of terms that are "well known in treatises" (or in special kinds of treatises) but not "well known in the world." In fact, with his broad knowledge of all of the sciences, he is able to recognize and analyze any strange and obscure terminology that he encounters. His total mastery means that he is able to keep a treatise and a teaching in its proper order, synopsizing it clearly while treating all of its parts with balance and fairness. And, he is able to prevent a false teaching from gaining ground.

It may be thought that my focus on the first two chapters of the *Gateway*, rather than the third, on debate, has caused me to overestimate Sa-paṇ's belief in scholarship as complete mastery of a perfect doctrine.[2] As Georges Dreyfus has argued, debate is an inherently deconstructive process. There is no telling ahead of time what position will prevail, and the result depends almost entirely on the respective abilities of the debaters in competition. Experts in debate are those who are able to undermine *any* argument, and thus training in debate consists in training oneself to recognize the instability of doctrine—a profoundly Buddhist ability.[3] I find Dreyfus's argument convincing, and I have no doubt that Tibetan debaters have enjoyed the unpredictability of debate since well before Sa-paṇ's time. But this is not the view of debate that Sa-paṇ presents in the *Gateway*. Although Sa-paṇ recognizes that debates among students must take place for the sake of sharpening the mind and clarifying views, for him master scholars should only debate to defend the view that they believe is correct:

> [Great masters] such as Dharmakīrti when debating with the non-Buddhist sectarians used to debate adhering to the philosophical tenets of the Buddhists and [with the opponent maintaining the tenets of a teacher] such as Kaṇāda. But for someone who has no capability of maintaining a doctrine to extract any sort of definition or fragment of texts and to say "Set forth a formal argument!" is the debate by which a childish person tests his knowledge. It is not the debate of scholars who adhere to tenets. Such [elementary debate] is explained as being debate that is proper to the occasion for explicating [texts], but it is not suitable as debate that is proper to the occasion of debating, for [by it one] cannot accept or reject tenets.[4]

As Dreyfus describes them, all of the great debates of the monastic colleges in Tibet are of a form that Sa-paṇ would consider mere classroom exercises, if not simply "childish." The third chapter of the *Gateway* addresses itself to the grown-up version alone. This is one of the reasons that, as Dreyfus has told me, in his view Sa-paṇ's descriptions of debate in the *Gateway* have had "no effect at all" on the actual practice of debate in Tibet.[5] Of course, there are no Tibetan *tīrthikas* with whom to debate. I would imagine that if a scholar from afar showed up at a Geluk monastery today to debate the existence of God, there would be a rather powerful incentive for the monks to revert to Sa-paṇ's approach, and to defend their own Buddhist doctrine—provisional as it may be—against the outside threat. Like his discussion of poetics, wherein the scholar must keep to proper form and express himself eloquently, lest the dharma be degraded before a literary public, Sa-paṇ's discussion of debate envisions a larger world stage, wherein Buddhist views are in contest with those of outsiders, and scholars are the defenders of the true doctrine. Sa-paṇ believed in the real value of doctrines, and he believed in real threats to those doctrines (conventionally real, but no less recognizable for that).

The *Gateway* gives ample evidence that Sa-paṇ was deeply interested in Tibet's place in the world. Sa-paṇ's unique intellectual vision takes into account the distinctive needs of the Tibetan dharma: its history as a recipient of the doctrine from India via translators who worked in accord with well-established royal proclamations; its distinctive language, with a grammar that only partially mapped the inflectional possibilities of Sanskrit; and its distinctive environment and social context, lacking knowledge of Indian traditions, legends, flora and fauna. As Sheldon Pollock has argued, the "social aesthetic" of Sanskrit poetry—the details of the social world in which the characters operated—was too obvious to Sanskrit literary theorists to allow it to become an "object of consciousness":

> The poetry is about the people and their world, and is intelligible only through that world. Yet it is a world occluded to theory because it is too far inside consciousness to be rendered an object of consciousness. In a word, literary suggestion is social, and sequesters the social from critical inspection.[6]

Sa-paṇ had the good fortune of having been born in a time, like ours, when theorization and change are born of the interaction of cultures.[7] Buddhist Sanskrit literature could be reexamined, through the lens of poetics as well as through the combined linguistic and epistemological sciences, by a scholar who was close enough to have first-hand knowledge of the tradition from his *paṇḍitas,* but not too close to be able to see and describe what in their methods and practices was new, vibrant, and useful for Tibetans.

Thus, when Sa-paṇ wrote of the dangers to the dharma in an age of decay, it was more than a rhetorical flourish. He understood that any doctrine that resulted from the localized context of an enlightened being's exercise of *skill in means* must rely upon the persistence of an interpretive community, or lose its connection to the original speaker's intention in that context. This is how skill in means leads to a conservative belief in the authority conferred by tradition and fame. There may be no perfect dharma in this world, but the best teachings are those that are known to have come via a well-preserved, well-authenticated lineage, and the best teachers are those who are well trusted to have mastered such well-known knowledge. This is the principle that motivated the Tibetan translators of the second diffusion of Buddhism to face the dangers of travel to India in search of authentic teachings (for a Sanskrit original was sure evidence of an authentic pedigree). Sa-paṇ did not travel to India, but he was able to study with Indian *paṇḍitas,* and through this study he came to accept the view that linguistic study was a powerful method to transform Tibetan scholars into a community able to maintain the true doctrine, and to prevent the proliferation of false "fabricated" doctrines.

This is why, as we have seen in many instances in the *Gateway*, Sa-paṇ conflates or homologizes the needs of the *saṅgha* with the abilities of the scholar of language. Sa-paṇ writes how letters combine into words, words into phrases, phrases into statements, and statements into the dharma. In each case, these combinations are the result of a speaker's intention—specifically, the Buddha's intention, which it is the scholar's role to decipher. The concept of "term generalities" connects Buddhist linguistic theory with the need for the scholarly practice of interpretation: words are as malleable as mental events, and so the scholarly community is necessary to maintain reliable paths between words and their meanings. Sa-paṇ uses Buddhist hermeneutic categories as the organizing principles of his discussions of linguistic subjects: these are not separate topics, but rather two theoretical approaches to the very same practice, the interpretation of the dharma. Figurative language, therefore, is as necessary to understand as is the "special intention" of the Buddha, and if you are ignorant of one you are likely to misconstrue the subtleties of the other. Buddhist scripture, too, is brought together on the same playing field with *kāvya.* Terms must be "well known" in Buddhist language just as they are in public poetry. The poetic concepts of the *rasas* can be used to distinguish Buddhist from non-Buddhist "heroes" as well as to illuminate the distinctive, "unfabricated" character of Buddhist religious literature—a quality that matches the pure, unfabricated truth of the dharma itself.

Sa-paṇ's vision of hyperrefined Buddhist linguist/philosopher/poets, noblemen bound to each other in defense of the dharma, was born of the royal family at Sakya, and perhaps appealed to the imperial aspirations of several Mongol rulers. I have mentioned the massive power and influence that the Sakyapa would earn as a result of their connection with the Mongols. Still, while the nobility of the king's court is unquestioned when one holds the throne, as when Sa-paṇ taught his own treatises at Sakya, there are disadvantages when other, greater powers are in the field. It is certain that Sa-paṇ's scholarly reputation contributed to his having been summoned to negotiate the treaty under which Tibet would submit to Mongol rule, and we know that he quite reasonably dragged his feet between when he received the summons in 1244 and he finally arrived in Liang-chou to negotiate with Ködän in 1247.[8] Apart from this story of Sa-paṇ's long, delaying procession east, giving teachings at every stop along the way, Sa-paṇ leaves no evidence of having regretted his political position, and there is no reason to think that he did, in fact regret it. But if we assume that he would rather not have had to go to Liang-chou, then we see a negative side to literary learning appear even in the story of the greatest icon of Tibetan literary scholarship. Unlike most other traditions, the Geluk monasteries near Lhasa never taught their monks how to write—on the argument that if they did not know how to write, they could never be drafted into government service. Elite literary skills were a requisite of governmental service under the Dalai Lamas and their regents. And, although the current Dalai Lama likes to say that he is, at heart, "just a simple Tibetan monk," in fact his training and position have meant that that path was never open to him. The same was true of Sa-paṇ, and of Sa-paṇ's nephew Pakpa, who would spend thirty-nine years administering Tibet from afar under Qubilai.[9]

The relationship between religious scholarship, literary skill, and royalty here in evidence makes Sa-paṇ's *Gateway* a potentially fruitful topic of cultural studies more generally. In conclusion, therefore, I would like to suggest that the most appropriate avenues for future research on this topic should locate Sa-paṇ more precisely in his own intellectual context, and then work to bring his views into dialogue with other religious views of scholarship. First, of course, more research needs to be done in locating the Indian and Tibetan sources of the various skills Sa-paṇ presents in the *Gateway*.[10] More importantly, though, is the question of whether Sa-paṇ's comprehensive vision resonates across other Indian and Tibetan topics. I hope that future discussions of Buddhist theories of meaning, especially those under the rubric of a "causal theory of meaning" will consider the nature of causation involved in a text's being perfected as a result of an "oath of composition" and a "verse of reverence." Sa-paṇ's theory of meaning, like Dharmakīrti's, is causal but not physical or natural. I am particularly interested in the degree to which Sa-paṇ's assumptions about the educated community as serving not just an example, but an epistemological foundation, might play out in Indian and other Buddhist philosophical contexts.[11] Indeed, the very question of whether there is some "Buddhist" justification for, or method of, interpretation, or translation, or scholarly training, strikes to the center of our concern.

As long as we keep the specificity of Sa-paṇ's intellectual context in mind, though, we can also begin to examine resonances between his views and those of scholars in other religious and historical contexts. Are there any conclusions we can already draw from Sa-paṇ's arguments that might teach us something about religion and scholarship more widely construed? For Sa-paṇ, the pursuit of scholarly excellence, even perfection, is a religious ideal: It makes one a protector of the true teachings, and it moves one toward achieving the intellectual completeness of a Buddha's omniscience. In this case, at least, scholarship is motivated by the desire for intellectual perfection, a religious goal that itself comes from the desire to correct for sacred scripture's being out of its original context: In a new location, a new time, a new language. This paradigm, then, gives us a set of questions we can use to inquire into the motives in the formation of other intellectual communities. Other religious traditions have dealt with similar issues, Medieval Christian scholastic communities being in many ways the most similar and therefore perhaps the most obvious comparative possibility.[12] But it may prove useful as well to move beyond the scholastics. Nineteenth-century critical Biblical scholarship erupted around the notion that the true intentions of the Christian scriptures had been lost in time and translation. The very notion of a "classical" liberal education can be seen as an attempt to recover an idealized state of learning from a distant and foreign civilization and make it "ours." How many intellectual communities across history are the result of a desire to preserve an original, "authentic" interpretation of texts as they move across cultures and across time? How difficult is it to see the religious yearning in the desire to transcend time with the intellect and recover the completeness, finality, and perfection of a text's original, or best, revelation? Might "Paṇḍitization" then be usefully added to the catalogue of translocal historical forces such as are listed in Pollock's epigraph to this chapter?

These questions suggest possible general avenues of comparative research, but before we can justifiably move to such a broad view, comparisons with Sa-paṇ ought to arise out of studies of individuals, specifically those most evidently similar to Sa-paṇ in their religious and intellectual interests. Most likely productive will be comparisons with either the great "well-known" scholastics, as Henderson has suggested,[13] or the "great translators" (*lo tsā ba chen po*) of other times and places. Among Buddhists, Sa-paṇ has a number of intellectual partners across history who struggled with parallel difficulties as the dharma was brought from one culture to another. As Sa-paṇ knew well, the translations themselves often effected major changes not only in the target culture, but in the dharma as well. It is certain that Buddhist intellectual history will come into clearer focus when we have a better sense of the beliefs and practices of the major players across the varied landscape of Buddhist translation projects.

A rather different kind of comparison would seek out Sa-paṇ's compatriots among Biblical translators in Europe. It is quite possible that serious comparison in this arena will be undermined by the extreme variance of intellectual contexts involved, but it should not be assumed hopeless before it is tried. Scholars across cultures have recognizably similar norms and practices, and their methods should serve religious needs in similar ways. As an example of a possible direction such inquiry might take, I will only mention, in conclusion, the figure of Launcelot Andrewes, don of the "great translators" of the King James Bible.[14] Andrewes was the scholar's scholar, closely allied to the royal court, a popular preacher with a very subtle literary sensibility—all qualities that made him one of the leaders of the King James translation. Perhaps most enticing for comparison with the issues of this book, though, is that Andrewes blamed the "newness" of the teachings of Puritan preachers for "God's wrath" in the form of the plague. As Adam Nicolson writes in his contemporary account (he begins quoting Andrewes):

> The people of England now "think it a goodly matter to be *wittie,* and to find out things our selves to *make to our selves,* to be Authors, and inventors of somewhat, that so we may seem to be as wise as God, if not wiser." What could be more wicked than the idea of being an Author? Let alone *wittie?* Newness was the sin and novelty was damnable. "That Sinn may cease, we must be out of love with our own inventions and not goe awhoring after them . . . otherwise, his anger will not be turned away, but his hand stretched out still."

The argument of Nicolson's book is that the magic of the King James Version is the tension—or, perhaps, the balance—between the translators' love of literary flower and their scholarly, and politically conservative, abhorrence of the "new." As Nicolson writes, this conservatism was an essential characteristic of the translation that was to be made "with the learned authority of Oxford and Cambridge (which, at least in their upper echelons, were profoundly conservative institutions, both of which had sent to the king long and high-flown refutations of every point in the Puritans' Millenary Petition)."[15]

Is there evidence here of a transcultural nexus of religious conservatism, scholarly and literary expertise, and royal patronage of translation? Is it outlandish to predict that we might find not only rhetorical, but also doctrinal resonances between the Oxford refutations of the Millenary Petition and Sa-paṇ's refutations of the "new Chinese" Drigung doctrine of "single intention"? Perhaps Bishop Richard Bancroft's royally sanctioned letter of instruction to the translators could fruitfully be compared with the decrees of the *Two-Volume Lexicon* and other similar pronouncements. We might well find it a commonality across traditions that elite communities attempt to assert their hegemony of interpretation. Should we be surprised if they find similar intellectual methods at their disposal? How many religious intellectual communities are in the business of establishing, as precisely as possible, what is acceptable for a person to say in what situation—for as many situations as possible? Only future research will show.

Appendix A
Outline

The Gateway to Learning: Introduction, Chapter 1, and Chapter 2 (GL 369–2459)

Sa-paṇ's *Gateway* contains no outline (*sa bcad*), nor does the text itself provide much guidance to the reader in the form of internal divisions and subdivisions. Where divisions are signaled, as where chapter 2 uses a verse from the *Vyākhyāyukti* as a kind of rough outline of the middle of the chapter, Sa-paṇ does not follow his own outline very closely, especially in the autocommentary. Of the five categories enumerated in the *Vyākhyāyukti* verse, one is treated not at all in Chapter 2, one at some length, one at great length (including what I am calling 2.3–2.9), and two very briefly. Thus if we use only Sa-paṇ's internal divisions we find some areas of the text very well outlined and other diverse areas simply spiraling in their own directions. A similar problem exists in the available commentaries, which tend either to leave the many twists and turns of Sa-paṇ's analysis uncharted, or follow them in such detail that the outline itself becomes a work needing careful analysis. For instance, Ngag dbang chos grags's commentary does an admirable job of organizing the topics in the *Gateway*, but its outline, as a result, occupies some 197 lines on 10 pages.[1] I have chosen, therefore, to put together a brief outline that fits the possibly idiosyncratic needs of readers of this book—so that readers can easily locate topics and passages mentioned herein. What follows is not intended as a comprehensive organizing scheme, but as a rough map, designed to facilitate the reader's understanding of this variegated and complex text, and to show the contexts in which the sections and subsections I have emphasized appear in the book.

I have supplied a translation of chapter 1 up to, but not including, the sections I call "1.3.4: Selected Topics from *Kāvyādarśa* I" and "1.3.5: Comprehensive Summary of *Kāvyādarśa* II.8–200." As the titles suggest, these sections consist in Sa-paṇ's paraphrase of verses from the Sanskrit literary theoretical work the *Kāvyādarśa* by Daṇḍin, with only a very few original comments and interpolations by Sa-paṇ himself. Since Daṇḍin's work is already available in English translation directly from the Sanskrit, my English translation of Sa-paṇ's Tibetan translation from the Sanskrit would be of interest primarily for the issues related to translation itself (some of which I mention in chapter 6 above). While such details are interesting in themselves, to make them (and the Sanskrit literary theory in which they are embedded) comprehensible to nonspecialist readers would have required an undue expansion of the work.

Appendix B
The Gateway to Learning

Translation of
Introduction and Chapter 1 (GL 369–405)

Introduction

In Sanskrit, *Vidagdhāvatāradvāra;*[1] in Tibetan, *Mkhas pa 'jug pa'i sgo.*

I prostrate with reverence before the guru and Mañjuśrī:

True meanings, classifications, confidence, and undefiled language;[2]
For one's own sake and that of others: realization, abandonment, and Buddhahood[3]**—**
[With these qualities] they declare the Buddha's dharma with a lion's roar;
I bow down at their feet, the guru and Mañjunātha.

Suppose someone should ask, what is the point of this verse of reverence at the beginning of the treatise? Well, the guru together with Mañjughoṣa is the essence of all the Buddhas of the three times.[4] So if you say even a part of his[5] qualities, the final result will be Buddhahood, and the temporary result will be the pacification of obstacles. The initial statement is said with this in mind.

This partial [listing] of qualities begins the treatise with [the guru's] own attainment of confidence in the four specific knowledges, and [his use] for others [of] the four fearlessnesses to roar like a lion in the midst of the assembly.

These [qualities] are, furthermore, the four specific knowledges—meanings, classifications, confidence, and definitive wording—by means of which [the guru] has attained mastery over everything that can be known; and, both for his own (*rang*) sake and the sake of others,[6] the four fearlessnesses—realization, abandonment, [teaching] the path to Buddhahood, and teaching its obstacles—which [he] has achieved by being invincible to others [such as] the *tīrthikas* together with [their] gods (*lha dang bcas pa'i mu stegs*). Through this method, in composing texts himself, explaining them to others, and clarifying wrong views, he fears nothing; and since this is the complete basis for the perfection of the lion's roar, [I] explained this at the beginning.

Some people, in [the fields of] grammar (*śabda*), and nominal inflection (*vibhakti*), verbal formation (*dhātu*[*-siddhi*]) and inflective impetus (*kāraka-pada*), comparison (*upamā*) and verbal ornamentation (*śabdālaṅkāra*), divisions and summaries, reckoning and ascertainment, and structure, are predominantly perplexed; seeing [this, I've written] this [treatise].

Some here in the snowy mountain ranges [of Tibet] who claim to be learned are not well trained in the analysis of sound itself, in providing the grammatical affixes for nominal inflection of a formed word, in providing the grammatical affixes for inflections (*ti ngan ta*) in verbal formation, in applying the four, six, etc. *kārakas,* in distinguishing such things as the object (*dngos, vastu*) and the reversal (*bzlog pa, viparyāsa*) in an analogy, in the nature of verbal ornamentation, in distinguishing among such things as expressions of substance and quality, in the different methods for divisions and headings, in how to summarize based on the general and subheadings in a summary, in deciding among opposing [positions] in reckoning and ascertainment (*grangs nges pa*), in eliminating wrong views, in how to get a definitive ascertainment by way of the purpose, and in joining the order of words and meanings in a structure that is pleasant to say and easy to understand, and so [they] are, for the most part, mistaken. This *Gateway to Learning* is related for their benefit.

If one should ask, who is teaching?

By having heard, seen, and grown accustomed to many [teachings]
And being able to give close instructions [upon them],
The glorious Kun-dga'
Rgyal-mtshan [371] is explaining something here;
Scholars, make yourselves happy: Listen up!

[As for the many teachings mentioned:][7]

Grammar treatises: Kalāpa and Candrapa[8], and so on;
Logic treatises: *Pramāṇasamuccaya* [of Dignāga] and the Seven Treatises [of Dharmakīrti],[9] and so on;
Poetry treatises: *Jātaka*[*-mālā* of Āryaśūra], the three great [poets] and the three small [works of Kālidāsa],[10] and so on;
Metrics treatises: The *Candoratnākara* [of Ratnākaraśānti] and the great work on metrics, and so on;
Alaṅkāra (poetics) treatises: the [*Kāvyādarśa* of] Daṇḍin and the *Sarasvatīkaṇṭhābharaṇa* [by Bhoja], and so on;
Lexicographic treatises: *Amarakośa* and *Viśvaprakāśa,* and so on;

Drama treatises: *Nāgānandanāṭaka* [of Harṣadeva], and the *Rūpamañjarī*,[11] and so on;

Medical treatises: *Aṣṭāṅga[hṛdaya]*, *Ayurveda*, and so on;

The Science of Crafts: The Iconography of the Divine Form, the Analysis of Earth, Water, and such;

Astronomical/calendrical calculations of external [causes], and internal [causes] such as the winds, including the *Kālacakra* of both Buddhists and non-Buddhists, and the treatise written by Śrīdhara;[12]

Among the Inner Sciences (i.e., dharma): The Three Baskets, i.e. Sutra, Vinaya, and Abhidharma, and the Four Tantra [classes], i.e. *kriyā*, *cārya*, *yoga*, and *anuttarayoga*

—[All of these teachings], together with most of their universally known *vṛtti* commentaries and *ṭīkā* commentaries, and so on, I have seen, heard, and grown accustomed to. So, since this exposition the *Gateway to Learning* is not a fabrication or based on ignorance, people with a clear mind [372] should abandon attachments and aversions, should bring about mental bliss and listen—this is the meaning [of the verse].

Who is a scholar? If he sees, just as it is, everything that can be known, he is accepted as a scholar. Also, someone who is knowledgeable in a specific field is a scholar in that.

If someone should ask, who gets called "scholar"?—He is someone who knows without error everything that can be known. Alternatively, for someone who knows teachings in some specific field, in that and that alone he gets the name (*ming*) "scholar."

The fields of study for that scholar are the five sciences:

The fields of grammar, reasoning,
Medicine, the inner, and the outer are called "the sciences."

Grammar is [the science of] language (*śabdavidyā*); reasoning is [the science of] logic (*hetuvidyā*); the outer science is crafts (*śilpakarmasthānavidyā*); the inner science is the transmitted [Buddha]dharma (*lung gi chos*—i.e., *adhyātmavidyā*); and medicine is the science of remedies (*cikitsāvidyā*)—[so are the sciences] explained.

Furthermore, as the *Mahāyānasūtrālaṅkāra* says:

Without becoming a scholar in the five sciences
Not even the supreme sage can become omniscient.

For the sake of refuting and supporting others,
And for the sake of knowing everything himself,
He makes an effort in these [five sciences].[13]

Other explanations which are given elsewhere
Should be known to have been condensed within these.

What are called in the sutras the "eighteen realms of knowledge" should be known to be condensed in these five.

There are three chapters here in the *Gateway to Learning:* Entry into Composition, Exposition, and Debate.

Chapter 1: Entry into Composition

1.1: Opening Statements

1.1.1: The Verse of Reverence

So, with the intent to explain the entry into composition first, we explain the verse of reverence (*mchod brjod*) at the start of a treatise:

> **An excellent author of a treatise [373] should give a verse of reverence to the teacher [i.e., the Buddha]. In order that the teachings may flourish, pure words are here seen to be proper and good.**

Verses of reverence have three [aspects]: the purpose, the summary, and the meaning of the words. There are two kinds of purpose: that which arises in the composer's own continuum, and that which is realized in the continua of others—[including both the people] who have explained and [those who have] listened to [the treatise]. The meaning in summary form is to whom, by whom, and in what manner the praise is offered, and so on. As for the meaning of the words: Once [the composer] has examined the statement meaning (*ngag don*) in the manner of a lion's glance, [he can then proceed to] explain the subject matter (*gzhung don*) with the gait of a tortoise.[14] Each subject matter must be understood at length in the context of its own composition and exposition.

Suppose someone should ask, is it certain that verses of reverence are of only one kind?

> **[Verses] whose nature are reverence, praise, homage, auspicious wish, etc. are commensurate (*mi 'gal*), because they all teach only the greatness of the teacher [i.e., the Buddha].**

Verses of reverence include verses that end with [an expression] of reverence, and likewise those ending with praise, going for refuge, or auspicious wish. As for the first, the *Madhyantavibhāgabhāṣya* [of Vasubandhu] says:

> Having honored the noble composer of this treatise, born of the nature of the well-gone one, and the ones who expounded [it] to myself and others, I will make an effort to analyze the meanings.[15]

Likewise praise, going for refuge, and auspicious wishes should be understood. Although these are different words, their meanings are commensurate (*mi 'gal*), because they are alike in stating the virtues of the Buddha or the favored deity. [374]

1.1.2: The Oath of Composition

As for the oath of composition and so forth, suppose someone should think that if you are going to give an exposition, it is unnecessary [to say what you are going to say again anyway], and if you are not going to give an exposition, [a promise to do so] is meaningless:

> **Oaths, exhortations, and so forth**
> **Indicate one's enthusiasm (*spro ba*) to give the exposition.**
> **Since it will bring about the achievement of supreme realization,**
> **There is no inconsistency (*'gal ba med*) in the promise.**

The oath of composition is threefold: The meaning in its intent, the meaning in summary form, and the meaning of the words.

First, the promise "[I] will give an explanation," indicates one's enthusiasm to give an exposition on this subject matter, and the cause of [that] enthusiasm is that one is starting in on a good topic. For instance, a king promises to give away the throne, or to turn the wheel of the dharma, but even though he does engage in lesser activities, such as playing dice and checkers, he does not promise to do so in the middle of the assembly. Additionally, because of the promise one is recognized by others as himself a scholar in that topic. If he is not a scholar how can he make the promise in the middle of the assembly? Furthermore, the oath will be the cause of achieving the [goal]. For, as it is said, "Noblemen will give up their life, but not their promise."

Likewise, exhortatory expressions such as "Come here to listen to the supreme dharma," or "Make yourself happy: Listen up!" and so on should be understood like that.

The meaning in summary form is threefold: Object, agent, and action. [For the first,] "What is being explained?" The treatise. [Second,] "By whom?"

By the composer. [Third,] "How is it being explained?" The statement meaning is summarized and taught in an expanded, middle-length, or concise version of the expression "It is being explained like this"[16] as is appropriate to the occasion. The word meaning [375] should be understood according to its subject matter.

1.1.3: The Expression of Humility

Now, if one should ask, what is the expression of humility (*kheng bskyung ba bshad pa*) [that appears] in some treatises?

> **Even though I may not have the ability, in accord with my effort**
> **I yet begin the treatise—such expressions exist,**
> **With respect to treatise and author,**
> **In order to demonstrate the nobility (*dam pa*) of both.**

"By nature I am of weak intellect, and by the condition that I have studied little, I may not be capable of composition. Nevertheless, I should make an effort for the sake of myself, those like me, and those inferior to me." This statement indicates [first] the nobility of the treatise. The examination comes when someone thinks, "Even if [the author] is not [fully] capable, if an effort like this is made, there [must be] a great prospect here. For instance, it's like the merchant who goes to get a jewel from [across] the ocean."

Also, the author is himself recognized to be a noble (*dam pa*) person. If one examines the humility like this, in which even such as a scholar of words and meanings (*tshig don*) [says] "I don't know," there is the [inevitable] recognition that the composer is a noble person.

Here too the summary and word meanings should be explained however it is appropriate.

1.1.4: The Outline

Now, if someone should ask, what is the purpose of placing an outline (*rnam par gzhag pa*) of the body [of the treatise] at the beginning:

> **For ease of explanation (*bshad sla ba*) and ease of comprehension (*gzung bde*), and also the elimination of disputes about the treatise, some scholars summarize the body of the treatise and place an outline at the beginning.**

There are three benefits to placing an outline of the body [of the treatise] at the beginning: ease of exposition by the expositor; ease of comprehension by the listener; and generation of certainty about the treatise.

First, [376] knowing the outline of the body [of the treatise] has three benefits [for the expositor]: it acquaints him with what will be said, keeps the order undisturbed, and by indicating the order brings about the meaning with ease.

Second, easy comprehension by the listener has three benefits: when hearing, easily becoming acquainted with what will be said; when contemplating, ease of comprehension without disturbing the order; and when meditating, due to the practice being in summary form, the quick arising of meditative wisdom.

Third, generating certainty about the treatise is where, since the body and limbs are connected, the conviction arises that "This treatise is perfect," because it is free from the faults of being disordered, broken, or unnecessarily long.

The meaning in summary form and the meaning of the words of these [outlines] should be explained [each] just as they are understood in their specific section of the treatise.

1.1.5: The Statement of Purpose

If one should ask, what is the purpose of placing a statement of purpose and relations at the beginning of the treatise?

> **In order to indicate the nobility of the treatise,**
> **The teacher [i.e., the Buddha] indicates the purpose in the beginning.**
> **If one with supreme knowledge is seen [doing] this,**
> **Why not begin [one's own] analysis as well?**

The up-front placement of the statement of purpose and relations is threefold: The purpose, the summary, and the meaning of the words. First, as the purpose is explained in the *Vyākhyāyukti:*

> Since, having heard the great significance of the sutra,
> Listening and accepting it, and so forth,
> That listener becomes faithful,
> The purpose should be stated up-front.

Here the purpose is, some say, to generate a beautiful text; some want to refute a wrong understanding of [some] meaning. It may be that these are not inappropriate as temporary goals. But the [final] purpose is the creation of an initial beginning (*'jug pa*).

The summarized [377] meaning is fourfold: The intended meaning (*brjod bya,* lit. "what is to be said"), the purpose, the ultimate purpose (lit. "the purpose of the purpose"), and the relations. With respect to these, there are three [topics] that should be understood at length as I have explained them elsewhere: Refuting an opposing tradition, presenting one's own position, and eliminating objections to it.[17]

1.2: The Linguistic Causes of Composition

1.2.1: Assembling Letters, Words, and Phrases

Having thus explained opening statements, if [now we] explain the composition of the body of the treatise, there are three causes (*rgyu*) of expression: assemblages of letters, words (*ming*), and phrases (*tshig*). First:

> **Without [themselves] indicating any speech intention,**
> **What will [nonetheless] be the basis for all expression (*brjod*),**
> **Are called "letters."**

"Letter" is defined as "the appearance of a term generality that does not indicate a meaning." Furthermore,

> **Vowels and consonants**[18]

are what have the nature of "a"-li and "ka"-li, [respectively].

Suppose [the following objection is raised]: [There is a problem] when [letters are defined] like this. When definitively stated, the letters, "a" and "ka" and so on are said to be [equivalent to] Mañjuśrī and Brahmā, and so forth, [in tantric symbolism]. And in Tibet as well, it is seen that individual letters can be words, so this [definition] is uncertain.

[Response: In fact] there is no mistake. Comprehension comes as a result of case endings or a speech intention (*brjod 'dod*), but no comprehension comes from the individual letters taken separately (*yi ge ldog pa*). For, [such an argument] would issue in an extreme consequence.

> **Their divisions and summary are not explained here.**

As for the divisions and summary of these letters, since I am not writing about them here out of fear of going on too long, they should be understood from such [texts as the] *Entry into Language* (*Smra sgo*).[19]

> **Having the nature of an assemblage of letters**
> **That indicates the substance of a meaning**
> **Is a word (*ming*).**

"Word" (*ming*) is defined as "the appearance of a term generality that indicates the substance of a meaning." That is, what arises out of a group of letters like "pillar" or "pot" and so on. [But] if it does not indicate the substance of a meaning with either case endings or a speech intention, [378] it will not become a word merely by being an assemblage of letters. For if even an assemblage of letters that doesn't indicate a meaning is [included, there is the fault again of an] extreme consequence [in the definition of] a word.

When specifications (*khyad par dag*) of these[20]
Are indicated, they are called "phrases" (*tshig*).

"Phrase" (*tshig*) is defined as "the appearance of a term generality that specifically indicates a meaning." [These are] assemblages of words, such as "tall pillar" and "good pot." If it does not specifically indicate a meaning, it will not become a phrase merely by being an assemblage of words. For if even a single word or an assemblage of words that do not specifically indicate [a meaning] are [included, there is the fault again of an] extreme consequence in [the definition of] a phrase.

What, by joining these [phrases] together
Clearly indicates a speech intention, is a statement (*ngag*).

When these are joined together, the understanding [that arises] in the intended combination of meanings is a statement.

By combining these, such things as a section (*rab byed*) and
Everything else up to a portion of the dharma is obtained.

By combining statements, [if] one indicates one's intended meaning from a particular perspective, it is a specialized thesis (*prakaraṇa*); indicating a few aspects, [it becomes] a chapter (*le'u*); giving it a full reckoning, it is a treatment (*brjod byed*); then a complete dissertation; or a compendium of stages—such linguistic formations are achieved, all the way up to a verbal portion of the dharma.

1.2.2: Proper Linguistic Application

1.2.2.1: Specific Problems in Word-Meaning Relations

How the old [linguistic inventors] (*rgan po*) of these words and phrases
Initially applied [them] is [called] "sign";
What is later analyzed [in them] is [called] "term."

Joining words and phrases with things, the linguistic inventors made [such] associations by force of mere speech intention (*brjod 'dod*)—such are [called] "signs." Later, secondary analysis of these is [called] "term."

> **The first of these is an autonomous expression (*'dod rgyal sgra*);**
> **Based on that, later on, [what is made to]**
> **Signify another meaning is a supervenient expression (*rjes sgrub sgra*).**

The first, where [379] whatever is suitable [is used] as an independent sign without looking to the reason, is an autonomous expression—such as "wood" or "ox." [The second type of expression] is a subsequent expression (*rjes 'jug sgra*), [which is] made based upon that [autonomous expression] for reasons such as similarity, association, and so on—as where [the meaning of] steadfastness[21] is superimposed on [the word] "wood," or stupidity on "ox."[22]

> **The Grammarians (*brda sprod byed pa*) [hold that new] autonomous expressions for which no strong established reason appertains are not applicable in these latter days (*slan chad*). For even if the sign refers to a meaning, [it may be] unintelligible.**

If scholars of grammar see that if they do not use a new sign, the meaning will not be established, there is no contradiction in using a new [sign]. Nevertheless, they do not apply a new sign for [some] small purpose, because of it being the cause of incomprehension, misconception, and doubt. For instance, the signs [invented by] doctors and magicians.[23]

> **As for differences among signs: What to some**
> **Is well known, to others is not well known**
> **[And] thus not understood. What in some [texts]**
> **Is well known is clearly well known.**

Some signs, while well known in scripture, are not well known in reasoning; and some are well known in reasoning but not well known in scripture. And even though the three baskets of the sutras and the four tantras are not mutually well known, each in the other, there is no fault, since to be well known somewhere is to be well known.

> **A fully enlightened Buddha in front of his disciples**
> **[Says things] that do not exist in mundane scriptures.**
> **Such signs are beyond the ken (*spyod yul min*) of ordinary people.**
> **Omniscient thought is incomprehensible.**

Expressions in the sutras and tantras such as "father and mother should be killed," "where the ocean changes," and "*kotakṣa*" are signs made up by the Buddha. [380] Even though some people appear to understand a trifling explanation [of these], [such expressions] do not have a definitive explanation (*nges pa*) from only one side. Consequently, those who look [only] from their own perspective have a hard time trying to explain them.

> **Even where they are not well known in other, previous [treatises],**
> **Signs that the scholars [can] understand**
> **Are supervenient (*rjes sgrub nyid*),**
> **Because they [can] see [their] reasons.**

Even where the sign is not elsewhere well known, some expressions, if they are analyzed, are accepted because they are supervenient [expressions] and figures of speech (*mtshungs*). The scholars are not at fault.

> **Similarity and opposition**
> **Are the two kinds of supervenient [expression].**

A supervenient expression of similarity is like saying "conch" for a white dog; a supervenient expression of opposition is saying what is dissimilar, such as "conch" for a black dog.

> **Being mutually related, and so forth—**
> **Once some reason like this is seen, they [i.e., the supervenient expressions, are understood].**

[Supervenient expressions made for the reason of] being mutually related are: Naming the cause after the result, as in [calling a] water spring "leg sickness"[24]; naming the result after the cause, as in "known thing" (*shes pa*) or "object possessor" (*yul can*);[25] naming the whole for the part, such as "sound of a drum" or "sprout of a seed";[26] naming the part for the whole, such as calling one side of a stretch of cloth that has been burnt a "burnt stretch of cloth" or, when seeing one side of a house, [saying we are] seeing the house. [Supervenient expressions] made by reason of similarity are, for instance, the medicine [called] "crows leg"[27] or calling a stupid person an "ox." [Supervenient expressions made by reason of] a reversal of similarity are, for instance, calling a stupid person "pleasing to the gods," and the reversal of a relation [gives us something] like "auspicious" for Tuesday,[28] or "good" for the *viṣṭi-kāraṇa*[29]—[381] all these ways of giving names should be understood after a thorough investigation.

Furthermore, contradiction between direct application (*'jug*) and
well-known use (*grags pa*),
Not being in contradiction, and being in contradiction with one
and not the other—
[Such are the] four kinds of linguistic application (*'jug tshul*)
Well known (*grags pa*) to the grammarians.

Having no contradiction between well-known use (*grags pa*) and direct application (*'jug pa*) is, for instance, calling a lotus that was born from a lake "lake born." Having a contradiction between direct application and well-known use is, for instance, using the expression "lake born" for [a lotus] that is not a lotus born in a lake. Direct application but not well-known use is like saying ["lake born"] of such things as lake-born plants and water animals that, though born in a lake, are not well-known as "lake born." Having neither well known use nor direct application is like saying ["lake born"] of rocks and wood on dry land.

Preceded by an earlier application,
[A usage that,] without giving any reason,
Gets its impetus from a mere speech intention
Is accepted as established in the reverse.

Relying upon a direct expression that precedes it, a later application in contradiction with both convention and ordinary usage—such as using the word "conch" for a black dog or "good" for something bad—looks only to speech intention. But if a reason is explained, expressions that generate misdirection are called "secondary expressions that establish a reversal."

Joy, great suffering, and amazement,
Cymbals too—sounds in accord with such things
That are said to closely adduce [their objects]
Are called imitating expressions (or, onomatopoeia: *rjes su byed*
***pa'i sgra*).**

Joy is indicated with "*ha ha*," etc.; great suffering with "*khi hud*," etc.; amazement with "*ah la la*," etc.; and cymbals with "*khral khrol*" and "*dar dir*," etc.[30] [Such] sounds, which are manifestly in accord with their objects, are [382] well known to the grammarians as "imitating expressions."

Visual forms, sounds, smells, tastes, tactile sensations, and
Thoughts (*sems las byung ba*) of several different kinds

That cannot be ascertained in only one way—
Indicating such are indefinite expressions.

For visual forms, "*'od lhag lhag po*"; for sounds, "*cal cal*"; for smells "*chil chil*"; for tastes, "*myog myog*"; for tactile sensations, "*'byor 'byor po*"; for thoughts, "*sems sems po*"—when made in the mind, the several things made that cannot be ascertained in only one way are [expressed by] what are called "indefinite expressions."

Statements (*ngag*) that use [words] like this, for the most part,
If they closely indicate [their objects], use repetitive sounds.

In the application of phrases like this, for the most part repeated sounds are used, such as "*lhag lhag,*" "*khral khrol,*" "*sems sems,*" and so forth.

1.2.2.2: General Problems in Signification

Whatever expressions set forth a meaning,
All are included (*'dus*) in two types: classification (*rigs*) or naming (*ming*).

As Dignāga says, "Every meaningful expression (*don brjod pa'i sgra*) is [either] a classificatory expression or a naming expression." If you should ask, what are these expressions like?

What has the opposite of that which it is not
Is equal to a generality in all aspects.
Through mutual acceptance and rejection [of qualities], similarity is achieved.
What has indicated that [achieved similarity] is a classificatory expression.

Having gained a definition that excludes what is non-tree and non-ox, and so forth by excluding [what does not have] branches and a hump, and so forth, things are defined as similar. By force of an erroneous mental construction, these [similar things] are grasped as (in) one generality "tree" or "ox." And then, [383] by conceiving as one (*gcig tu zhen pa*) the particular (*rang mtshan*) and the generality (*spyi mtshan*), one begins accepting and rejecting trees and oxen—this is classificatory expression.

Having focused upon the object (*don*), the thing is to be defined (*mtshon bya, lakṣya*);
Its defining property (*don ldog*) is the definition.

Having focused upon the definition of [qualities] such as branch and hump, the designation of a sign is a classificatory expression. It itself is the thing to be defined. For instance, the tree and the ox, and so on.

> **Whether or not there is a reason, it is acceptable.**
> **A reverse reason is also okay (*bla*).**
> **When no reason for the definition is seen,**
> **All designations are naming expressions (*ming gi sgra*).**

[Names] given autonomously without looking to any defining characteristic such as Devadatta or Puja, and so on; or with a real reason, such as Siddhartha or Manibhadra (*nor bzang*); or with a reverse reason, such as Fire born (*me skye*) and Dog born (*khyi skye*), etc.—giving names to people and animals, etc., whatever one desires to designate with a speech intention, there is no fault: it is a naming expression.

> **In the ultimate nothing is negated or asserted;**
> **The specific (*rang*) and the general (*spyi*) both belong to convention.**

Since the ultimate is devoid of elaboration (*spros pa*), conventional [mental] objects such as existents and nonexistents, negations and assertions, do not exist, since objects of knowledge do not exist. Among knowable things of the conventional world are both [kinds of] meanings, [both] particulars and generalities.

Particulars are not objects of language and conceptual construction; objects of language and conceptual construction are generalities.

> **The grasping of a particular is a [mere] appearance;**
> **The grasping of a generality is the elimination of other (*gzhan sel, anyāpoha*). [384]**

Whereas the particular itself is the object of an appearance, it is not the object of linguistic and conceptual construction (*sgra rtog*). Consequently, it is not directly signified in language. [Conversely, whatever] is an object of linguistic and conceptual construction is a generality. Moreover, when they are being explained the generality and the particular are kept separate, but when they are conventionally made they are mistaken as one, and applied through generating a reversal—as it has been explained in the *Treasury of Reasoning.*[31]

> **Elimination of the other includes both negation and assertion;**
> **Assertions include [both] "exits" and "is";**
> **Negations include "does not exist" and the negation "is not."**

Among assertions, there are two kinds: saying such things as "it is a pot" and "there is a pot," which are, respectively, methods of asserting [something] being of a particular nature, and of asserting the existence of some other nature. [Among negations, expressions] such as "there is no pot," which is a simple negation that is not associated with an assertion, are called "nonimplicative negation" (*med dgag, prasajyapratiṣedha*). Negations such as "this region has no pots" and "uncontaminated wisdom," which are associated with assertions,[32] are called "implicative negation" (*ma yin dgag, paryudāsa*). If this [implicative negation] is made with the assertion foremost, then it even gets named an assertion. If the negation is made foremost, it may be named a negation. Negating one particular nature is an assertion of one [other as well]. In the linguistic treatises, the verbal application of nonimplicative negation and implicative negation is made easy to understand by giving examples of expressions such as lowly (*dman pa*), feeble (*zhan pa*), despondent (*zhum pa*), and so forth. So for fear of going on too long, I will not write about it here. Moreover, the methods of negating and asserting meanings should be understood from [my] *Treasury of Reasoning.*

Sometimes [what appear to be] casting aside (*'gog*) are [in fact] assertions;
Some assertions contain expressions of negation.
Some, while they start off as if expressing a meaning
Are in essence probable conditions. [385]

"Why isn't it true?"; "Why is this not known?"; "How is there no benefit from seeing a Buddha?"—such expressions negate a thing's nonexistence and so suggest (*'phen*) its existence. While in part negating a meaning, they are associated with a positive statement.

As for the reverse of the former: "For example, why is it there?"; "Why is this known?"; "What benefit is there to having eyes that have never seen the Buddha?"—such verbal assertions suggest a negation. So, by the strength of the particle (or affix, *'phrad, pratyaya*) that expresses either a reason (*'thad pa*) or a question such as "Why" and "How" and so on, an expression of an existent suggests a nonexistent. [And] an expression of a nonexistent suggests an existent.

Some expressions start off as if [asserting] a meaning, as in "Where there is wisdom there are no mental afflictions," and so on. The application of expressions such as these must be understood according to the strength of the words and the context (*don gyi skabs*).

When explaining such phrases:

In the formation of nominals there is "*supanta*";[33]
It has twenty-four kinds.

While this method of establishing sounds according to "*supanta*" may be very important in Sanskrit, since it is not important in Tibetan language, I will keep it short (*re zhig bzhag go*). If we explain how to apply in sounds just the small bit of [the Sanskrit] cases that are called for here in Tibet:

> **Nature (*ngo bo*), object, agent, purpose,**
> **Source, relation, location, and vocative.**
> **By dividing [these each] into single, dual, and plural,**
> **There are twenty-four categories of case endings.**

The endings to a word such as "tree," and so on are: First, nature; second, object; third, agent; fourth, purpose; fifth, source; sixth, relation; seventh, location; and eighth, vocative. If we display them in full: "Tree" [386] understood merely as what has branches and leaves is a nature inflection (*tshig, pada*). As in looking at or cutting down that tree, the expression "with respect to a tree" associates [the tree] with an action. Thus, the second is an action [-related, or object] inflection. As in "with a tree, the house was built," the third is the agent. "Water is poured for the tree"—so the fourth is the purpose inflection. "Fruit comes from the tree"—such is the fifth, the source. As in "Branch of a tree" the sixth is a relation inflection. As in "A bird's nest is located in the tree," the seventh is a location inflection. As in "O tree!," the eighth is a vocative inflection. These [each] also have for one, singular inflections, for two, dual inflections, and for many, plural inflections, which makes three eights, [or] twenty-four. For instance, separately applying expressions such as "tree," "two trees," and "many trees" [to each case], this will be understood.

Moreover, if it is asked, how do linguists (*sgra pa dag*) explain the methods of [applying] inflectional endings (*rnam par dbye ba, vibhakti*)?

> **"To words with particular vowel endings**
> **The three genders are separately assigned;**
> **Thus are applied the different inflectional endings**
> **And a single meaning is correctly established."**
>
> **Following [in line with the rules of] Sanskrit,**
> **Grammarians say this of [their] language.**

Sounds (*sgra nams*) that end in the long and short [vowels] *a, i, u,* and so forth are separately assigned [one of] the three genders: masculine, feminine, and neuter. For instance, [to words such as] "tree" (*vṛkṣa*) and so on are assigned the masculine gender; to "wisdom" (*prajñā*) and so on, the feminine gender; [and] to "merit" (*puṇyam*) and so on, the neuter gender. Once the application of the inflectional endings to these [words] is complete, even a single case ending, due to the particulars of [its] expression, [387] brings about many ways of being expressed. [To understand] this is a necessity in Sanskrit language (*sgra*); but since this is not necessary for Tibetan language, it is not explained here.

If it should be asked, what will happen if you make an explanation in Tibet that is like the tradition of Sanskrit word formation (*sgra sgrub*)?

> **Here [in Tibet, word formations] cannot be made and are unnecessary.**
> **In grammatical case endings we have no station.**
> **Since the [various] uses are different as well,**
> **We will keep the proliferation of these meanings short.**

The grammatical affixes in Sanskrit expressions cannot establish the Tibetan language. Since Tibetan signage (*brda nyid*) comprehends its own conventions, the morphological formations based on Sanskrit's affixes are unnecessary [to explain here]. The fact that the three genders in Sanskrit have different case endings does not begin to get into the specifics of Tibetan gender. And the various morphological constructions (*sgra sbyor*)[34] for Sanskrit words ending in vowels have are inappropriate for combining similar sounds in Tibetan; so I will not lay out here the proliferations of traditional Sanskrit morphological constructions.

Suppose it is asked, if the morphological constructions are not made in this way [i.e., according to Sanskrit rules], how is one to understand the meaning of a Sanskrit expression from a translation into Tibetan?

> **Take this word "citizen" (*grong khyer pa*).**
> **We don't have all of its aspects, [like its] length.**
> **Its gender structure (*rtags*) is also completely different;**
> **Even its more definite qualities (*nges pa dag*) cannot be made.**

This is a Tibetan word, "citizen" (*grong pa'i skye bo*). [So,] certain things definitively known about a word that are associated with its sign—[in what context it is] well known, its length, its verbal force, etc.—do not exist [because the Sanskrit uses a different sign]. Also, the sound of "*pho mo*" and so on are nothing like Sanskrit, so in this the [different signs] are out of wack (*phan tshun 'khrugs pa*, lit. "in mutual contention"). For this reason, the Tibetan linguistic inventors made up no method for forming words with case endings.

> **Now, [in Tibetan], due to the speech intention**
> **And the strength [of some expression], a word of a particular inflectional ending [388]**
> **Becomes [several] expressions with one and the same meaning;**
> **This comes about because of the suffix letters.**

Furthermore, through a person's expressive intention and the meaning's context, and the strength of the inflected word, there comes about in Tibetan language a single meaning in different words, which arises predominantly because of suffix letters. For instance, in the sixth case, even though there is no difference [in the meaning], the [relation to the term "heap"] in the expressions "form heap" (*gzugs kyi phung po*), "heap of feeling" (*tshor ba'i phung po*), and "compositional factor's heap" (*'du byed kyi phung po*) come in different words.

Scholars applying expressions like these
Formerly were concerned only with how well known [the expression] was.

For these expressions in Tibetan, the linguistic inventors had as their main concern how well known [the expressions] were, but [word formation] was not the main concern. Furthermore,

Some, out of fear of bringing about a mistake,
Even when making an effort will change it into something different.

For instance, [the expressions] "in the vow," "in the dharma" and "in form." For fear of mistaking them with the seventh case, some, in order to make the expressions easier to say, where needing to say "Dharma [means] the path to be known" or "For what reason is there a vow," [make] the translation "vow" or "dharma" [in the nominative]. And, for instance, [they] will translate "Water is poured on the tree" for "Water is poured for the sake of the tree"; and "I bow down to the Buddha" for "I bow down for the sake of the Buddha"; and "Making auspicious wishes to the king" for "Making auspicious wishes for the sake of the king." And as in, "There being smoke, there is fire here," all reasons (*gtan tshigs, hetu*), while [originally] in the fifth case, are translated "Because of there being smoke," or "Because of performing a function" [which is the fourth case].

Some use the particularities of what is well known [389]
To effect a disconnection with inflectional endings.

For instance, [translating] "you may work or sit" as "you may work, you may sit," or [translating] "the story from Devadatta" as "Devadatta's story," and so on.

Nonetheless, these very ones
Are consistent even though they are constructed differently.
There is no such thing as an essential relation.
Therefore only a speech intention is achieved.

Since there is no substance to the connection between a sound and a meaning, its application (*'jug*) relies on the power of a speech intention. For this reason, no matter how it is applied there is no contradiction. As the [*Pramāṇa*]*vārttika* says:

> Apart from reliance upon the speech intention,
> No language exists anywhere.[35]

> **By force of the speech intention, in the three numbers**
> **And the three genders mix-ups are seen.**
> **The suggestions (*'phen pa*) of these [forms], which are the grammatical affixes for the inflected forms,**
> **Are established either explicitly (*dngos*) or inexplicitly (*mi mngon pa*).**

By force of the speech intention, it is seen that expressions of one, two, and many are confused one with the other. "Sand" and "woman", though singular, are [given] plural expressions. Expressions such as "the six families" and "a string of good houses," though plural, appear as singular inflections. Also, the three affixes for masculine, feminine, and neuter genders are seen to be confused, one with the other. The affixes by which the expression suggests these, such as [the dual marker] "*dag*" and [the plural marker] "*rnams*," and so on, are either explicit or made inexplicit. The affixes for masculine, feminine, and so on as well are either explicit or made inexplicit.

> **As to the sound [which has a particular] length and verbal force, etc.,**
> **Whether or not it gets into the meaning,**
> **They are intended to be understood from context, [390]**
> **Setting aside direct presentation.**

In Tibet, a statement with [a particular] length and verbal force, such as "*ka wa ka wa*," and "*sang sang*," and so on, although there is [something] in the meaning, the linguistic inventors did not set up their characteristics. The purpose is to understand [them] from the context and the meaning.

> **Conjugation of verbal roots is "*tiṅanta*."**
> **These are of three kinds, according to person.**

Tiṅanta refers to the linguistic affixes for formations out of verbal roots (*khams*, *dhātu*). It has three persons: First person [i.e., "third person"] is "Devadatta," and so on; the middle person [i.e., "second person"] is "you" and so on; and the highest (*mchog*) person [i.e., "first person"] is an expression such as "I," etc. These each also have singular, dual, and plural words, which makes them nine [different kinds]. For instance, "Devadatta," "both Devadattas," and "[many] Devadattas"; likewise "you," "both of you," and "you all"; "I," "both of us," and "we." If they are formed according to the different affixes for conjugation in past, future, and present [tense], they become countless.

These are completely necessary for the Sanskrit language, but inflection does not exist in Tibetan language, and moreover, our own linguistic inventors generated understanding through the strength of how well known a word is. Therefore, the expressions for establishing verbal inflection (*kriyā-pada, byed pa'i tshig*) are not explained here. Aside from having correct or incorrect expressions, there is no difference in comprehending the meaning.

> **In short, the noun is formed with case endings,**
> **The verbal formation with verbal inflection (*byed pa'i tshig*).**
> **The indication of what is to be said is called a "statement."**
> **These are the basics of grammar.**

All nouns are established through the case ending affixes [391]. All verbal roots are established through the verbal affixes. The comprehension of an intended meaning is a "statement." For, as the *Amarakośa* says:

> *sup* and *tiṅ* -ending things are statements.

Thus, sound (*sgra*)[36] and verbal root (*khams*) formation are the basics of grammar.

1.3: Poetic Composition

1.3.1: General Considerations

Having understood the application of words thus, in order to begin [the section on] the composition of poetry [I] will explain verbal ornamentation.

> **Upon nature, quality, and action,**
> **The ways of expressing praise and censure of a thing**
> **With denotation and connotation, word and meaning,**
> **Through direct and indirect analogies (*dpe*),**
> **Are superimposed, and verbal ornament**
> **Is applied and developed with the flavor (*rasa, ro*) of the nine emotions (*bhāva, nyams*).**

Nature is simply the expression of the substance of a person, etc. Qualities are handsome body and joyous thoughts, etc. Actions are things to do such as going, coming, and talking.

Suppose one should ask, just what are the ways of expressing such things as the praise and censure of the faults and positive traits associated with the situation of the thing, as well as praise and censure of the thing [itself]? The direct expression of the situation is denotation. Understanding one thing indirectly through the direct expression of another is connotation.

Both word and meaning are understood directly, for example, in the denotative expression "There is no scholar like me anywhere else." Both word and meaning are indirectly understood, for example, in the implicit statement "The ocean and the flower [say] to the swan and the bee: 'You have seen all the directions; is there a greater body of water than me?—is there anything sweeter smelling than a flower?'" By such an expression in speech or in writing, it is indirectly stated: "You people who have traveled in all the directions, have you seen a scholar like me?" [392].

With directly and indirectly [stated] analogies, etc., good language and ornamentation become superimposed [with exaggerated meaning] (*sgro btags*), and in applying the nine emotions (*bhāvas, nyams*) the poetry of Passion (*rol sgegs dang bcas pa'i snyan ngag, śṛṅgāra-kāvya*) is written.

1.3.2: The Poetic Emotions

If it is asked, What are the nine emotions?

> **Passion (*śṛṅgāra, sgeg*), heroism (*vīra, dpa' ba*), repulsiveness**
> **(*bibhatsa, mi sdug pa*),**
> **Comedy (*hāsya, dgod*), violence (*raudra, drag shul*), horror**
> **(*bhayānaka, 'jigs su rung*),**
> **Compassion (*karuṇa, snying rje*), awesomeness (*adbhuta, ngam*),**
> **and tranquility (*śānta, zhi ba*) are the nine.**
> **In the *Amarakośa* ('*chi med mdzod*) it is abridged into eight.**

Their specific definitions and divisions should be explained.

> **Passion is a kind of beauty**
> **In body, speech, appearance, and place, etc.**[37]

Passion, being beautiful, is an appearance that arrests the mind. Suppose we divide it into parts: Inner passion has the distinction of (*khyad par can*) beautifying the demeanor of body and speech. Outer erotic passion arises out of the place, etc. Such things as the village and the park, things like flowers, fruit, water, clouds, mountains, meadows, pleasant plains, birds and animals, wealth such as jewelry, clothes, tooth-paint, and maroon dye, and the summer wind, the sun and moon and lamps, etc., [all] please the body and mind. And, by [bringing about] amazement (*ngo mtshar*) they become examples which show the meaning (*dpe don 'byor*). And words that generate this amazement foster passion.

Heroism is residence in the discipline of fearlessness.
If we divide it: giving (*dāna*) and moral behavior (*śīla*), etc.
Is supreme dharma [heroism];
With regard to enemies in battle,
Being the conqueror, etc.,
Should be known as worldly heroism.

Heroism is a kind of fearlessness. If we further divide that, [393] the one who is able fearlessly to practice giving and moral behavior, etc. [i.e., the *pāramitās*], is the hero of dharma. The world-conquering hero is fearless with respect to enemies in battle, wild beasts and demons, etc.

Repulsiveness is the opposite of beauty.
It is distinguished as an aspect by way of
Such things as body, speech, appearance, and place.

Repulsiveness in body has such descriptions as having the three: a hunch, blindness, and a goiter. Repulsiveness in speech is spitting and stuttering, etc. The various repulsivenesses in appearance are being ugly, dirty, and indistinct, etc. Repulsiveness in place is uneven ground with ditches (*rad rod*), tree stumps, and thorns—words which generate loathing (*yid 'byung*).

Comedy is language that generates laughter.
It excites [laughter] in another [person]
By way of good or bad deeds, together with
Gestures of body, speech, and appearance.

What have the ability to generate laughing, exciting [it] in another [person] by presenting actions and gestures of body and speech—those words that cause laughter are comedy.

Violence is the vicious use of force.
Where the two obscurations together with their latencies
Are conquered through exertion, etc., is dharma [violence];

In suppressing opponents with body, speech, and mind,
The quality of viciousness is worldly violence.

Violence is subduing one's enemies through viciousness. "He pulls out negative afflicted emotions from the root," so to speak, and so forth. (1) Cutting out the roots of such afflicted obscurations and obscurations of wisdom, with their latent tendencies (*vāsanā*), [394] and (2) the Buddha's subduing the Maras, and (3) Vajrapāṇi subduing Rudra, etc., are [all instances of] violence conducive to the dharma. As a way of suppressing one's opponents, to subdue one's enemies with rage, which is a great commotion of body, speech, and mind, is worldly violence.

Horror is a method of making [someone] shrink back.
An unbearable gesture of body and speech,
Such as making a gift, etc., is the dharma [type] which is difficult to practice.
Other than that is the worldly [type].

Horror (*bhayānaka*) is driving away the opponent and making [him or her] frightened. It may be a quality of mind, but is generally best [exemplified] through gestures of body and speech. To relate examples in the six perfections (*pāramitā*): The cutting away of son and daughter by Vessantara; of [his] eye by the king of the Śibis; of [one's] flesh through the power of love (compassion); of [his] head by king Moonlight; and of the upper and lower parts of the body by Suvarṇavarṇa, for example. Likewise for the other perfections, such as moral behavior, etc. For others (ordinary people), [these acts that are] difficult to perform surpass even the imagination. All [these things] that bring about "terror" (*skyi bung*) are dharmic horror.

Other than that is worldly [horror], such as the appearance of demons and ogres, and the terrifying behavior of wild animals, etc., [vertigo in] canyons [and] mountain slopes, and dark forests, oceans, great fires, frightening winds, etc. One fears these things and they work to exemplify the fears. And they also, since they have the nature [of horror], can be used in combination[38] without opposition in this method of poetry (*kāvya*) [395].

Compassion (*rnying rje*) is a mind that generates loving kindness.
By seeing an inferior person, and by hearing of
The wondrous compassionate (*thugs rje*) acts of the bodhisattva
There arises the distinction [between the two kinds of] compassion.

Feeling loving kindness in the heart for one who has fallen into evil, in the three lower existences, lack of refuge, disease, misery, hunger, poverty, being tormented by others, old age, trouble, and death, etc., is the arising of compassion for an inferior person. Having heard of the splendid acts of the bodhisattva, the heart is overwhelmed, one's hair stands up. Tears flow. Being amazed, loving kindness arises; this is the compassion which arises for the superior person.

Awesomeness[39] is the thought of superiority to another.
By the fortune of a worldly person and
The perfected qualities of a scholar
One suppresses the opponent with splendor.

Caste, physical form, power, wealth, sovereignty, etc., are worldly awesomeness. When, by being singly superior to others in intelligence, virtues (*yon tan*), confidence, renunciation, and attainments, etc., one suppresses the opponent with splendor, it is dharmic awesomeness.

Tranquility is the quality of conquering conceit
And seeks the very dispelling of awesomeness.

Tranquility is abandonment of the qualities of pride, haughtiness, and conceit. If we divide it, there is abandonment of worldly pride and dharmic pride; [Each] dispels the mentality of [one of the types of] awesomeness explained above.

As for the ways of using these ornaments in combination:

With the ornament of passion, the ornaments of repulsiveness,
Fierceness and awesomeness do not apply.

The body and possessions being beautiful, passion is poetry which generates gladness in the mind. In addition, [396] in conformity with that, the example and the verbal ornament bring about beauty, bringing about what is appealing to the mind. But repulsiveness does not settle in the mind. And, neither generating fear by way of violence nor being timid at heart toward another because of [his] awesomeness applies with the ornament which sustains beauty.

In the ornament of heroism, avoid the ornaments
Of comedy, compassion, and tranquility.

With heroism, which is a combination of words of courage, the [following] ornaments should not be used: Comedy, which is words that bring about laughter; compassion, which generates loving kindness; and tranquility, by which, being timid, the mind is subdued. For, the mutual opposition (contradiction) would crush the potency of the words. If it does not crush the potency, and if there is no opposition, there is no fault in [their] combined use in accordance with the context.

> **With repulsiveness, the ornaments of passion,**
> **Compassion, and tranquility do not apply.**

Because while repulsiveness is in opposition to beautification, passion is closely related to beautification; and because while compassion is a thought that grasps the other, repulsiveness is a cause of shunning [the other]; and because while tranquility is disciplined and conforms to quietude, repulsiveness conforms to a way of the mind's seeking to avoid something and being caught up in it, there is no [sic.?] mutual opposition.

> **In the ornament of comedy, avoid violence,**
> **Horror, compassion, and tranquility.**

Where comedy is a combination of words which have brought about laughter, violence brings about viciousness. And viciousness is connected with making one cry; it is distinct from comedy. Compassion is also similar to that (i.e., it makes one cry). Tranquility too, is associated with a kind of heavy-heartedness (*yid skyo;* repentance?), and so because of its distinction from comedy it is an opposition and is therefore [397] unsuitable as an ornament.

> **In both violence and horror, avoid,**
> **Similarly, compassion and tranquility.**

Violence and horror, being vicious, are qualities of doing harm to others. Since compassion and tranquility, being tender, benefit [others], they are mutually opposed.

> **In both compassion and tranquility, avoid the six:**
> **Passion, heroism, comedy,**
> **Violence, horror, and awesomeness.**

Since, while compassion and tranquility, being beneficial, are kinds of discipline, passion—quivering and distracting—is a quality of extreme disquiet. And since, on the one hand, compassion and tranquility, with the mind serene, are disciplines, and on the other hand, heroism, comedy, violence, and horror are hindrances to those [disciplines].

If some of them, like heroism and horror, etc., do not oppose the perfections (*pāramitā*) such as giving, etc. in contexts associated with the dharma, then the application in context is explained as was explained in the context of heroism above.

> **In the ornament of awesomeness, completely**
> **Avoid both compassion and tranquility.**

Because, while awesomeness is a kind of pride, compassion and tranquility are kinds of discipline.

> **Compassion, awesomeness, and tranquility can be used (*'jug*)**
> **In the ornament of passion.**

Even though compassion and the others are in some small aspect opposed to the context of magnifying passion, if the force of the speech intention is flawless [398] and brings about the virtues—if it is suitable to the context and is not in opposition with the method of the poetry—there is no flaw.

> **To the ornament of heroism, the ornaments of**
> **Violence, horror, and awesomeness are not opposed.**

Since in the context of magnifying heroism, no aspect of these others is in opposition to it there is no flaw if one knows [how to] combine them in poetry. In some contexts it will even generate good qualities.

> **With repulsiveness there is no opposition to**
> **Violence and horror in some contexts.**

Since amongst repulsiveness and these others as well there is no opposing aspect, if one knows how to combine them in words, there is no opposition.

> **The ornaments of compassion and tranquility can also**
> **Have no opposition in the context of their mutual [appearance].**

Since compassion and tranquility have no mutual opposition, in context [their] ornament also has no mutual opposition. Even if some opposition occurs by reason of the strength of their combination, the ornaments are not mistakenly combined. Examine the context such as this yourself, and you should understand.

> **With the ornament of comedy, the ornaments of passion,**
> **Heroism, repulsiveness, and awesomeness can be combined.**

In the context of conveying the ornament of comedy, the ornaments of passion, heroism, repulsiveness, and awesomeness can be used. Relying upon these, they are words [by which] the poet has the ability to draw out laughter. For example: "When the gods are having a dance, because of the jumping, Shiva's snake stumbles and falls on the ground. At that instant the Garuda enters the dance. The snake, being afraid, and finding no place of refuge, enters the nostril of Gaṇapati (*tshogs bdag*), who is dancing. [399] Gaṇapati is unable to bear him there, and shakes his head. Seeing that, all the gods start to laugh. May such good fortune be yours!" There is a poem with a good story like this at the start of a Mīmāṃsā treatise.

In both aspects of violence and horror,
Heroism, repulsiveness, and awesomeness apply.

In the ornaments which magnify violence and horror, the ornaments of heroism, repulsiveness, and awesomeness do not obstruct [their] application.

In the ornament of awesomeness, passion,
Comedy, violence, and horror are used (*'jug*).[40]

On the occasion of magnifying the ornament of awesomeness, if one understands the use of these qualities such as passion, etc., there is no flaw in their use as a group.

With regard to the three aspects of passion, comedy, and awesomeness:
Physical display of emotion, holding things aloft, and humbling others,
And the various examples, ornaments, and hyperboles,
Are manifested, [making] an entry into attractive verbal ornamentation.

The expression of passion, etc., being deepened, is fit together with [everything] it includes, and with the generation of happiness, the fulfillment of the external ornament, various examples, various verbal ornaments and hyperboles (*sgra btags pa*); being manifest in accordance with the meaning, it is an entry into poetry which has passion.

With regard to the three aspects of heroism, violence, and horror:
Appearing to eat the three realms,
Being naturally terrifying,

[And] having the character of causing goose bumps
Should be fitted together with rough verbal ornaments.

In relation to the three [aspects]—heroism, etc.: One should fit together words which are able to cause great fear and goose bumps, [like descriptions of] being unwavering oneself but causing fear in others; [400] causing internal and external fear through a nature unending in its internal commotion and external appearance of body, speech, weaponry, etc.; and having an appearance of being able to eat the three worlds. Furthermore, such things as furrowed eyebrows are the bodily qualities. Such things as harsh weapons are associated with the body. Such things as the terrifying sound HUM are associated with speech. Such things as tiger skins and snake canopies are associated with costume. Such things as cemeteries, dense thickets, deep ravines and gorges, darkness, and being near wild animals are associated with the place.

Repulsiveness is [of] body, speech, and mind.
It is an appearance associated with faults
Which are [both] spontaneously generated and attached.
It is a way of causing loathing.

Repulsiveness of body is irregularity of color and build. Repulsiveness of speech is coarseness, raving, and sounding forth expressions which should not be let out in public. Repulsiveness of mind is thoughts of harming someone who should be assisted, and thoughts of cheating proper objects of praise. By merely hearing about [such things] the whole world, together with the gods, can have loathing. Furthermore, such things that arise from within [the body, speech, and mind] are spontaneously generated repulsiveness. Such things as bodily stench, smearings of ashes, and torn and tattered clothing are [repulsiveness] which is associated with costume. Such places as are bad, unclean, mucky, uneven, gritty, having burnt tree trunks, [401] hair, bones, stumps, and putrid water are [repulsiveness] associated with the surroundings (*gnas*).

The ornament of comedy is of two kinds:
Naturally arisen, and arisen through attainment.
Mostly, fools have the natural [kind].
Scholars have the attained [kind].

In relation to comedy: Laughter which is drawn out naturally is mostly arisen from the appearance of a shameless fool. Attainment is a kind of study, such as [by a] poetics scholar, drama scholar, or comedy scholar. Furthermore, laughter which arises from body, speech, and mind is internal, while laughter which arises from such things as the setting and the props is external. [You] should know examples of these, such as the *Nāgānandanāṭaka* [of Harṣadeva] (*klu rnams rab tu dga' bar byed pa'i zlos gar*).

> **With regard to compassion and tranquility:**
> **Both are destroyed if they are mixed with verbal ornaments**
> **Such as passion and heroism.**
> **Therefore, abandon fabricated ornamentation!**

Compassion and tranquility are both by nature soothing. Thus, expressions that come from the main ornament with a nature in conformity with that [natural serenity] are able to generate love and discipline (*dul*). Therefore, the most excellent ornament is unfabricated, like what is said by parents to a suffering child. Here, fabricated verbal ornaments should not be mixed in, because if they are mixed in, the spontaneously arisen compassion and discipline become as if fabricated. Examples of compassion should be understood by looking at the *Vessantara Jātaka*, and examples of tranquility [should be understood by looking at] the *Iron House Jātaka* [402]

> **In such things as passion, examples of tranquility should not be used,**
> **Just like in tranquility, such things as passion [should not be used].**
> **In all cases one should recognize for oneself and apply,**
> **In this way, the mutually contradictory examples.**

Just as in tranquility you should not use an example of passion, so with an example of tranquility in passion. And just as in violence you should not use an example of compassion, so with an example of violence in compassion, etc. You should realize [this] with your own mind, and understand it.

1.3.3: Proper and Improper Poetic Language

> **For the most part, analogies**
> **Are applied in conformity with their respective quality (*rang gi chos*).**
> **If the analogy is not in accord with the meaning,**
> **The poetics scholars may ridicule [you].**

Everything, such as analogies and ornaments, [must be] applied in conformity with its respective meaning, because if the analogy is in opposition to the meaning, there might be a situation of mockery from the poetry scholar. For example, the *Sarasvatīkaṇṭhābaraṇa* [of Bhoja] (*dbyangs can gyi mgul rgyan*) explains expressions such as "A mountain ridge with one tree, a thick forest, water falls," as having the fault of expressions such as "On the mountain range, from inside the thick forest, from inside a rock crevice, water falls."[41] If one thinks according to my comprehension:

> Geese (*chu skyar*), cats, and thieves
> By advancing silently and stealthily,
> Attain the object of their highest desire.
> The sage [i.e., the Buddha] always behaves like this.

Furthermore, one must not make any mistake in meaning. If there is [a mistake] in the context of poetry, the non-Buddhists will question [you] and tease, "Does your Buddha act like this?"

In the *Jātakas,* the Bodhisattva was called the King of the Fish [403]. The expression "Don't make the ravens (*khwa*) happy" is not suitably elegant as a verbal ornament of a Bodhisattva. If he says, "May we be saved from this danger of the ravens," it is realized as elegant. Examples such as this are given at length in the *Sarasvatīkaṇṭhābaraṇa,* and out of fear of extending the text, I will not write [more about it]. Having duly realized it yourself, know it.

> **"In the example of fame: Whiteness,**
> **Height, shine, and a banner, etc.**
> **Are applied"—so says the *Sarasvatīkaṇṭhābaraṇa.***

As a pleasant-sounding example which expresses fame, it is said that one should use examples such as a banner on a snow mountain, or some such, white, high up, and shaken by the wind.

> For heroism, such things as the lion and the tiger
> For cowardice, such things as the fox and the hyena
> For scholarship, Mañjuśrī; for power, Nārāyana (*sred med*)
> For foolishness, a bull; for violence, a snake.
> For clarity, the lamp of beings (the sun), etc.
> [Are what] scholars call the "well-developed connection" (*rgyas par sbyar*).

"Use the example of a lion, etc. for fearlessness; a fox, etc., for cowardice; Mañjuśrī, etc., for scholarship; Narāyana, etc., for power; the bull for foolishness; the snake for aggression; the sun for clarity; and, likewise, such things as the lotus for being unstained by error." This is how the poetic treatises explain [it].

> **[Certain] words, expressed in the assembly,**
> **Are words with a lowly purpose in Sanskrit.**
> **The poetry scholar should avoid them.**

In the context of poetry, words which can be used in the assembly are expressions that make scholars happy, [404] and apply. But [words] that are inappropriate for use in the assembly, even if they make fools happy, are sounds that are likely to bring ridicule from the scholars upon [oneself], and do not apply.

> **For example, "the body of the excellent one" (*mchog lus*), "stand by" (*nyer gnas*), "excite" (*bskul*), and "moving lightly" (*yang zhing g.yo*).**

If you should ask just how these sounds are unsuitable for use in the assembly: "the body of the excellent one" is, in the Sanskrit language, *varāṅga*; "stand by" is *upasthā*, which means the male and female organs; the word for "excite" is *codana*, which in common usage means to be adulterous; "light movement" is said *haraṇa* in Sanskrit; so, you could enter into a shameful situation. What is faultless in ordinary usage is counted as a verbal fault in the context of poetry. Thus, since when the Sanskrit terms *nas* and *yabh* are spoken, if they are said [together with] *bhaya*, they mean to act adulterously, if they are well used in the context of the composition, they can be faultless. But if they [are used] wrongly, they can be counted as faulty. Walk flawlessly (that is, carefully so you don't make a mistake) with Sanskrit words like these. In Tibet one goes into fault.

> **If one hears [such mistakes] from many people of faith,**
> **What need is there for the burning expressions of opponents?**

Such was said by one utterly faultless in Sanskrit. In Tibet, occasionally it is possible even to go to ridicule. "Kinds of colors of flowers," "wanting to make distinctions," "incense cup," "smelling the incense," and such expressions—even though they are faultless—since in some circumstances they become words unsuitable for use in the assembly, you should examine the context and apply them appropriately. In some treatises of scripture and reasoning, the examples are not beautiful and the sounds, arising in a manner unsuitable for use in the assembly, do indicate the meaning and are therefore faultless. In poetry, since the main thing is the sound, [405] it must fit without fault in any way.

Notes

Chapter 1. The Lion's Roar in the Assembly

1. Faure (1991).

2. The story as a whole, Lhalungpa (1977), pp. 153–57, is cited by Kapstein (2003), p. 776. The quotation is from pp. 154–55.

3. Chang (2006), pp. 381–82.

4. The term "Neoconservative Movement" is Davidson's (2005), and my discussion of this movement depends greatly upon him, especially pp. 151–54. See below for why this movement poses a challenge to Milarepa's followers. I will elaborate upon "Indianization" below. The term draws upon Kapstein's (2003) discussion of "*Indianité,*" pp. 768–76, and his description of Sa-paṇ's interests as "Indological," p. 776, as well as Ruegg's (1995) distinction between "Indian" and "Indic," pp. 141–43—on which, more below.

5. For discussion of Sa-paṇ as the "model of conceit," see Kapstein (2003), pp. 776–78, and my discussion of "relative omniscience" below.

6. As Kapstein (2000), writes, p. 56: "[T]here can be little doubt that the very great efforts made to establish Buddhism and Buddhist learning in the Tibetan empire do reflect in part the value attributed to them by Tibet's rulers during the eighth and ninth centuries: monastic, clerical Buddhism, with its trained scholars and scribes, its language sciences and methods of translation, its libraries and catalogues, its systematization of reasoning and debate, provided medieval Tibet with an ideal model of organized knowledge." Kapstein also suggests: (1) that the legitimation of laws within a large and diverse empire required moral universals, which of course Buddhism provided as well and (2) that tantric Buddhism supplied the Tibetan kings with a transnational, "cosmopolitan" language of power spanning medieval Asia, pp. 58–59.

7. See Simonsson (1957), Ruegg (1983), and Scherer-Schaub (2002) on the official translation methods established under the old Tibetan empire.

8. Whorf (1956).

9. See Beyer (1992), pp. 36–38.

10. Ruegg (1995), pp. 96–97.

11. Ruegg (1995), p. 143: "typologiquement 'indianisant' (*Indic*) sans être indien (*Indian*) au sens strictement historique."

12. For a correction of the traditional claim as to a "dark age" blackout across Tibet, see Kapstein (2000), pp. 10–17.

13. Kapstein (2003), p. 755.

14. Kapstein (2003), p. 775.

15. Davidson (2005).

16. Davidson (2005), pp. 144–47.

17. Davidson (2005), p. 149.

18. I am not including here Davidson's second form of neoconservatism, which simply disregarded doctrines on the basis of their inappropriateness, as opposed to their inauthenticity.

19. See Rhoton (2002), pp. 166–67, and p. 196, n. 103, for Sa-paṇ on spurious scriptures.

20. Jackson (1987).

21. See appendix A for an explanation of why I do not include these final sections of the first chapter of the *Gateway*.

22. GL 370.7–19: *mkhas par khas 'che ba 'ga' zhig sgra tsam gyi rnam gzhag dang/ming sgrub pa la rnam par dbye ba'i rkyen ster ba dang/khams sgrub pa la ti ngan ta'i rkyen ster ba dang/byed pa'i tshig la bzhi dang drug la sogs pa'i sbyor ba dang/dpe la dngos dang bzlog pa la sogs pa'i khyad par dang/tshig gi rgyan la rang bzhin dang/rdzas dang yon tan brjod pa la sogs pa'i dbye ba dang/dbye ba sgo tha dad pa'i tshul dang/bsdu ba la spyi bye brag gi sgo nas ji ltar sdud pa dang/grangs nges pa la dngos 'gal rnam par gcod pa dang/log rtog bzlog pa dang/dgos pa'i sgo nas ji ltar nges pa dang/go rims la tshig dang don gyi rim pas brjod bde zhing rtogs sla ba'i sbyor ba la gangs can gyi khrod 'di na legs par ma sbyangs pa'i skye bo phal cher 'khrul par mthong nas/de la phan pa'i don du mkhas pa 'jug pa'i sgo 'di bshad do.*

23. Examples abound. See, especially, Sa-paṇ's best-known and longest "polemical" work, *A Clear Differentiation of the Three Codes*, Rhoton (2002).

24. Kapstein (2000), p. 120.

25. Sa-paṇ begins another short work, the *Lung rigs rnam dag dang mthun par 'chad dgos tshul*, in a similar vein: "The Monk who, having abundantly heard the [Buddha's] Collection [of teachings] from the learned, Possesses the intelligence that appropriately discriminates what is to be accepted and rejected, Properly guards his morality, is endowed with the correct view, [And] has the name Kun-dga' (Ananda), speaks these words." Translation by Schoening and Sørensen (1988), p. 43. Their edition, p. 42: *mkhas pa rnams las sde snod mang thos shing/blang dor legs par 'byed pa'i blo gros can/tshul khrims legs srung lta ba dag ba can/kun dga'i ming can dge slong 'di skad smra.*

26. GL 370.20–371.1: *mang du thos shing mthong nas goms pa dang/man ngag dbang gis dpal ldan kun dga' yi/rgyal mtshan 'di na* [371] *'ga' tsam 'chad pa la/mkhas pa rnams kyis dga' ba skyed de nyon.*

27. See appendix B for translation. Sa-paṇ's list of his own accomplishments in learning has been translated and studied by Kapstein (2003), pp. 779–80, and Verhagen (2005), pp. 189–91, both of which contain extensive resources in the notes.

28. Jackson (1987) has made an excellent study of Sa-paṇ's education and accomplishments.

29. Stearns (2001), p. 163: "When he was twenty years old he received the first section of the *Pramāṇaviniścaya* four times and the last section twice, from the spiritual friend Mtshur ston Gzhon nu seng ge at Rkyang thur in upper Nyang, and mastered absolutely the meaning of the words." Cf. Jackson (1987), p. 25.

30. See Tucci (1949), pp. 334–39, for an introductory discussion of Śākyaśrī's life, including a translation of Thropu Lotsāwa's biographical verses of reverence to Śākyaśrī. The occasion for this translation is Tucci's description of a remarkable thanka (no. 9, plates 6 and 7) of Śākyaśrī, representing thirty-one scenes from Śākyaśrī's life that correspond with the first thirty-one verses from Thropu's biography. See Jackson (1990b) for the Tibetan text of Thropu's biography and Bsod nams dpal bzang po's commentary, as well as a brief study of the current state of research on this central figure in Tibetan intellectual history. For this section I have also made extensive use of van der Kuijp (1994), Jackson (1987), and Roerich (1959 and 1976).

31. Van der Kuijp (1994), p. 599, and Stearns (1996), p. 127, both calculate that Śākyaśrī was in Tibet 1204–1214. Counting back the three years spent in Jagaddala would place Śākyaśrī's visit to Magadha in 1200–1201.

32. According to Chak Lotsāwa's biography (Roerich 1959, p. 64), Vikramaśīla was entirely destroyed by the time of the latter's visit in 1235, though the *mahāvihāra* had still stood amid the wreckage when Śākyaśrī was there, some three decades earlier.

33. This quote is from the penultimate verse of the *Gateway* (III 77), trans. D. Jackson (1987), p. 366. His edition, p. 298: *'bab chu zad pa'i rdzing bzhin.*

34. The texts in the Tibetan canons (the *Bstan 'gyur* and *Bka' 'gyur*) written or translated by Śākyaśrī's two disciples Vibhūticandra and Dānaśīla alone count almost up to one hundred. I have not counted them myself: For a listing of Vibhūticandra's work in the Peking *Bstan' gyur*, see Stearns (1996), pp. 159–64; Dutt (1988), p. 379, cites the list of Dānaśīla's texts from Phanindra Nath Bose's *Indian Teachers of Buddhist Universities* (Madras: Theosophical Publishing House, 1923), pp. 151–54.

35. Van der Kuijp (1994), p. 613: "Tibet's subsequent intellectual history is unthinkable without [Śākyaśrī]."

36. Sa-paṇ took monastic vows with Śākyaśrī in 1208, according to D. Jackson (1987), p. 27, and van der Kuijp (1994), p. 612.

37. Stearns (2001) pp. 158–69. Stearns (1996) would add Vibhūticandra to this list. Tāranātha records that Vibhūticandra refused to prostrate before Trakpa Gyeltsen, and thus although Sa-paṇ had already learned grammar from Saṅghaśrī and logic from Dānaśrī, he requested no teachings from Vibhūticandra because of this alleged disrespect to his uncle. Since this story does not ap-

pear in the earlier account by Padma gar dbang, Stearns thinks that it was probably fabricated to explain the later rift between the Sakyapa and Vibhūticandra's followers, in particular the 'Bri-gung-pa. See Stearns (1996), p. 134 and p. 133, n. 23. Even if Vibhūticandra was not Sa-paṇ's official teacher, he was surely an influential part of Śākyaśrī's entourage who was in dialogue with the Sakyapas. And, as Jackson (1990a), p. 21, writes: "Sanskrit manuscript materials in Vibhūticandra's hand survived at Sa-skya and were discovered there in the 1930s by Rāhula Sāṃkrtyāyana." Yet Vibhūticandra's writings do manifest disagreements with Trakpa Gyeltsen, especially on the notion of "transmutation" (*gnas 'gyur*) of the three vows.

38. D. Jackson (1987), pp. 26–27.

39. I rely upon Roerich (1959), pp. 1057–59, (1976), and Rhoton (2002), pp. 205–209, for Chag Lo-tsā-ba's life story. This is Roerich (1976), pp. 102–103, also cited by Rhoton (2002), p. 206.

40. Roerich (1976), p. 1057: "He obtained many doctrines from the Saskya lo-tsā-ba (sa-lo) in gTsaṅ, Khro-lo (Khro-phu lo-tsā-ba), Myaṅ-stod lotsā-ba, Gro-ston bDud-rtsi-grags, and others."

41. This is my translation of Roerich (1959), p. 2: *spyir rigs pa'i gnas lnga dang/khyad par du sngags dang sgra dang/mtshan-nyid kun la mkhas pa te.*

42. Śākyaśrī was said to have four great students who established learning in four separate fields: Sa-paṇ in *pramāṇa* studies, Thropu Lotsāwa in (tantric) oral instructions, Dpyal Lotsāwa in tantric theory and practice, and Gtsang so ba in the *vinaya*. Van der Kuijp (1994), p. 613. Thropu is also known as a great disciple of Śākyaśrī's because of having built, with Śākyaśrī's help, a famous temple dedicated to Maitreya. Ruegg (1966), p. 43.

43. These were Mitrayogin, Buddhaśrī, and Śākyaśri. Jackson (1990b), p. 3.

44. This from Jackson (1990b), pp. 12 and 33–34, and van der Kuijp (1994).

45. Ruegg (1995), pp. 134–35. Kapstein (2003), n. 102, provides comprehensive evidence for his claim that "from the fourteenth century onwards virtually every Tibetan author of note, whether monk or layman, tried his hand at some *kāvya*." This is also Kapstein's motive, p. 777, for comparing Sa-paṇ's ideals to the Western, post-Rennaisance notions of a "classical" education, where "it was poetic excellence that was regarded as a touchstone of moral and intellectual refinement." Van der Kuijp (1996), p. 400, writes that the forms of metaphor described in the *Kāvyādarśa* in particular are used to display literary mastery by several great luminaries, including Longchenpa.

46. For GL III, I use Jackson's translation (1987), here p. 329, and his edition, p. 256: *gang zag dam pa rang rang gi bstan pa gzung bar bya ba'i don du 'khrul pa bzlog cing ma 'khrul ba'i don go bar bya ba'i phyir/rgol phyir rgol brtsad kyi.*

47. GL 372.12–15: *rig pa'i gnas lnga dag la mkhas par ma byas par // 'phags mchog gis kyang thams cad mkhyen nyid mi 'gyur te // gzhan dag tshar gcad rjes su gzung bar bya phyir dang // rang nyid kun shes bya phyir de la de brtson byed.* MSA 11.60, p. 70: *vidyāsthāne pañcavidhe yogam akṛtvā sarvajñatvaṃ naiti kathaṃcit paramāryaḥ/ityanyeṣāṃ nigrahaṇānugrahaṇāya svājñārthaṃ vā tatra karoty eva sa yogam.* On the five sciences, see Griffiths (1990), pp. 99–100, Kapstein (2003), and Dudjom (1991), pp. 97–101.

48. See Ruegg (1995), pp. 103–104, n. 13, for the use of the five sciences not just in the MSA and the *Bodhisattvabhūmi,* but in a range of hagiographic writings describing the education of major Buddhist figures.

49. GL 372.9–11: *brda sprod pa sgra dang/rtog ge tshad ma dang/phyi rol rig pa'i bzo dang/nang rig pa lung gi chos dang/gso ba rig pa sman spyad do.*

50. Asaṅga (1907), p. 70: *bhedena punar hetuvidyāṃ śabdavidyām ca paryeṣyate nigrahārtham anyeṣāṃ tadanadhimuktānāṃ/cikitsāvidyām śilpakarmas-thānavidyāṃ cānyeṣām anugrahārthaṃ tadarthakānāṃ/adhyātmavidyām svayam ājñārthaṃ.* See also Dudjom (1991), p. 98.

51. See D. Jackson (1987), pp. 191–206, for a concise summary of the contents of the *Gateway,* with an emphasis on the third chapter. See appendix A for my outline of the first two chapters.

52. Asaṅga (1907), p. 70: *sarvajñatvaprāptyartham abhedena sarvaṃ.*

53. Asaṅga (1907), p. 70: *adhyātmavidyām svyayam ājñārthaṃ.*

54. Though, since Jackson (1987) has made a thorough study of the *Gateway*'s chapter on debate, I focus my attention on the skills Sa-paṇ discusses in his earlier chapters, on composition and exposition.

55. GL 372.5–7: *mkhas pa zhes bya ba gang yin zhe na/shes bya thams cad phyin ci ma log par shes pa yin la/gzhan yang bye brag gang bslabs pa shes pa de la'ang de nyid la mkhas pa zhes bya ba'i ming thob po.*

56. GL 369.12–370.4: *yon tan gyi cha shas de'ang rang gis so so yang dag par rig pa bzhi'i spobs pa thob pa dang/gzhan la mi 'jigs pa bzhis 'khor gyi nang du seng ge'i sgra sgrogs pa las brtsams pa yin no // de dag kyang don dang chos dang spobs pa dang nges pa'i tshig ste/so so yang dag par rig pa bzhis shes bya thams cad la dbang 'byor ba thob cing/rang gi don dang gzhan gyi don mkhyen pa dang/spangs pa dang/nges par 'byung ba'i lam dang gegs ston pa la lha dang bcas pa'i* [370] *mu stegs gzhan gyis mi rdzi bas mi 'jigs pa bzhi brnyes pa ste/tshul 'dis rang gis rtsom pa dang/gzhan la 'chad pa dang/log rtog sel ba la mi 'jigs shing seng ge'i sgra sgrogs pa'i rgyu phun sum tshogs pa yin pas thog mar bshad do.*

57. This according to official PRC usage.

58. Bo thar Bkra shis chos 'phel (1998), pp. 74.4–19: *de la so so yang dag rig pa bzhi ni/'khor 'das kyi chos rnams kyi ngo bo dang dbye ba sogs tshul bzhin mkhyen cing/bstan bya'i don der ma rtogs log rtog/the tshom gyi nyes pa cha tsam yang mi mnga' ba ni don bzang so so yang dag par rig pa dang/shes par bya ba'i don

de dag gi rjod byed kyi ngag rnam dag dang/chos rnams kyi ming gi rnam grangs sogs tshul bzhin mkhyen pa ni chos so so yang dag par rig pa dang/bcu phrag rig gnas kyis bsdus pa'i shes bya kun la 'chad rtsod rtsom pa'i spobs pa rgyas shing/skal ldan rjes su 'dzin pa dang/log smra tshar gcod pa la bsam gyis mi khyab pa'i mthu dang ldan pa ni spobs pa so so yang dag par rig pa dang/rgyal khab dang mi rigs so so'i skad bzhin du/sgra mi gsal ba dang/zur ma phyin pa dang/rkyen dang rkyen can gyi sdeb nor ba sogs kyi skyon med par tshig 'bru bzang pos don ston nus pa ni nges tshig so so yang dag par rig pa'o // bzhi po 'di ni 'khor gyi nang du seng ge'i sgra sgrog cing/rang gis rtsom pa dang/gzhan la 'chad pa dang/log rtog sel ba la mi 'jigs pa'i spobs pa thob pa'i thun min gyi nang rgyu yin la.

59. GL 371.1–18 provides Sa-paṇ's listing the *bstan bcos* (treatises) he has mastered in *sgra* (linguistics), *tshad ma* (epistemology), *snyan ngag* (poetry), *bsdeb sbyor* (metrics), *tshig gi rgyan* (poetics), *ming gi nges brjod* (synonymics), *zlos gar* (drama), *sman dbyad* (medecine), *bzo rig pa* (crafts), *rtsis* (astronomical calculations), and *nang rig pa* (Buddhist/Inner sciences).

60. GL 372.7–8: *mkhas pa des bslab par bya ba'i yul ni rig pa'i gnas lnga ste.* GL 372.5–6: *shes bya thams cad phyin ci ma log par shes pa yin la.*

61. Though, in other contexts *sarvākārajñatā* is considered an expression indicating "full enlightenment." Makransky (1997), p. 32. The topic of omniscience in Buddhism deserves fuller treatment. In the ninth chapter of his *Treasury of Reasoning,* when Sa-paṇ explains the fruit of valid knowledge—of *pramāṇa*—he goes on to give a definition and discussion of the ominiscience of Buddhahood. If Sa-paṇ holds the view that I have sketched here, this work, though early, would be an appropriate place to find it.

62. Stearns (2001), p. 70.

63. This is why Sa-paṇ says that a good teacher must be famous, for the sake of his students: "If he is not famous as a scholar, they will be ridiculed, "Where does your [learning] come from, when [your] teacher has none?" GL 429.7–8: *mkhas par ma grags na slob dpon la med par khyod la gar yod ces brnyas par 'gyur te.*

64. Translation from Kapstein (1987), pp. 252–53.

65. See Griffiths (1990), pp. 96–97, on the distinction between "specific content omniscience" and comprehensive knowledge of general characteristics. Ārya Vimuktasena concurs in his *Abhisamayālaṅkāra* commentary, for as Makransky (1997) points out, pp. 205–206, he approves of Bhadrapāla's view of *sarvākārajñatā* as "the quintessence (Tib., *snying po;* Skt. *sāra*) contained in [all] objects of knowledge," i.e., their "perfected nature" (*pariniṣpanna*). In this context, since the *ākāra* is the nature that all things share, *sarvākārajñatā* should perhaps be translated "knowledge of the mode of appearance [nature] of all [things]."

66. TR 81.2–4.

67. Ruegg (1966), p. 15.

68. Roerich (1959), p. 2.

69. Yijing (1896), p. 181.

70. Yijing (1896), p. 181.

71. Xuanzang (1969), pp. 170–71.

72. Xuanzang (1969), pp. 171–72.

73. The *Blue Annals* also records Drogmi's meetings with these six *dvāra-paṇḍitas* just before recieving the Lamdre teachings from Ḍombi-heruka, a disciple of Virūpa. Roerich (1976), pp 205–206. See also Stearns (2001), pp. 85–87, and Davidson (2002), pp. 281–83.

74. Jackson (1987), p. 7.

75. Stearns (2001), p. 85.

76. Jackson translates *mkhas pa,* which I have been calling "the scholar" and "learning," as "the wise" (1987), 2:366. His critical edition (1987), p. 297, reads: *thub pa'i bstan pa phyogs su 'phel ba dang//'jig rten khams 'dir yun ring gnas bya'i phyir//mkhas pa'i lugs 'dzin mkhas pa 'jug pa'i sgo//rnam gsum phye 'dir mkhas rnams 'jug par bya.*

77. Jackson (1987), p. 366. His edition, p. 298: *blo gros gsal ba'i skye bo rnams thar pa chen po'i grong khyer du 'jug pa'i sgo/dam pa rnams kyis bgrod par bya ba'i 'jug ngos/rtsom pa dang 'chad pa dang rtsod pa'i tshul gtan la 'bebs par byed pa/mkhas pa rnams 'jug pa'i sgo zhes bya ba'i bstan bcos 'di ni yul byang phyogs kyi rgyud.* Here the term translated as "establishes" is *gtan la 'bebs,* which would seem to reflect the exact wording of the royal translation edict in the *Sgra sbyor bam po gnyis pa* (see chapter 2), which says that "the new terms not previously established and ratified/fixed were established as terms and ratified/fixed (*ming du btags shing gtan la phab ste*)." This is Scherrer-Schaub's translation (2002), p. 284.

78. D. Jackson (1987), p. 366. His edition p. 298: *deng sang śākya seng ge'i bstan pa 'di//'bab chu zad pa'i rdzing bzhin nyin re 'bri//blo gsal rnams kyis tshul 'di legs rtogs la//thar pa 'dod pa dag gis 'bad dgos so.*

79. When Sa-paṇ describes the decline of the doctrine, he may well have specific doctrinal views in mind, as mentioned above. His retelling of the story of the degenerate views of the "Chinese monk" that led up to the bSam-yas debate is among the best studied passages of his work, but it is worth recalling for the direct connection it depicts between the general state of the doctrine's decline and some very particular, historical doctrinal shifts (this is R. Jackson's (1982) translation, p. 91): "The *ācārya* Śāntarakṣita left the following testament: . . . 'because it is the nature of causality that both day and night, right and left, waxing and waning, and pure and impure *dharmas* (all) arise, after my death will come a Chinese master (*mkhan po*) who will negate method and wisdom and will say that one attains Buddhahood only by the examination of the mind called the White Panacea."

80. GL 453.4–9: *de ltar tshig gi don legs par shes par 'dod na/rig pa'i gnas lnga ka la ci rigs par sbyang dgos/khyad par du sgra dang sdeb sbyor dang snyan ngag dang/ming gi mngon brjod la sogs pa la 'dris par bya'o // spyir shes bya thams cad la dbang 'byor pa la gzungs kyi sgo shes dgos.*

81. Cabezon (1998), p. 5.

CHAPTER 2. BEWARE OF THE DHARMA IN TRANSLATION

1. Stearns (2001), p. 135. Stearns's translation of *Zhib mo rdo rje* 132.14–15: *ma gcig na re/khyod kyi pha'i slob dpon kyang lo tsha ba yin nyid kyang lo tsha ba'i slob dpon zhig la chos slob dgos zer te.*

2. Stearns (1992), pp. 158–59: *bla ma lo tsha ba.*

3. Stearns (2001). p. 163. See discussion below.

4. This is true even if we set aside Davidson's (2005) argument that the translators developed their own tantric monopolies.

5. See my discussion of the "dharma language" (*chos skad*) in chapter 1.

6. GL 433.9–455.15.

7. These are listed, as well, as topics of study in Chak Lotsāwa's biography, Roerich (1959), p. xli. See chapter 1, above, and Simonsson (1957), Ruegg (1983), and Scherer-Schaub (2003) on the official translation methods established under the old Tibetan empire.

8. Ishihama and Fukuda (1989) and Ishikawa (1990).

9. GL 451.10–11: *bod kyi tshig bzang ngan la go bde bar sgyur cig ces skad gsar bcad las 'byung ba ltar shes par bya'o.* See Kapstein (2003), pp. 756–57, for "ease" as a rule in the *Two-Volume Lexicon.*

10. GL 450.9–10: *mkhas pas bshad mi dgos.*

11. I use the expression "the translators" to indicate the standard practices of translators, including those articulated in the *Mahāvyutpatti,* etc.

12. See chapter 1.

13. GL 443.16–19: *chos de'ang chos kyi gzugs brnyan nam/chos ltar bcos pa zhes gsungs pa de yin/'di 'dra'i rigs can bstan pa la mi phan pa'i steng du bstan pa 'jig pa'i rgyur 'gro.*

14. See chapter 1 for my discussion of "fabrication" as the bugbear of the Neoconservative Movement, of which Sa-paṇ is the chief proponent.

15. My categories follow Sa-paṇ's organization of these issues fairly closely, though I have changed the order to show increasing difficulties for the interpreter, and I have created and named the last category. Also, Sa-paṇ spends many pages on these topics, while I have included only selective examples and summarizations.

16. GL 446.8–10: *A ma ra ko ṣā dang/bi sha pra kā sha la sogs pa ming gi mngon brjod rnams legs par shes pa tshig gi don thams cad la the tshom chod pa yin no.*

17. GL 446.10–11: *'di'i phyogs tsam kho bos tshig gi gter du bshad pa ltar shes par bya'o.*

18. Sa-paṇ in fact gives *five* divisions of reasons that an interpretation might go wrong due to a misunderstanding of translation terms. I have moved the missing one—terms translated as derivatives from a different root, such as translating *kāya* as "shout"—into my category of unintelligible context. By shifting Sa-paṇ's categorization this way I am emphasizing the methods Sa-paṇ suggests for avoiding errors. That is, I separate potential misinterpretations that can be avoided by studying a word list from those that cannot. It seems to me unlikely that Sa-paṇ assumed that a standard synonymic word list such as the *Amarakośa* would include the full range of interpretive alterations that can be provided to a word by Indian commentators. I do not, however, have a good explanation for Sa-paṇ's having classified such changes with the other obscure terms for which studying a word list is useful, except that they also fall under the general description of difficult words.

19. GL 446.15–16: *lo tsā ba snga rabs pa dang phyi rabs pa dag gis brda gsar rnying gi khyad par la byung ba'ang yod.*

20. GL 446.21–447.3: *dper* [447] *na hwags la bye ma ka ra dang/gla gor zho sha la go yu dang/rin chen tog la rin chen dbal dang/nam yang la gzhar yang la sogs pa bod kyi brda rnying pa rnams deng sang go dka' ba dang.*

21. Rhoton (2002), pp. 169–70 and n. 190 on p. 197.

22. GL 447.12–17: *gzhan yang rang rang gi yul gyi skad du bsgyur bas/mda' la nyag phran/gzhu la gnam ru/. . . la sogs pa yul phan tshun du ma grags pa bsgyur bas go dka' ba yod.*

23. GL 447.3–6: *gzhan yang śākya la phod par bsgyur/go pa la sa 'tshor bsgyur/ma ga dhā la byings 'dzin/wā rā ṇa sī la 'khor mo 'jig/. . . bsgyur ba la sogs pa.*

24. GL 446.18: *la las sgra 'gyur la don 'gyur du byas pa'ang yod.*

25. GL 447.6–8: *gzhan yang gdugs dkar la tshad skyob dkar po/smon lam la yongs su bsgyur ba/dge ba la ngan 'byol la sogs pa lta bu sgra'i khams mi shes na go dka'.*

26. For this reason, this issue might also have been classified as a problem due to translation technique, rather than due to simply failing to understand obscure words.

27. GL 446.6–8: *legs par sbyar ba'i skad la mdzes pa byung na/'jig rten phal cher la ma grags pa'i saṃ skṛ tas sbyar ba yin pas.*

28. See my chapter 4 for a treatment of these terms.

29. "Though the Sanskrit language does not have it, a small part is added and [put in the] translation. Even [where] the Sanskrit has no expression ['jewel', the Tibetan shows] 'Vaidharbya jewel', and 'Padmarāga jewel', and so on. And though the Sanskrit has no expression 'flower', [the Tibetan] extends it to 'Utpala flower', and 'padma flower', and 'Saugandhika flower', and so on." GL 450.10–15: *legs par sbyar ba'i skad la med kyang bod kyis go bde bar bya ba'i*

phyir tshig gi rgyan cung zad bsnan nas bsgyur ba yod de/rgya gar la sgra med kyang rin po che bai dūrya dang/rin po che padma rā ga zhes bya ba la sogs pa dang/rgya gar la me tog gi sgra med kyang me tog ūtpala dang/me tog padma dang/me tog sau gandhi ka zhes bya ba la sogs pa bsnan pa dang.

30. GL 451.11–14: */gzhan yang rgya gar la lha'i me tog dang/lha'i bdug spos dang zhes bya ba la sogs pa la 'ga' zhig gis rdzas kyi sgra bsnan nas/lha rdzas kyi me tog dang lha rdzas kyi bdug spos dang zhes bya ba la sogs par bsgyur ba dang.*

31. GL 451.3–6: *de bzhin du ye shes dang/phyag rgya dang/go rims la sogs pa la rgya gar na ye dang/phyag dang/go la sogs pa'i sgra med kyang bod la tshig sbyar ba bde ba'i don du bsnan nas bsgyur ba dang.*

32. "For example, the *Eight Thousand* says, 'winged one bird.' If someone should understand the meaning to be 'the winged one and the bird,' and think that there is no reason [other than this] that the two should be repeated, it is not so. 'Winged one' in Sanskrit is *pakṣi,* and since this expression is used [to mean] many things, such as 'side,' etc., [the expression] 'bird' is said to eliminate these. Also, 'bird' in Sanskrit is *śakuna,* and since this [expression] is used [to mean] other [things] as well, such as 'fortune' (*bkra shis*) and 'lucky omen' (*dge mtshan*), [the expression] 'winged one' is said to eliminate these. There is no fallacy of duplication. " GL 452.5–12: */dper na brgyad stong pa las/'dab chags bya zhig ces 'byung ste/'dab chags dang bya gang rung gis don go mod gnyis ka bzlas pa don med do snyam na ma yin te/'dab chags la saṃ skṛ tas pa kṣi zer la/sgra de phyogs la sogs pa mang po la 'jug pas de spang ba'i don du bya zhes smos so // yang bya la saṃ skṛ ta'i skad sha ku na zhes zer la/de bkra shis dang dge mtshan la sogs pa gzhan la yang 'jug pas/de gcad pa'i don du 'dab chags zhes smod pa zlos pa'i skyon med do/*

33. GL 453.4–7: */de ltar tshig gi don legs par shes par 'dod na/rig pa'i gnas lnga ka la ci rigs par sbyang dgos/khyad par du sgra dang sdeb sbyor dang snyan ngag dang/ming gi mngon brjod la sogs pa la 'dris par bya'o.*

34. "Although Sanskrit expressions rarely differentiate the honorific from the non-honorific, [the Tibetan] translation uses [the expression] 'he bestows the gift of speech' for the Buddha addressing someone else, [the expression] 'he beseeches [him]' for someone else speaking to the Buddha, and 'he speaks' for a reciprocal inquiry among equals. Likewise, all words are either honorific or non-honorific. As the new language determination (*skad gsar bcad*) [of Khri-lde-srong-btsan] says, 'In relation to the honorific level of Tibetan expressions, translate so as to [achieve] ease of understanding.'" GL 451.6–11: *rgya gar la zhe sa'i sgra dang phal pa'i sgra phal cher khyad med kyang/sangs rgyas kyis gzhan la smras pa la bka' stsal/gzhan gyis sangs rgyas la zhus pa la gsol ba/mnyam po phan tshun 'dri ba la smras pa zhes bya bar bsgyur/de bzhin du zhe sa dang zhe sa ma yin pa'i tshig thams cad/bod kyi tshig bzang ngan la go bde bar sgyur cig ces skad gsar bcad las 'byung ba ltar shes par bya'o.*

35. The Sanskrit word *khaḍga* can mean either "sword" or "rhino [horn]."

36. The Sanskrit word *bāla* can mean, among other things, "child," "sand," or "hair."

37. GL 447.20–448.2: */saṃ skṛ ta'i rnam grangs kyi sgra // bse ru la ral gri ral gri la bse rur bsgyur ba dang / rjes dang rkang pa'i sgra bzlog nas bsgyur ba dang/* [448] *byis pa dang bye ma dang skra'i sgra phan tshun 'chol bar bsgyur ba la sogs pa dang.*

38. "Some do not know the expressions, and so, without understanding, translate in ignorance. [For instance], 'essence' (*snying po*) is translated as 'arrow' (*mda'*—that is, the Sanskrit word *sāra* has been mistaken for *śāra*); 'green' (*ljang gu*) as 'rob' (*'phrog pa*—that is, the Sanskrit adjective *harita* has been mistaken for a form derived from the verb root *hṛt*); and [the proper name] Indrabhūti (*'byung po'i dbang po*) as *indrabodhi* (*brgya byin byang chub*)—by force of such erroneous translations we see a failure to comprehend the intended meaning just as it is." GL 448.7–11: *la la sgra mi shes pas ma rtogs te mun sprul du bsgyur ba snying po la mdar bsgyur ba dang / ldang* [sic?] *gu la 'phrog pa dang / 'byung po'i dbang po la brgya byin byang chub tu bsgyur ba la sogs pa 'l par bsgyur ba'i stobs kyis brjod bya'i don ji ltar yin pa mi rtogs pa mthong ngo.*

39. "Some mistakes of word division [include] either mistakenly construing the sound *na* of the third case ending as an expression of negation of a succeeding word or construing the *na* that is an expression of negation of a succeeding word as the sound *na* of the third case ending of a preceding word. [Either] translate into an incorrect expression." GL 448.2–5: *la la sa mtshams 'chugs pa yod de / rnam dbye gsum pa'i na'i sgra tshig 'og ma'i dgag pa'i sgrar 'og tu sbyar ba dang / tshig 'og ma'i dgag sgra'i na / gong ma'i rnam dbye gsum pa'i na'i sgra yar sbyar ba'i stobs kyis sgra 'khrul par bsgyur ba dang.*

40. GL 447.19–20: *log par bsgyur ba go ba dka'*. Emphasis added.

41. GL 437.21–441.7

42. GL 438.21–439.2: *ka ya'i sgra drang por sku la 'jug / khams kyis drangs* [439] *na kai / gai rai / shabha zhes brjod na / sgrogs pas na / sku zhes sku'i sgra sgrogs pa la bshad du rung.*

43. GL 441.2–4: *slob dpon mi thub zla bas lus kyi sgra lhar 'chad pa na / lus la de ha zer / ha'i gnas su ba bzhag pas de bar bsgyur ba dang.*

44. GL 440.20–441.2: *yang mtshan brjod las / thig le stong pa yi ge brgya // zhes bya ba'i don dus 'khor bas 'chad pa na yi ge la sha ta ā kṣa* [441] *ra zer la / sha'i gnas su ṣa / ta'i gnas su ṭa bzhag nas yi ge drug tu 'chad pa dang.*

45. The commentarial style of the Sanskrit *śāstra* would thus seem a peculiarly clear example of what André Lefevere, following Bourdieu, calls a textual "grid," "the collection of acceptable ways in which things can be said," which may or may not be recapitulated in a translation, depending on method and context. Bassnett and Lefevere (1998), p. 5.

46. GL 454.10–21: *lha rnams dga' ba zhes bya ba ni/ra dang ma he la sogs pa'i mchod sbyin dag la lha rnams dga' bas/khyod kyi blo yang dud 'gro dang 'dra'o zhes bsting pa'i tshig go // 'byung po dang mgul chings bzhin no zhes pa ni/'byung po mchod pa dag gis srog chags kyi gzugs brnyan mi 'dra ba mang po'i mgrin par me tog gi phreng ba la sogs pa'i srad bu gcig gis bcings pa ltar/bye brag du ma la spyi gcig gis khyab pa'i dpe'o // bya rog dang ta la'i tshul zhes pa ni/ta la'i yal ga rang nyid chag pa'i steng du bya rog babs pa na/bya rog gis ta la bcag ces 'jig rten sgrogs pa ltar stes dbang gis don 'grub pa'i dpe'o // bya rog gi dri ba zhes bya ba ni/gzhung lugs 'chad pa na rngar ma bsams pa glo bur du dgos pa dran nas/de ci zhes pa bab col du 'dri ba'o.*

47. GL 455.7–11: *g.yem ma mu cor gyis rgyal lo zhes bya ba yang 'phyon mas log par spyod pa bdag pos mthong ba'i tsh/bdag pos 'thabs pa na khyod kyi mig chu bur bems po la yid brtan ci/nga snying dang 'dra ba bden no zhes ser ba ltar/khyod kyi lung rigs la yid brtan cing/nga'am nga'i bla ma gsung ba bden no zhes zer ba'i dpe'o.*

48. Vettam Mani (1975), p. 199, summarizes the story: "When Śrī Kṛṣṇa was a small boy, Yaśodā tied him to a mortar-stone. The boy ran about, dragging the heavy stone with him and the rope snapped. Part of the rope still remained round his abdomen. From that he got the name Dāmodara. 'Dama' means rope and 'Udara' means abdomen."

49. GL 449.17–19: *dha mo da ra'i sgra nor lha'i bu byis pa'i gnas skabs na tha gu lto ba la dkris pas tha gu lto zhes 'thad mod kyi khyab 'jug tu bsgyur ba dang.*

50. The Tibetans may also have been inspired by the goddess' epithet Vāgmatī.

51. GL 448.17–449.1: *dper na sa ra swa tī sgra sngon rgya mtsho bsrubs pa las byung bas mtsho las byung ba yin mod kyi/gtam rgyud ma gzigs pa dang bod kyis go bde bar bya ba'i don du dbyangs can mar bsgyur ro // sa ra swa tī zhes sgra bzlog na dbyangs can yin mod kyi/'dir sa ra swa tī yin pas dbyangs can du bsgyur du mi* [449] *rung ngo.*

52. GL 448.14–17: *mu stegs byed kyi sngon rabs dang/mdo'i rtog pa brjod pa sna tshogs las/sems can gyi ming dang yul gyi ming tha dad du 'dogs pa rnams sngon rabs kyi gtam rgyud ma shes pas/lo tsā ba mkhas kyang phyin ci log tu bsgyur ba mthong ste.*

53. I do not mean to suggest, however, that Sa-paṇ is satisfied with substandard translations. My point here is only that he considers the general practices of the translators to be acceptable, except on a few particular issues—which are predominantly related to ignorance of non-Buddhist Indian literature. This is one reason that Sa-paṇ believes the literary arts of India must be imported into Tibet.

54. See, famously, the linguistic relativity of Quine (1960) and Whorf (1956). For a brief survey of Western theories of translation, see Bassnett-McGuire (1991), which is now the main introductory text of the field of translation studies and which has a useful bibliography, as well, pp. 148–61. Steiner

(1992) remains essential and contains the crucial Translation Studies bibliography, pp. 500–16.

55. Stearns (2001). p. 163, which is Stearns's translation of his p. 163.12–21. I present the translation without Stearns's typographical distinction between the original and the interlinear manuscript notes.

56. Stearns (2001), p. 77: "The *Zhib mo rdo rje* is the companion volume to the *Gsungs sgros ma*, used to establish the authentic lineage and the spiritual qualities of previous masters."

57. Stearns (2001), p. 260, n. 272.

58. GL 390.14–16: */'di dag legs par sbyar ba'i sgra la shin tu dgos kyang/bod kyi skad la sgra'i stobs kyis sgrub pa med cing/rang gi rgan po rnams la grags pa'i stobs kyis go ba'i phyir.* See chapter 4 for Sa-paṇ's various uses of the expression "well known" (*grags pa*).

59. GL 387.13–14: *de ltar sgra'i sbyor ba ma byas na saṃ skṛ ta'i sgra la bod du bsgyur ba las don go ba ji ltar yin zhe na.*

60. Ruegg (1992), p. 370 has addressed this issue in a different context, quite rightly stating that "The use of different canonical languages is . . . in harmony with Mahāyānist docetism according to which the teaching of the Dharma is carried out by a Buddha's *nirmāṇakāya* in conformity with the capacities and requirements of each of his disciples." Although, of course, *paramārtha* as "ultimate truth" is ineffable, Ruegg continues, p. 380, the expositions in *sūtra* and *śāstra* are effable, and "such effability of course implies translatability."

61. In fact, he says that where Sanskrit has determined every vowel's length and strength, in Tibetan these are undetermined and disorganized: GL 387.17–18: *ring thung dang drag zhan la sogs pa'i sgra'i nges pa med pa dang.*

62. "Furthermore, through a person's expressive intention and the meaning's context, and the strength of the word, there comes about in Tibetan expression a single meaning in different words, which arises predominantly because of suffix letters. For instance, in the sixth case, even though there is no difference [in the meaning], the [relation to the term 'heap'] in the expressions 'form heap,' 'heap of feeling,' and 'compositional factor's heap' come in different words." GL 388.2–6: *'on kyang bod kyi sgra la gang zag gi brjod 'dod dang/don gyi gnas skabs dang/tshig gi shugs kyis don gcig la'ang sgra tha dad du 'gyur ba phal cher mthar gnas kyi yi ge'i stobs las 'byung ste/dper na drug pa'i sgrar khyad med kyang gzugs kyi phung po/tshor ba'i phung po/'du byed kyi phung po zhes sgra tha dad du 'gyur ba lta bu'o.*

63. "And as in, 'There being smoke, there is fire here,' all reasons (*gtan tshigs, hetu*), while [originally] in the fifth case, are translated 'Because of their being smoke,' or 'Because of performing a function' [which is the fourth case]." GL 388.19–21: *du ba yod pa la 'di na me yod ces bya ba lta bu/gtan tshigs thams cad lnga pa'i sgrar yod pa la du ba yod pa'i phyir byas pa'i phyir zhes bya bar bsgyur ba dang.*

64. GL 389.3–7: *de lta na yang de dag nyid // gzhan du sbyar yang mi 'gal phyir // ngo bo nyid kyis 'brel med pa // des na brjod 'dod kho nar grub // sgra don la 'brel pa dngos po med pas brjod 'dod kyi dbang gis 'jug pa'i phyir ji ltar sbyar yang 'gal ba med de.*

65. Sa-paṇ supports this claim by citing the great Indian Buddhist epistemologist Dharmakīrti: "As the [*Pramāṇa*]*vārttika* says, 'Apart from what arises by force of the speech intention, what expressions are there?'" GL 389.7–9: *rnam 'grel las/brjod par 'dod pa'i gzhan dbang phyir // sgra rnams gang la'ang med ma yin // zhes gsungs pas so.* For a discussion of Dharmakīrti's arguments against an "essential relation" between words and meanings, see Tillemans (2000), pp. 219–28.

66. I treat these expressions in detail in chapter 4.

67. Kapstein (2000), p. 11.

CHAPTER 3. THE DHARMA IS ONLY WORDS

1. Nonetheless, there is often order to this multiplicity. Many Buddhists use the doctrine to establish a clear hierarchy of teachings, often with their own favored view at the top. As Lopez (1988a), p. 6, writes, the doctrine of *upāya* is not just a "hermeneutics of accommodation," it is also a "hermeneutics of control." Sa-paṇ is not alone in using the doctrine of skill in means as support for a particular variety of intellectual authority.

2. This is the section I title "1.2.1: Assembling Letters, Words, and Phrases (GL 377–78)."

3. Of the many works on this, Pye's monograph (1978) has yet to be surpassed.

4. See discussion of a "portion of the doctrine" (*chos phung*) below and Cabezón (1994), pp. 34–35.

5. This is the central theme of Sa-paṇ's famous polemical work, *A Clear Differentiation of the Three Codes* in Rhoton's translation (2002).

6. Jackson (1987), p. 354. For passages from the third chapter of the *Gateway*, I use Jackson's excellent published translation.

7. When referring to the "Hīnayāna" (Lesser Vehicle) here, I am simply transmitting Sa-paṇ's perspective on the so-called Individual Liberation Buddhist traditions. According to this view, which he shares with the entire Tibetan tradition, the non-Mahāyāna traditions are fundamentally selfish because they focus on achieving liberation for oneself, rather than for all beings, as opposed to the goal of Universal Liberation pursued by *bodhisattvas* of the Mahāyāna. This is a false, ahistorical view invented to serve the polemical needs of the Mahāyāna tradition in India when its innovations were contested by many rivals. D'Amato (2000) is a useful analysis of the issues here.

8. Again, see discussion of "portion of the doctrine" below.

9. Jackson (1987), p. 354.

10. Jackson's *sa bcas* (1987), p. 530, extracted from Glo-bo Mkhan-chen's Commentary on the GL calls this section: *sgra'i rgyu yi ge dang ming dang tshig gi tshogs gsum bshad pa.* In the translation below I call this section "1.2.1: Assembling Letters, Words, and Phrases."

11. My simplified presentation bypasses the question of whether *yi ge* is equivalent to *phoneme,* and the complex issues of interpreting *ming* and *tshig.* Verhagen (1993–2001), Miller (1993), and Simonnson (1982, 1984) disagree as to how these terms ought to be translated based on analysis of the *Rtags 'jug.* Verhagen makes the (I think correct) distinction between *ming* as stem form and *tshig* as built out of inflected forms, but Simonsson argues (also correctly) that a *tshig* must be a multiword phrase linked by grammatical connectors. I think that Sa-paṇ presents a kind of compromise between Simonsson's and Verhagen's views, and for the sake of this discussion I keep to the standard translations "word" and "phrase" instead of adopting either the Verhagen/ Miller or Simonsson translations. At the least, this makes for a smoother discussion of the building-block quality of the linguistic causes. In fact, since I am concerned only to show how Sa-paṇ integrates elements of the epistemological tradition into an otherwise standard (that is, similar to *Rtags 'jug,* SDL and EW) discussion of the linguistic causes, my argument holds whether Sa-paṇ would agree with Verhagen's or Simonsson's understanding of the linguistic causes.

12. Though, it is less than obvious that these were basic concepts for Tibetans of Sa-paṇ's time. Still, they are treated in the *Abhidharmakośa,* and they provide the organizational impetus for Smṛtijñānakīrti's *Smra sgo mtshon cha* (*SDL*), "the basic Tibetan work on [Sanskrit grammar] until the thirteenth century." Smith (1974), pp. 4–5. Sa-paṇ based a large portion of his own linguistic analyses on the latter text, to which he refers his reader for further study at several points, including at the end of this section, GL 377.17.

13. See Anacker (1998), pp. 66–71, for Vasubandhu's discussion of the *citta-saṃprayukta-* and *citta-viprayukta-saṃskāras* in his later work, the *Pañcaskandhaprakaraṇa.* See Buswell (1997) for interesting analysis of the use of the category of *citta-viprayukta-saṃskāras* among the Vaibhāṣikas. Among Tibetan scholars after Sa-paṇ, there is little doubt that the even better known locus classicus for this terminology is the *Rtags 'jug* attributed to Thönmi Saṃbhoṭa, the inventor of the Tibetan script. Miller (1993) has shown convincingly that while Sa-paṇ probably had access to some early version of the text(s) that *later* came to be the *Rtags 'jug,* he did not consider it/them to be composed by Thönmi, and it could not yet have been a standard fixed text at his time.

14. Vasubandhu (1967) 62.14: *ime saṃskārā na cittena saṃprayuktā na ca rūpasvabhāvā iti cittaviprayuktā ucyante.* See Biardeau (1964), p. 393, n. 1.

15. For Sanskrit text, see Vasubandhu (1967) 80.12–81.28. French translation in La Vallée Poussin (1923–1931), pp. 238–43, cited in full by Biardeau (1964), pp. 392–94. Simonsson (1982) translates some significant passages with Yaśomitra's commentary.

16. Biardeau (1964), p. 394: "Il n'est pas exagéré de dire que ce texte bouddhique, rapportant une discussion entre bouddhistes de deux écoles réputées voisines, nous fournit le schéma d'ensemble des développements brahmaniques autour de la philosophie du langage."

17. Like the SDL, the EW is organized topically around *yi ge, ming,* and *tshig gi tshog.* Verhagen (2001) lists other similarities between the SDL and the EW. Of course, *yi ge, ming* and *tshig* are the building blocks of language best known in the *Rtags 'jug.* But since Sa-paṇ most likely did not have access to the *Rtags 'jug* (see note 13), I restrict my comparison to the SDL.

18. The SDL's analysis, in turn, would appear to be based on a combination of the definitions from Asaṅga's *Abhidarmasasmuccaya* and/or Haribhadra's *Abhisamayālaṃkārāloka,* where we find the notion that *nāmakāyas* express the "substance" of a meaning whereas *padakāyas* express a "particularity" of a meaning (but which declare *vyañjanakāyas* to be the basis for both), and other sources such as the *Abhidharmakośa,* which make the *vyañjanakāyas* building blocks for the *nāmakāyas,* which are in turn the building blocks for *padakāyas.* See Jaini (1959), p. 97.

19. EW 506.19–20: *mtshan nyid ni/sgra gang zhig 'brur chags pa'o.*

20. EW 507.18–19: *don gyi ngo bo nyid mtshon par nus pa'o.*

21. EW 511.9: *mtshan nyid ni/don gyi khyad par ston nus pa ste.*

22. GL 377.8–9: *yi ge'i mtshan nyid ni/don mi ston pa'i sgra spyi snang ba zhes bya ba yin la.*

23. GL 377.19–20: *ming yin zhes ming gi mtshan nyid ni don gyi ngo bo ston par byed pa'i sgra spyi snang ba'o.*

24. GL 378.3–4: *tshig gi mtshan nyid ni don gyi khyad par ston pa'i sgra spyi snang ba ste.*

25. SDL 35.12–14: *mdor na chos kyi ngo bo nyid tsam ston nus la khyad par mi ston pa'i yi ge 'dus pa'i gnas skabs la ming zhes bya'o.*

26. SDL 41.8–9: *rang gi ngo bo ni de 'dus pas don gyi khyad par brjod pa'o.*

27. In each text, each definition is followed by a discussion whose elucidation here would complicate matters but in no way undermine the obvious parallels among the texts. In fact, some tangential issues are treated similarly in all three texts. For instance, all address a possible objection to the sharp distinction between individual letters and words on the basis of single-letter words such as *nga* ("I") and *ma* ("mother," "causal potency").

28. Sa-paṇ has based a large part of his linguistic analyses on the SDL, and there is no mention of *sgra spyi* in either the SDL or in Trakpa Gyeltsen's commentary on that work. Sa-paṇ also claims to be expert in the Sanskrit gram-

matical systems of Kātantra and Cāndra traditionally used by Buddhist scholars in India, and, while these are extensive and difficult grammatical systems which I have not mastered, their traditional definitions and divisions do not contain references to the *term generality*. See Liebich (1919 and 1920), Scharfe (1977), and Saini (1999). While Buddhist discussions of grammar lack such terminological usage, the same cannot be said of non-Buddhist grammatical philosophy. In fact, it is probable that this terminology was first developed in Bhartṛhari's *Vākyapadīya* as discussed in Herzberger (1986), pp. 28 ff., and was later borrowed by Buddhist epistemologists. Perhaps Sa-paṇ has unwittingly reintroduced the terminology of *sgra spyi* and *don spyi* into the grammatical context out of which it was born.

29. I speak in this section of "Sakyapa" epistemology, although it is almost certain that any Sakyapa *pramāṇa* tradition before Śākyaśrībhadra would have to have been derived from the Rngog-lugs, the tradition of the great translator Rngog lo-tsā-ba Blo-ldan shes-rab (1059–1109), centered around Gsang-phu monastery. On the early tradition of *pramāṇa* studies in Tibet, see Smith (1970), now reprinted in Smith (2001), pp. 111–16, and recent scholarship noted there on pp. 352–53, especially Dreyfus (1997a) and van der Kuijp (1983). As his recently published works show (Jackson 1993a and 1993b), Rngog's interests were diverse, and although he is known as the founder of Tibetan *pramāṇa* studies, he should perhaps also be recognized, as Jackson (1993a) suggests, as the founder of a wide range of Tibetan scholastic traditions.

30. My analysis in this section is entirely in agreement with Kapstein's discussion of *don spyi* (2000), pp. 89–97, which he calls "objective generalities." I extend the discussion to include an analysis of *sgra spyi,* which is the term of central importance to the *Gateway*. Dreyfus (1997a), p. 274, also discusses these terms, arguing that in this distinction the Sakyapa seem to align themselves, perhaps inadvertently, with the older epistemological tradition of Dignāga and the non-Buddhist Indian grammarian tradition of Bhartṛhari. Whether or not it is similar to Dignāga, the distinction was also used by Sa-paṇ's uncle Sönam Tsemo, and so could well be derived from the epistemological tradition that predates Sa-paṇ, the Rngog-lugs (see above note). It is possible that the importance of this terminology for the Sakyapa may be rooted more in its utility for characterizing the linguistic workings of the dharma (see below) than in its "preserving the integrity of Buddhist epistemology," as Dreyfus claims—though these may simply be two ways of talking about the same thing. Also, at the current time I set aside analysis of the all-important term "*snang ba*" (*pratibhā*) from the phrase *sgra spyi snang ba.* It is Dignāga's term, and will probably need to be unpacked in the context of a discussion of *apoha.*

31. The *Gateway* contains a brief synopsis and reference to this passage at GL 383.19–384.5.

32. Dreyfus (1997), pp. 272–75, treats these same issues, and the entirety of his chapter 15, pp. 261–80, places the traditional Sakya interpretation in dialogue with the Geluk.

33. For "conceived signifier" (*zhen pa'i brjod bya*), see the table below. Go rams pa's commentary on the TR, the *Sde bdun rab gsal,* defines "spyi" as "commonly appearing superimpositions" (*thun mong bar snang ba'i sgro grags*), and then defines "don spyi" as: "Superimpositions that mistakenly take appearance and concept as one and the same" (*snang btags gcig tu 'khrul ba'i sgro btags*). Go rams pa Bsod nams seng ge, pp. 84–85. I am grateful to Geshe Ngawang Gyatso for this reference.

34. See below for my discussion of similarities and differences between Sa-paṇ's terms and Saussure's well-known terms *sign, signified,* and *signifier* (1959), pp. 65–67. Broido (1982), n. 68, and (1983a) argues repeatedly against the simple translation of *sgra* and *don* as "word" and "meaning" in contexts that call for linguistic precision, since he considers the English terms to "flout the principle" that "the linguistic meaning of a word is just the rules governing its use in the language of which it is a part." Thus, a word is nothing apart from its meaning. But there is a significant and meaningful distinction between *sgra* and *don.* Broido's terminology of choice for the *sgra/don* distinction is *convention* and *intention* (and related elements of these categories), but he also cites favorably K. K. Rāja's translation of *śabda/artha* as *signifiant/signifié* as well as Williams's (1980) translation of *rjod-byed/brjod-bya* as "language"/"referents of language." Although I have not followed Broido's advice all the way down the line in translating *sgra* and *don,* my translation inherits this tradition of interpretation and I hope not to conflate Broido's quite correct distinctions. See note 46 below.

35. TR 167.15–16: *dngos kyi brjod byed sgra spyi dang zhen pa'i rjod byed sgra rang gi mtshan nyid yin no zhes rnam par dbye ba.*

36. Alternatively, you may have heard the sound not as a sound, but as a *cough,* in which case you *did* create a conceptualization, since no two coughs are the same either. But this time you still did not create a *term generality;* you created an *object generality.*

37. TR 167.14–16: *sgra'i dngos kyi brjod bya sgra don dang zhen pa'i brjod bya don rang mtshan yin la . . . zhes rnam par dbye ba.*

38. This "more or less" is suggested by Dreyfus (1997), p. 274: "By asserting that things are conceived signified, that is, are signified from the conventional point of view of conception, Buddhist epistemology can pretend to do justice to our precritical intuitions, [in] which we use language to refer to reality."

39. TR 167.14–19: *'chad pa'i tshe . . . rnam par dbye ba shes nas gnas lugs la mkhas par 'gyur ro / 'jug pa'i tshe rang mtshan dang spyi so sor ma phye bar gcig tu 'khrul pa la brda sbyar bas tha snyad kyi tshe don rang mtshan thob pa yin no.*

40. TR 158.14: *brjod bya dang rjod byed rtogs pa'i tshul*

41. Here I have translated only the first two of these three parts.

42. TR 167.1–19: *gnyis pa rang 'dod pa la gsum ste/mtshan nyid dang/rab tu dbye ba dang de'i don gtan la dbab pa'o // dang po ni/brda las go bya go byed yin // brjod bya'i mtshan nyid brdas go bar bya ba yin la/rjod byed ni don go bar byed pa'i brda'o // nyis pa rab tu dbye ba ni/'chad dang 'jug pa'i gang zag gi // dbye bas gnyis gnyis rnam pa bzhi // 'chad pa dang 'jug pa'i dus kyi brjod bya rjod byed gnyis gnyis bzhi'o // 'chad tshe rnam par phye bas mkhas // 'jug tshe gcig tu 'krul pas thob // 'chad pa'i tshe sgra'i dngos kyi brjod bya sgra don dang zhen pa'i brjod bya don rang mtshan yin la dngos kyi rjod byed sgra spyi dang zhen pa'i rjod byed sgra rang gi mtshan nyid yin no zhes rnam par dbye ba shes nas gnas lugs la mkhas par 'gyur ro/'jug pa'i tshe rang mtshan dang spyi so sor ma phye bar gcig tu 'khrul pa la brda sbyar bas tha snyad kyi tshe don rang mtshan thob pa yin no.*

43. TR 170.4–5: *des na sgra'i dngos kyi brjod bya med la zhen pa'i brjod bya 'jug yul nyid yin no.*

44. Dreyfus (1997a), pp. 272–73. See also Raja (1969), p. 25. In truth, I am dubious about the use of the term "sign" to translate *brda,* as Dreyfus does. Precritically, *brda* can mean "symbol" or "word." In the passage I translated from the TR, Sa-paṇ uses *brda* to indicate the cause of "what is to be understood" (*go bar bya ba*), and then, qualifying it as "what brings about understanding of an object," *equates* it with the "signifier" (*rjod byed*). Saussure (1959), p. 67, of course, uses "sign [*signe*]" to mean the unity of *both signifier and signified.* While, for Sa-paṇ, *brda* has a part to play in each, it seems more appropriate to say that *brda* means something like the ordinary English word "sign," which, as I understand it, leans toward the *signifier* side of Saussure's *sign.*

45. These terms have a long history in Sanskrit grammatical analysis, and I have no intention of defending a Saussurian translation for any context other than Sa-paṇ's works. My analysis is limited enough in its treatment of Sa-paṇ alone. For instance, given more space I would prefer not to have to discuss a passage from Sa-paṇ's TR without referring directly to the works of the Indian philosopher Dharmakīrti, since the TR purports to be an analytical introduction to Dharmakīrti's works. And, much work needs to be done to distinguish more clearly Sa-paṇ's understanding of this terminology from that of other Tibetans. For the time being, however, I am satisfied if I can illuminate Sa-paṇ's purposes in including the "term generality" in the *Gateway.*

46. Dreyfus's Saussurian translation is useful for this chapter's "first pass" at Sa-paṇ's linguistic argument, but I am also fairly well convinced by Broido's (1983a), p. 27 ff., more nuanced discussion of these terms in his analysis of *bshad thabs* ("methods of explaining the Tantras"). Broido's view is that *brjod bya sgra* refers to linguistic *convention* and *rjod byed don* refers to the *intention,* rather than the *word meaning* of a textual unit. This is not in contradiction to the general

point of this chapter, though it would appear to disallow my rather simplistic parallels between Sa-paṇ and Saussure. My belief, however, is that Sa-paṇ sees no difference between the *intended meaning* and the *meaning* of a term—for, to understand a word is to understand the intention of the speaker. Given that a speaker's intention (*brjod 'dod*) is at work at every level of linguistic construction (see below), the meaning of the words *is* the words' *intention.* As long as this is understood, we need not adhere to Broido's rejection of the translation of *don* as "meaning."

47. Saussure (1959), p. 66.

48. Saussure (1959), p. 66.

49. GL 377.8–9: *yi ge'i mtshan nyid ni/don mi ston pa'i sgra spyi snang ba zhes bya ba yin la.*

50. GL 377.19–20: *ming yin zhes ming gi mtshan nyid ni don gyi ngo bo ston par byed pa'i sgra spyi snang ba'o.*

51. GL 378.3–4: *tshig gi mtshan nyid ni don gyi khyad par ston pa'i sgra spyi snang ba ste.*

52. Saussure (1959), p. 67 ff.

53. Saussure (1959), p. 68.

54. Tillemans (2000), pp. 219–28, gives a useful introduction to the Buddhist epistemologists' critique of the Mīmāṃsā and the Vyākaraṇa views on the intrinsic fitness (*yogyatā*) between words and meanings. See also Raja (1969).

55. See chapter 2

56. TR 167.18–19: *brda sbyar bas tha snyad kyi tshe don rang mtshan thob pa yin no.*

57. The other, longer, part of this argument requires a more detailed understanding of the Buddhist epistemologists' description of the conceptual apparatus, in particular the doctrine of "elimination of other" (*anyāpoha, gzhan sel*). See Siderits (1987), pp. 335 ff., for an analysis of how Dharmakīrti's argument provides for the proper functioning of conceptualization within a larger context of error.

58. GL 430.7–12: *rgyas par shes par 'dod na/bdag nyid chen po bsod nams rtse mos mdzad pa'i chos la 'jug pa'i sgo las gsungs pa ltar/dpon slob kyi mtshan nyid dang/chos bshad nyan bya ba'i tshul dang/bdud kyi sde tshar gcad pa'i gzungs sngags la sogs pa legs par gsungs pas der blta bar bya'o.*

59. GD 527.1: *chos lugs zhes bya ba ci zhe na/rang rang gi thabs dang thabs las byung ba'i rnam par gzhag pa'i gzhung lugs te/de ni de la blo 'chos pa'i phyir ram/blo 'dul bar byed pa'i phyir chos zhes bya'o.*

60. This bidirectional authentication of the Buddha's doctrine is present in the standard structure of Buddhist *sūtras,* which always begin with a description of the context for a Buddha's speech (justification of the authenticity of the source), and always end with a description of the delight of the audience (justification of the authenticity of the effect, or goal).

61. In my translation, I have reversed the order of "realization" (*rtogs pa*) and "scripture" (*lung*) in order to make the verse and commentary (below) easier to follow.

62. GD 533.3: *mdzod las / ston pa'i dam chos rnam gnyis te // lung dang rtogs pa'i bdag nyid do // de 'dzin byed dang smra byed pa // sgrub par byed pa kho na yin // zhes gsungs te.*

63. GD 533.3: *de la rtogs pa'i chos ni gang zag 'phags pa rnams la 'byung ba ste / dbyings glo bur gyi dri ma las grol ba 'gog pa mthar thug dang / de snang ba med pa'i shes pas bskyed pa lam mthar thug pa'o / lung gi chos ni de thob par byed pa'i thabs su gyur pas te / rang gi rnam par rtog pa la sgra spyi dang don spyi 'dres pa can gyi rnam par snang ba yin la / de'i rkyen byed ba sgra rang gi mtshan nyid dang / glegs bam la sogs pa la'ang btags te gzhag go.*

64. For an explanation of the different goals of Hīnayāna and Mahāyāna Buddhism at play here, see Mario D'Amato's study of *vimukti* in the *Mahāyānasūtrālaṃkāra* (2000), pp. 76–98. See also my note 7 on the derogatory implication of the term "Hīnayāna."

65. GL 378.12–15: *ngag 'dus pa las brjod bya phyogs re ston pa rab byed dang / phyogs 'ga' zhig ston pa le'u dang / de nyid la rnam grangs rjod byed dang / yongs su bcad pa dang / rim par phye ba la sogs pa'i ming can chos kyi phung po'i bar du 'grub bo.*

66. Cabezón (1994), pp. 34–35.

67. The Tibetan *brjod 'dod* is the standard Tibetan translation of *vivakṣā* but interestingly it also literally translates the very old, perhaps Vedic, term *vaktur icchā*—"the desire to speak"—from which the notion of *vivakṣā* developed. Radicci (1993), pp. 221–22.

68. The same may not be said of *alaṃkārika* texts, since, as Radicchi (1993), pp. 229–30, notes, Ānandavardhana thematized *vivakṣā* as a poetical/stylistic element.

69. GL 371.2.

70. *vivakṣāvyāpter iṣṭāvasāyaḥ*. Radicci (1993), p. 228: "It is what one wants to express that commands the desiderata of grammar, that indicates what forms we want to see regularized by grammar."

71. PV 2.16: *vivakṣā-paratantratvān na śabdāḥ santi kutra vā*. Sa-paṇ cites this passage at GL 389.7–8: *brjod par 'dod pa'i gzhan dbang phyir // sgra rnams gang la'ang med ma yin.*

72. It is not as though Sa-paṇ combined separate terms. Ruegg (1989), pp. 28–29, describes a development of Patañjali's use of *vivakṣā* as a simple "intention to express" through the later grammarians' understanding of intention justifying a particular word form, to Dharmakīrti's view in the passage Sa-paṇ cites below.

73. GL 377.10–15: *de lta na yi ge re re'i nges brjod las / A dang ka la sogs pa la 'jam dpal dang / tshangs pa la sogs par shad pa dang / bod la yang yi ge re res*

ming du 'gyur ba mthong bas ma nges so zhe na/mi 'gal te rnam dbye 'am brjod 'dod kyi sgo nas go ba yin gyi/yi ge ldog pas go ba ma yin te/ha cang thal bar 'gyur ba'i phyir ro.

74. Sa-paṇ brings up this issue again in the EW, 507.17 ff., using as examples the Tibetan words *nga* and *ma*. In Tibetan, both are printed with a single character—as is the English word *I*, for that matter.

75. The "or" in "case endings *or* the speech intention" seems to imply the possibility of case endings without a speaker's intention, but this possibility is vitiated by the grammatical principle, cited above, that all case endings are universally concomitant with the speech intention.

76. GL 378.1: *yi ge 'dus pa tsam gyis ming du mi 'gyur te.*

Chapter 4. The Expert Knows the Context

1. For a lucid introduction to the relevant issues in Buddhist scriptural interpretation, see Davidson (1990). Most of the current discussion of Buddhist hermeneutics dates from the late 1970s, though Lamotte's 1949 article was a crucial contribution (on which much later work relies), and a few streams of discussion began earlier, such as Bhattacarya (1928) and Wayman (1968, 1973). For issues of relevance to this chapter, see especially Bond (1988), Broido (1980, 1982, 1983a, 1983b, 1984a, 1984b, 1985a, 1985b, 1988a, and 1988b), Cabezón (1992, 1994), Hallisey (1994), Hamlin (1983), Kapstein (1988, 1989), Katz (1983), Lopez (1988a, 1988b), Ruegg (1977, 1985, 1988), Steinkellner (1978), Thurman (1978, 1988), and Williams (1980). It should be noted that Broido (1983a, especially, but also elsewhere) resists using the term "hermeneutics" with regard to what Tibetans call *bshad thabs,* "methods of explanation [of the tantras]."

2. Kapstein (1988), pp. 164–66, argues that Buddhism is ultimately a "hermeneutical endeavor" in the sense that the "continuing integrity of the Buddha's teaching in the world" relies upon the proper "interpretation" both of the teachings themselves and, from practicing them, of reality itself.

3. Cabezón (1994), p. 55.

4. Broido (1988a), pp. 86–87.

5. See Kapstein (1988), p. 149 ff., for the useful distinction between *interpretations, rules for interpretation,* and "a complete *theory of interpretation.*" This chapter describes, in Kapstein's terms, an *implicit theory of interpretation.*

6. One can probably most easily imagine a conservative against gay marriage making this claim in order to shore up the position that heterosexual marriage is the traditional standard, but one can also imagine a liberal pointing out that while marriage might conventionally mean a heterosexual union, this convention is *only* a convention, and not an ultimate reality. But the position in fa-

vor of legalized gay marriage would perhaps be better served by rejecting the claim that the word "marriage" has a heterosexual implication, and positing that in fact "marriage" does *not* conventionally refer to men or women, but only to a union between two people.

7. GL 379.16: *la lar grags pa nyid grags par 'gyur bas.*

8. Like Kripke, Sa-paṇ appeals to experts as the guardians of truth in a causal theory of meaning.

9. Van der Kuijp (1983), p. 5.

10. Van der Kuijp (1983), p. 258, n. 10.

11. Van der Kuijp (1983), p. 258, n. 10. Broido has also repeatedly pointed out that Tibetan interpretive schemes tend to be classified under the rubric of "methods of exposition" (*bshad thabs*), using the exact word *bshad* that is the title of the *Gateway's* second chapter ("[On] Exposition").

12. For a survey of the *Gateway*'s hermeneutic categories and terms, see Verhagen (2005).

13. Probably as filtered through Haribhadra's *Abhisamayālaṃkāra-Sphuṭārthā.*

14. Broido (1983a), p. 23, points out that Sönam Tsemo is perhaps the clearest and most comprehensive of Tibetan writers on the issues of tantric hermeneutics that he addresses.

15. See chapter 3.

16. See Broido (1983a, 1988a), Steinkellner (1978), and Thurman (1978 and 1988).

17. Sa-paṇ's arguments against the *dgongs gcig* doctrine and other so-called new Chinese doctrines have been the subject of much research in Sakyapa scholarship. See especially David Seyfort Ruegg (1989), D. Jackson (1990, 1994), Broido (1987), van der Kuijp (1983, 1986), and R. Jackson (1982), and, for a concise statement of the current state of research, Kapstein (2000), p. 253, n. 33. The most comprehensive treatment is Jackson (1994), and my discussion of Jigten Gonpo here as well as my translations from *Gateway* chapter 2 rely on Jackson (1994), p. 108, n. 254, which appears in the midst of Jackson's translation of this same concluding section of *Gateway* chapter 2 (Jackson's pp. 107–109).

18. GL 457.20–458.6: */'ga' zhig sangs rgyas kyi gsung thams cad nges don kho na yin gyis drang don mi srid de/gal te drang don yod na sangs rgyas* [458] *brdzun gsung bar 'gyur ro zhes zer ro // de dag gis mdo rgyud kyi dgongs pa ma shes par zad de/nges don kho na yin na sku gsum dang sde snod gsum dang bslab pa gsum la sogs pa'i rnam gzhag tha dad pa phal cher 'gal bar 'gyur te/rnam gzhag tha dad don dam pa nges pa'i don la gar yod/tha snyad kun rdzob drang ba'i don la brten nas mdzad do.*

19. In refuting the single-intention doctrine, Sa-paṇ does not need to survey the scriptures and show the differences between doctrinal claims in dif-

ferent words of Buddhas and Bodhisattvas. Instead, he simply makes reference to the doctrinal systematizations themselves, which are attested in various scriptures. The adversary must not only account for a variety of contradictory views as being all of "definitive meaning." He must also explain how his own view of a single intention can stand in the face of clear doctrinal statements that the scriptures have multiple intentions, without contradicting his own view that *these doctrines too* must be of definitive meaning only.

20. GL 457.6–14: *dgongs pa bshad pa ni mnyam pa nyid la sogs pa dgongs pa bzhi dang/gzhug pa la ldem por dgongs pa la sogs pa ldem dgongs bzhi shes pas sangs rgyas dang byang chub sems dpa'i tshig don 'gal bar snang ba rnams dgongs pa shes pas mi 'gal bar 'gyur ro // 'di dag rgyas par yi ge mangs kyis dogs pas ma bris te/mdo sde rgyan la sogs par blta bar bya'o // dgongs pa ma yin pa bshad pa ni/de ltar dgongs pa gzhan btsal mi dgos par tshig don de nyid kyis sangs rgyas kyi dgongs pa dngos su 'phrod pa'o.*

21. GL 458.11–18: *bsgra ji bzhin pa ni/sbyin pas longs spyod khrims kyis bde // zhes bya ba la sogs pa dge ba dang bsod nams dang ye shes kyi tshogs la sogs pa sgra ji lta ba bzhin don la 'jug pa'o // sgra ji bzhin ma yin pa ni // pha dang ma ni gsad bya zhing // zhes bya ba la sogs pa sgra de don gzhan la 'jug pa ste/mdo rgyud rnams dang snyan ngag gi bstan bcos 'ga' zhig la ji ltar 'byung ba ltar ro // 'di dag gi tshul rgyas par yi ge mangs kyis dogs pas ma bris so.*

22. GL 458.19–459.1: */mtha' drug mi shes na mdo rgyud gang bshad kyang nor bar 'gyur te/slob dpon zla ba grags pas/mtha' drug bral bas nges par rtogs zhes gang smra ba // zla ba lta 'dod sor mo'i rtse la lta dang mtshungs // zhes gsungs* [459] *pa ltar ro/*

23. GL 379.17–380.3: *rdzogs sangs rgyas kyis gdul bya'i ngor // 'jig rten bstan bcos la med pa'i // brda ni skye bo'i spyod yul min // kun mkhyen dgongs pa bsam mi khyab // mdo rgyu dag las/pha dang ma ni bsad bya zhing // zhes bya ba dang/rgya mtsho gang du ldog par 'gyur // zhes bya ba dang/ko taksh la sogs pa'i sgra sangs rgyas kyis brda mdzad pa* [380] *ni/'ga' zhig gi rgyu mtshan cung zad shes par snang yang/phyogs gcig kho na yin pa'i nges pa med pas tshu rol mthong ba rnams kyis dpyad dka' ba'i phyir/ji ltar gsungs pa de ltar gzung bar bya'o.*

24. See Broido (1988a). Thurman (1988), p. 139, translates the relevant passage from the *Pradīpodyottanā* as follows: "The special communications of Buddha,/Using (coined) words such as *koṭākhyā*,/Not found in the mundane sciences;/These are symbolic teachings."

25. I will elaborate upon each of these passages below. It may be objected that these parallels are overdetermined, since the hermeneutic categories are sufficiently general to resemble any number of linguistic categorizations. While there is some truth to this, my discussion below will evince further connections between hermeneutic categories and linguistic analyses, and in any event, such a general argument would fail to account for similarities such as the repetition

of example and target interlocutor that appear in the quote just cited. If it is objected that there is no evidence of "mixing" of disciplines here since four of the six limits *simply are* linguistic categorizations, I would submit that this is not so much an objection to my argument as it is a question-begging expectation of Sapaṇ's conclusion: It fails to ask why hermeneutic categories of linguistic analysis, which are ordinarily indexed in each case to specific categories of the Buddha's intentions, have been effaced into the general linguistic categories that they resemble.

26. GL 457.3–4: */mtha' drug gang gis shes pa de // gzhung bshad pa la shin tu mkhas.*

27. GL 458.19–20: *mtha' drug mi shes na mdo rgyud gang bshad kyang nor bar 'gyur te.*

28. 1.2.2: Proper Linguistic Application (GL 378.16–391.4).

29. This refers to the section I call "Proper Linguistic Application" in the outline to chapters 1 and 2 of the *Gateway,* Appendix A. Ngag dbang chos grags's commentary (1998), whose primary genius is in its systematization of the *Mkhas 'jug,* does a brilliant job of making order out of this jumble of topics. But in order to do so it makes use of forty subheadings in less than fourteen pages of commentary (see his *dkar chag,* pp. 6–7). Tashi Chöpel (1998) doesn't bother to explain the order, and instead calls the whole section *ming tshig bye brag tu bshad pa,* including therein even the discussions of *ngag* and *ngag tshogs* which are, I think, more logically connected with the earlier section. See his *dkar chag,* p. 2.

30. GL 378–82: "Specific Problems in Word-Meaning Relations." See appendix.

31. GL 382–91. "General Problems in Signification." See appendix.

32. A note on the Buddha's intentionality: While the classification of a Buddha's intentions pose some significant problems for Buddhists—see Griffiths (1994) and Dunne (1996)—it is a mistake to assume that a lack of intentions in a Buddha's mental state ought to disqualify the intentionality of the statements of the Buddha. As Searle (1983), pp. 27–28, and others have made clear, speech acts include a two-fold intentionality: we have an intention in expressing our words (such as to declare our belief in a proposition, or to propose a hypothesis, or to vow to do something), and we also endow the words themselves with intentions with specific "conditions of satisfaction" (as Searle puts it). This latter act of endowing sounds with intentions is an ordinary human capability, like walking or chewing. We need not know exactly how it is done to recognize that the Buddha might be able to endow words with specific intentions, without himself having more than the first kind of intention, which could be a very general intention to free all beings from suffering. For example, I can ask someone the time in order to see if he is awake. While my words would have been

endowed with a certain intention (which would not be satisfied except by an appropriate response to the question), I need not actually care what time it is, or even believe that time matters at all.

33. I will not waste space arguing what I take to be obvious, that the section as a whole displays the scholar to be the authoritative mediator of the signifier/signified relation. In addition, however, for the sake of brevity I am setting aside several other points deserving of special note, such as Sa-paṇ's repeated use of the term *brjod 'dod* and his integration of linguistic and epistemological issues both in his discussion of classifying and naming expressions (GL 382.13–383.14), and in his lengthy discussion of assertions and negations (GL 383.15–385.11).

34. GL 378.16–19: *ming tshig de dag rgan po yis // thog mar sbyar ba brda yin la // phyis nas dpyod pa tha snyad yin // dngos po rnams la ming dang tshig tu btags pa rgan po rnams kyis brjod 'dod kho na'i dbang gis sbyar ba ni brda yin la / phyis de'i rjes su dpyod pa ni tha snyad ces bya'o.* Interestingly, the discussion that follows never again takes up this term "term" (*tha snyad*), using instead the term "secondary expression" (*rjes sgrub sgra*). The first is from the SDL, the second more in line with Dignāga's grammatical discussions from the *Pramāṇasamuccaya* as Sa-paṇ presents them in the *Treasury*. It would seriously delay our argument to point out all of Sa-paṇ's combinations and equations of terms from various literatures, but this is one of his methods of displaying the unity and comprehensiveness of the scholar's knowledge.

35. I take *brtan* from D 13.12 as a correction of GL 379.2 *brten*.

36. GL 378.20–379.4: *de yi dang po 'dod rgyal sgra // de la brten nas phyis nas don // gzhan la sgro 'dogs rjes sgrub sgra // dang po rgyu mtshan la ma ltos par* [379] *rang dgar brda ci'ang rung ba ni 'dod rgyal gyi sgra lte / shing dang ba lang la sogs pa'o // de la brten nas 'dra ba dang 'brel pa la sogs pa rgyu mtshan du byas te / brten* [?*brtan*] *pa la shing dang / blun po la ba lang la sogs par sgro 'dogs pa ni rjes 'jug gi sgra'o.* Note that here "subsequent expression" (*rjes 'jug sgra, anuvartana-śabda*) is a gloss on the verse's "supervenient expression" (*rjes sgrub sgra, anusiddha-śabda*). The terms "autonomous expression" (*'dod rgyal sgra*) and "supervenient expression" (*rjes sgrub sgra*) take up a large port of the SDL's *ming gi tshogs* section, in a position parallel to Sa-paṇ's placement of his linguistic subsection (SDL 35 ff.). The important difference between these verses in the GL and the SDL, then, is Sa-paṇ's insertion of the verses on the *rgan po*-s and the invention of words based on *brjod 'dod* alone.

37. The *Triṃśikāvijñapti-bhāṣya* attributed to Sthiramati, for instance, defines *upacāra* (metaphor; figure) with the statement that "A word is used figuratively with regard to something which is not there, as when [one calls] a Bahīkan [person] an ox." Lévi (1925), p. 16: *yac ca yatra nāsti tat tatropacaryate / tad yathā bahīke gauḥ.* There are resonances between the terms here

delineated and the traditional grammatical analysis of words as having four kinds of meanings: *yaugika, rūḍha, yogarūdha,* and *yaugikarūḍha.* See Raja (1969), pp. 59–63.

38. GL 379.5–11: *slan chad mi sbyar don de la // brda 'jug na yang mi rtogs phyir // brda spyod pa'i mkhas pa dag gis // brda gsar pa ma sbyar na don mi 'grub pa mthong na gsar pa sbyar ba mi 'gal mod/'on kyang dgos pa chung ngu la brda gsar pa mi sbyar te/ma rtogs pa dang/log par rtogs pa dang/the tshom gyi rgyu yin pa'i phyir ro/dper na sman pa dang/mngon dpyod [spyod?] mkhan po'i brda bzhin no.* Here, on the suggestion of K. N. Mishra (personal communication), I read *mngon spyod mkhan po,* meaning *abhicārin,* "magician," rather than *mngon dpyod mkhan po,* so the point is that black magicians, like doctors, make up all sorts of words appropriate to the particulars of their technical arena, but that these are not applicable to a general context.

39. GL 380.4–6: *mkhas pa rnams kyis ngo 'phrod pa'i // brda ni rjes sgrub nyid yin te // rgyu mtshan dag la ltos phyir ro.*

40. Because drinking from the spring causes a leg sickness.

41. The knowledge, *shes pa,* is named after its cause, the knowing (*shes*), and the holder of a cognitive object (*yul can,* less literally translated as "subject") is named after the cognitive object (*yul*).

42. The sound of a drum comes not only from the drum, but also from the stick and the drummer, and likewise the sprout comes not only from the seed but also from the soil and water, and so forth.

43. This is a medicine that looks like a crow's leg.

44. Indian astrology has Tuesday as an inauspicious day.

45. Indian astrology divides the day into eleven *kāraṇas,* and the seventh, *viṣṭi,* is considered inauspicious.

46. GL 380.13–381.1: *phan tshun 'brel pa ste rgyu la 'bras bu'i ming btags pa lteng ka rkang nad lta bu'o // 'bras bu la rgyu'i ming btags pa shes pa'am yul can lta bu'o // tshogs pa la ya gyal gyi ming btags pa rnga'i sgra'am nas kyi myu gu lta bu/ya gyal la tshogs pa'i ming btags pa/ras yug gi phyogs gcig tshig pa la ras yug tshig pa'am/khang pa'i phyogs gcig mthong ba la khang pa mthong ba lta bu/'dra ba rgyu mtshan du byas pa/sman bya rog rkang ngam/mi blun po la ba lang du btags pa lta bu/'dra ba bzlog pa mi blun po la lha rnams dga' ba dang/'brel pa bzlog pa gza' mig dmar la bkra shis sam/byed pa biṣṭi la bzang po zhes* [381] *btags pa lta bu thams cad du brtags la shes par bya'o.*

47. TR 167.14–19: *'chad pa'i tshe . . . rnam par dbye ba shes nas gnas lugs la mkhas par 'gyur ro/'jug pa'i tshe rang mtshan dang spyi so sor ma phye bar gcig tu 'khrul pa la brda sbyar bas tha snyad kyi tshe don rang mtshan thob pa yin no.*

48. TR 305.7–10: *ming la bshad 'jug rnam pa gnyis/bshad pa'i rgyu mtshan can gyi sgra thams cad mkhyen pa la sogs pa yi ge so sor bshad pa las thob pa dang 'jug pa'i rgyu mtshan can shing la sogs pa'i ming ngo.*

49. This terminological distinction is undoubtedly related to the traditional Sanskrit grammatical distinction between meaning that is analyzed through grammatical rule, *yoga*, and that which is merely convention, *rūḍha*. But since Sa-paṇ's usage here is different from his usage in the *Gateway*, where he also seems to be at least partially employing the traditional fourfold characterization *yaugika, rūḍha, yogarūḍha*, and *yaugikarūḍha,* I have decided to opt for simplicity and simply use Sa-paṇ's Tibetan presentation instead of tracing each usage back to its closest Sanskrit original. See Abhyankar (1977), p. 326.

50. TR 305.14–306.2: *bshad 'jug 'gal ba'i sgra bye'u til 'thung ngam/bya lug rdzi mo la sogs pa'o // mi 'gal ba'i sgra thams cad mkhyen pa'am rnam par shes pa la sogs pa'o // 'gal zhing mi 'gal ba ni 'gal 'du mu gsum pa ste/dper na mtsho skyes lta bu ste/'jug pa ni padmo la 'jug la bshad na mtsho las skyes pa'i phyir mtsho skyes so // de la mu gsum ste/mtsho las skyes pa'i padmo la bshad 'jug gnyis ka yod la/skam las skyes pa'i padmo la 'jug pa 'ba' zhig yod cing/mtsho las skyes pa'i srog chags la bshad pa 'ba' zhig yod pas so // 'o na skam sa'i sdong dum la bshad* [306] *'jug gnyis ka med pas mu bzhi pa ma yin nam zhe na/yin mod kyi mtsho skyes zhes pa'i ming la mi 'jug pas mu bzhi par mi bgrang ngo.*

51. This makes "lake born" a special case where two terms which have a relation of "fourfold *logical* possibility" in fact find only three *reasonable* possibilites. This is a clever but anomalous use of the notion of a "threefold logical possibility," which generally refers only to pairs of terms that are related through necessity, such as "tree" and "oak": there really is no ("fourth") possibility of having something which is "oak" but not "tree."

52. Again, these levels of linguistic analysis resemble, but do not exactly exactly match, the traditional Sanskrit grammarians' distinction between *yaugika* and *rūḍhi.* See Abhyankar (1977), p. 326, and note 49 above.

53. See chapter 2, above.

54. Michael Broido's work consists largely in an analysis of these issues.

55. On Smṛtijñānakīrti and the SDL see Smith (2001), p. 192.

56. SDL 45.19–20: *grags pa'i yan lag bsdu ba la yang 'jig rten la grags pa dang/bstan bcos la grags pa gnyis te.*

57. SDL 46.1–3: *'jig rten la grags pa ka ba bum pa la sogs pa'i tha snyad byas pa lta bu'o // bstan bcos la grags pa ni las la sogs pa'i byed pa'i tshig byed pa lta bu'o.* Note that the SDL refers to "pot" and "pillar" as *tha snyad,* "conventional."

58. Cardona (1974), Scharfe (1977), Matilal (1990), pp. 40–48, and Saini (1999).

59. Again, these terminological distinctions reflect Sa-paṇ's familiarity with the Indian grammatical traditions. See, for instance, Raja (1969), pp. 63 ff., on "*Etymology versus Popular Usage.*" Further research is needed to determine where Sa-paṇ concurs and where he differs from other traditional grammatical analyses.

60. Broido (1983a) discusses both sixfold schemes, and their relation, in the GATC and other Tibetan sources.

61. Interestingly, the GATC's classification of well-known usages is somewhat different from the SDL's (45.14–20), which distinguishes *grags pa'i yan lag bsdu ba* from *don gyi yan lag bsdu ba* in a listing of *bsdu ba bzhi* (the other two are *'brel ba'i yan lag bsdu ba* and *go rim gyi yan lag bsdu ba*). Although I am arguing here that Buddhist hermeneutical concerns predominate in the *Gateway*, the SDL's linguistic categorizations also underlie these structures, and it is exceedingly difficult to separate out the methods of explanation of linguists and of hermeneuts. This chapter remains a first attempt to untangle Sa-paṇ's complexly intertwined influences.

62. GATC 64b1–4: *yan lag gi don ni/'jig rten las grags pa'i sgra dang bcas/bstan bcos las grags pa'i sgra dang bcas/sgra 'jug pa'i rgyu mtshan nges pa'i tshig dang bcas pas gzhung dngos kyi don la 'jug pa'o // de'ang 'jig rten las grags pa ni dper na rgyu me shel las grub pa nam mkha' la gnas pa tsa ba 'od can de la nyi ma zhes grags so // de nyid la bstan bcos las bcu gnyis pa dang/'od zer brgya pa dang/padmo'i gnyen dang/snang byed dang/nyin mor byed pa la sogs pa grags pa bzhin no // sgra 'jug pa'i rgyu mtshan yang nyi ma la khyim bcu gnyis yod pas dang/padmo kha 'byed pas dang/mun pa sel ba mtshan mo 'joms pa la sogs pa yon tan du ma yod pas de dang de dag tu gdags su rung bas tshul 'di lta bu rnams la yan lag gi don gyis bshad do.* Broido (1983a), p. 30, discusses this passage in his summary of *bshad thabs* from the GATC. The following is his translation, in which he has left an unfortunate ellipsis:

> *yan lag gi don gyis bshad pa* means manifesting the point of the text having *sgra* well known in the world, *sgra* known from the *śāstras*, and etymologies which cause *sgra* to become manifest . . . for instance the cause for *sgra* to become manifest is the fact that the sun has twelve stations in the sky, that it causes lotuses to open, that it dispels the darkness, defeats the night and so forth, and by these many properties it becomes suitable to designate (*gdags su rung ba*).

By leaving out the examples of terms "well known in the world" and "well known in treatises," Broido makes it unclear that the "etymologies which cause *sgra* to become manifest" are explanations of the terms well known in treatises. Then, in his analysis, Broido distinguishes between the first part of his translation, which "is a description of ordinary lexical or literal interpretation," and the second part, which "is a description of how it comes about that the use of 'sun' is governed by linguistic *convention*." As my translation and analysis make clear, however, the first and second "parts" of the passage both describe ordinary lexical or literal interpretation: It is just that ordinary interpretation *depends upon* linguistic convention, and in cases of possible confusion, *refers to* it.

63. TR 305.8–9: *yi ge so sor bshad pa las thob pa*. The main difference is that Sa-paṇ points specifically to the "letters" (*yi ge*, perhaps closer, "phonemes"), rather than what Sönam Tsemo calls the meaning's "parts" (*yan lag*), which I translate as "linguistic elements." In fact, as I will explain below, Sa-paṇ includes both of Sönam Tsemo's *first two* categories—that is, both *yi ge'i don* and *yan lag gi don*—under the umbrella category of "well known in treatises."

64. GL 437.10–437.20: *thog mar sgra dang mi 'gal tshig rnam par phye ste bshad do // de la 'jig rten la grags pa/bstan bcos la grags pa/thun mong ma yin pa la grags pa'i sgra gsum/dang po ni 'jig rten thams cad la thun mong du grags pa ka ba dang bum pa la sogs pa'o // gnyis pa ni sgra pa dag la grags pa rnam par dbye ba dang byed pa'i tshig la sogs pas bsgrubs pa mkhas pa rnams kyis go ba'i brda'o // gsum pa ni 'jig rten dang bstan bcos la ma grags pa/sgra 'jug pa'i rgyu mtshan nges pa'i tshig bshad dka' zhing/'phags pa'i gang zad la dgos pa shin tu che ba/mdo sde dag las kyang cung zad bshad mdo/rgyud sde rnams las mang du bshad pa/de bzhin gshegs pa'i brda zhes grags pa'o/'di rgyud sde bshad pa na dgos kyi 'dir skabs ma yin pas re zhig bzhag go.*

65. GL 438.3–5: *bstan bcos la grags pa'i sgra la/sgra drang por bshad pa/drangs nas bshad pa/phan tshun bsgyur te bshad pa'o.*

66. As I have noted, Sa-paṇ cites the *Treasury* at several points within the *Gateway*. See Jackson (1987), pp. 57–69, for a discussion of the relative chronology of Sa-paṇ's works, and p. 66 for a chart of internal citations and references.

67. GL 381.2–9: *de yang grags 'jug 'gal ba dang // mi 'gal 'gal zhing mi 'gal ba'i // sgra yi 'jug tshul rnam pa bzhi // brda sprod byed pa rnams la grags // grags pa dang 'jug pa mi 'gal ba/mtsho las skyes pa'i padma la mtsho skyes lta bu/grags 'jug 'gal ba mtsho las skyes pa'i padma ma yin pa la mtsho skyes lta bu/'jug kyang ma grags pa mtsho las skyes pa'i ldum bu'am srog chags la sogs pa la mtsho las skyes kyang mtsho skyes su ma grags pa lta bu/grags 'jug gnyis ka med pa skam sa'i rdo dang sdong dum la sogs pa lta bu'o.*

68. GL 388.7–9: *'di 'dra'i sgra sbyor mkhas rnams la // sngon chad grags pa kho nar zad/bod kyi sgra 'di ni rgan po rnams la grags pa gtso bo yin gyis bsgrub pa gtso bo ma yin no.*

69. GL 379.11–16: *brda yi khyad par gzhan dag tu // ma grags gzhan du grags pa la // de ltar mi bsam gzhan dag tu // grags pa grags pa nyid du gsal // brda gang zhig lung la grags shing rigs pa la ma grags pa dang/rigs pa la grags pa lung la ma grags pa dang/sde snod gsum dang/rgyud sde bzhi phan tshun gcig la gcig ma grags kyang/la lar grags pa nyid grags par 'gyur bas skyon med do.* I am grateful to John Dunne for his thoughts on this passage.

70. It may be objected that Sönam Tsemo's hermeneutical discussions are quintessentially Buddhist. But the point I am making is that Sa-paṇ uses Buddhist examples in explicating *grags pa*, which Sönam Tsemo restricted to the di-

rect, literal meanings that (presumably) ought to be comprehensible across sectarian boundaries.

71. GL 372.6–7: *bye brag gang bslabs pa shes pa de la'ang de nyid la mkhas pa zhes bya ba'i ming thob bo.*

72. See chapter 3, note 7 on the polemical nature of the term "Individual Liberation" here.

73. This is in the chapter "Vows of Individual Liberation," verses 26–28 in Rhoton (2002), pp. 44–45.

74. GL 379.17–380.3: *rdzogs sangs rgyas kyis gdul bya'i ngor // 'jig rten bstan bcos la med pa'i // brda ni skye bo'i spyod yul min // kun mkhyen dgongs pa bsam mi khyab // mdo rgyu dag las / pha dang ma ni bsad bya zhing // zhes bya ba dang / rgya mtsho gang du ldog par 'gyur // zhes bya ba dang / ko taksh la sogs pa'i sgra sangs rgyas kyis brda mdzad pa* [380] *ni / 'ga' zhig gi rgyu mtshan cung zad shes par snang yang / phyogs gcig go na yin pa'i nges pa med pas tshu rol mthong ba rnams kyis dpyad dka' ba'i phyir / ji ltar gsungs pa de ltar gzung bar bya'o.*

75. GL 372.5–7: */mkhas pa zhes bya ba gang yin zhe na / shes bya thams cad phyin ci ma log par shes pa yin la / gzhan yang bye brag gang bslabs pa shes pa de la'ang de nyid la mkhas pa zhes bya ba'i ming thob bo.*

76. Sa-paṇ may have used Bhāmaha's presentation in the *Kāvyālaṃkāra* for his discussion of *rasa* in the *Gateway*. I use Vāmana's commentary here to provide a standard interpretation, though Sa-paṇ makes no explicit reference to having learned it (though, on GL 371.18–19 he does write that he is familiar with "[all of these teachings] together with most of their univerally known *vṛtti* commentaries and *ṭīkā* commentaries, and so on." *de dag gi 'grel pa dang / 'grel bshad la sogs pa'i yongs su grags pa*). Still, it is perhaps not necessary to postulate that Sa-paṇ knew of these particular texts. I present these terms as typical examples of poetic virtues of which Sa-paṇ would have had general exposure as part of his education in poetics.

77. Jha's translation from Vāmana (1928) of Vāmana (1927, vs. 8): *śāstramātraprayuktamapratītam.*

78. Jha's translation from Vāmana (1928) of Vāmana (1927, vs. 13): *aprasiddhārthaprayuktaṃ gūḍhārtham.*

79. GL 429.18–21: *mnyan bya'i chos kyang sangs rgyas kyi gsungs / mkhas pa las brgyud / grub thob kyis bsgoms // paṇḍi tas bshad / lo tsā bas bsgyur / rgya gar dang / bod kyi sde snod 'dzin pa mkhas pa thams cad la legs par grags pa'i chos la nyan bshad byed dgos.*

80. GL 446.6–8: *legs par sbyar ba'i skad la mdzes pa byung na / 'jig rten phal cher la ma grags pa'i saṃ skṛ tas sbyar ba yin pas.*

81. GL 429.4–8: *spyir bla ma mkhas shing chos bzhin byed pa mkhas par grags pa zhig la mnyan / mi mkhas na the tshom gcod mi nus / mi btsun na slob ma'i spyod pa chud 'dza' / mkhas par ma grags na slob dpon la med par khyod la gar yod ces brnyas par 'gyur te.*

CHAPTER 5. THE MESSAGE IN THE MEDIUM

1. The only mention of private rumination on scholarly treatises is in fact in Sa-paṇ's description of the activities of the *student* at GL 376.3ff., which I discuss below.

2. See chapter 7, where I discuss a possible response Sa-paṇ might give to Richard Nance's critique of Śāntarakṣita.

3. On this, it is important to note that the word "meaning" (*don*) is generally extended to all three of the explanatory categories, so that all are understood as aspects of the verse's meaning, or point. When Sa-paṇ makes this explicit, I translate the first two topics as "the meaning in its intent" (*dgos don*) and "the meaning in summary form" (*bsdus don*).

4. Here we are to understand that a lion is so proud that he looks across to the horizon, taking everything in at once. Thus, the "lion's glance" is present in the verse of invocation, which thus gives a broad, comprehensive view of the meaning of the treatise.

5. GL 372.21–373.9: *bstan bcos byed* [373] *pa'i dam pa yis // ston pa la ni mchod brjod bya // bstan pa spel phyir dag pa'i tshig // 'di la 'thad pa bzang po mthong // mchod par brjod pa la dgos pa dang/bsdus pa dang/tshig gi don gsum las/dgos pa la gnyis te/rtsom pa po rang gi rgyud la 'byung ba dang/bshad nyan byed pa gzhan gyi rgyud la 'thob pa'o // bsdus pa'i don la gang la gang gis ji ltar bstod pa la sogs pa'o // tshig gi don ni seng ge'i lta stangs kyis ngag don btsal la/rus sbal gyi 'gros kyis gzhung don bshad pa ste/rgyas par rang rang gi gzhung rtsom dang 'chad pa'i skabs su shes par bya'o.*

6. Here the Tibetan leaves out the subject, which makes for elegant Tibetan but unacceptable English; so I have chosen to insert the guru as subject.

7. GL 369.8–12: *bstan bcos kyi thog mar mchod par brjod pa 'dis ci bstan zhe na/bla ma dang 'jam pa'i dbyangs dus gsum gyi sangs rgyas thams cad kyi ngo bo yin pas de'i yon tan cha tsam brjod na'ang mthar thug 'tshang rgya zhing/gnas skabs bar chad zhi ba'i rgyur 'gyur bar bsams nas ngag dang po brjod do.*

8. For instance, Sa-paṇ's verse of reverence from the *Treasury* is prominent in the Sakyapa monastic liturgy.

9. GL 428.1–2: *'chad par byed pa slob dpon dang // bshad par bya ba'i yul slob ma // bshad par bya ba'i chos so.*

10. "What is the definition of a scholar? Pure, scholarly and with a desire to benefit others. . . . The definition of a student is: A clear mind, a desire to understand, and devotion to the master." GL 428.2–8: *de la slob dpon gyi mtshan nyid gang zhe na/gtsang mkhas gzhan la phan par 'dod/. . . . blo ma'i mtshan nyid ni/blo gsal shes 'dod bla mar gus.*

11. "A mind of indolence that wanders in the ten directions, when you explain fears of this life such as old age, death, etc., and fears of later lives, such

as hell, etc.—dangers of samsara into which one has fallen for all time—should settle into a mind of dharma." GL 444.16–19: *sems rgod pas phyogs bcur rnam par g.yeng ba la rga shi la sogs pa tshe 'di'i 'jigs pa dang/ngan song la sogs pa tshe phyi ma'i 'jigs pa dang/dus thams cad du skabs su bab pa'i 'khor ba'i nyes dmigs rnams bshad la/sems chos la 'bab par bya'o.*

12. "For those who are sluggish, an amazing/Tale should be told, making them listen." GL 444.19–20: *rmugs pa rnams ni ngo mtshar gyi // gtam bshad nas ni nyan du gzhug.*

13. Faith is therefore a central component in the student's education: "If he does not trust in even the subtle points [of the dharma], he does not know the meaning, the words, and the syllables flawlessly." GL 429.13–14: *tshig don phra mo la yang rton pa ma byas na don dang tshig 'bru phyin ci ma log par mi shes.* Dreyfus (2003), p. 279, believes that the best of Tibetan training takes the form of a dialectical process that requires both faith and a probing, questioning inquiry: "Tibetan scholastic training starts with some belief in the validity of the tradition, some commitment to the inquiry; otherwise, students would not put up with the considerable hardships that this training sometimes entails. It continues with interpretive practices—commentary and debate—that seek to deepen that confidence. To that end, students question the tradition in order to reach their own conclusions." Cf. p. 392, note 22.

14. GL 373.5–6: *bsdus pa'i don la gang la gang gis ji ltar bstod pa la sogs pa'o.*

15. GL 434.8: *las dang byed po bya ba yi // tshig don sprel.*

16. "In this way, whatever texts are being explained, having summarized the basis of characterization (*khyad par gyi gzhi*) from the text, you get the statement meaning; explaining the qualities of characterization (*khyad par gyi chos*), you should classify the words. . . . With the glance of a lion grasp the basis of characterization. With the jumps of a frog, divide up meaning into individual contexts. With the gait of a turtle explain the meaning of the words in pleasant tones (*'jebs par*)." GL 436.18–437.4: *de bzhin du gzhung lugs gang bshad kyang/gzhung las khyad par gyi gzhi bsdus la ngag don blang/khyad par gyi chos bshad de tshig rnam par dbye bar bya'o/. . . .* [437] */seng ge'i lta stangs kyis khyad par gyi gzhi blang/sbal pa'i 'phar bas skabs don so sor dbye/rus sbal gyi 'gros kyis tshig don 'jebs par bshad.*

17. GL 373.8–9: *rgyas par rang rang gi gzhung rtsom dang 'chad pa'i skabs su shes par bya'o.*

18. GL 374.1–4: *bshad par dam bca' ba la sogs pa gal te 'chad na mi dgos la/mi 'chad na don med do snyam na/dam bca' ba dang bskul tshig sogs/'chad phyir spro ba ston pa ste // mchog rtogs 'grub pa'i rgyur 'gyur bas // khas len pa la 'gal ba med.*

19. GL 374.6–10: *dang po bshad par bya'o zhes khas blangs pas gzhung 'chad pa la spro ba ston la/spro ba'i rgyu don bzang po la 'jug ste/rgyal po rgyal sar 'byin pa*

dang/chos kyi 'khor lo bskor ba lta bu la khas len gyi/sho dang mig mangs la sogs pa bya ba ngan pa byed du 'jug kyang tshogs kyi dbus su khas mi len to.

20. The term "illocutionary act" is, of course, J. L. Austin's term for an intentional act one completes through speaking, "i.e., performance of an act *in* saying something as opposed to performance of an act *of* saying something" (Austin and Searle 1986, p. 835). Is it a coincidence that Searle's paradigmatic analysis of the rules governing the illocutionary act also takes the promise as its starting point? (Adams and Searle 1986, pp. 65–68). Searle shares Sa-paṇ's interest in the promise for its innauguration of a complex relationship of responsibility, a linguistically constituted status in relation to the "promisee."

21. GL 374.10–12: */gzhan yang khas blangs pas de'i don la rang nyid mkhas par gzhan gyis rtogs pa yin te/mi mkhas na tshogs kyi dbus su khas len ga la nus.*

22. GL 374.12–14: *yang dam bcas pas de 'grub pa'i rgyur 'gyur te/ya rabs rnams ni/srog ni gtong gi dam bca' min // zhes gsungs pa ltar ro.*

23. All that is left to close the circle is the explicit guarantee that the proposed or promised exposition does, in fact, satisfy an authentic, socially sanctioned goal. This role is served by the "statement of purpose," which I will explain below. Sa-paṇ does not explain any other social mechanisms for maintaining the legitimacy of reference, so this analysis hardly amounts to a complete theory of meaning. Nonetheless, the *Gateway* is dedicated to the analysis of *scholars*, and to whatever degree scholars are legitimate, *their* meanings are regulated by the scholarly community. Unless you are a scholar, however, Sa-paṇ has not explained the social forces that *get you your dumplings* (see chapter 3).

24. GL 374.14–17: *de bzhin du bskul ba'i tshig/dam pa'i chos nyan phyir ni 'dir shog shog // ces bya ba'am/yid la dga' ba skyed de nyon // zhes bya ba la sogs pa'ang de dang 'dra bar shes par bya'o.*

25. GL 370.20–371.1: *mang du thos shing mthong nas goms pa dang // man ngag dbang gis dpal ldan kun dga' yi // rgyal mtshan 'di na* [371] *'ga' tsam 'chad pa la // mkhas pa rnams kyis dga' ba skyed de nyod.*

26. GL 375.2: *bstan bcos 'ga' zhig du.*

27. GL 375.3–4: *nus pa med kyang 'bad bzhin du // bstan bcos la yang 'jug pa'i tshig // bstan bcos dang ni ston byed pa.*

28. GL 375.10–11: *dper na tshong pas rgya mtsho las rin po che lon pa bzhin no.*

29. GL 375.12–14: *'di ltar tshig don la mkhas bzhin du'ang mi shes so zhes khengs pa med pa la dpyad na rtsom pa po gang zag dam par rtogs pa yin no.*

30. See Kapstein (2003), pp. 776–78, for further thoughts on Sa-paṇ's self-aggrandizing rhetoric and the reputation it would gain him for being "the very type of the self-inflated scholar, a model of conceit."

31. GL 375.19–21: *lus rnam gzhag thog mar bkod pa la dgos pa gsum ste/'chad pa pos 'chad sla/nyan pa pos gzung bde/bstan bcos la nges pa skye ba'o.*

32. GL 427.21–428.1: *'chad byed bshad par bya ba'i yul // bshad par bya ba rnam pa* [428] *gsum.*

33. GL 375.21–376.9: *dang po ni lus rnam* [376] *gzhag shes pas brjod bya ngos zin / go rims mi 'khrug / go smos pas don bde blag tu bya ba'i dgos pa ste gsum mo // gnyis pa nyan pa pos gzung bde ba la gsum ste / thos pa'i skabs su brjod bya bde blag tu ngos zin / bsam pa'i skabs su go rims mi 'khrugs par rtogs sla / bsgom pa'i skabs su bsdus nas nyams su len pas bsgoms byung gi shes rab myur du skye ba'i dgos pa'o / gsum pa bstan bcos la nges pa skye ba ni / lus dang yan lag rjes su 'brel bas lhag pa dang chad pa dang 'khrugs pa'i skyon las grol bas bstan bcos yang dag pa'o zhes nges shes skye ba'o.*

34. GL 429.1–2: *dbyangs kyi yan lag phun sum tshogs pas gsal la dag par bshad do.*

35. Literally "wandering around" (*byil byil po*)—i.e., saying "um, uh, well, uh . . . where was I?"

36. GL 442.17–443.5: *mi 'chad pa dang / legs par mi 'chad pa dang / the tshom gyis 'chad pa dang / dka' ba'i gnas la byil byil po dang / dgos pa'i gnas su mi spro ba dang / mi dgos par spro ba dang / gong 'og 'khrugs pa mi bsdeb pa dang / mi dgos pa dkrugs te bshad pa dang / gong du bshad rgyu 'og tu 'dor ba dang / 'og tu bshad rgyu gong du len pa* [443] *dang / skabs su ma bab pa bshad pa dang / bab pa mi bshad pa dang / brjod pa mtho dman can dang / mi gsal pa dang / sub sub po dang / myur ches pa dang / bul ches pa dang / tshig dang don legs par brda mi sprod pa la sogs pa 'chad pa'i skyon rnams spangs te mkhas pa rnams kyis legs par bshad do.*

37. GL 430.19–433.8.

38. GL 431.15–17: *don 'dus tshig gsal brjod pa bde // ngag nyung tshig snyoms gzung ba sla // bsdus don nyid kyis gzhung go ba // de 'dra gang gis shes de mkhas.*

39. GL 431.18–432.1: *brjod bya'i don ma lus pa phyogs gcig tu 'dus pa / nang gses kyi dbye ba spyi don gyi khongs su ma shor ba / spyi don gyi ming nang gses kyi dbye bar ma shor ba / brjod bya tha dad kyi sa mtshams ma 'chugs pa / don gyi brjod bya* [432] *phyogs phyogs su ma 'dres shing dril bas phan tshun chod che ba'o.*

40. GL 432.13–16: *bsdus don de nyid kyis gzhung go ba ni / bsdus pa'i don nyid khong du chud pas gzhung gi dgongs pa 'di lta bu zhig yin zhes brjod bya'o don bde blag tu rtogs pa'i nus pa yod pa'i tshig go.*

41. GL 432.19–20: *bsdus don gong 'og ring thung can du shor bas tshig gi khrigs mi mdzes pa.* There is no need to "use your own words," as modern academics tell their students.

42. GL 432.10–11: *gzung ba sla ba ni tshig bde bas rnar snyan cing yid la gcags pa ste / bsdus don snga ma'i tshig gi phrad kyis phyi ma'i tshig 'bad mi dgos par 'dren nus pas.*

43. GL 372.4–5: *bye brag sbyangs pa'i don shes pa // de yang de la mkhas pa yin.* Another instance is where, as discussed in chapter 4, the scholar is defined as having mastery over the "Six Alternatives": "If one understands well methods of explanation such as these, one understands well the intentions of the

sutras and tantras, and will be a scholar who settles [the matter] via objections and replies." GL 459.2–4: *'di lta bu'i bshad pa'i tshul legs par shes na/mdo rgyud kyi dgongs pa legs par shes shing/brgal lan gyis gtan la 'bebs pa mkhas par 'gyur ro/* As I will discuss in my conclusion, these are both instances where the scholar is defined as one with comprehensive mastery.

44. GL 433.6–8: *des na rang gis brjod bde/gzhan gyis rtogs sla/gnyis ka la mar snyan pa zhig shes na mkhas pa yin no.*

45. GL 432.16–433.6: */'di lta bu'i don shes pa de mkhas pa yin la/de las bzlog na mi mkhas te/brjod bya'i don ma 'dus pa/bsdus don gyi tshig mi gsal ba/'chad pa na brjod mi bde ba/ngag mang bas dbugs thog re'i bar du brjod dgos pa/tshig ma snyoms pa bsdus don gong 'og ring thung can du shor bas tshig gi khrigs mi mdzes pa/gzung dka' ba ste tshig don mi 'phrod pas yid la gzung dka'/ngag tu brjod dka'* [433] *ba'o // bsdus don brjod pas gzhung gi dgongs pa mi go ba ste/bsdus don dang gzhung tshig don mi 'phrod pas bsdus don la brten nas gzhung go ba'i nus pa med pa'o // 'di lta bu'i bsdus don mtho dman can mang po mthong ste/de lta bu'i sa gcod 'ga' zhig don yang 'chug nus don ma 'chugs kyang slob dpon gyis brjod dga' // slob mas gzung dka' ba'i phyir kho bos btang snyoms su bshag go.*

46. GL 431.4–9: *gzhung gi thog mtha' ma lus pa blo yul du byas te/brjod bya rigs mthun mi mthun blos phye nas spyi'i sdom chen po rnams so sor gzhag // nang gi dbye ba rnams mi 'gal bar phye/de'i yan lag gi dbye ba dgos pa rnams so sor bsdus/mi dgos pa 'ga' zhig de'i yan lag gi nang du bsdus te bshad.* Jackson (1993), pp. 2–5, relying on Glo-bo Mkhan-chen's commentary, interprets the "summarized meaning" (*bsdus don*) explained in this passage as referring to a subgenre of commentary—that is, as a *written* commentary, rather than as an oral one.

47. GL 457.3–4: *mtha' drug gang gis shes pa de // gzhung bshad pa la shin tu mkhas.*

48. GL 370.5–7: *'ga' zhig sgra dang rnam par dbye ba dang // khams dang byed tshig dpe dang tshig gi rgyan // dbye bsdu grangs dang nges pa go rims la // 'di la phal cher rmongs par mthong nas 'di.*

49. GL 376.11.

50. GL 376.21–377.2: *bsdus pa'i* [377] *don la bzhi ste/brjod bya/dgos pa/dgos pa'i dgos pa/'brel pa'o.*

51. GL 430.16–18: *thog mar dgos pa'i don dgos 'brel gyi ngag yin la/de thams cad la grags pas re zhig bzhag go.* Sa-paṇ also assimilates this categorization to the *dgag bzhag spang gsum* method of disputation, which he discusses in GL chapter 3, Jackson (1987), and in the TR, Beckwith (1990).

52. GL 376.12–14: *bstan bcos dam par bstan pa'i phyir // ston pas thog mar dgos pa bstan // yongs su rtogs pas de mthong na // dpyod pa la yang cis mi 'jug.*

53. GL 376.16–17: *mdo don che ba nyid thos nas/ . . . /nyan pa po de gus 'gyur bas.*

54. GL 376.18–20: *de la dgos pa ni 'ga' zhig gzhung mdzes pa skyes ces zer/'ga zhig don gyi log rtog ldog par 'dod.*

55. GL 376.20–21: *de dag kyang gnas skabs su 'gal ba med mod kyi/mthar mjug par 'gyur ba nyid dgos pa yin no.* Note that in GL, the term under discussion as *'jug pa* is printed as *mjug pa.* I translate this passage using *'jug* based on the Sakya College's (1987) print of the Derge edition (*tha* 165a) and T. G. Dhongtog Rinpoche's handscript edition, D: 11. See below for discussion of the significance of the different versions.

56. This interpretation also makes sense of an alternate text reading that appears in one version of the *Gateway,* where the term is written *mjug,* "end, consequence," instead of *'jug,* "entry, beginning." The two words are essentially opposites, but in a strange way the transformation in the overall meaning is not that great. With the alteration, Sa-paṇ's comment reads: "The [final] purpose is to place the end result up front" (GL 376.21: *mthar mjug par 'gyur ba nyid dgos pa yin no/*). This reading fits better with Vasubandhu's idea that expressing the goal will generate faith in the listener, and with Sa-paṇ's later statement that the purpose of the "purpose and relations" is to state the ultimate goal of the treatise up front, but given that this has already been indicated earlier in the commentary, it does not add much. Of course, both versions cannot be the "correct" reading, but both readings suggest to me a similar point: one provides a significant entry into the text only by beginning with a statement of its most salient end goal.

57. GL 431.1–2: *de la nye bar mgo na dngos su med kyang lung dang rigs pa'i gzhung gzhan nas blangs te.*

58. GL 372.12–15: *rig pa'i gnas lnga dag la mkhas par ma byas par // 'phags mchog gis kyang thams cad mkhyen nyid mi 'gyur te // gzhan dag tshar gcad rjes su gzung bar bya phyir dang // rang nyid kun shes bya phyir de la de brtson byed.* MSA 11.60, p. 70: *vidyāsthāne pañcavidhe yogam akṛtvā sarvajñatvaṃ naiti kathaṃcit paramāryaḥ/ityanyeṣāṃ nigrahaṇānugrahaṇāya svājñārthaṃ vā tatra karoty eva sa yogam.* On the five sciences, see Griffiths (1990), pp. 99–100, Kapstein (2003), Dudjom (1991), pp. 97–101, Ruegg (1995) and chapter 1, above.

59. GL 374.21–375.1: *tshig gi don ni rang rang gi* [375] *gzhung du shes par bya'o.* This is a comment on the "oath of composition."

60. Sa-paṇ in fact exemplifies this kind of exposition on three texts. After the MMK, he also analyzes the opening verse to Haribhadra's *Abhisamayālaṅkāra* commentary, and then a few verses from the end of the *dharaṇī* text, the *Vajravidharaṇa* (*rdo rje rnam 'joms*). GL 435.16–436.18.

61. Or, ". . . who do not know the eighth case . . ."

62. GL 433.21–434.6: *gzhung* [434] *gang zhig 'chad par byed pa na/byed pa'i tshig drug la sogs pa dang sbyar te/tshig don legs par sbrel nas mi dgos pa mi 'chad/dgos pa mi 'dor bar dpyis phyin par bshad pa ni sgra pa dag gi lugs so/bod sgra mi shes pa la legs par bshad kyang 'byor dka' bas 'dir ma bshad do // gal te shes par 'dod na kho bos byas pa'i sgra'i bstan bcos su blta bar bya'o.*

63. GL 434.7–8: *'dir bod la nye bar mkho ba'i bshad tshul cung zad brjod par bya ste.*

64. The *kārakas* are syntactic-semantic class categories through which parts of a sentence are classified according to how they partake in the action of the verb. Ordinarily the verb itself—that is, the "action" (*kriyā*) is not considered a *kāraka*. Thus Sa-paṇ's method is to isolate the verb and two, not three (or six), *kārakas*. I am calling these three items *kārakas* for the sake of simplicity of explanation here. See Cardona (1974), Scharfe (1977), Matilal (1990), pp. 40–48, and Saini (1999).

65. GL 434.8–10: *las dang byed po bya ba yi // tshig don sbrel la ngag don blang/las ni 'bras chan la sogs pa'o // byed pa po ni lhas byin la sogs pa'o // bya ba ni 'ched par byed pa'o.*

66. What Sa-paṇ expects his readers to know is, of course, the Tibetan translation, DGTG 96.2.2–3: *gang gis rten cing 'brel par'byung // 'gag pa med pa skye med pa // chad pa med pa rtag med pa // 'ong ba med pa 'gro med pa // tha dad don min don gcig min/spros pa nyer zhi zhi bstan pa // rdzogs pa'i sangs rgyas smra rnams kyi // dam pa de la phyag 'tshal lo.*

67. GL 434.16–19: *tshig dang po gang gis zhes bya ba dang/drug pa'i bstan pa zhes bya ba dang/brgyad pa'i de la phyag 'tshal lo zhes sbrel la gang gis bstan pa de la phyag 'tshal lo zhes khyad par gyi gzhi blang ngo.*

68. GL 434.19–435.2: *des na khyad par gyi chos bshad do // gang bstan/gang gis bstan/ji ltar bstan zhes don gyi dri ba bkod la/gang bstan na rten cing 'brel bar 'byung ba bstan // gang gis bstan na* [435] *rdzogs pa'i sangs rgyas des bstan/ji ltar bstan zhe na zhi ba bstan/zhes sbrel lo.*

69. See Dudjom (1991), vol. 2, p. 191, for the "Eight extremes" (*mtha' brgyad*). For Je Tsongkhapa's commentary on this verse of exposition, see Tsong Khapa (2006), pp. 24 ff.

70. GL 435.3–16: *de dag gi don legs par bshad na/rten cing 'brel bar 'byung ba ji lta bu zhe na/'gag pa med pa skye med pa // 'ong ba med pa 'gro med pa // chad pa med pa rtag med pa // tha dad don min don gcig min // zhe de lta bu'i rten cing 'brel bar 'byung ba mtha' brgyad dang bral ba de rten 'brel gyi khyad par gyi chos su sbyar ro // gang gis bstan pa'i sangs rgyas de ji lta bu zhe na/smra ba rnams kyi dam pa zhes sbyar te/smra ba ni drag po dang 'phrog byed la sogs pa lha chen po rnams sam/ser skya dang gzegs gzan la sogs pa drang srong chen po rnams yin gyi/smra ba gang ci'ang rung ba phal pa rnams mi gzung ngo // rten cing 'brel bar 'byung ba de ji ltar bstan zhe na/spros pa nyer zhi zhi bstan pa // zhe sbrel la/de rten cing 'brel bar 'byung ba de'ang/spros pa thams cad nye bar zhi ba'i zhi ba yin gyi/dbang phyug la sogs pa la zhi bar 'dogs pa'i zhi ba ma yin gyi/yod med la sogs pa spros pa thams cad nye bar zhi'o zhes bshad par bya'o.*

71. See Martin (1996).

72. This paragraph is indebted to the observations of Matthew Kapstein (personal communication).

73. Fish (1999), and Adams and Searle (1986), pp. 524 ff.

74. Adams and Searle (1986), pp. 360 ff.

75. Adams and Searle (1986), pp. 164 ff.

76. Related to this is the fact that these theorists also share Sa-paṇ's concerns with the pragmatic efficacy of language, rather than its ultimate meaning. As Iser writes, "What is important to readers, critics and authors alike is what literature *does* and not what it *means*." Adams and Searle (1986), p. 360. Sa-paṇ will more resemble philosophers of language that emphasize linguistic *use* rather than truth-conditionality.

CHAPTER 6. APPEALING TO THE TRANSLOCAL

1. "Pages" here refer to the main edition I have used for my translation, GL 391.5–427.16.

2. For a basic introduction to the Tibetan traditions of interpreters of Daṇḍin, see Van der Kuijp (1996). Kapstein (2003) places Sa-paṇ's literary interests at the forefront of the twelfth- and thirteenth-century renewal of Tibetan interest in *kāvya*. See also my note 45 in chapter 1.

3. GL 391.5–402.8. In this chapter I do not discuss Sa-paṇ's introductory subsection, which I call "General Considerations" in my outline in appendix A. Subsections 1–4 here thus reflect sections 1.3.2–1.3.5 in that outline.

4. *Hevajra-Tantra* II.v.26a–c, in: Snellgrove (1959), vol. 2, p. 81.

5. Kuijp (1996), p. 403.

6. GL 402.8–405.2.

7. Ingalls (1968), p. 15.

8. GL 405.2–410.15.

9. GL 410.15–427.16.

10. Daṇḍin treats the *rasas* in Kā II.280–92, where he writes that they consist in intensified forms (*rūpa-bāhulya,* cf. II. 281) of other emotions, but does not set them apart, or above the other *alaṅkāras*. For instance, *rasavat* appears along with all of the other generally applicable *alaṅkāras* at the opening of Kā II, and then appears again along with *preyas* and *tejas* as the three *alaṅkāras* that indicate the greatness of a character (*yuktotkarṣa,* cf. II.275).

11. This was suggested to me by Sheldon Pollock, but I have not yet had the opportunity to study Bhoja's work. It is an obvious next step to substantiate and expand the argument of this chapter.

12. GL 402.12–14: *dper na dbyangs can gyi mgul rgyan las/ri sul shing gcig pa/nags tshang tshing can/chu 'bab pa zhes bya ba la sogs pa dang/* . . . and GL 403.3–8: *'di lta bu'i dper brjod dbyangs can gyi mgul rgyan las mang du brjod kyang/yi ge mangs kyis dogs pas ma bris te/rang gis legs par brtags la shes par bya'o // grags pa'i dpe la dkar ba dang // mtho dang 'od dang ba dan sogs // sbyar zhes dbyangs can mgul rgyan smra.*

13. GL 392.1–3: *dpe drang po dang zur mig la sogs pa'i sgo nas yi ge dang rgyan bzang pos sgro btags te / rol sgegs dang bcas pa'i snyan ngag nyams dgu dang sbyar la brtsam mo.* Here I am borrowing Sheldon Pollock's convention (1998), p. 126 ff., from his translation of Bhoja's *Śṛṅgāraprakāśa,* of capitalizing "Passion" when it refers to "the capacity for emotional intensity as such," as opposed to just one of the many affective states. My references to Bhoja here also rely on Pollock (1995, 1998, 2001).

14. It is also worth noting the vagueness of this passage. Bhoja, following Bharata, paints a detailed process of the development of the poetic emotions, distinguishing between contributing and direct causes of emotional development, transitory and stable emotions, etc. There is no evidence here that Sa-paṇ is aware of these distinctions, or even that he distinguishes systematically between *rasas* and *bhāvas.*

15. This point needs more research, in particular, to track Sa-paṇ's sources of influence through the known Sanskrit sources that might have been available to him.

16. "If one is explaining the Tantra Basket this is necessary, but since here is not [such a] context, for the time being I will set it aside." GL 437.19–20: *'di rgyud sde bshad pa na dgos kyi 'dir skabs ma yin pas re zhig bzhag go.*

17. GL: 392.4–5: *sgeg cing dpa' ba mi sdug pa // dgod cing drag shul 'jigs su rung // snying rje ngam dang zhi ba dgu.*

18. Sa-paṇ is not directly citing the *Hevajra Tantra* text. He gives a slightly different version of the same list, and finishes the verse with a different *pada* of his own construction: "In the *Amarakośa* they are abridged to eight." GL 392.6: *'chi med mdzod las brgyad du bsdus.* In spite of differences, the all-important first words, which are the memory trigger for all Sakyapas, are the same, which makes this most definitely a reference to the *Hevajra,* indirect though it may be. The *Hevajra Tantra* verse is II.v.26a–c in Snellgrove's (1959) edition. Snellgrove's (1959) translation, vol. 1, p. 111, reads: "He is possessed of the nine emotions of dancing: passion, heroism, loathsomeness, horror, mirth, frightfulness, compassion, wonderment, and tranquility." His Sanskrit and Tibetan editions, vol. 2, pp. 81–82, read (respectively): *śrṅgāravīrabībhatsaraudrahāsyabhayānakaiḥ // karuṇādbhūtaśāntaiś ca ravanādyarrasair yutaṃ // sgeg ciṅ dpaḥ bo mi sdug pa // dgod ciṅ drag śul ḥjigs ruṅ ba // sñiṅ rje rṅam daṅ źi ba yis // gar dguḥi ro daṅ ldan pa ñid.* The first three lines do not include the last words "are the nine" from Sa-paṇ's verse, since they are wrapped into the fourth pada. The only other differences from Sa-paṇ's passage are: The *Hevajra*'s *dpa' bo* instead of *dpa' ba,* probably an error; the insignificant difference of *'jigs rung ba* instead of *'jigs su rung;* and the more comprehensible (I think) *rngam* instead of Sa-paṇ's *ngam.*

19. GL 392.21–393.3: *dpa' ba ni 'jigs pa med pa'i khyad par te / de'ang dbye na sbyin* [393] *pa dang / tshul khrims la sogs pa la 'jigs pa med par spyod nus pa chos*

kyi dpa' ba/g.yul ngor dgra dang/gcan gzan dang/gnod sbyin la sogs pa la 'jigs pa med pa ni 'jig rten gyi dpa' ba'o.

20. GL 393.19–394.4: *drag shul ni rtsub pa'i sgo nas mi mthun phyogs 'dul ba ste/nyon mongs nyams smad rtsad nas bton/zhes bya ba la sogs pa nyon mongs pa dang shes bya'i sgrib pa bag chags dang bcas pa* [394] *rtsad gcod pa dang/sang rgyas kyis bdud btul ba dang/phyag na rdo rjes drag po btul ba la sogs pa/chos dang mthun pa'i drag shul yin la/pha rol gnon pa'i sgo nas lus ngag yid rnam par 'khrugs pa'i zhe sdang gis dgra bo 'dul ba ni 'jig rten pa'i drag shul lo.*

21. GL 394.7–19: *'jigs su rung ba ni pha rol bskad cing bag 'khums par byed pa ste/de yang sems kyi chos la'ang yod mod kyi gtso bor lus ngag gi rnam 'gyur phul du byung ba/pha rol tu phyin pa drug la dper brjod na/thams cad sgrol gyis bu dang bu mo dang/shi bi pa'i rgyal pos mig dang/byams pa'i stobs kyis sha dang/rgyal po zla 'od kyis mgo dang/gser mdog gis lus kyi stod smad bcad pa la sogs pa dper bya'o // de bzhin du tsul khrims la sogs pa pha rol tu phyin pa gzhan yang/gzhan kyis spyad par dka' ba blo'i yul las 'das pa/skyi bung zhes byed pa thams cad chos kyi 'jigs su rung ba'o // de las gzhan pa ni 'jig rten pa ste/gnod sbyin dang srin po'i cha lugs dang/seng ge/glang chen/stag la sogs pa'i spyod tshul 'jigs su rung ba dang/g.yang za/'brog stong/nags thibs po/chu klung/me chen/'jigs pa'i dus kyi rlung la sogs pa 'jigs shing.*

22. GL 395.3–8: */log par ltung ba ngan song gsum dang/mgon med pa/nad/mya ngan/bkres pa/phongs pa/gzhan gyis mnar ba/rgas pa/rgud pa/'chi ba la sogs pa la snying brtse ba ni dman pa la snying rje skye ba yin la/byang chub sems dpa'i spyod pa rlabs pa che thos nas sems mi bzod cing/spu ldang/mchi ma g.yo/ngo mtshar zhing brtse ba skye ba ni mchog la skye ba'i snying rje'o.*

23. GL 395.11–14: */rigs/gzugs/stobs/longs spyod/rgyal srid la sogs pa ngam pa ni 'jigs rten pa'i yin la // blo gros/yon tan/spobs pa/spangs pa dang thob pa la sogs pa gzhan las khyad par du 'phags pas pha rol zil gyis gnon pa ni chos kyi ngam pa yin no.*

24. GL 395.16–18: *zhi ba ni nga rgyal dang rgyags shing dregs pas chos spang ba'o // de'ang dbye na/'jig rten pa'i dregs pa dang chos kyi dregs pa spang ba ste/sngar bshad pa'i ngam pa nyid go bzlog pa'o.*

25. Dhanañjaya (1969) IV.73, p. 243.

26. This is not to say that Sa-paṇ has, necessarily, isolated distinctive emotional styles that are exclusively Buddhist. On the contrary, we could find examples analogous to each of his "dharmic" stories in many non-Buddhist traditions. But it seems quite clear from his selection of examples that Sa-paṇ's use of the word "dharma" is not intended to include, for instance, the dharma explained by Krishna to Arjuna.

27. GL 394.14: *gzhan gyis spyad par dka' ba blo'i yul las 'das pa.*

28. GL 395.6–8: *byang chub sems dpa'i spyod pa rlabs pa che thos nas sems mi bzod cing/spu ldang/mchi ma g.yo/ngo mtshar zhing brtse ba skye ba.*

29. In fact, the description of compassion here does not divide compassion into "worldly" and "dharmic" types. Instead, it is compassion for "superior" and "inferior" persons. It makes sense, I think, to have avoided claiming that any kind of compassion would be nondharmic, but the category division is still one where superior acts of great beings are distinguished from inferior acts of ordinary beings. We might also read this as an implicit criticism of so-called Hīnayāna practitioners.

30. GL 393.21–394.1: *nyon mongs pa dang shes bya'i sgrib pa bag chags dang bcas pa* [394] *rtsad gcod pa dang.*

31. This is a similar list to that in Sa-paṇ's commentary to his *Eight Affirmations of the Ego,* wherein he defends self-aggrandizing rhetoric in respect to dharmic accomplishments, rather than worldly ones for, as Kapstein (2003) explains, "truly learned persons would be ashamed to engage in *that* sort of braggadocio."

32. GL 397.2–18: *drag shul 'jigs rung rnam gnyis la'ang // de bzhin snying rje zhi ba spang // drag shul 'jigs su rung ba ni rtsub cing gzhan la gnod pa'i chos yin la/snying rje dang zhi ba ni 'jam zhing phan 'dogs pa yin pas phan tshun 'gal ba'i phyir ro // snying rje zhi ba rnam gnyis la // sgeg dang dpa' dgod drag shul dang // 'jigs rung ngam pa drug po spang // snying rje dang zhi ba ni phan 'dogs shing dul ba'i yan lag yin la/sgeg pa ni 'phyar ba dang g.yeng zhing rnam par ma zhi ba'i chos yin/de bzhin du snying rje dang zhi ba ni yid bde zhing dul ba yin la/de bzhin du dpa' ba dang dgod pa dang/drag shul dang/'jigs su rung ba ni de dag las bzlog pa yin pa'i phyir ro // gal te chos dang 'brel ba'i skabs su sbyin pa la sogs pa pha rol tu phyin pa rnams la dpa' ba dang 'jigs su rung ba la sogs pa 'ga' zhig mi 'gal ba ni // gong du dpa' ba'i skabs su bshad pa ltar skabs dang sbyar la bshad par bya'o // ngam pa'i rgyan la snying rje dang // zhi ba gnyis ni rnam par spang // ngam pa ni nga rgyal gyi yan lag yin la snying rje dang zhi ba ni dul ba'i yan lag yin pa'i phyir ro.*

33. ED 527.1: *de ni de la blo 'chos pa'i phyir ram/blo 'dul bar byed pa'i phyir chos zhes bya'o.* I discussed this passage in chapter 3.

34. Apte (1957), p. 537, gives the following as an example of *karuṇa rasa* from the *Uttararāmacarita* 3.1, 13: *puṭapākapratīkāśo rāmasya karuṇo rasaḥ.*

35. GL 401.13–402.1: *snying rje zhi ba rnam gnyis la // sgeg cing dpa' ba la sogs pa'i // tshig rgyan sbyar na gnyis po 'jig // de phyir bcos ma'i dpe rgyan spang // snying rje dang zhi ba gnyis rang bzhin gyis nye bar zhi ba yin pas de dang mthun pa'i rang bzhin gyis rgyan rkang gi khong nas skyes ba'i tshig brtse ba dang dul ba bskyed nus pas pha mas bu sdug pa la brjod pa lta bu ma bcos pa nyid rgyan gyi dam pa yin no // 'di la bcos ma'i tshig rgyan mi sbyar te/sbyar na brtse ba dang dul ba ngang gis skyes pa bcos nas byas pa lta bur 'gyur ba'i phyir ro // snying rje'i dpe brjod pa thams cad sgrol dang/zhi ba'i dpe brjod pa lcags kyi khyim du skyes pa'i* [402] *rabs la sogs pa ltar shes par bya'o.*

36. This is mentioned in chapter 5.

37. As Pollock (1998) argues, the emphasis on reader response in later Sanskrit literary theory has overshadowed the interpretation of literary theory before the *Dhvanyāloka*. In spite of the known Kashmiri influence from Śākyaśrī, I do not see any evidence of the later approach in the *Gateway*.

38. GL 443.13–20: *chos mi shes pa'i bla ma dag gis rnam rtog phyin ci log dang/rang gis ci dran dran rnams bshad nas/mdo rgyud kyi dgongs pa 'gog pa ni chos kyi sbyin pa ma yin/de 'chad mkhan de yang mi dge ba'i bshes gnyen yin zhes sangs rgyas kyis gsungs/chos de'ang chos kyi gzugs brnyan nam/chos ltar bcos pa zhes gsungs pa de yin/'di 'dra'i rigs can bstan pa la mi phan pa'i steng du bstan pa 'jigs pa'i rgyur 'gro // chos ma yin pa'i sbyin pa yin gyi/chos kyi sbyin pa ma yin no.*

39. GL 402.16–18: *chu skyar byi la chom rkun dag // sgra med 'jab cing 'gro ba yis // mngon par 'dod pa'i don sgrub pa // thub pas rtag tu de bzhin spyad.* Interestingly, Sakya Khenpo Sangyey Tenzin cites this verse at the end of his TAJ commentary, Davenport (2000), pp. 303–304, with the statement that the verse itself is perfect, but that critics "assert that Buddha Śākyamuni . . . is being likened to a robber or an animal by use of this citation." He continues: "Therefore, I fold my palms together at my heart and request these skeptics not to get snarled up in the literal designation of words." Sangyey Tenzin obviously does not feel the same obligation to correcting his predecessors as Sa-paṇ is evincing in this example. Perhaps the more important worry is that the apparent author of the verse in question is the great Śāntideva.

40. GL 402.19–20: *nyan ngag gi skabs yin na/mu stegs dag gis khyed kyi thub pa de ltar spyod dam zhes co 'dri'i dogs pa la.*

41. GL 404.13–14: *dad pa can mang bzung nyes na // cig shos bsregs pa smos ci dgos.*

42. GL 403.14–18: *'jigs pa med pa la seng ge la sogs pa/zhum pa la wa skyes la sogs pa/mkhas pa la 'jam dpal la sogs pa/stobs la sred med kyi bu la sogs pa/blun po la ba lang/zhe sdang la sprul/gsal ba la nyi ma/de bzhin du skyon gyis ma gos pa la padma la sogs pa dper bya'o.*

43. GL 404.1–3: *chogs par dbyung du mi rung ba blun po dga' ba bskyed kyang/mkhas pa rnams kyis 'phyas gdags su rung ba'i sgra mi sbyar ro.*

44. GL 404.4–8: *chags par dbyung du mi rung ba sgra ji lta bu zhe na/mchog gi yan lag ni saṃ skṛ ta'i skad du wa rā ga/nyer gnas ni U pasthā ste pho mo'i dbang po la 'jug/skul ba'i sgra tso da yin la/'phral skad du mi tshangs par spyod pa la 'jug/yang zhing g.yo ba la saṃ skṛ tas ha ra ṇa zhes zer la/ngo tsha ba'i gnas la 'jug mod.*

45. GL 404.15–18: *bod la skabs 'gar bzhad gad du 'gro ba'ang srid/me tog kha 'bye ba dang/'bye 'dod pa dang/pog phor dang/spog gis bdug pa la sogs pa sgra la skyon med kyang yul 'ga' zhig na tshogs par dbyung du mi rung ba'i ngag du 'gyur bas skabs brtags te sbyar bar bya'.*

46. GL 404.19–405.1: *lung dang rigs pa'i bstan bcos 'ga' zhig tu dpe mi mdzes pa dang/sgra tshogs par dbyung du mi rung ba byung yang don la rton pa yin pas*

skyon med do // snyan ngag ni sgra gtso bo yin pas thams cad du skyon [405] *med par sbyar bar bya'o.*

47. Pollock (1995), p. 123.

48. Pollock (1995), p. 124.

49. This is Pollock's (1995, p. 124) translation and citation from the *Śṛṅgāraprakāśa.* See his work for reference to Bhoja's original, which I have not used.

50. See my discussion in chapter 3.

51. Jackson (1987), p. 194. Leonard van der Kuijp wrote an entire article (1986) on Sa-paṇ's treatment of just one of Daṇḍin's verses (Kā I.11), and the interest in this topic came from the fact that Sa-paṇ's translation differed significantly from Daṇḍin's original, and caused subsequent controversy in Tibetan literary circles—a fact that distinguished this verse from the majority. John Eppling's (1989) Ph.D. dissertation on the second chapter of the *Kāvyādarśa* includes a detailed list of which of Daṇḍin's verses Sa-paṇ translates. Dragomir Dimitrov's (2002) recent work on the *first* chapter of the *Kāvyādarśa* briefly discusses the process of Sa-paṇ's translation (sensibly arguing that Sa-paṇ did not translate alone, but probably had the assistance of Indian *paṇḍitas* of his circle), and helpfully prints Sa-paṇ's Kā I verses next to the later, Tibetan translation from the *Tanjur,* which is far more of a direct translation than Sa-paṇ's.

52. Jackson (1987), p. 194, does note that "the longest part of the section on composition" is "his treatment of the poetical figures of meaning (*don rgyan : arthālaṃkāra*)."

53. In these verses Sa-paṇ represents Daṇḍin's extensive list of comparative terms with his own list of similar terms in Tibetan.

54. GL 412.1–2: *de lta'i dpe yi rab dbye ba // sngon gyi mkhas pas 'di ltar bshad.*

55. GL 412.3–5: *chos dang dngos po bzlog pa dang // phan tshun dpe dang nges pa'i dpe // nges pa med dang sdud pa'i dpe/de sogs dpe ni spros te bshad.*

56. GL 415.17: *dpe yi dbye ba mi mngon pa'i // nyid ni rū pa ka zhes 'dod.*

57. GL 418.7–11: *'di dag nye bar mtshon pa tsam yin/rgyas par rang gis brtags la shes par bya ste/rgyan las/rnam rtog rnams kyi mtha' med pas // rū pa ka dang dpe dag ni // phyogs tsam bstan to mkhas rnams kyis // brjod pa gzhan yang rjes su dpag // ces bshad pa ltar ro.*

58. GL 426.19–21: *'di lta bu'i snyan ngag rgya gar la gtsigs che yang/bod snyan ngag gi tshul la blo mi 'jug pas/spros pa de tsam zhig las re zhig bzhag go.*

59. GL 405.19–20: *'di dag shes par 'dod na kho bos byas pa'i sdeb sbyor me tog gi chun por blta bar bya'o.*

60. GL 430.7–12: *gryas par shes par 'dod na/bdag nyid chen po bsod nams rtse mos mdzad pa'i chos la 'jug pa'i sgo las gsungs pa ltar/dpon slob kyi mtshan nyid dang/chos bshad nyan bya ba'i tshul dang/bdud kyi sde tshar gcad pa'i gzungs sngags la sogs pa legs par gsungs pas der blta bar bya'o.*

61. GL 433.16–18: *bsdus nas bshad na don mi go bas/kho bos byas pa'i sgra'i bstan bcos gzhan dang/smra sgo la sogs par blta bar bya'o.*

62. GL 441.4–7: *de la sogs pa'i sgra'i bshad pa dpag tu med pa yod mod kyi/mkhas pa rnams la shin tu 'thad kyang blun po rnams kyis go bar dka' bas 'dir rgyas par ma bris so // cung zad blta bar 'dod na mdo rgyud kyi 'grel pa rnams su blta bar bya'o.*

63. GL 446.8–11: A *ma ra ko ṣā dang/bi sha pra kā sha la sogs pa ming gi mngon brjod rnams legs par shes pa tshig gi don thams cad la the tshom chod pa yin no // 'di'i phyogs tsam kho bos tshig gi gter du bshad par ltar shes par bya'o.*

64. On the other hand, it does seem that although his treatment is quite lengthy for an introduction, Sa-paṇ did make an effort to keep his passage as brief as possible. A close comparison of Sa-paṇ's transposition with Daṇḍin's verses is beyond the scope of this chapter, but it can be stated that in a great number of cases Sa-paṇ transposes only half—usually the *first* half—of Daṇḍin's verses, and the verses of Daṇḍin's that Sa-paṇ skips are often arguably redundant.

65. Kapstein (2000), pp. 151–54.

66. Petech (1990).

67. Pollock (1995), p. 131.

68. In his "Letter to the Tibetans," trans. Tucci (1949), pp. 10–12, Sa-paṇ writes that the Tibetans really have no choice but to submit to the Mongol prince Köden, but he says also that they should not worry about ill effects coming from submitting to him, since "This king is a bodhisattva, who has the greatest faith in the Buddhist teachings generally, and in the three gems in particular. He protects the universe by good laws, and particularly he has a great attachment for me, far above others. He said (to me): 'Preach religion with a tranquil mind, I will give you what you wish. I know that you do good, heaven knows if I do so also.'" Sa-paṇ thus felt that he had succeeded, at least, in gaining the king's trust: "The king is bound to me as he is to no one else." The relative advantages accruing to the Sakyapa in this circumstance are obvious. Though, see my conclusion for discussion of the negative side of this coin.

CHAPTER 7. CONCLUSION

1. Jackson (1987), vol. 2, p. 366. His edition, vol. 1, p. 298: *bstan pa'i mjug 'dir bstan la rab gus shing/bstan pa mtha' dag bsrung zhing 'dzin 'dod pa // shākya'i dge slong kun dga' rgyal mtshan dpal // bzang pos bstan la phan phyir 'di sbyar ro // deng sang shākya seng ge'i bstan pa 'di // 'bab chu zad pai rdzing bzhin nyin re 'bri // blo gsal rnams kyis tshul 'di legs rtogs la // thar pa 'dod pa dag gis 'bad dgos so.*

2. I have not treated the *Gateway*'s third chapter at length because David Jackson (1987) has already made an excellent study of it.

3. Dreyfus (2002).

4. Jackson (1987), vol. 2, pp. 330–31. In his edition, vol. 1, p. 258: *chos kyi grags pa la sogs pa dag mu stegs byed dang rtsod pa na/sangs rgyas pa dang gzegs zan la sogs pa'i grub mtha' bzung nas rtsod kyi/bstan pa 'dzin mi nus pa gang yang rung ba'i mtshan nyid dang gzhung dum bur bton nas sbyor ba khod ces zer ba ni byis pa'i skye bo nyams sad pa'i rtsod pa yin gyi/mkhas pa'i skye bo grub mtha' 'dzin pa'i rtsod pa ma yin no // 'di lta bu 'chad pa'i skabs kyi rtsod par bshad kyi/rtsod pa'i skabs kyi rtsod par mi rung ste/grub mtha' blang dor mi nus pa'i phyir ro.*

5. Personal communication. But see Dreyfus (2003), pp. 103–105 and n. 19, p. 357, for his more general assessment of Sa-paṇ's influence upon Tibetan monastic practices.

6. Pollock 2001, p. 208.

7. Perhaps Sa-paṇ's dual membership in distinct intellectual communities—Indian *paṇḍitas* and Tibetan scholars—is one of the factors that gave him enough of an outsider's perspective to come up with his "social" analysis of the "oath of composition," as I discuss in chapter 5.

8. Jackson (1987), p. 28, and Petech (1990).

9. Szerb (1980b).

10. Throughout this book I have mentioned many aspects of the available Tibetan and Sanskrit literature that deserve closer analysis, and the main topics are: the available works of Phya-pa and Sa-paṇ's other interlocutors on *pramāṇa* from the TR, as well as the TR itself; the hermeneutic works of early Sakyapa masters; the SDL and its Indian grammatical predecessors; the *Two-Volume Lexicon* and its relationship to Sa-paṇ's views of translation; the *Vyākhyāyukti* of Vasubandhu and its Tibetan readership; and the *Sarasvatīkaṇṭhābharaṇa* of Bhoja for its influences on Sa-paṇ's approach to *rasa* and the notion of propriety in poetic composition.

11. For instance, Richard Nance recently criticized the Buddhist scholar Śāntarakśita for mistakenly imagining that the fact of linguistic conventions guiding our speech might resolve the philosophical difficulty that a Buddhist causal account of meaning must face when someone speaks inappropriately, or incoherently. Yet in describing the interpreter of such speech, Śāntarakśita uses the term "*vidagdha*"—the word that Sa-paṇ uses as the Sanskrit for his "*mkhas pa*," "learning/scholar" in the title of the *Gateway to Learning.* Is it not possible that Śāntarakśita is assuming, as Sa-paṇ is arguing, that a scholar *can* discern the proper intention of any speech act worth considering? Nance (2004), pp. 42–59.

12. Ruegg (1995), p. 136, suggests that such a comparison would be fruitful, but must not be expected to be too closely parallel, since Tibetan Buddhists adopted Indian learning from Buddhists, and therefore would have no need, as the Church Fathers felt, to separate the wheat from the chaff among the "pagan sciences."

13. Henderson (1988).

14. I rely here on Adam Nicolson's recent compelling popularization (2003) and Lynne Long's brief but elegant literary history (2001).

15. Nicolson (2003), p. 30.

16. Nicolson (2003), p. 60.

APPENDIX A: INTRODUCTION AND OUTLINE

1. Ngag dbang chos grags (1998), pp. 5–14.

APPENDIX B: TRANSLATION

Leonard van der Kuijp translates the title to the *mkhas 'jug,* "An Introduction to Scholarship," which I consider very close to my own translation, though I felt the notion of "gate" or "door" in *'jug pa'i sgo* also to be important. David Jackson's resonant translation, "Entrance Gate for the Wise" feels quite close to the Tibetan, but loses van der Kuijp's implication, in the title, of an introductory textbook—which is clearly present in the Sanskrit *avatāra.* Kapstein's "Scholar's Gate" is elegant in the extreme, but left me difficulties in merging the title's words into other contexts. I chose to opt for "Gateway to Learning" in order to capture the notion of an entryway as well as an introduction, while still allowing for the possibility that with "*mkhas pa*" Sa-paṇ intended (as he often does) not simply the learned person, but the characteristic value that the community of learning embodies. That is, I followed van der Kuijp in supplying the abstract noun form that Tibetan language lacks. I chose "learning" over "scholarship" in order to imply the breadth of the *value* of study, over against mere expertise. From here forward the translator will keep a proper silence. See Kuijp (1996), Jackson (1987), and Kapstein (2003).

Bold, italicized headings are translator's insertions, indicating section divisions outlined in Appendix A. All other bold text indicates lines from Sa-paṇ's root text, which he includes within his autocommentary.

1. The Tibetan script reads: *bi ta ga tā wa tā ra dwā ra.*

2. These are the four specific knowledges, as described by Bkra shis chos 'phel (1998), pp. 71.4–19.

3. These are the first three of the four fearlessnesses, as described by Bkra shis chos 'phel (1998), p. 75.5–18.

4. The three times are past, present, and future.

5. Here and in the commentary section that follows (as throughout the text), the Tibetan leaves out the subject, which makes for elegant Tibetan but unacceptable English; so I have chosen to insert the guru as subject. It should be understood that here the guru is taken to be identical with Mañjuśrī and all the Buddhas of the three times as well, and it is that full essence that is the

proper subject. Sa-paṇ's root guru is his uncle Trakpa Gyeltsen, as he has written explicitly in answer to question 21 of his *Snyi mo sgom chen gyi dris lan*, cited in Bkra shis chos 'phel (1998), p. 72.

6. The first two fearlessnesses are achieved for one's on sake (*rang don*), the second two for the sake of others (*gzhan don*).

7. Sa-paṇ's list of his own accomplishments in learning has been translated and studied by Kapstein (2003), pp. 779–80, and Verhagen (2005), pp. 189–91, both of which contain extensive resources in the notes.

8. These are the two Buddhist post-Pāṇinian Sanskrit grammatical systems, the Kātantra and the Cāndra systems, both well known in Tibet.

9. The Seven Treatises of Dharmakīrti are: *Pramāṇavārttikakārikā*, *Pramāṇaviniścaya*, *Nyāyabindu*, *Sambandhaparīkṣā*, *Vādanyāya*, *Saṃtānāntarasiddhi*, and *Hetubindu*.

10. This is an early reference to the *bṛhattrayī* and the *laghutrayī* of Sanskrit poetry.

11. The reference here is unclear. K. N. Mishra (personal communication) has suggested that perhaps this was a common name of Rājaśekhara's *Karpūrmañjarī*, which has a character called *Rūpamañjarī*. Kapstein (2003), p. 780, mentions the similarity of this title to the very popular Tibetan drama *Gzugs kyi nyi ma*, but notes that this drama postdates Sa-paṇ by several centuries.

12. Probably Śrīdhara's *Triśatika*.

13. MSA 11.60, p. 70: *vidyāsthāne pañcavidhe yogam akṛtvā sarvajñatvaṃ naiti kathaṃcit paramāryaḥ/ityanyeṣāṃ nigrahaṇānugrahaṇāya svājñārthaṃ vā tatra karoty eva sa yogam.*

14. Here we are to understand that a lion is so proud that he looks across to the horizon, taking everything in at once. Thus, the "lion's glance" is present in the verse of invocation, which thus gives a broad, comprehensive view of the meaning of the treatise. cf. Verhagen (2005), pp. 197–99.

15. MAVBh, p. 424: *śāstrasyāsya praṇetāramabhyarhya sugatātmajam/ vaktāraṃ cāsmadādibhyo yatiṣye 'rthavivecane.*

16. The word "this" stands for whatever the treatise actually means.

17. See Beckwith (1990) for discussion of this threefold method of disputation, called the "*dgag bzhag spang gsum*."

18. This is indented to show it is a continuation of the previous line from the root verses.

19. This refers to SDL.

20. This is indented to show it is a continuation of the previous line from the root verses.

21. I take *brtan* from D 13.12 as a correction of GL 379.2 *brten*.

22. Note that here "subsequent expression" (*rjes 'jug sgra, anuvartanaśabda*) is a gloss on the verse's "supervenient expression" (*rjes sgrub sgra, anusiddha-śabda*).

23. Taking *mngon spyod mkhan po* (*abhicārin*) for GL 379.10: *mngon dpyod mkhan po.*

24. Because drinking from the spring causes a leg sickness.

25. The knowledge, *shes pa,* is named after its cause, the knowing (*shes*), and the holder of a cognitive object (*yul can,* less literally translated as "subject") is named after the cognitive object (*yul*).

26. The sound of a drum comes not only from the drum but also from the stick and the drummer, and likewise the sprout comes not only from the seed but also from the soil and water, and so forth.

27. This is a medicine that looks like a crow's leg.

28. Indian astrology has Tuesday as an inauspicious day.

29. Indian astrology divides the day into eleven *kāraṇas,* and the seventh, *viṣṭi,* is considered inauspicious.

30. Really *dar dir* is the sound used to indicate drums—presumably they go with the cymbals.

31. I discuss this passage from the TR in chapter 3 above.

32. That is, the assertions "There are pots in other regions" and "Not all wisdom is uncontaminated," respectively.

33. This is the Sanskrit grammarian Pāṇini's abbreviation for case endings; *sup* means locative plural, so it literally means "the list ending in *sup,*" or, just "case endings."

34. *śabdayojanā*—'grammatical construction of a word'.

35. PV 2.16: *vivakśā-paratantratvān na śabdāḥ santi kutra vā.*

36. Here Sa-paṇ appears to be using *sgra* as a substitute for *ming.*

37. For the sake of ease of comprehension in English, I have slightly altered the word order in translating a number of verses in this section. Separate lines reliably reflect only the number of translated Tibetan *padas.*

38. Here I translate the word *sbyor* (*saṃyoga,* among other things) as "use in combination." Needless to say, it has the meanings of "use" as well as "combine," and in what follows I use it in these ways and others ("combined use," as a noun), depending on context. Also, I use the word "apply" or "apply appropriately" in some contexts, as well as "fit." But I do not think that in Tibetan there is a difference in the sense of its use from one instance to the next. I am hoping that this is a case of what Sa-paṇ calls *sgra 'gyur la don 'gyur,* a translation with a semantically faithful transformation of the expression.

39. *Ngam pa* is a difficult word to translate. It is clear, in the discussion that follows, that the person with *ngam pa* is seen by others as superior and attractive, while at the same time exhibiting egotism and ruthlessness.

40. These verse lines do not appear in the 1998 Beijing root text (T).

41. This passage, GL 402.13–16, needs to be clarified in light of the *Sarasvatīkaṇṭhābaraṇa* verse.

Tibetan Orthographic Equivalents

Butön Rinchendrup = bu-ston rin-chen-grup
Chak Lotsāwa = chag lo-tsā-ba chos-rje-dpal
Chakna = phyag-na rdo-rje
Drokmi = 'brog-mi lo-tsā-ba
Je Tsongkhapa = rje rin-po-che tsong-kha-pa blo-bzang grags-pa
Jigten Gonpo = 'jig-rten mgon-po
Lamdre = lam-'bras
Longchenpa = klong-chen rab-'byams-pa
Lowo Khenchen = glo-bo mkhan-chen
Marpa = mar-pa chos-kyi blo-gros
Martön = dmar-ston
Milarepa = rje-btsun mi-la ras-pa
Pakpa = 'phags-pa blo-gros rgyal-mtshan
Sakya = sa-skya
Sakyapa = sa-skya-pa
Sa-paṇ = Sakya Paṇḍita = sa-skya paṇ-ḍi-ta kun-dga' rgyal-mtshan
Sönam Tsemo = bsod-nams rtse-mo
Songtsen Gampo = srong-btsan sgam-po
Tashi Chöpel = bkra-shis chos-'phel
Thönmi Saṃbhoṭa = thon-mi saṃ-bho-ṭa
Thri Desongtsen = khri lde-srong-btsan
Thri Songdetsen = khri srong-lde'u-btsan
Thropu Lotsāwa = khro-phu lo-tsā-ba
Trakpa Gyeltsen = grags-pa rgyal-mtshan

Abbreviations

B: Sa-skya Paṇḍita Kun-dga'-rgyal-mtshan (1979)

CSI: *Clarification of the Sage's Intent* = Sa-skya Paṇḍita Kun-dga'-rgyal-mtshan (1992d)

D: Sa-skya Paṇḍita Kun-dga'-rgyal-mtshan (1967)

DGTG: Sde-dge Bstan-'gyur

EW: *Entry into Words* = Sa-skya Paṇḍita Kun-dga'-rgyal-mtshan (1992b)

GATC: *General Analysis of the Tantra Classes* = Bsod-nams rtse-mo (1992b)

GD: *Gateway to the Dharma* = Bsod-nams rtse-mo (1992a)

GL: *Gateway to Learning* = Sa-skya Paṇḍita Kun-dga'-rgyal-mtshan (1992a)

Glo-bo: Glo-bo mkhan-chen Bsod-nams-lhun-grub (1979)

Kā: *Kāvyādarśa* of Daṇḍin, Sanskrit text from Belvalkar (1924)

MAVBh: *Madhyāntavibhāgabhāṣyam* of Vasubandhu = Anacker (1998)

MSA: *Mahāyānasūtrālaṅkāra* = Asaṅga (1907)

PV: *Pramāṇavārttika* = Dharmakīrti (1997)

SDL: *Sword Doorway into Language* = Smṛtijñānakīrti (2000)

T: Sa-skya Paṇḍita Kun-dga'-rgyal-mtshan (1998)

TAJ: *Treasury of Aphoristic Jewels* = Bosson (1969)

TR: *Treasury of Reasoning* = Sa-skya Paṇḍita Kun-dga'-rgyal-mtshan (1992c)

Bibliography

Abhyankar, K. V. (1977) *A Dictionary of Sanskrit Grammar.* Second revised edition. Baroda: Oriental Institute.

Adams, Hazard, and Leroy Searle, eds. (1986) *Critical Theory Since 1965.* Tallahassee: Florida State University Press.

Anacker, Stefan. (1998) *Seven Works of Vasubandhu, the Buddhist Psychological Doctor.* Delhi: Motilal Banarsidass.

Apte, Vaman Shivaram. (1957) *The Practical Sanskrit-English Dictionary.* Revised and enlarged edition. Poona: Prasad Prakashan. Reprinted, Kyoto: Rinsen, 1992.

Asad, Talal. (1993) *Genealogies of Religion: Discipline and Reasons of Power in Christianity and Islam.* Baltimore and London: Johns Hopkins University Press.

Asaṅga. (1907) *Mahāyāna-Sūtrālaṃkāra.* Sylvain Lévi, ed. and trans. Vol I: Text. Paris: Librarie Honoré Champion.

Bassnett-McGuire, Susan. (1991) *Translation Studies.* Revised edition. London and New York: Routledge.

Bassnett, Susan, and André Lefevere, eds. (1990) *Translation, History, and Culture.* London and New York: Pinter.

———. (1998) *Constructing Cultures: Essays on Literary Translation.* Topics in Translation 11. Philadelphia: Multilingual Matters.

Beckwith, Christopher. (1990) "The Medieval Scholastic Method in Tibet and the West," in Lawrence Epstein and Richard F. Sherburne, eds., *Reflections on Tibetan Culture: Essays in Memory of Turrell V. Wylie.* Lewiston: Mellen Press, pp. 307–313.

Belvalkar, S. K. (1924) *Kāvyādarśa of Daṇḍin: Sanskrit Text and English Translation.* Poona Oriental Series 33. Poona: Oriental Book-Supplying Agency.

Beyer, Stephan V. (1992) *The Classical Tibetan Language.* SUNY Series in Buddhist Studies. Albany: State University of New York Press.

Bhattacarya, Vidhusekhar. (1928) "Sandhābhāṣā," *Indian Historical Quarterly,* p. 287.

Biardeau, Madeline. (1964) *Théorie de la connaisance et philosophie de la parole dans le brahmanisme classique.* Monde d'outre-mer, passé et présent. Première série, Etudes 23. Paris: Mouton.

Bkra shis chos 'phel, Bo thar. (1998) *mkhas pa 'jug pa'i sgo'i rnam bshad 'chad rtsom gsal ba'i me long,* in Padma Tshul-khrims, ed., *Sa paṇ mkhas 'jug rtsa 'grel bzhugs.* Si gron mi rigs dpe skrun khang [Sichuan Regional Printing House], Si gron zhing chen zhing hwa dpe tshong khang [Sichuan Province Library]. pp. 47–288.

Bond, George D. (1988) "The Gradual Path as a Hermeneutical Aproach to the *Dhamma,*" in Donald S. Lopez, Jr., ed., *Buddhist Hermeneutics.* Kuroda Institute Studies in East Asian Buddhism 6. Honolulu: University of Hawaii Press, pp. 29–47.

Bosson, James E. (1969) *A Treasury of Aphoristic Jewels: The Subhāṣitaratnanidhi of Sa skya Paṇḍita in Tibetan and Mongolian.* Indiana University Publications Uralic and Altaic Series 92. Bloomington: Indiana University.

Bourdieu, Pierre. (1977) *Outline of a Theory of Practice.* Richard Nice, trans. Cambridge Studies in Social and Cultural Anthropology 16. Cambridge, UK and New York: Cambridge University Press.

———. (1991) *Language and Symbolic Power.* Gino Raymond and Matthew Adamson, trans. John B. Thompson, ed. Cambridge, Mass.: Harvard University Press.

Broido, Michael. (1980) "The Term *Dgnos-po'i Gnas-lugs* as Used in Padma Dkar-po's Gzhung-'grel," in Michael Aris and Aung San Suu Kyi, eds., *Tibetan Studies in Honour of Hugh Richardson.* Proceedings of the International Seminar of Tibetan Studies, Oxford 1979. Warminster, England: Aris & Phillips, pp. 59–66.

———. (1982) "Does Tibetan Hermeneutics Throw Any Light on *Sandhābhāṣa?*" *Journal of the Tibet Society* 2, pp. 5–39.

———. (1983a) "*Bshad thabs:* Some Tibetan Methods of Explaining the Tantras," in Ernst Steinkellner and Helmut Tauscher, eds., *Contributions on Tibetan and Buddhist Religion and Philosophy.* Proceedings of the Csoma de Körös symposium held at Velm-Vienna, Austria, 13–19 September 1981. Vol. 2. Vienna: Arbeitskreis für Tibetische und Buddhistische Studien, Universität Wien, pp. 15–45.

———. (1983b) "A Note on Dgos-'brel" *Journal of the Tibet Society* 3, pp. 5–19.

———. (1984a) "Padma Dkar-po on Tantra as Ground, Path and Goal" *Journal of the Tibet* Society 4, pp. 5–46.

———. (1984b) "Abhiprāya and Implication in Tibetan Linguistics," *JIP* 12, pp. 1–33.

———. (1985a) "Padma Dkar-po on Integration as Ground, Path, and Goal," *Journal of the Tibet Society* 5, pp. 5–54.

———. (1985b) "Intention and Suggestion in the Abhidharmakośa: Sandhābhāṣā Revisited," *JIP* 13, pp. 327–381.

———. (1987) "Sa-skya Paṇḍita, the White Panacea and the Hva-Shang Doctrine," *JIABS* 10(2), pp. 27–69.

———. (1988a) "Killing, Lying, Stealing, and Adultery: A Problem of Interpretation in the Tantras," in: Donald S. Lopez, Jr., ed., *Buddhist Hermeneutics*. Kuroda Institute Studies in East Asian Buddhism 6. Honolulu: University of Hawaii Press, pp. 71–118.

———. (1988b) "Veridical and Delusive Cognition: Tsong-kha-pa on the Two Satyas," *JIP* 29, pp. 29–63.

Bsod-nams rtse-mo. (1992a) *chos la 'jug pa'i sgo zhe bya ba'i bstan bcos bzhugs*, in: *Bsod nams rtse mo'i bka' 'bum. The Collected works of Slob-dpon bSod-nams-rtse-mo* (Part 2). *dpal ldan sa skya pa'i bka' 'bum: Collected Writings of the Great Founding Masters of Sa-skya*. Volume 4 (*nga*). Reproduced from the 1736 Derge Edition. Dehra Dun, India: Sakya Centre, 1992, pp. 525–634.

———. (1992b) *rgyud sde spyi'i rnam par gzhag pa*, in: *Bsod nams rtse mo'i bka' 'bum. The Collected works of Slob-dpon bSod-nams-rtse-mo* (Part 1). *dpal ldan sa skya pa'i bka' 'bum: Collected Writings of the Great Founding Masters of Sa-skya*. Volume 3 (*ga*). Reproduced from the 1736 Derge Edition. Dehra Dun, India, Sakya Centre, 1992. pp. 1–147.

Buswell, Robert E. (1997) "The Proliferation of the *Cittaviprayuktasamskāra*-s in the Vaibhāṣika School," *JIP* 25, pp. 451–66.

Cabezón, José Ignacio. (1992) "Vasubandhu's *Vyākhyāyukti* on the Authenticity of the Mahāyāna *Sūtras*," in Jeffrey Timm, ed., *Texts in Context: Traditional Hermeneutics in South Asia*. Albany: State University of New York Press, pp. 221–243.

———. (1994) *Buddhism and Language: A Study of Indo-Tibetan Scholasticism*. Albany: State University of New York Press.

———, ed. (1998) *Scholasticism: Cross-Cultural and Comparative Perspectives*. Albany: State University of New York Press.

———, and Roger R. Jackson, eds. (1996) *Tibetan Literature: Studies in Genre*. Ithaca, N.Y.: Snow Lion.

Cardona, George. (1974) "Pāṇini's *kārakas*: Agency, Animation and Identity," *JIP* 2, pp. 231–306.

Chang, Garma C. C., trans. (2006) *The Hundred Thousand Songs of Milarepa*. Whitefish, Mont.: Kessinger Publishing.

Coady, C. A. J. (1992) *Testimony: A Philosophical Study*. Oxford, Clarendon.

D'Amato, Mario A. (2000) *The Mahāyāna-Hīnayāna Distinction in the* Mahāyānasūtrālaṃkāra: *A Terminological Analysis*. 2 vols. Ph.D. Thesis, University of Chicago.

Davenport, John T., trans. (2000) *Ordinary Wisdom: Sakya Pandita's Treasury of Good Advice*. With a commentary entitled *A Hive Where Gather Bees of*

Clear Understanding, by Sakya Khenpo Sangyay Tenzin. Sallie D. Davenport and Losang Thonden, asst. trans. Boston: Wisdom.

Davidson, Ronald M. (1990) "An Introduction to the Standards of Scriptural Authenticity in Indian Buddhism," in Robert E. Buswell, Jr., ed., *Chinese Buddhist Apocrypha*. Honolulu: University of Hawaii Press, pp. 291–325.

———. (1992) "Preliminary Studies on Hevajra's *Abhisamaya* and the *lam-'bras Tshogs-bshad*," in Steven D. Goodman and Ronald M. Davidson, eds., *Tibetan Buddhism: Reason and Revelation*. Albany: State University of New York Press, pp. 107–32.

———. (2002) *Indian Esoteric Buddhism: A Social History of the Tantric Movement*. New York: Columbia University Press.

———. (2005) *Tibetan Renaissance: Tantric Buddhism in the Rebirth of Tibetan Culture*. New York: Columbia University Press.

Dhanañjaya. (1969) *The* Daśarūpaka *of Dhanamjaya with the Commentary* Avaloka *by Dhanika, and the Subcommentary* Laghutīikā *by Bhattanrsimha*. T. Venkatacharya, ed. Madras: Adyar Library and Research Centre.

Dharmakīrti. (1968) *Pramāṇavārttika of Dharmakīrti with the Commentary "Vritti" of Acharya Manorathanandin*. Dwarikadas Shastri, ed. Varanasi: Bauddha Bharati.

———. (1972–1977) *Pramāṇavārttika-kārikā: Sanskrit and Tibetan*. Y. Miyasaka, ed. Acta Indologica 2, 3, 4.

———. (1997) *Pramāṇavārttika* [e-text]. Prepared by Motoi Ono. http://www.logos.tsukuba.ac.jp/~nagasaki/dharmakirti/pv.txt.

Dimitrov, Dragomir. (2002) *Mārgavibhāga: Die Unterscheidung der Stilarten. Kritische Ausgabe des ersten Kapitels von Daṇḍins Poetik* Kāvyādarśa *und der tibetischen Übertragung* Sñan ṅag me loṅ *nebst einer deutschen Übersetzung des Sanskrittextes*. Indica et Tibetica: Monographien zu den Sprachen und Literaturen des indo-tibetischen Kulturraumes 40. Marburg: Indica et Tibetica Verlag.

Dreyfus, Georges B. J. (1995) "Is Dharmakīrti a Pragmatist?" *Asiatische Studien* 49(4), pp. 671–91.

———. (1997a) *Recognizing Reality: Dharmakīrti's Philosophy and Its Tibetan Interpreters*. Albany: State University of New York Press.

———. (1997b) "Tibetan Scholastic Education and the Role of Soteriology," *JIABS* 20(1), pp. 31–62.

———. (2003) *The Sound of Two Hands Clapping: The Education of a Tibetan Monk*. Berkeley: University of California Press.

Dudjom Rinpoche, Jikdrel Yeshe Dorje. (1991) *The Nyingma School of Tibetan Buddhism: Its Fundamentals and History*. 2 vols. Gyurme Dorje and Matthew Kapstein, trans. Boston: Wisdom.

Dunne, John D. (1996) "Thoughtless Buddha, Passionate Buddha," *JAAR* 64, pp. 525–56.

———. (1999) *Foundations of Dharmakīrti's Philosophy: A Study of the Central Issues in His Ontology, Logic and Epistemology with Particular Attention to the* Svopajñavṛtti. Ph.D. Thesis, Harvard University.

Dutt, Sukumar. (1988) *Buddhist Monks and Monasteries of India: Their History and Their Contribution to Indian Culture.* Delhi: Motilal Banarsidass.

Eppling, John Frederick. (1989) *A Calculus of Creative Expression: The Central Chapter of Daṇḍin's "Kāvyādarśa."* Ph.D. Thesis, University of Wisconsin, Madison.

Faure, Bernard. (1991) *The Rhetoric of Immediacy: A Cultural Critique of Chan/Zen Buddhism.* Princeton, N.J.: Princeton University Press.

Fish, Stanley. (1980) *Is There a Text in This Class? The Authority of Interpretive Communities.* Cambridge, Mass: Harvard University Press.

———. (1999) *The Stanley Fish Reader.* H. Aram Veeser, ed. Malden, Mass.: Blackwell.

Foucault, Michel. (1972) *The Archaeology of Knowledge and The Discourse on Language.* A. M. Sheridan Smith, trans. New York: Pantheon.

Gerow, Edwin. (1977) *Indian Poetics.* A History of Indian Literature, vol. 5, fasc. 3. Wiesbaden: Harrassowitz.

Glo-bo mkhan-chen Bsod-nams-lhun-grub. (1979) *Mkhas pa rnams 'jug pa'i sgo'i rnam par bshad pa rig gnas gsal byed.* New Delhi: N. Topgye.

Go-rams-pa Bsod-nams seng-ge. *tshad ma rigs pa'i gter gyi dka' ba'i gnas rnam par bshad pa sde bdun rab gsal*, in *Sa skya pa'i bka' 'bum: The Complete Works of the Great Masters of the Sa skya Sect of the Tibetan Buddhism.* Sde dge edition. Vol. *ga*, pp. 1–334a.

Griffiths, Paul J. (1990) "Omniscience in the *Mahāyānasūtrālaṅkāra* and Its Commentaries," *IIJ* 33(2), pp. 85–120.

———. (1994) *On Being Buddha: The Classical Doctrine of Buddhahood.* Albany: State University of New York Press.

———. (1998) "Scholasticism: The Possible Recovery of an Intellectual Practice," in José Ignacio Cabezón, ed., *Scholasticism: Cross-Cultural and Comparative Perspectives.* Albany: State University of New York Press, pp. 201–35.

———. (1999) *Religious Reading: The Place of Reading in the Practice of Religion.* Oxford: Oxford University Press.

Halbfass, Wilhelm. (1997) *Beyond Orientalism: The Work of Wilhelm Halbfass and Its Impact on Indian Cross-Cultural Studies.* Eli Franco and Karin Preisendanz, eds. Atlanta: Rodopi.

Hallisey, Charles. (1994) "In Defense of a Rather Fragile and Local Achievement: Reflections on the Work of Gurulugomi," in Frank E. Reynolds and David Tracy, eds., *Religion and Practical Reason: New Essays in the Comparative Philosophy of Religions.* Albany: State University of New York Press, pp. 121–60.

Hamlin, Edward. (1983) "Discourse in the *Laṅkāvatāra-sūtra*," *JIP* 11, pp. 267–313.

Haribhadra. (1993) *Abhisamayālaṅkāravṛttiḥ Sphuṭārthā by Ācārya Haribhadra*. Ramshankar Tripathi, ed. Bibliotheca Indo-Tibetica Series 2. Varanasi: Central Institute of Higher Tibetan Studies.

Harrison, Paul. (1996) "A Brief History of the Tibetan bKa' 'gyur," in José Ignacio Cabezón and Roger R. Jackson, eds., *Tibetan Literature: Studies in Genre*. Ithaca, N.Y.: Snow Lion.

Hayes, Richard P. (1984) "The Question of Doctrinalism in the Buddhist Epistemologists," *JAAR* 52(4), pp. 645–70.

Henderson, John B. (1988) "Neo-Confucian Scholasticism," in José Ignacio Cabezón, ed., *Scholasticism: Cross-Cultural and Comparative Perspectives*. Albany: State University of New York Press, pp. 159–75.

Herzberger, Rhadika. (1986) *Bhartṛhari and the Buddhists*. Studies of Classical India 8. Dordrecht: Kluwer Academic Publishers.

Horváth, Zoltán. (1984) "Structure and Content of the *Chad-ma Rigs-pa'i Gter*, an Epistemological Treatise of Saskya Paṇḍita," in Louis Ligeti, ed., *Tibetan and Buddhist Studies: Commemorating the 200th Anniversary of the Birth of Alexander Csoma de Körös*. Bibliotheca Orientalis Hungarica 29(1). Budapest: Akadémiai Kiadó, pp. 267–302.

Ingalls, Daniel H. H. (1968) *Sanskrit Poetry from Vidyākara's "Treasury."* Cambridge, Mass.: Harvard University Press.

Ishihama, Yumiko, and Yoichi Fukuda. (1989) *A New Critical Edition of the* Mahāvyutpatti: *Sanskrit-Tibetan-Mongolian Dictionary of Buddhist Terminology*. Studia Tibetica 16, Materials for Tibetan-Mongolian Dictionaries, vol. 1. Tokyo: Tōyō Bunko.

Ishikawa, Mie. (1990) *A Critical Edition of the* Sgra sbyor bam po gnyis pa: *An Old and Basic Commentary on the* Mahāvyutpatti. Studia Tibetica 18, Materials for Tibetan-Mongolian Dictionaries, vol. 2. Tokyo: Tōyō Bunko.

Jackson, David P. (1985) "Madhyamaka Studies among the Early Sa-skya-pas," *The Tibet Journal* 10(2), pp. 20–34.

———. (1987) *The Entrance Gate for the Wise (Section III): Sa-skya Paṇḍita on Indian and Tibetan Traditions of Pramāṇa and Philosophical Debate*. 2 vols. Wiener Studien zur Tibetologie und Buddhismuskunde, Heft 17 (I–II). Wien: Arbeitskreis für Tibetische und Buddhistische Studien.

———. (1990a) "Sa-skya Paṇḍita the 'Polemicist': Ancient Debates and Modern Interpretations," *JIABS* 13(2), pp. 17–116.

———. ed. (1990b) *Two Biographies of Śākyaśrībhadra: The Eulogy by Khro-phu Lo-tsā-ba and Its "Commentary" by bSod-nams-dpal-bzang-po*. Tibetan and Indo-Tibetan Studies 4. Stuttgart: Franz Steiner Verlag.

———. (1992) "A Recent Translation of Sa-skya Paṇḍita's *Thub pa'i dgongs gsal*." Rev. of *Illuminations: A Guide to Essential Buddhist Practices*, by Geshe

Wangyal and Brian Cutillo. *Studien zur Indologie und Iranistik,* vol. 16/17, pp. 93–99.

———. (1993a) "Foreword: rNgog Lo-tsā-ba's Commentary on the *Ratnagotravibhāga,*" in *Theg chen rgyud bla ma'i don bsdus pa: Commentary on the* Ratnagotravibhaga *by Rṅog Lotsaba Blo ldan Śes rab (1059–1109)*. Dharamsala: Library of Tibetan Works and Archives.

———. (1993b) "Foreword: rNgog-lo's Commentary on the *Abhisamayālaṃkāra,*" in *Lotsaba Chen po'i Bsdus don Bzugs so: Commentary on the* Abhisamayalamkara *by Rṅog Lotsaba Blo ldan Śes rab (1059–1109)*. Dharamsala: Library of Tibetan Works and Archives.

———. (1994) *Enlightenment by a Single Means: Tibetan Controversies on the "Self-Sufficient White Remedy" (dkar po chig thup)*. Beiträge zur Kultur- und Geistesgeschichte Asiens, No. 12. Vienna, Der Österreichischen Akademie der Wissenschaften.

———. (1995) "The Status of Pramāṇa Doctrine According to Sa skya Paṇḍita and Other Tibetan Masters: Theoretical Discipline or Doctrine of Liberation?" in T. Skorupski and U. Pagel, eds., *The Buddhist Forum, Volume III (1991–1993): Papers in Honor and Appreciation of Professor David Seyfort Ruegg's Contribution to Indological, Buddhist and Tibetan Studies*. New Delhi: Heritage, pp. 85–129.

Jackson, Roger. (1982) "Sa-skya Paṇḍita's Account of the bSam-yas Debate: History as Polemic," *JIABS* 5(2), pp. 89–99.

Jaini, Padmanabh S. (1959) "The Vaibhāṣika Theory of Words and Meanings," *Bulletin of the School of Oriental and African Studies, University of London* 22(1), pp. 95–107.

Kapstein, Matthew. (1987) *Self and Personal Identity in Indian Buddhist Scholasticism: A Philosophical Investigation*. Ph.D. Thesis, Brown University.

———. (1988) "Mi-pham's Theory of Interpretation," in Donald S. Lopez, Jr., ed., *Buddhist Hermeneutics*. Kuroda Institute Studies in East Asian Buddhism 6. Honolulu: University of Hawaii Press, pp. 149–74. Reprinted in Kapstein, *Reason's Traces,* pp. 317–43.

———. (1989) "The Purificatory Gem and Its Cleansing: A Late Tibetan Polemical Discussion of Apocryphal Texts," *HR* 28(3), pp. 217–44.

———. (2000) *The Tibetan Assimilation of Buddhism: Conversion, Contestation, and Memory*. New York: Oxford University Press.

———. (2001) *Reason's Traces: Identity and Interpretation in Indian and Tibetan Buddhist Thought*. Boston: Wisdom.

———. (2003) "The Indian Literary Identity in Tibet," in Sheldon Pollock, ed., *Literary Cultures in History: Reconstructions from South Asia*. Berkeley: University of California Press, pp. 747–802.

Katz, Nathan. (1983) "Tibetan Hermeneutics and the *Yāna* Controversy," in Ernst Steinkellner and Helmut Tauscher, eds., *Contributions on Tibetan and Buddhist Religion and Philosophy*. Proceedings of the Csoma de Körös symposium held at Velm-Vienna, Austria, 13–19 September 1981. Vol. 2. Vienna: Arbeitskreis für Tibetische und Buddhistische Studien, Universität Wien, pp. 107–30.

Kolmaš, Josef. (1978) "The Aphorisms (*legs-bshad*) of Sa-skya Paṇḍita," in *Proceedings of the Csoma de Körös Memorial Symposium: Held at Mátrafüred, Hungary, 24–30 September 1976*. Louis Ligeti, ed. Budapest: Akadémiai Kiadó, pp. 189–203.

Kuijp, Leonard W. J. van der. (1978) "Phya-pa chos-kyi Seng-ge's Impact on Tibetan Epistemological Theory," in *JOIP* 5, pp. 355–69.

———. (1979a) "Introductory Notes to the *Pramāṇavārttika* Based on Tibetan Sources," *Tibet Journal* 4(2): 6–28.

———. (1979b) "Tibetan Contributions to the *Apoha* Theory: The Fourth Chapter of the *Tshad-ma Rigs-pa'i Gter*," *JAOS* 99.

———. (1983) *Contributions to the Development of Tibetan Buddhist Epistemology: From the Eleventh to the Thirteenth Century*. Alt- und Neu-Indische Studien 26. Wiesbaden: Franz Steiner.

———. (1985) "Miscellanea Apropos of the Philosophy of Mind in Tibet: *Mind in Tibetan Buddhism*," *Tibet Journal* 10(1), pp. 32–43.

———. (1986a) "Sa-skya Paṇḍita Kun-dga' rgyal-mtshan on the Typology of Literary Genres," *Studien zur Indologie und Iranistik* 11/12, pp. 41–52.

———. (1986b) "On the Sources for Sa-skya Paṇḍita's Notes on the bSam-yas Debate," *JIABS* 9(2), pp. 147–53.

———. (1987) "An Early Tibetan View of the Soteriology of Buddhist Epistemology: The Case of 'Bri-gung 'Jig-rten Mgon-po," *JIP* 15, pp. 57–70.

———. (1994) "On the *Lives* of Śāyaśṛībhadra (?–?1225)," *JAOS* 114(4), pp. 599–616.

———. (1996) "Tibetan Belles-Lettres: The Influence of Daṇḍin and Kṣemendra," in José Ignacio Cabezón and Roger R. Jackson, eds., *Tibetan Literature: Studies in Genre. Essays in Honor of Geshe Lhundup Sopa*. Ithaca, N.Y.: Snow Lion, pp. 393–410.

Lakoff, Robin Tolmach. (2000) *The Language War*. Berkeley: University of California Press.

Lamotte, Étienne. (1949) "La critique d'interprétation dans le bouddhisme," in *Annuaire de l'institut de philologie et d'histoire orientales et slaves* 9 (Mélanges Henri Grégoroire). Université libre de Bruxelles, pp. 341–61. English translation by Sara Boin-Webb, "Assessment of Textual Interpretation in Buddhism," in Donald S. Lopez, Jr., ed., *Buddhist Hermeneutics*. Kuroda Institute Studies in East Asian Buddhism 6. Honolulu, University of Hawaii Press, 1988, pp. 11–27.

La Vallée Poussin, Louis de, trans. (1923–1931) *L'Abhidharmakośa de Vasu-*

bandhu. 6 volumes. Paris: Paul Geuthner. Rept. 1971 as Mélanges Chinois et Bouddiques, 16. Bruxelles: Institut Belge des Hautes Études Chinois.

Lévi, Sylvain, ed. (1925) *Vijñaptimātrasiddhi: Deux Traités de Vasubandhu: Viṃśatikā et Triṃśikā.* Paris: Champion.

Lhalungpa, Lobsang P., trans. (1977) *The Life of Milarepa.* New York: Dutton.

Liebich, Bruno. (1919) "Zur Einführung in die indische einheimische Sprachwissenschaft: 1. Das Kātantra," *Sitzungsberichte der Heidelberger Akademie der Wissenschaften: Philosophisch-historiche Klasse.* Heidelberg: Carl Winter's Universitätsbuchhandlung, March 1919, pp. 1–13.

———. (1920). "Zur Einführung in die indische einheimische Sprachwissenschaft: 4. Analyse der Candra-Vṛtti," *Sitzungsberichte der Heidelberger Akademie der Wissenschaften: Philosophisch-historiche Klasse.* Heidelberg, Carl Winter's Universitätsbuchhandlung, June 1920, pp. 1–28.

Long, Lynne. (2001) *Translating the Bible: From the Seventh to the Seventeenth Century.* Ashgate New Critical Thinking in Theology and Biblical Studies. Aldershot, England: Ashgate.

Lopez, Donald S., Jr. (1988a, ed.) *Buddhist Hermeneutics.* Kuroda Institute Studies in East Asian Buddhism 6. Honolulu: University of Hawaii Press. "Introduction," pp. 1–10; "On the Interpretation of the Mahāyāna Sūtras," pp. 47–70.

———. (1988b) "Do *Śrāvakas* Understand Emptiness?" *JIP* 16, pp. 65–105.

Makransky, John J. (1997) *Buddhahood Embodied: Sources of Controversy in India and Tibet.* Albany: State University of New York Press.

Mani, Vettam. (1975) *Purāṇic Encyclopaedia: A Comprehensive Dictionary with Special Reference to the Epic and Purāṇic Literature.* First English edition. Delhi, Patna, and Varanasi: Motilal Banarsidass.

Martin, Dan. (1996) "Tables of Contents (*dKar chag*)," in José Ignacio Cabezón and Roger R. Jackson, eds., *Tibetan Literature: Studies in Genre.* Ithaca, N.Y.: Snow Lion, pp. 500–14.

Matilal, Bimal Krishna. (1990) *The Word and the World: India's Contribution to the Study of Language.* Delhi: Oxford University Press.

Miller, Roy Andrew. (1993) *Prolegomena to the First Two Tibetan Grammatical Treatises.* Vienna: Arbeitskreis für Tibetische und Buddhistische Studien, Universität Wien.

Mohanty, Jiten N. (1987) "Sense, Reverence, and the Ineffable in Indian Philosophy," *Journal of Chinese Philosophy* 14, pp. 401–18.

Nance, Richard F. (2004) *Models of Teaching and the Teaching of Models: Contextualizing Indian Buddhist Commentary.* Ph.D. Thesis, University of Chicago.

Ngag dbang chos grags. (1998) *bstan bcos chen po mkhas pa 'jug pa'i sgo'i rnam par bshad pa blo gsal mgrin pa'i dpal yon,* in: *Sa paṇ mkhas 'jug rtsa 'grel bzhugs.* Padma Tshul-khrims, ed. Si gron mi rigs dpe skrun khang [Sichuan

Regional Printing House]: Si gron zhing chen zhing hwa dpe tshong khang [Sichuan Province Library]. pp. 289–373.

Nicolson, Adam. (2003) *God's Secretaries: The Making of the King James Bible.* New York: Harper Collins.

Nussbaum, Martha C. (1995) *Poetic Justice: The Literary Imagination and Public Life.* Boston: Beacon.

Obermiller, E. (1987) *The Jewelry of Scripture by Bu Ston.* Bibliotheca Indo Buddhica No. 42. Delhi: Sri Satguru.

Onoda, Shunzo. (1992) *Monastic Debate in Tibet: A Study on the History and Structures of* Bsdus grwa *Logic.* Wiener Studien zur Tibetologie und Buddhismuskunde 27. Vienna: Arbeitskreis für Tibetische und Buddhistische Studien Universität Wien.

Petech, Luciano. (1990) *Central Tibet and the Mongols: The Yüan Sa-Skya Period of Tibetan History.* Rome: Istituto italiano per il Medio ed Estremo Oriente.

Pollock, Sheldon. (1995) "Literary History, Indian History, World History," *Social Scientist* 23(10–12), pp. 112–42.

———. (1996) "The Sanskrit Cosmopolis, A.D. 300–1300: Transculturation, Vernacularization, and the Question of Ideology," in J. E. M. Houben, ed., *Ideology and Status of Sanskrit: Contributions to the History of the Sanskrit Language.* Leiden: Brill.

———. (1998) "Bhoja's *Śṛṅgāraprakāśa* and the Problem of Rasa: A Historical Introduction and Annotated Translation," *ES/ÉA* 52(1), pp. 117–92.

———. (2001) "The Social Aesthetic and Sanskrit Literary Theory," *JIP* 29, pp. 197–229.

———. (2003) *Literary Cultures in History: Reconstructions from South Asia.* Berkeley: University of California Press.

Pye, Michael. (1978) *Skillful Means: A Concept in Mahāyāna Buddhism.* London: Duckworth.

Quine, W. V. (1960) *Word and Object.* [Cambridge, Mass.:] Technology Press of the Massachusetts Institute of Technology.

Radicchi, Anna. (1993) "Vivakṣā in the *Vākyapadīya*," AS/ÉA 47(1) (Proceedings of the Bhartṛhari Conference, Poona University, Jan. 6–8, 1992), pp. 221–33.

Raja, K. Kunjunni. (1969) *Indian Theories of Meaning.* Second edition. Adyar Library Series 91. Madras: Adyar Library and Research Centre.

Rescher, Nicholas. (1998) *Communicative Pragmatism and Other Philosophical Essays on Language.* Lanham, Md.: Rowman & Littlefield.

Reynolds, Frank, and David Tracy, eds. (1992) *Discourse and Practice.* Albany: State University of New York Press.

Rhoton, Jared Douglas, trans. (2002) *A Clear Differentiation of the Three Codes: Essential Distinctions among the Individual Liberation, Great Vehicle, and Tantric Systems. The* sDom gsum rab dbye *and Six Letters by Sakya Pandita*

Kunga Gyaltshen. Victoria R.M. Scott, ed. Albany: Stae University of New York Press.

Rigzin, Tsepak. (1993) *Nang don rig pa'i ming tshig Bod-Dbyin sang sbyar: Tibetan-English Dictionary of Buddhist Terminology*. Second revised edition. Dharamsala: India, Library of Tibetan Works and Archives.

Roerich, George, trans. (1959) *Biography of Dharmasvāmin (Chag lo-tsā-ba Chos-rje-dpal) a Tibetan Monk Pilgrim*. Patna: Jayaswal Research Institute.

———. (1976) *The Blue Annals*. 2 vols. Delhi: Motilal Banarsidass.

Ruegg, D. Seyfort. (1966) *The Life of Bu ston Rin po che, with the Tibetan Text of the Bu ston rNam thar*. Roma: Istituto Italiano per il Medio ed Estremo Oriente.

———. (1977) "The Uses of the Four Positions of the *Catuṣkoṭi* and the Problem of the Description of Reality in Mahāyāna Buddhism," *JIP* 5, pp. 1–71.

———. (1983) "On Translating the Buddhist Canon (A Dictionary of Indo-Tibetan Terminology in Tibetan and Mongolian: *Dag yig mkhas pa'i 'byuṅ gnas of Rol pa'i rdo rje*)," in Perala Ratnam, ed., *Studies in Indo-Asian Art and Culture*. Vol. 3, pp. 243–61.

———. (1985) "Purport, Implicature and Presupposition: Sanskrit *Abhiprāya* and Tibetan *Dgoṅs pa/Dgoṅs gži* as Hermeneutical Concepts," *JIP* 13, pp. 309–25.

———. (1988) "An Indian Source for the Tibetan Hermeneutical Term *Dgoṅs Gži* 'Intentional Ground,'" *JIP* 16, pp. 1–4.

———. (1989) *Buddha-nature, Mind and the Problem of Gradualism in a Comparative Perspective: On the Transmission and Reception of Buddhism in India and Tibet*. Jordan Lectures, 1987. London: University of London School of Oriental and African Studies.

———. (1992) "Some Reflections on Translating Buddhist Philosophical Texts from Sanskrit and Tibetan," AS/ÉA 46(1), pp. 367–91.

———. (1995) *Ordre Spirituel et Ordre Temporel Dans la Pensée Bouddhique de l'Inde et du Tibet*. Paris: De Boccard.

Saini, R. S. (1999) *Post-Pāṇinian Systems of Sanskrit Grammar*. Delhi: Parimal.

Śāntideva. (1995) *The Bodhicaryāvatāra*. Kate Crosby and Andrew Skilton, trans. Oxford World's Classics. New York: Oxford University Press.

Sa-skya Paṇḍi-ta Kun-dga'-rgyal-mtshan. (1967) *'jam mgon sa skya paṇḍi tas mdzad pa'i mkhas pa 'jug pa'i sgo zhes bya ba'i bstan bcos bzhugs so. Way of the Wise: Guide to Propagation, Disputation and Composition of Classics by Sa sKya Pan Dita Kun dga' rGyal mTsan*. T. G. Dhongtog Rinpoche, ed. Delhi: ALA Press.

———. (1979). *Byis pa bde blag tu 'jug pa'i rnam par bśad pa mkhas pa 'jug pa'i sgo*, in *Bśes pa'i 'phrin yig gi tīka and 'phags pa klu sgrup kyi rtogs brjod mdor bsdus: Commentary on the Suhṛllekha of Nāgārjuna with a Brief Biography by*

Nag-gi-dbaṅ-phyug-dge-legs-rgya-mtsho'i-sde and *Byis pa bde blag tu 'jug pa'i rnam par bśad pa mkhas pa 'jug pa'i sgo: An Introduction to the Principles of Tibetan Buddhist Scholasticism by Sa-skya Paṇḍita Kun-dga'-rgyal-mtshan*. Reproduced from rare manuscripts from Pha-jo-ldiṅ Monastery in Bhutan. Thimphu: Tulku Kunsang Gyatso, c/o Kunsang Tobgyay, pp. 131–255.

———. (1992). *Sa paṇ kun dga' rgyal mtshan gyi gsung 'bum*. Three volumes. Gangs can rig pa mdzod [Tibetan Treasures of Reasoning Series], vols. 23–25. Chab spel tshe brtan phun tshog, gtsho 'gan dpe sgrig pa [Editor in Chief]. Bod ljongs bod yig dpe rnying dpe skun khang [Lhasa: Old Tibetan Text Publishers].

———. (1992a). *mkhas pa rnams 'jug pa'i sgo zhes bya ba'i bstan bcos*, in *Sa paṇ kun dga' rgyal mtshan gyi gsung 'bum*. Legs bam dang po [vol. 1]. Chab spel tshe brtan phun tshog, gtsho 'gan dpe sgrig pa [Editor in Chief]. Gangs can rig mdzod [Tibetan Treasures of Reasoning Series] 23. Bod ljongs bod yig dpe rnying dpe skun khang [Lhasa: Old Tibetan Text Publishers], pp. 367–501.

———. (1992b). *sgra la 'jug pa zhes bya ba'i bstan bcos*, in: *Sa paṇ kun dga' rgyal mtshan gyi gsung 'bum*. Legs bam dang po [vol. 1]. Chab spel tshe brtan phun tshog, gtsho 'gan dpe sgrig pa [Editor in Chief]. Gangs can rig mdzod [Tibetan Treasures of Reasoning Series] 23. Bod ljongs bod yig dpe rnying dpe skun khang [Lhasa: Old Tibetan Text Publishers], pp. 503–23.

———. (1992c). *tshad ma rigs pa'i gter gyi rang 'grel*, in *Sa paṇ kun dga' rgyal mtshan gyi gsung 'bum*. Legs bam gnyis pa [vol. 2]. Chab spel tshe brtan phun tshog, gtsho 'gan dpe sgrig pa [Editor in Chief]. Gangs can rig mdzod [Tibetan Treasures of Reasoning Series] 24. Bod ljongs bod yig dpe rnying dpe skun khang [Lhasa: Old Tibetan Text Publishers], pp. 55–538.

———. (1992d). *thub pa'i dgongs pa rab tu gsal ba*, in *Sa paṇ kun dga' rgyal mtshan gyi gsung 'bum*. Legs bam dang po [vol. 1]. Chab spel tshe brtan thun tshog, gtsho 'gan dpe sgrig pa [Editor in Chief]. Gangs can rig mdzod [Tibetan Treasures of Reasoning Series] 23. Bod ljongs bod yig dpe rnying dpe skun khang [Lhasa: Old Tibetan Text Publishers], pp. 1–212.

———. (1998) *mkhas pa rnams 'jug pa'i sgo zhes bya ba'i bstan bcos* [root text only], in Padma Tshul-khrims, ed., *Sa paṇ mkhas 'jug rtsa 'grel bzhugs*. Si gron mi rigs dpe skrun khang [Sichuan Regional Printing House], Si gron zhing chen zhing hwa dpe tshong khang [Sichuan Province Library], pp. 3–46.

Saussure, Ferdinand de. (1959) *Course in General Linguistics*. Wade Baskin, trans. Charles Bally and Albert Sechehaye, eds. New York: Philosophical Library. Reprinted New York: McGraw-Hill, 1966.

Scharfe, Hartmut. (1977) *Grammatical Literature*. History of Indian Literature, vol. 5, fasc. 2. Wiesbaden, O. Harrassowitz.

Scherrer-Schaub, Christina A. (1999) "Translation, Transmission, Tradition: Suggestions from Ninth-Century Tibet," *JIP* 27(1/2), pp. 67–77.

———. (2002) "Enacting Words: A Diplomatic Analysis of the Imperial Decrees (*bkas bcad*) and Their Application in the sGra sbyor bam po gñis pa Tradition," *JIABS* 25(1–2), pp. 263–340.

Schoening, Jeffrey D., and Per K. Sørensen. (1988) "Two Minor Works by Sa-skya Paṇḍita," *Studies in Central and East Asian Religions* 1, pp. 35–49.

Searle, John R. (1983) *Intentionality: An Essay in the Philosophy of Mind.* New York: Cambridge University Press.

Siderits, Mark. (1987) "The Sense-Reference Distinction in Indian Philosophy of Language," *Journal of Chinese Philosophy* 14, pp. 331–55.

Simonsson, Nils. (1957) *Indo-tibetische Studien: Die Methoden der Tibetischen Übersetzer, untersucht im Hinblick auf die Bedeutung ihrer Übersetzungen für die Sanskritphilologie.* Imprint Uppsala: Almqvist & Wiksells.

———. (1982) "Reflections on the Grammatical Tradition in Tibet," in L. A. Hercus, et al., eds., *Indological and Buddhist Studies. Volume in Honour of Professor J. W. de Jong on His Sixtieth Birthday.* Canberra, Australia: Faculty of Asian Studies.

———. (1984) "Reflections on the Grammatical Tradition in Tibet and Its Connection with Indian Buddhistic Speculation on Language," *Indologica Tarinensia,* vol. 12. (Proceedings of the Scandinavian Conference-Seminar of Indological Studies, Stockholm, June 1–5, 1982.) Torino, Italy: Edizioni Jollygrafica.

Smith, E. Gene. (1970) "Introduction," in Lokesh Chandra, ed., *Kongtrul's Encyclopaedia of Indo-Tibetan Culture: Parts 1–3.* New Delhi: International Academy of Indian Culture, pp. 1–78.

———. (2001) *Among Tibetan Texts: History and Literature of the Himalayan Plateau.* Kurtis R. Schaeffer, ed. Boston: Wisdom.

———. (1974) "Introduction," in S. T. Kazi, ed., *Encyclopedia Tibetica: The Collected Works of Bo-dong Paṇ-chen Phyogs-las-rnam-rgyal.* New Delhi: Tibet House, 1969–1981, vol. 3, pp. 1–10.

Smṛtijñānakīrti (dran pa'i ye shes grags pa). (2000) *smra ba'i sgo mtshon cha lta bu zhes bya ba.* Second edition. Beijing: mi rigs dpe skrun khang [Ethnic Groups' Publishers], 2000.

Snellgrove, David L. (1959) *The Hevajra Tantra: A Critical Study.* 2 vols. London Oriental Series, volume 6. London: Oxford University Press.

———. (1987) *Indo-Tibetan Buddhism: Indian Buddhists and Their Tibetan Successors.* 2 Vols. Boston: Shambhala.

Stcherbatsky, Th. (1992) *Buddhist Logic.* Bibliotheca Buddhica 26. Delhi: Motilal Banarsidass.

Stearns, Cyrus. (1996) "The Life and Tibetan Legacy of the Indian *Mahāpaṇḍita* Vibhūticandra," *JIABS* 19(1), pp. 127–71.

———. (2001) *Luminous Lives: The Story of the Early Masters of the Lam 'bras Tradition in Tibet.* Studies in Indian and Tibetan Buddhism. Boston: Wisdom.

Steiner, George. (1992) *After Babel: Aspects of Language and Translation.* Second edition. New York: Oxford University Press.

Steinkellner, Ernst. (1978) "Remarks on Tantristic Hermeneutics," in *Proceedings of the Csoma de Körös Memorial Symposium: Held at Mátrafüred, Hungary, 24–30 September 1976.* Louis Ligeti, ed. Budapest: Akadémiai Kiadó, pp. 445–58.

———. (1983) "*Tshad ma'i skyes bu:* Meaning and Historical Significance of the Term," in Ernst Steinkellner and Helmut Tauscher, eds., *Contributions on Tibetan and Buddhist Religion and Philosophy. Proceedings of the Csoma de Körös symposium held at Velm-Vienna, Austria, 13–19 September 1981.* Vol. 2. Vienna: Arbeitskreis für Tibetische und Buddhistische Studien, Universität Wien, pp. 275–84.

Strong, John. (1989) *The Legend of King Aśoka: A Study and Translation of the* Aśokāvadāna. Delhi: Motilal Banarsidass.

Szerb, János. (1980a) "Glosses on the Oeuvre of Bla-ma 'Phags-pa: I. On the Activity of Sa skya Paṇḍita," in Michael Aris and Aung San Suu Kyi, eds., *Tibetan Studies in Honour of Hugh Richardson.* Proceedings of the International Seminar of Tibetan Studies, Oxford 1979. Warminster, England: Aris & Phillips, pp. 290–300.

———. (1980b) "Glosses on the Oeuvre of Bla-ma 'Phags-pa: II. Some Notes on the Events of the Years 1251–1254," *Acta Orientalia Hungarica* 34, pp. 263–85.

Tauscher, Helmut. (1999) "Phya pa chos kyi seng ge's Opinion on *Prasaṅga* in His *Dbu ma'i shar gsum gyi thong thun,*" in Shoryu Katsura, ed., *Dharmakīrti's Thought and Its Impact on Indian and Tibetan Philosophy: Proceedings of the Third International Dharmakīrti Conference, Hiroshima, November 4–6, 1997.* Österreichische Akademie der Wissenschaften Philosophisch-Historische Klasse Denkschriften, 281. Beiträge Zur Kultur- und Geistesgeschichte Asiens. Vienna: Verlag der Österreichische Akademie der Wissenschaften.

Thurman, Robert A. F. (1978) "Buddhist Hermeneutics," *JAAR* 46(1), pp. 19–39.

———. (1984) *The Central Philosophy of Tibet: A Study and Translation of Jay Tsong Khapa's* Essence of True Eloquence. Princeton Library of Asian Translations. Princeton, N.J.: Princeton University Press.

———. (1988) "Vajra Hermeneutics," in Donald S. Lopez, Jr., ed., *Buddhist Hermeneutics.* Kuroda Institute Studies in East Asian Buddhism 6. Honolulu: University of Hawaii Press, pp. 119–48.

Tillemans, Tom J. F. (1986) "Identity and Referential Opacity in Tibetan Buddhist *Apoha* Theory," in B. K. Matilal and R. D. Evans, eds., *Buddhist Logic and Epistemology*. Studies in Classical India 7. Dordrecht: Kluwer Academic Publishers, pp. 207–27.

———. (1999) *Scripture, Logic, Language: Essays on Dharmakīrti and His Tibetan Successors*. Studies in Indian and Tibetan Buddhism. Boston: Wisdom.

———. (2000) *Dharmakīrti's* Pramāṇavārttika. *An Annotated Translation of the Fourth Chapter (Parārthānumāna)*. Volume 1.

Tsong Khapa, rJe. (2006) *Ocean of Reasoning: A Great Commentary on Nāgārjuna's* Mūlamadhyamakakārikā. Geshe Ngawang Samten and Jay L. Garfield, trans. New York: Oxford University Press.

Tucci, Giuseppe. (1949) *Tibetan Painted Scrolls*, vol. 2. Rome: La Libreria dello Stato.

———. (1980) *The Religions of Tibet*. Translated from the German and Italian by Geoffrey Samuel. Berkeley: University of California.

Vāmana. (1927) *Kāvyālaṃkārasūtravritti of Vamana with Extracts from Kamadhenu*. Narayan Nathaji Kulkarni, ed. Poona Oriental Series 34. Poona: Oriental Book Agency.

Vāmana. (1928) *Vāmana's Kāvyālaṃkāra-sūtra-vrtti*. Ganganath Jha, trans. Poona Oriental Series 35. Poona: Oriental Book Agency.

Van der Kuijp (see Kuijp).

Vasubandhu. (1925) Lévi, Sylvain, ed. *Vijñaptimātratāsiddhi: deus traités de Vasubandhu, Viṃśatikā (La Vingtaine) accompagnée d'une explication en prose, et Triṃśikā (La Trentaine), avec le commentaire de Sthiramati*. Paris: Libraire Ancienne Honoré Champion.

———. (1967) *Abhidharmakośabhāṣyam of Vasubandhu*. Prahlad Pradhan, ed. Tibetan Sanskrit Works Series, 8. Patna: K. P. Jayaswal Research Institute. Reprint 1975.

Venuti, Lawrence, ed. (2000) *The Translation Studies Reader*. Mona Baker, advisory ed. London and New York: Routledge.

Verhagen, Pieter C. (1993–2001) *A History of Sanskrit Grammatical Literature in Tibet*. 2 vols. Leiden & New York: Brill.

———. (1996) "Tibetan Expertise in Sanskrit Grammar: Ideology, Status and Other Extralinguistic Factors," in Jan E. M. Houben, ed., *Ideology and Status of Sanskrit: Contributions to the History of the Sanskrit Language*. Brill's Indological Library 13. New York: Brill, pp. 275–87.

———. (2005) "*Studies in Indo-Tibetan Buddhist Hermeneutics (5). The mKhas pa rnams 'jug pa'i sgo by Sa skya Paṇḍita Kun dga' rgyal mtshan*," *JIABS* 28(1), pp. 183–219.

Wangyal, Geshe, and Brian Cutillo. (1988) *Illuminations: A Guide to Essential Buddhist Practices*. Novato, Calif.: Lotsawa.

Watson, Burton, trans. (1993) *The Lotus Sutra*. Bibliotheca Indo-Buddhica Series No. 202. New York: Columbia University Press. Reprint: Delhi, India: Sri Satguru Publications, 1999.

Wayman, Alex. (1968) "Concerning *Saṃdhābhāṣā / saṃdhi-bhāṣā / saṃdhyā bhāṣā*," in *Melanges d'Indianisme à la Mémoire de Louis Renou*. Paris: E. de Boccard, pp. 789–96.

———. (1973) *The Buddhist Tantras: Light on Indo-Tibetan Esotericism*. New York: Weiser.

Whorf, B. L. (1956) *Language, Thought, and Reality: Selected Writings*. John B. Carrol, ed. Cambridge: Technology Press of the Massachusetts Institute of Technology.

Williams, Paul. (1980) "Some Aspects of Language and Construction in the Madhyamaka," *JIP* 8. pp. 1–45.

Xuanzang. (1969) *Si-yu-ki: Buddhist Records of the Western World. Translated from the Chinese of Hiuen Tsiang (A.D. 629)*. Samuel Beal, trans. 2 vols. Delhi: Oriental Books Reprint.

Yijing. (1896) *A Record of the Buddhist Religion as Practised in India and the Malay Archipelago (A.D. 671–695) by I-Tsing*. J. Takakusu, trans. Oxford: Clarendon.

Index